Lecture Notes in Computer Science 10441

Commenced Publication in 1973
Founding and Former Series Editors:
Gerhard Goos, Juris Hartmanis, and Jan van Leeuwen

More information about this series at http://www.springer.com/series/7409

Andrea Kő · Enrico Francesconi (Eds.)

Electronic Government and the Information Systems Perspective

6th International Conference, EGOVIS 2017
Lyon, France, August 28–31, 2017
Proceedings

 Springer

Editors
Andrea Kő
Department of Information Systems
Corvinus University of Budapest
Budapest
Hungary

Enrico Francesconi
Italian National Research Council
Institute of Legal Information Theory
    and Techniques
Florence
Italy

ISSN 0302-9743   ISSN 1611-3349 (electronic)
Lecture Notes in Computer Science
ISBN 978-3-319-64247-5   ISBN 978-3-319-64248-2 (eBook)
DOI 10.1007/978-3-319-64248-2

Library of Congress Control Number: 2017947036

LNCS Sublibrary: SL3 – Information Systems and Applications, incl. Internet/Web, and HCI

Printed on acid-free paper

This Springer imprint is published by Springer Nature
The registered company is Springer International Publishing AG
The registered company address is: Gewerbestrasse 11, 6330 Cham, Switzerland

Preface

The 6th International Conference on Electronic Government and the Information Systems Perspective, EGOVIS 2017, took place in Lyon, France, during August 28–31. The conference belongs to the 28th DEXA Conference Series.

The international conference cycle EGOVIS focuses on information systems and ICT aspects of e-government. Information systems are a core enabler for e-government/governance in all its dimensions: e-administration, e-democracy, e-participation, and e-voting. EGOVIS brought together experts from academia, public administrations, and industry to discuss e-government and e-democracy from different perspectives and disciplines, i.e., technology, policy and/or governance, and public administration.

The Program Committee accepted 20 papers from recent research fields such as open data and government cloud, identity management and e-government architectures, innovation, open government, intelligent systems, and semantic technologies applications. Beyond theoretical contributions, papers cover e-government experiences from all over the world; cases are presented from Europe and South America.

This proceedings volume is organized in, during seven sections according to the conference sessions.

We were honored that the EGOVIS 2017 keynote speech was given by Prof. Roland Traunmüller: He is one of the pioneers in e-government studies and has contributed for years to identify limits and opportunities in the field. Prof. Traunmüller's speech discussed digitalization as challenge for e-government.

The chairs of the Program Committee wish to thank all the reviewers for their valuable work; the reviews raised several research questions to be discussed at the conference. We would like to thank Gabriela Wagner for the administrative support and helping us with the scheduling.

We wish our readers a beneficial learning experience, and we hope that the discussions at the conference will continue after the event between the researchers and contribute toward building a global community in the field of e-government.

June 2017

Enrico Francesconi
Andrea Kő

Organization

General Chair

Roland Traunmüller   University of Linz, Austria

Program Committee Co-chairs

Enrico Francesconi   Italian National Research Council, Italy
Andrea Kő   Corvinus University Budapest, Hungary

Honorary Chairs

Wichian Chutimaskul   King Mongkut's University of Technology, Thailand
Fernando Galindo   University of Zaragoza, Spain

Program Committee

Luis Álvarez Sabucedo	Universidade de Vigo, Spain
Jaro Berce	University of Ljubljana, Slovenia
Francesco Buccafurri	Università degli Studi Mediterranea di Reggio Calabria, Italy
Alejandra Cechich	Universidad Nacional del Comahue, Argentina
Wojciech Cellary	Poznan University of Economics, Poland
Wichian Chutimaskul	King Mongkut's University of Technology, Thailand
Flavio Corradini	University of Camerino, Italy
Vytautas Cyras	Vilnius University, Lithuania
Joan Francesc Fondevila Gascón	Universitat Pompeu Fabra, Spain
Enrico Francesconi	Italian National Research Council, Italy
Ivan Futo	National Tax and Customs Administration, Hungary
András Gábor	Corvinus University of Budapest, Hungary
Fernando Galindo	University of Zaragoza, Spain
Francisco Javier García Marco	University of Zaragoza, Spain
Stefanos Gritzalis	University of the Aegean, Greece
Henning Sten Hansen	Aalborg University, Denmark
Christos Kalloniatis	University of the Aegean, Greece
Nikos Karacapilidis	University of Patras, Greece
Evangelia Kavakli	University of the Aegean, Greece
Bozidar Klicek	University of Zagreb, Croatia
Hun-yeong Kwon	Korea University, South Korea
Andrea Kő	Corvinus University Budapest, Hungary

Herbert Leitold	E-Government Innovation Center EGIZ, Austria
Marian Mach	Technical University of Kosice, Slovakia
Peter Mambrey	University of Duisburg-Essen, Germany
Mara Nikolaidou	Harokopio University of Athens, Greece
Javier Nogueras	University of Zaragoza, Spain
Monica Palmirani	University of Bologna, Italy
Aljosa Pasic	Atos, Spain
Andrea Polini	UNICAM, Italy
Reinhard Posch	Technical University Graz, Austria
Aires J. Rover	Federal University of Santa Catarina, Brazil
Erich Schweighofer	University of Vienna, Austria
Ella Taylor-Smith	Edinburgh Napier University, UK
Costas Vassilakis	University of the Peloponnese, Greece
Gianluigi Viscusi	EPFL, CDM, CSI, Switzerland
Robert Woitsch	BOC Asset Management, Austria
Chien-Chih Yu	National ChengChi University, Taiwan

Additional Reviewers

Lise Schrøder	Aalborg University, Denmark
Andres Flores	University of Comahue, Argentina
Agustina Buccella	University of Comahue, Argentina

Contents

E-Government Research and Intelligent System

mGovernment and Inclusion

E-Government Cases - Data and Knowledge Management

Knowledge Management in the Context of e-Government

Digitalization and Transparency

Digitalization as Challenge for Electronic Government

Roland Traunmüller[✉]

Johannes Kepler Universität Linz, Altenbergerstrasse 69, 4040 Linz, Austria
traunm@ifs.uni-linz.ac.at

Abstract. Digitalization is a megatrend that conveys key challenges for
e-Government and touches several hot topics. Knowledge is the fundamental
bridge bringing together diverse extensions. Important developments include:
Administrative Work, Collaborative Platforms, Open Government Data,
e-Participation, Mobile Government etc.

Keywords: Digitalization · Electronic government · Digital government ·
Knowledge management

1 Digitalization as Megatrend

Digitalization is a megatrend determining current situation. The impact is acting
together and in synergy with other major developments such as globalization, universal
competition, cyber-physical networks, demographic change and migration. Digitalization aims at the integration of digital technologies into everyday life; hence it stands
for making digital everything that can be digitized and converting information into
digital format. These procedures improve the efficiency of data collection/analysis and
so speed and quality of political and administrative ventures. At large it indicates
progress; yet occasionally it also may trigger disruptions.

At start let us consider some fundamental demands. Digitalization must be acted
with a focus on innovation. Thus, connectivity means tapping the knowledge of specialists as well as non-professional persons. Thus, the collaborative energy of people
creates a powerful knowledge engine. Another obvious request is that Digitalization
should be intertwined with administrative culture. That implies that public employees
sense a better understanding on their importance in pushing the change process.
Ultimately, they ought to comprehend themselves as knowledge workers.

2 Knowledge Matching Diverse Problem Areas

In concrete projects for Digitalization diverse procedures are triggered so matching
distinct problem areas. Consequently, in the following we touch some aspects of high
burning issues. Thus, we deal with some facets of the following topics: Administrative
Work, Open Government Data (OGD), Collaborative Platforms, e-Participation and
Mobile Government.

© Springer International Publishing AG 2017
A. Kő and E. Francesconi (Eds.): EGOVIS 2017, LNCS 10441, pp. 3–8, 2017.
DOI: 10.1007/978-3-319-64248-2_1

Knowledge is the bridge connecting all these topics - hence will be treated in a wider way. Starting with some basics about knowledge. All in all, knowledge can be regarded as information combined with experience, context, interpretation, and reflection. The content of the human brain is extensive so comprises besides knowledge also skills, intuition, imagination and fantasy. The forms in which knowledge becomes visible are various: knowledge about people and society; knowledge on ethics; knowledge about procedures and structures; knowledge about events, objects and relationships; knowledge about knowledge such as assessments or evaluation. Summarizing, knowledge is purpose-oriented and goal-directed holding important features such as subject-relevant and context-sensitive.

3 Knowledge and Government

Next turning to the topic "knowledge in organisations". There, knowledge may be regarded as the decisive success factor. It is perceived as intellectual capital, as productive resource, as competitive factor and as instrument of power. Knowledge is a comprehensive perception encompassing various segments: procedures, products, formal organisation, cooperative work, information resources, employees, external partners and stakeholders etc. As consequence, analysing knowledge in organisations is high on the agenda. Observations and interviews are the basis and relevant techniques can be found under various names (Groupware Task Analysis, Participatory Design, Ethnographic Studies).

Now we turn treating a specific realm of organisations, namely Government. The role of knowledge is predominant as the central part of administrative work is on information and data sharing. Accordingly, integrating managing knowledge in governmental work will improve public services as well as internal efficiency and quality. In technically handling that issue a KMS (Knowledge Management System) is used. Such systems integrate a lot of features such as content repositories, domain ontologies, collaborative tools, content integration, knowledge dissemination, legal drafting etc.

Administrative work: Work in Government can be regarded from various points of view. Without question, of utmost importance is the understanding as employment of knowledge. Accordingly, officials are knowledge workers par excellence. Most administrative tasks are informational in nature, especially the case of those tasks that are closely related to the core functions of Public Administration. Consequently, the scope of knowledge work is rather broad. It comprises building administrative repositories, sustaining decision models, enhancing administrative procedures, assisting planning ventures and improving citizen participation.

It should be annotated that this regained focus on decisions means somehow going back to roots. It is closely connected with cybernetic thinking, an approach which in the Sixties has been widely used for explaining control in the governmental realm. Now turning to an important issue - one must become aware of some obstacles which Government work meets. Here we treat two cases, namely a high diversity and a high multitude of actors.

First obstacle concerns the high diversity in functions. It starts with the fact, that the three principal realms, legislation, public administration and justice, have quite different features. Further, various layers ought to be considered. These include governance as a strategic-political layer, diverse administrative bodies as tactical layers and agencies as executive layers. Adding to such structural complexity is a high material diversity. There is a necessity to operate within quite many factual domains ranging from social welfare to human resources.

A second innate obstacle is rooted in a high number of entities/actors getting involved and the need to establish smooth cooperation between them. Most actors are embedded in different situations - so have different policies, visions and attitudes. They diverge in standpoints, even if this may not be apparent at first glance. As first objective common goals and a shared comprehension of the task should be established. Then the persons in charge will guide towards a win-win approach which would provide an impression for most involved actors showing that the benefits are balanced.

4 Knowledge Repositories

(a) Registers: Government has three principal categories of repositories. Registers are traditional and cover the basic items such as persons and land, then going to refinements as real estate, property rights, entitlements, and a plenitude of geographical data. Other conventional repositories concern income taxes, tariffs, duties, and excise. In practical work problems using these data occur. There is a history problems as in some collections the semantics of data might be defined long time ago and also might have changed. Entity integration is another issue concerning objects which belong together but may be identified in differing mode due to quite heterogeneous resources.

(b) Legal databases: The legal structuring of administrative work can be seen both as a restricting and as a guiding force. Legal norms are a standard vehicle of communication between central authorities and executive agencies. Often norms establish a framework and leave leeway for interpretation and situation-bound decisions. Here consensus building and negotiation come in as supplementary mode of work. Besides legal norms give meaning to administrative structures: protecting the rights of citizens, procedures bound to the rules of law, safeguarding legal validity etc.

(c) Management information: A third category to mention is the plenitude of repositories containing controlling and management information. The list of items belonging is long so following some examples. Basically, management information comprises knowledge about the own resources and abilities to influence the setting. In any case, knowledge about the internals of the administrative system is an important part. Not to forget the expertise about applying the general knowledge to individual cases. Numerous specific knowledge items are essential in managing. Such as to name: knowledge about standards, about attitudes of stakeholders or how to protect basic citizen rights. Further, included is the knowledge about the potential effects induced by the communication of an administrative act.

5 User Interfaces and Usability

Knowledge enhancement: Enhancing interfaces is a fundamental topic and is central for achieving a high up take. Special repositories are directed to quite specific goals and get filled with service knowledge. A typical example is handling a demand starting with a real-life description. After analysing the service demanded the factual elements are translated into administrative terms. This example is an important application used in most administrative help-systems.

Now going into more details on the issue of improving the user interface with knowledge. In-depth-analyses made for typical interaction processes have revealed that users often cannot cope with the logic of administrative thinking and frequently do not comprehend the administrative jargon and so navigate helplessly through the jungle of information. Accordingly enhancing usability is demanded.

There are several systemic enhancements such as building clarifying dialogues and scenarios and providing static and dynamic help. A static support may include thoroughly editing and working on better comments, drawing clearer scenarios, adding better help-functions. Instruments for dynamic help are software agents and knowledge based techniques. This may mean that knowledge is incorporated into software and personal assistants are combined with public services portals.

Under the label of ease of use many current developments can be named - even if their prime intention was not paired with usability. Paradigmatically, we treat the Internet of things (IoT). This means the inter-networking of physical devices, vehicles, buildings, and other items which have evolved due to a convergence of multiple technologies. These objects are embedded with electronics, software, sensors, actuators, and network connectivity which enable them to collect and exchange data. Result is the inter-connectivity of everything from urban transport to household appliances. Even if it was not the explicit intention the indirect effect on the usability is high. In deed IoT has an eminent capability for making every-da-life more comfortable for citizens.

6 OGD and Big Data

Open Government Data: The state acts as driver and spurs a lot of activities that give leverage to progress. Thus, providing public information is utmost important. In that respect, the development of Open Government Data is a top actual issue. The overall goal of Open Government is making public value from such data. Public value is linked to individual and societal interests and is created in several ways. We just mention improving accountability and transparency as well as efficiency and effectiveness. These marks are the main traits of good governance and so these features should be mirrored in the way authorities act. In OGD the fan of relevant data is broad comprising geographical coordinates, micro-census, regulations, traffic data etc. Thus, many business-related projects flourish with an opening of the Governmental data and with novel applications extracting value from such data.

Big Data: This is a term for data sets that are so large or so complex that traditional data processing application software is inadequate to deal with them. In concrete, this means a utilization of predictive analytics from a set of advanced data analytics method. At the centre is a collection of rather heterogeneous data repositories containing data of diverse type format that are originated from different sources. In principle selection of data always was considered as a critical issue; now in the field of Big Data extra sophisticated questions arise focussing on "which data to take and which data to neglect".

Big Data Analytics shares two problems common to most decision issues, namely information quality and the restricted scope of models. Guaranteeing information quality has become both, more important and more difficult as the number and variety of information sources continue to grow. Further, it is genuine to many decision models that in core they are restricted. They map a limited segment of the real world and mainly focus on "the hard data". In that way results reached in modelling should be regarded "with a grain of salt".

7   Collaboration

Collaboration is marked by a lack of pre-arranged coordination; its metaphor is the discussion performed at a round-table. Historically seen collaboration is the remedy to overcome the intrinsic limitations of formalised work procedures. A central charge is sustaining the collaboration part which is the main element of such essential and important tasks as "negotiation" and "participation".

Portals and platforms serve for enabling collaboration as they offer a broad choice of methods and tools. Some tools are easy to use and low-cost, as in the case of discussion forum and mailing lists. Even the phone plays an important role in some countries. Prepaid phone cards provide a frequently used means to ensure safeguarding the anonymity of the users involved.

More advanced approaches include meeting support, brainstorming software, issue-based information systems (IBIS) and spatial technology for visualization. Meeting support systems attempt to support the meeting process itself and perform various sub tasks, including synchronization of communications, agenda setting, problem structuring, evaluation of solutions, and discussion facilitation. It follows that such working environments must blend collaborative methods with strictly structured phases such as distributing information by workflow or delegating sub-tasks such as searching for information. Argumentation systems (issue-based information systems) list issues and give pro and con arguments so clarifying and documenting the decision process. Often facilitators perform an important part as they will bundle and/or split arguments. With such means they influence the course of discussion and the outcome.

8   Participation

Citizen Participation is a prime application which bundles the shared energy of people. As an example of a challenge we regard shortfalls in communication, a deficit urging for reconnecting citizen with politics. For this charge participation becomes a powerful instrument and opens new ways for politics. Active participation is central and consequently supports community development and the building up of a democratic culture. In general, a lot of actual trends spur interest in participation.

The list of high-level policy goals is long and includes enhancing transparency, reducing bureaucracy as well as fostering democratic culture and empowerment in the broad. Paradigmatically, one can regard the connection between transparency and participation as well as their mutual promotion. This connection provides a chance to fight for more clarity. Transparency means giving relevant information on budgets, plans, events and so can be regarded as essential contributions to any decision process. An essential objective of such decision processes is the building of a social environment. Accordingly, virtual communities emerge and grow by means of group's news, special forums and chat rooms.

One should be aware of various types of user roles. Only a small group produces content with blogs and wikis, others provide ratings and reviews. More often we find rather marginal activities, so employment of user-generated content and providing general attention. Respective groups show activities such as using on-line services or going to a most-read page.

In e-Campaigning citizens may become quite active in supporting their representatives at elections. E-Campaigning is concerned with raising awareness about political issues. It works by engaging with people and encouraging people to engage with each other. Hence it channels the power of public opinion to advance a progressive drive. Campaigning has a long history. Earlier it was performed by print media, party meetings, rallies, public speeches. Then electronic media, radio and TV, arrived. Since the mid-Nineties the Web 1.0 got used, a new medium but an old message. Now Web 2.0 as new medium bring additional messages. In evaluating one should be aware that the scope as well as the context of campaigning is quite special. Central features comprise traits such as citizen-based, decentralized, individualistic and using social micro-networks.

9   Mobile Government

Mobile Government is the next issue and e-Participation may serve as an outstanding example for understanding of this topic. Mobile Government means that citizens communicate with the devices at hand which commonly are tablets and smartphones. Turning to a deeper comprehension of mobility, we see that our reaction is equivocal. Mobility it is something we love and sometimes we hate as well. There is a genuine urge to mobility; maybe it is in the genes, or in our evolution or in a lifestyle we learn and adopt. Mobility has a corollary namely connectivity which creates ubiquity.

Technically, ubiquity can be realized by two ways. One way is distributing technical means for shared use, the other way is the existence of personally owned items/means. Such considerations may be directed toward many quite different fields such as cars, holiday habitats, phones, computer utilization. Regarding phones mobile phones are preferred over telephone booths. Mobile phones bring several advantages as to mention increased productivity, personalization and elevated feedback rooted in a higher number of users reached. The core intention is: Keeping in touch with your Business.

Tyrant Leaders as e-Government Service Promoters: The Role of Transparency and Tyranny in the Implementation of e-Government Service

Yuting Lin[1], Andreas Eisingerich[1], and Hersen Doong[2(✉)]

[1] Imperial College London, Imperial College Business School,
South Kensington Campus, London SW7 2AZ, UK
{y.lin14, a.eisingerich}@imperial.ac.uk
[2] Department of Management Information Systems, National Chiayi University,
No. 580, Sinmin Rd., Chiayi 60054, Taiwan
hsdoong@mail.ncyu.edu.tw

Abstract. While prior studies offer significant insights into the extent of EGS (Electronic Government Service) implementation from productivity-transparency trade-off perspectives, critical questions remain about how transparency of government department/agency facilitates the implementation timing of EGS. Such questions are important because transparency is an explicit indicator to outsiders, such as IT (Information Technology) vendors, to help them plan their marketing strategies in advance. Drawing insights from signaling and upper echelon theories, this research contributes to the electronic government literature by proposing that the government department/agency performance transparency is closely aligned to its timing of EGS implementation. Moreover, this relationship varies as it depends both on the size of the government department/agency and the level of tyranny of its leader or head. Empirical findings indicate that, in order to gain a competitive advantage, a tyrannical manager in a smaller organization accelerates the speed of IT implementation to use it as a strategic weapon to elicit favorable public response. This research, thus, complements and extends extant knowledge by exploring the key roles of both a government department/agency performance transparency and its tyrannical leadership on the timing of EGS implementation.

Keywords: Electronic government service · Implementation · Performance transparency · Signaling · Tyranny · Upper echelon

1 Introduction

Implementing a successful EGS (Electronic Government Service) has become a critical issue for government administration [1]. EGS uses computer hardware, computer software, database management technology, and networking and telecommunication technology to enhance the accessibility and delivery of government information and service for citizens [2]. Thus, understanding the key determinants of EGS implementation is a critical and constructive way for IT (Information Technology) infrastructure providers to determine market segmentations and help them evaluate relevant

© Springer International Publishing AG 2017
A. Kő and E. Francesconi (Eds.): EGOVIS 2017, LNCS 10441, pp. 9–18, 2017.
DOI: 10.1007/978-3-319-64248-2_2

promotional tactics [3]. Transparency is likely to play an important role in the context of ICT (Information and Communication Technologies) as it may have a facilitative impact on various relationship outcomes such as gaining trust [4], enhancing purchase intention and strengthening information exchanges between sellers, buyers and external stakeholders [5–8]. More specifically, many governments have worked to increase transparency. As EGS is viewed as a cost-effective and convenient means to promote transparency, it has been widely employed in many comprehensive transparency efforts [9, 10].

While prior studies offer significant insights into the extent of IT implementation from a productivity-transparency trade-off perspective [3], questions remain about whether transparency will affect the timing of organizational technological artefact implementation [11]. This question is important as transparency is an explicit indicator for outsiders such as IT vendors to plan their target markets in advance. Moreover, organizational performance has been shown to be affected by the risk-taking propensity of its leader such as chief executive officer (CEO) [12].

While organizations are the reflection of their top management team [13], it is essential to discuss organizational moves from its leadership point of view. Upper echelon theory suggests that, in most cases, this reflection is attributed to the disposition of CEOs alone [14]. Since it is they who play the decisive roles by setting the direction of the organization, making general decisions and building the organizational culture. Hence, an organization, either informally or formally, implements IT through each interaction when the top manager sets his or her own priorities [15].

For instance, as the CEO of Apple, which has been a highly visible firm in terms of media attention and accessible information, the authoritarian Steve Jobs was described by Walter Isaacson as the "creative entrepreneur whose passion for perfection and ferocious drive revolutionized many industries". Arguably, Apple is a highly innovative business with a tendency to adopt and implement novel technology, whereas, in contrast, Bill Gates, the head of Microsoft, being relatively democratic, spends his time communicating with his information technology specialists about how new products can become standard industry products [16]. An example of the consequences of this democratic approach is Microsoft's tendency to provide less accessible information for stakeholders by using lengthy descriptions rather than the simpler Q&A format, hence its implementation speed when adopting IT might be argued to be somewhat slower than Apple's. Because the combined effect of organizational characteristics and executive characteristics is worth exploring [17], this research explores the interaction effects between the tyrannical leadership of government department/agency head and performance transparency on setting the timing for the implantation of electronic government service.

Drawing insights from signaling and upper echelon theories, this research theorizes that a government department/agency with a high level of performance transparency will be relatively fast in EGS implementation and it will examine how a tyrannical government department/agency head may sharpen the relationship between the government performance transparency and the timing of EGS implementation. The theoretical framework, propositions and managerial implications are discussed next.

2 Theoretical Background

2.1 Transparency as a Signal

The concept of transparency has been investigated across different academic disciplines. The innovation management literature, for example, has examined it in the context of openness or scientific disclosure in innovation activities [18–20]. In the marketing field, researchers have explored information disclosure in the context of customers' responses to nutritional information and drug risk information [21, 22] and in IS (information system) literature, relevant concepts, such as business to consumer relationships and digital markets, have also been examined [23–26]. These works defined information transparency as the level of availability and accessibility of market information to its participants, implying the inclusion of both the quantity of information available and the quality of interface to make information accessible.

We define transparency as the extent to which stakeholders view the information provided by an organization as being both accessible and objective [7]. Transparency in business-to-business (B2B) communication among stakeholders such as governments, investors, media, vendors and service providers may improve an organization's performance in terms of efficiency and effectiveness [8]. In this respect, signaling theory may be applied in order to explain how transparency can benefit an organization [7]. This theory holds that, in a market characterized by information asymmetries, one exchange partner communicates unobservable elements, such as intention, ability, skill levels, quality and performance, by providing an observable signal [25, 27, 28]. Indeed, information transparency in contrast to information availability or information sharing, is deliberate, which implies the intention of the sellers to disclose or withhold electronic mercantile information that can affect policies and decisions with opportunities provided by e-commerce technologies [25].

Hence, IT service implementation is significantly affected by degrees of transparency because visibility from enforcement and auditing encourages businesses to be more likely to adopt modern efficiency-enhancing technologies [3]. Such operational clarity might be systematically correlated with organizational performance that leads a firm to initiate a "see through" approach that signals its competence in delivering its promises [7]. As such, transparency becomes a fundamental method of signaling different cues in the marketplace, thus enabling outsiders, such as IT service providers, to identify potential markets. Thus, exploring how sending different types of information transparently shapes the message being sent regarding its IT implementation strategy is an important issue for IT service providers.

2.2 The Upper Echelon in Strategic IT Decision Making

According to Hambrick and Mason [13], firms are a reflection of their top management teams or leadership, although most of the time, the reflection could be of the CEO [14]. Hayward and Hambrick [29] researched organizations along psychological lines and their findings were affirmed by more recent studies by Dwivedi et al. [15] and Gerstner et al. [30] who explored it from both a cognitive perspective and in terms of individual dispositions, such as hubris and narcissism in order to understand how these factors translate to decisions and outcomes at organizational and technological levels. For instance, Chatterjee and Hambrick [14] were of the opinion that narcissistic CEOs do not generate big wins or big losses in terms of their companies' performances, although they favor relatively bold or risky actions that attract attention. Therefore, from a psychological cognitive perspective, such executives' characteristics are manifested in their strategic choices, particularly in terms of IT adoption strategies, since this is one area that can earn them admiration and reinforce their self-image [15].

While narcissism is one of the destructive business leadership taxonomies, a CEO's tendency for tyrannical behavior has been suggested to act as another major contribution to an organization's extraordinary performance [31, 32]. Ashforth [33] defined a "petty tyrant" as "someone who uses power and authority oppressively, capriciously, and perhaps vindictively" although such leaders may behave in accordance with the legitimate goals, tasks, and strategies of their organizations [31]. Therefore, despite the fact that tyrannical leaders may be viewed as abusive, it is often apparent that they also engender employee satisfaction; hence, they may perform well on work-related assignments [34]. Skogstad [35] argued that leaders who behave badly toward subordinates may be highly constructive in their relations with customers or business partners or toward upper management; they may, of course, also have important professional or technical skills, which Ma et al. [32] described as "the paradox of managerial tyranny". More importantly, the dispositions explored in earlier research are from self-evaluation of the CEOs [14, 15, 30].

In this research, a tyrant is characterized by general public consensus together with perceptions and evaluations from subordinates, stakeholders (citizens) and media. Therefore, the role of tyrannical heads in influencing their organizations' strategies may prove to be contradictory factor, hence a matter worth investigating.

3 Proposition Development

3.1 The Effect of Transparency on EGS Implementation

Being transparent in a B2B context might be considered important for organizations as it could enhance their bargaining power by gaining the trust of service providers in attempt to negotiate preferable deals such as low interest rate, price reduction, aftercare service extension and so on. Many organizations have adopted innovative transparency policies to help stakeholders reduce uncertainty or perceived risk, and furthermore, gain their trust [6]. Such policies, which may be assisted by e-services, include offering unbiased information from the integration of various media channels, disclosing stakeholder reviews on websites, and providing accessible and comprehensive information across devices [24, 25].

However, transparency through technologies is a double-edged sword as it puts organizations in a situation where on the one hand it helps them to both increase productivity and signal their competitive advantages, while, on the other hand, such transparency of transactions leaves a clear audit trail, thus potentially making operational costs higher than they are for those who do not use IT systems [3, 26]. The dilemma between productivity and transparency causes the "Peter Pan Syndrome" whereby organizations prefer to stay small than to grow, thus impeding computer technology implementation. It is noticeable, therefore, that the preference for productivity-enhancing technologies has been empirically confirmed to be higher when organizations are motivated to be transparent [3]. As such, transparency predicts IT implementation in a way that organizations expect their IT functions to enable them to exploit new opportunities relatively quickly while also reacting to unanticipated changes.

Indeed, timeliness is an essential component of IT implementation as it results in better responsiveness to external changes and also to either attain or maintain competitiveness [11]. The focus of much IS research has been on the influences that impact those stages that come near the end of the IT innovation decision-making process; hence, the objective of this research is to identify the drivers that influence the earlier stages of the decision-making process.

In sum, government departments/agencies may rely heavily on EGS in a way that they can either easily distribute the information or manage content in order to abide by principles. Therefore, whether or not government departments/agencies are instructed or voluntarily requested to disclose their operational performance in an accessible and unbiased form for potentially interested parties, a high level of performance transparency could lead them to implement EGS quickly. In contrast, government departments/agencies with low performance transparency that retain their existing systems are less likely to be in the spotlight, which may result in a relatively slow pace in switching to EGS. We thus proposed that:

- P1: Government departments/agencies with high (versus low) transparency have a relatively fast EGS implementation timing.

3.2 The Interaction Between Tyrannical Leadership and Transparency

With the preceding discussion in mind, we argue that tyrannical leadership of a head of government department/agency could strengthen the positive relationship between performance transparency and his or her department/agency timing of EGS implementation. Thus, if both these elements come into play a firm's speed of EGS implementation will be fast.

The concept of petty tyranny or tyrannical leadership was originally introduced by Ashforth [33] as a description of leaders who exercise their powers over subordinates in a lordly manner and behave in arbitrary ways. However, tyrannical CEOs can influence strategic choices extensively and efficiently [32]. This is akin to the endorsement of a celebrity whose skills, output and charisma may attract media attention and then gain wide public attention. At the same time, a strict and authoritative managerial style of the executives may assist employees to clearly understand the direction of their firm.

Given the publicity generated by transparent performance, the autocratic leaders who make up mind according to their own beliefs accelerate the timing of IT implementation, since they tell their subordinates what to do and they make sure they have sufficient controllable resources on hand to facilitate their decisions [32, 33]. Consequently they elicit favorable public response by means of their IT, using it as a strategic weapon in order to gain a competitive advantage.

Furthermore, in an intriguing line of research on diffusion and implementation of IT, power and politics have been examined and have suggested that technology usage depends on superiority for the purpose of manipulation, control and coercion [36–38]. Tyrannical leaders tend to avoid resistance to technology implementation by emphasizing managerial authority as well as by encouraging user involvement through office politics.

When government departments/agencies have a highly transparent performance policy, tyrannical leaders have a greater tendency to implement EGS, but not when their performance transparency is low. Hence, once department/agency heads are put on the spot, they are more likely to invest in technological discontinuities to be impressed by bold and daring actions [30]. The higher government department/agency transparency in terms of visibility, the more favorably accepted will be the leader's tyrannical management style. This is because the interpretation of leader's oppressive action is more likely to be colored by intentional signals, transforming dictatorship into the dogged and resolute characteristics of a strong and capable leader. Although transparency does not always guarantee high performance in government, the exposure could trigger government with below average performances to long for external supports [10]. In such circumstance, tyrannical government department/agency heads may implement EGS more rapidly owing to them having plenty controllable resource on hand. Thus:

- P2: Tyrannical leadership positively moderates the relationship between transparency and timing of EGS implementation, such that transparency has a greater positive effect on timing of EGS implementation for government departments/agencies with more (vs. less) tyrannical tendencies of their leadership.

3.3 The Three Way Interaction Between Tyrannical Leadership, Transparency and Size of Department/Agency

In order to unpack the key mechanisms behind transparency and the timing of EGS implementation, this research explores in top management teams, namely their leaders' tyranny. The impact of transparency, however, is likely to depend on the size of the government department/agency. We hence expect that the return on transparency is more pronounced in certain conditions of size, than in others.

Organizational size has been shown to influence decisions, including the way information is processed [3, 17]. Organizations with varying levels of size may make quite different decisions, therefore, this research was further extended by predicting that the moderating role of tyrannical leadership in regard to the speed of EGS implementation will be influenced by how large the government department/agency is. The government department/agency is determined by the number of employees. Since perceived risk differs across business sizes, the implementation of new technology is generally perceived as bringing greater risks for smaller firms since they operate in a highly competitive environment and are thus likely to suffer from financial constraints, lack of professional expertise, and are more likely to be adversely affected by varying managerial styles of CEOs [17].

It has already been demonstrated that tyrant managers are more likely to be daring or risk takers and these personal tendencies may lead to bold choices [14, 31]. As such, when they are in the spotlight, they tend to act like innovators by trying out their new ideas as soon as possible despite suffering from occasional early setbacks. Building on the work of Mishina et al. [39], this study suggests that, particularly in small businesses, even though a moderate to strong negative character of a tyrant manager will have a greater influence on their reputation, tyrannical leaders rely less on group norms in relation to widespread beliefs than on their own self-confidence in their ability to lead them on to pioneer or apply new IT systems.

In contrast, when organizations are large, they are not so strongly affected by their CEOs decision making as there are other stakeholders involved whose collective knowledge may be relied upon to drag down the adoption time [11]. Consequently, this study argues that a tyrannical leadership is more likely to influence the relationship between transparency and EGS implementation timing when the government department/agency size is small rather than large. Therefore:

- P3: The moderating effect of tyrannical leadership on the relationship between transparency and timing of EGS implementation is stronger when the government department/agency size is small (versus large).

Figure 1 shows the conceptual framework including the research three propositions.

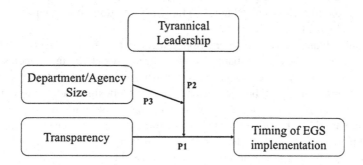

Fig. 1. Conceptual framework

4 Conclusion and Implications

This research theorizes that government departments/agencies with a higher level of performance transparency will be relatively quick in EGS implementation and explores how a tyrannical leader may sharpen such a relationship when the government department/agency size is small. This research complements existing knowledge about electronic government and contributes to the literature on signaling leadership in three important ways.

First, because signaling theory examines communication between individuals, there is room for it taking a new direction [40]; hence this research sheds light on the relationship between the signaled message, in this case performance transparency, and the sender, the leaders, which shows that the same form of transparent information from different degrees of tyrannical executives influences the timing of IT implementation. Second, although the results confirm that transparency affects organizational IT implementation [3, 24, 25], when looking at both the timing of implementation and executives' leadership, we also theorize an additional affect that consists of variance. Third, the link between organizational size and IT service implementation remains mixed. Many studies have reported that small size organizations are vulnerable to waiting for long-term value returns on their IT investments, whereas some claimed that small size organizations are more flexible in their implementation of new IT systems. This research, however, has theorized the key role played by a tyrannical leader in formulating and consolidating an organizational decision to obtain a new IT system.

This research offers some critical practitioners in the IT industry for finding better ways to promote their services. For example, marketers eager to promote IT can specify target leader segments by classifying heads in relative order of their tyrannical tendencies together with the transparency levels of their departments/agencies. It would therefore make strategic sense for tyrant leaders who manage highly transparent departments/agencies to be targeted first in order for them to receive positive messages about their innovative IT products and also have information about them more widely disseminated around the industry.

By taking advantage of the interaction effects between a leaders' tyranny and organizational performance transparency, IT service providers' investments in new product development may result in more fruitful benefits in that their operating objectives are more likely to be met. Therefore, by proposing and mounting a theoretical based research model backed up with an extensive literature review, the current research uncovered the pitfalls that may befall those IT vendors using other studies' results. Enterprise IT providers then understand why and how they could prioritize government departments when introducing innovative IT systems.

References

1. Krishnan, S., Teo, T.S.H., Lymm, J.: Determinants of electronic participation and electronic government maturity: Insights from cross-country data. Int. J. Inf. Manage. 37, 297–312 (2017)

2. Das, A., Singh, H., Joseph, D.: A longitudinal study of e-government maturity. Inf. Manag. **54**(4), 415–426 (2016)
3. Sudhir, K., Talukdar, D.: The "peter pan syndrome" in emerging markets: the productivity-transparency trade-off in IT adoption. Mark. Sci. **34**, 500–521 (2015)
4. Kang, J., Hustvedt, G.: Building trust between consumers and corporations: the role of consumer perceptions of transparency and social responsibility. J. Bus. Ethics **125**, 253–265 (2014); Park, C.W., MacInnis, D., Eisingerich, A.B.: Brand Admiration: Building a Business People Love. Wiley, New Jersey (2016)
5. Cannon, J.P., Perreault Jr., W.D.: Buyer-seller relationships in business markets. J. Mark. Res. **36**, 439–460 (1999); Ren, S., Tsai, H.T., Eisingerich, A.B.: Case-based asymmetric modeling of firms with high versus low outcomes in implementing changes in direction. J. Bus. Res. **69**, 500–507 (2016)
6. Hung, H., Wong, Y.: Information transparency and digital privacy protection: are they mutually exclusive in the provision of e-services? J. Serv. Mark. **23**, 154–164 (2009)
7. Liu, Y., Eisingerich, A.B., Auh, S., Merlo, O., Chun, H.E.H.: Service firm performance transparency how, when, and why does it pay off? J. Serv. Res. **18**(4), 1–17 (2015); Eisingerich, A.B., Bell, S.J.: Perceived service quality and customer trust: does enhancing customers' service knowledge matter? J. Serv. Res. **10**, 256–268 (2008)
8. O'Toole, J., Bennis, W.: A culture of candor. Harvard Bus. Rev. **87**, 54–61 (2009)
9. Pieterson, W., Ebbers, W.: The use of service channels by citizens in the Netherlands: implications for multi-channel management. Int. Rev. Admin. Sci. **74**, 95–110 (2008); Eisingerich, A.B., Chun, H., Liu, Y., Jia, H., Bell, S.J.: Why recommend a brand face-to-face but not on Facebook? How word-of-mouth on online social sites differs from traditional word-of-mouth. J. Consum. Psychol. **25**, 120–128 (2015)
10. Brito, J., Perraut, D.: Transparency and performance in government. NCJL Tech. On. **11**, 161–259 (2010)
11. Ciganek, A.P., Haseman, W., Ramamurthy, K.: Time to decision: the drivers of innovation adoption decisions. Enterp. Inf. Syst. **8**, 279–308 (2014)
12. Kraiczy, N.D., Hack, A., Kellermanns, F.W.: What makes a family firm innovative? CEO risk taking propensity and the organizational context of family firms. J. Prod. Innov. Manag. **32**, 334–348 (2015)
13. Hambrick, D.C., Mason, P.A.: Upper echelons: the organization as a reflection of its top managers. Acad. Manag. Rev. **9**, 193–206 (1984)
14. Chatterjee, A., Hambrick, D.C.: It's all about me: narcissistic chief executive officers and their effects on company strategy and performance. Adm. Sci. Q. **52**, 351–386 (2007)
15. Dwivedi, Y.K., Papazafeiropoulo, A., Chuang, T.-T., Nakatani, K., Zhou, D.: An exploratory study of the extent of information technology adoption in SMEs: an application of upper echelon theory. J. Enterp. Inf. Manag. **22**, 183–196 (2009)
16. Schlender, B.: All you need is love, $50 billion, and killer software code-named longhorn. Fortune **146**, 56–58 (2002)
17. Thong, J.Y., Yap, C.-S.: CEO characteristics, organizational characteristics and information technology adoption in small businesses. Omega **23**, 429–442 (1995)
18. Henkel, J., Schöberl, S., Alexy, O.: The emergence of openness: how and why firms adopt selective revealing in open innovation. Res. Policy **43**, 879–890 (2014)
19. Laursen, K., Salter, A.J.: The paradox of openness: appropriability, external search and collaboration. Res. Policy **43**, 867–878 (2014)
20. Simeth, M., Raffo, J.D.: What makes companies pursue an open science strategy? Res. Policy **42**, 1531–1543 (2013)

21. Cox, A.D., Cox, D., Mantel, S.P.: Consumer response to drug risk information: the role of positive affect. J. Mark. **74**, 31–44 (2010); Park, C.W., Eisingerich, A.B., Park, J.W.: Attachment-aversion (AA) model of customer-brand relationships. J. Consum. Psychol. **23**, 229–248 (2013)

22. Howlett, E.A., Burton, S., Bates, K., Huggins, K.: Coming to a restaurant near you? Potential consumer responses to nutrition information disclosure on menus. J. Consum. Res. **36**, 494–503 (2009)

23. Granados, N., Gupta, A., Kauffman, R.J.: The impact of IT on market information and transparency: a unified theoretical framework. J. Assoc. Inf. Syst. **7**, 7 (2006)

24. Granados, N., Gupta, A., Kauffman, R.J.: Designing online selling mechanisms: transparency levels and prices. Decis. Support Syst. **45**, 729–745 (2008)

25. Granados, N., Gupta, A., Kauffman, R.J.: Information transparency in business-to-consumer markets: concepts, framework, and research agenda. Inf. Syst. Res. **21**, 207–226 (2010)

26. Zhu, K.: Information transparency of business-to-business electronic markets: a game-theoretic analysis. Manage. Sci. **50**, 670–685 (2004)

27. Kirmani, A., Rao, A.R.: No pain, no gain: a critical review of the literature on signaling unobservable product quality. J. Mark. **64**, 66–79 (2000)

28. Rao, A.R., Qu, L., Ruekert, R.W.: Signaling unobservable product quality through a brand ally. J. Mark. Res. **36**(2), 258–268 (1999)

29. Hayward, M.L., Hambrick, D.C.: Explaining the premiums paid for large acquisitions: evidence of CEO hubris. Adm. Sci. Q. **42**, 103–127 (1997)

30. Gerstner, W.-C., König, A., Enders, A., Hambrick, D.C.: CEO narcissism, audience engagement, and organizational adoption of technological discontinuities. Adm. Sci. Q. **58**, 257–291 (2013)

31. Burke, R.J., Cooper, C.L.: Risky Business: Psychological, Physical and Financial Costs of High Risk Behavior in Organizations. Gower Publishing, Ltd., Farnham (2010)

32. Ma, H., Karri, R., Chittipeddi, K.: The paradox of managerial tyranny. Bus. Horiz. **47**, 33–40 (2004)

33. Ashforth, B.: Petty tyranny in organizations. Hum. Relat. **47**, 755–778 (1994)

34. Tepper, B.J.: Consequences of abusive supervision. Acad. Manag. J. **43**, 178–190 (2000)

35. Skogstad, A.: Effects of leadership behaviour on job satisfaction, health and efficiency. Department of Psychosocial Science, University of Bergen, Norway (1997)

36. Dub, L., Par, G.: Rigor in information systems positivist case research: current practices, trends, and recommendations. MIS Q. **27**, 597–636 (2003)

37. Markus, M.L.: Power, politics, and MIS implementation. Commun. ACM **26**, 430–444 (1983)

38. Romm, C.T., Pliskin, N.: The office tyrant-social control through e-mail. Inf. Technol. People **12**, 27–43 (1999)

39. Mishina, Y., Block, E.S., Mannor, M.J.: The path dependence of organizational reputation: how social judgment influences assessments of capability and character. Strateg. Manag. J. **33**, 459–477 (2012)

40. Connelly, B.L., Certo, S.T., Ireland, R.D., Reutzel, C.R.: Signaling theory: a review and assessment. J. Manag. **37**, 39–67 (2011)

Electronic Forms-Based Model of Public Administration Operations

Péter József Kiss$^{(\boxtimes)}$ and Gábor Klimkó

MTA Information Technology Foundation, Budapest, Hungary
mtaita@t-online.hu

Abstract. The traditional model of public administration operations has an inherent productivity flaw as it focuses on the activities of processing as opposed to the data of the cases to be processed. It is argued that an electronic forms-based model of operations in which the focus is laid on data would result in significant productivity increase. The paper presents the concept of the electronic forms-based processing as well as it describes the architectural elements of a unified integrated system in the context of the current Hungarian electronic government technical infrastructure. The conclusion is that existing architectural elements, if pragmatically applied, can be utilized into a system able to support hybrid, that is, both paper-based and computer system supported operations.

Keywords: Adaptive case management · Public administration efficiency · Public administration operations

1 Introduction

The improvement of the efficiency of public administration is a recurring issue often found in the literature and in the governance of different countries [1–6]. The Hungarian government declared the importance of developing public administration as early as 1992 and since then it has implemented a series of organizational and legislative reforms but the basic problem of low efficiency remained.

The implementation of computer support for basic registers of public administration did not solve the efficiency problem and, eventually, the necessity of using electronic solutions has been recognized. The "first generation" approach to the problem was the obvious "electronization" of the traditional "paper based" procedures and the implementation of the required supporting processes (e.g. scanning the paper documents). At this stage the administrative procedures were carried out with the scanned electronic version of the documents instead of using paper. This approach, however, did not bring the improvement hoped for [7, 8]. Earlier when using the former paper-based method, if the official in charge (the clerk or civil servant) received a paper document with a number of attachments, he placed the papers side by side to study them and thus he was able to complete the procedure in a few minutes. In the "electronic" process the task of the clerk became more difficult as scanned documents were shown on traditional sized screens and their handling required many screen changes, as well as up and down

© Springer International Publishing AG 2017
A. Kő and E. Francesconi (Eds.): EGOVIS 2017, LNCS 10441, pp. 19–31, 2017.
DOI: 10.1007/978-3-319-64248-2_3

scrolling in the windows. Thus it is not surprising that the clerk often resorted to printing all electronically submitted documents to be able to complete the tasks faster.

As this type of digitalization did not achieve the breakthrough hoped for, it was recognized that a new model of public administration was necessary to achieve any real change in Hungary [7]. This new model was not only expected to able to function together with the existing one but it was also expected to have the feasibility to replace the former approach gradually, thus ensuring significant improvement in efficiency.

In this paper we shall show a model of operations reshaped according to these requirements and present an overview of the architectural elements of a unified and integrated system that would support the model. Section 2 elaborates the problem statement and the research question. In Sect. 3 the concepts of the e-document and the electronic forms-based processing are discussed. A possible architecture for the electronic forms-based processing in Hungary is outlined in Sect. 4 (note that some architectural elements are already deployed.). Conclusions are summarized in Sect. 5.

2 Problem Statement and Research Question

2.1 The Traditional Processing Model of Public Administration Operations

We will illustrate the basic concept of the traditional processing model in the Hungarian public administration with a procedure initiated upon the client's request, as shown in Fig. 1.

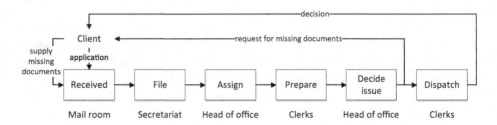

Fig. 1. Traditional processing logic in public administration.

It is an apparent characteristic of the traditional procedure that it involves a large number of steps and a lot of inside actors. Preparation and decision making are the only actions of added value, all the other steps are practically unproductive (in lean terminology they are waste, '*muda*'). The traditional procedure is focused on the file of the case and on the operations on the file the case itself is of secondary importance.

It is an attribute of all administrative organizations that process paper-based documents that if they do not possess any data managed by other administrative organizations then these data must be officially requested. Consequently, the traditional procedure will be repeated within these other authorities. For example if we consider the process when the acting authority "A" has to ask for data from authority "B" then we will immediately realize the highly bureaucratic nature of the whole procedure. The process is shown in Fig. 2.

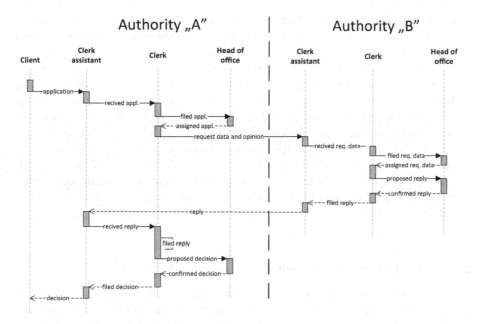

Fig. 2. Processing example with two involved authorities (traditional model).

These problems with the traditional way of operations in public administration have been recognized for a long time. There are basically two types of attempts to overcome these obstacles:

- **Switching to the digitized** (scanned) **form of the original paper-based documents.** The simple conversion from paper to electronic format, where an electronic signature is used for authentication, is not a new approach. When using this method the procedural and processing rules remain the same as with paper-based documents. Consequently only the proper mapping of the objects have to be ensured (i.e. handwritten signature to electronic signature, registration book to an electronic filing register). Scanned documents are processed exactly the same way just as shown in the earlier figure. Therefore, the only thing that became simpler was the dispatch (delivery) but not the processing of the documents. Unfortunately, this approach sometimes makes the efficiency of the whole procedure even worse. In the course of the years in public administration, the traditional document management became optimized for manual procedures. Hence, this became the basis of the format, size, and content of the documents (e.g., the amount of data required in a form). When paper documents are processed they can be laid side-by-side for comparison, but this cannot be achieved using an average sized monitor, and sorting tasks and pictures is even less efficient than in the course of paper based processing. Automatic conversion of paper-based documents to digital ones did not result in improved efficiency.

- **The development of customized and targeted IT systems resulted** in moderate but still only partial success as these individual developments often led to a number of isolated applications. If the clerk, who does the work, relies purely on his IT system, there is no problem. In practice, however, this is rather the exception than the rule. Typically, there are many actors as shown in the previous example where the acting authority "A" requested the help of authority "B". The ineptness of this model became evident when the Hungarian system of Government Windows (one stop shops for public administration services) was implemented [9]. The idea was to have a single unified client service (competent for most of the cases) that is able to serve the whole public administration. This lead to the necessity of accessing different IT systems from the same place but that again lead to technical accessibility problems and using paper-based documents was the only common form of documenting the events.

2.2   Research Question and Method

Due to the aforementioned problems there was a need for a new model of administration operations. There were basic requirements that had to be considered during the development of a new model that is expected to improve significantly the efficiency of public administration.

- The model has to be able to improve both the efficiency of the internet based "self-service" procedures handled by the clients from their home on their own as well as to improve the efficiency of the work of public administration clerks.
- The newly developed model and the traditional administration one are expected to work in co-operation and in parallel in the foreseeable future (i.e. there will be a hybrid operation). It is not possible to re-develop and convert all the individual specialized IT systems in a single step. Such an attempt would be technically unfeasible, risky and it would be also impossible to finance.
- In general it is possible to make some progress by simplifying the logics of traditional administration, automating wherever possible and eliminating unnecessary and repeated data entries and verifications. The objective is to reduce the number of steps that do not contribute materially to completing the case (this is the lean approach). The rationalization of the procedure is often specific to the professional branch therefore too much result cannot be expected from it.
- Authorities need to concentrate on specific issues of the case itself instead of focusing on the internal procedures of the professional branch. That is, we should get rid of the primacy of institutional document management.

The question was how to propose such a model that fulfills these requirements. We followed the usual research approach by studying the relevant literature and pieced together such an approach in which well-known techniques will be utilized but not according to the usual manner. The distinguishing feature of the proposed model lies in its focus on the data to be processed as opposed to the flow of processing. Note that it is a similar approach that is taken by the adaptive (or dynamic) case management where information of the case is put in the center and the workflow (the sequence of processing) is of secondary importance [11, 12].

The highly regulated environment of the public sector leads in continuous tracking of what has been done instead of looking at what should be done. As a consequence, attention is usually is paid to the activities of the processing and not to the processed data in the public sector. In technical terms the usual approach is to focus on the work-flow and not on the data. However, it was noted a long time ago that achieving interoperability in administration is also possible by "information integration" [13]. We argue that this approach is proper and suitable to satisfy the above listed requirements.

2.3   The Necessity of Using Structured Data

The basis of the new model is the introduction of such procedures (office work) that are supported by structured data suitable for at least partially automated processing. In this manner instead of having scanned pictures displayed, individual data elements can be processed and interpreted by the computers, too. Note that using structured data is a characteristics of the customized, targeted IT systems that support public administration operations.

From the technical point of view, the usage of structured data was surveyed and described as part of the Interoperability Solution for European Public Administration (ISA) programme in Action 2.1.5 on e-Documents[1] [14]. In that research, e-document is defined as any document in electronic format containing structured data (and possibly also unstructured data) used in the context of an administrative process. Here it has to be pointed out that a key requirement of the model was its ability to cooperate with the existing model of operations (and infrastructure) in order to allow for gradual implementation and deployment. **As a consequence, the new processing model is to be based on embedded forms of structured data that allow *both* humans and machines to read and process it.** The Portable Document Format (PDF) is suitable for traditional processing by showing it on a monitor and it can be complemented with an embedded XML code that contains the data in structured form, which allows for automated processing, too. If the computerized system uses such complemented PDF documents and these (electronic) documents are authenticated, then during the different stages of processing the case the same document can be automatically processed as well. Hybrid operations will be possible: for example, the computer system can receive and file the electronic documents while in the subsequent stages of processing a clerk (the acting official) will read them directly.

---

[1] See also https://joinup.ec.europa.eu/asset/isa_edocuments/home/.

3   The Data-Centric Model of Public Administration Operations

3.1   The Concept of Electronic Forms-Based Processing

The other conceptual basis of the new model is the broad use of electronic forms throughout the processing. Electronic forms with structured data fields will be introduced for the different procedures reducing the number of free text fields to the minimum.

The logics of the new model can well be illustrated through the computer representation of a contract that is an accompanying document of a case. According to the traditional model of administration there were as many different contracts as there were lawyers. In the new forms-based model all important data in the contract will have to be captured via an electronic form. Data contained in the contract must be entered according to a predefined structure: the subject, term, sum, and adverse conditions all to be filled in the usual way and separately but attached to a grouping concept. Whilst in the traditional model the clerk has to find the important data of the contract, in the new model the important data of the contract can be picked out automatically due to the form that breaks the contract into specific sections and fields. Capturing the structured data from the contract, however, will not replace the contract itself. The new processing model is expected to coexist with the traditional one.

There are some important steps required to allow the simultaneous handling of "self-servicing electronic" and traditional public administration processing. In the case of "self-servicing electronic" administration certain filling standards can be enforced (e.g. mandatory data, compulsory attachments): This enforcement cannot be achieved in the paper based administration.

In order to implement the new model gradually and widely in Hungary, the traditional paper-based processing (e.g. in the case of welfare issues) cannot be fully eliminated. The co-existence of the traditional and the new model will be ensured by the Central Register and Document Access Center service. In the Hungarian public administration the central receiving and registration postal packages to the public administration was introduced in 2015. All postal documents to public administration authorities (with certain exceptions) are now centrally scanned and the digital form is forwarded to the recipients. The digitized form now is a picture as opposed to the structured format. In the new model the essential data of the documents must be scanned (entered) into forms. If the presence of the paper-based-documents were to be standardized than it would facilitate the capture of structured data.

Many tasks performed earlier by the administration staff can be automated in the new model. It is important to underline that certain feedbacks and partial decisions can be automated, too. In the traditional model if the submitted set of documents was incomplete (e.g. absence of mandatory attachments) then the clerk had to call for the submission of the missing documents. In the new processing model there is no need for the intervention of the clerk. Note also that the risks, that are stemmed from the electronic way of conducting business with public administration authorities such virus infected electronic documents or electronic certification of documents, can also be treated by automated means.

3.2   The Concept of the e-Document

There are a number of categories of electronic forms as

- **starting form** that is mandatory to have for each case. Both the clerk and the client can fill in the starting form. It also includes a list of the steps that are required to create it;
- **working forms,** that are the basis of the preparation of the decision for the case;
- **transfer request** (also answer) **forms** which supplies the requested information;
- **decision form** on which the decision of the case is recorded;
- **supply of missing documents form** on which an authority might request certain data from the client. It is similar to the transfer request form but the contact with the client is different; and
- **data transfer form** on which data can be officially submitted to a register for recording.

We call the unit of information transfer as the e-document. This is an umbrella category that includes the basic data of the document (the type of the case and client data), its status data (who handled the case, what was done with it) as well as all the forms and attachments of the case.

3.3   Steps Involved in Electronic Forms-Based Processing

In the new model all processing is carried out using different electronic forms that are stored in complemented PDF format. When a client submits a case he is expected to provide only the absolutely necessary amount of data on the "starting form". In the traditional model the client was often asked to supply such data that the acting authority itself could have obtained. In the new model all data available in the achievable registers of the public administration are automatically obtained and shown on the forms for both the client and the clerk at all stages of the process.

If the data item required for processing cannot be obtained automatically then the so-called "working form" is the clerk's aid in the processing. In this case the system that manages the forms will create a "transfer request form" and send it without human intervention to the clerk of the authority which has the required data. The clerk of that authority replies by filling out the form. Note that if there is an independent third party service which certifies the availability and transfer of the requested data, then there is even no need to keep a separate register on the replies.

If we apply electronic forms then the processing shown in the previous example (see Fig. 2), becomes significantly more efficient due to the automated acquisition of data. There is no need to request data and there is no need to retype it. The improved processing is shown in Fig. 3.

Note that it may happen that the authority (for instance non-government or foreign organization) from which the data was requested, is not able or does not want to reply in the form structure. In this case the clerk will send the reply by postal means to the central receiving service where it will be scanned and electronically forwarded to the requesting party in PDF format.

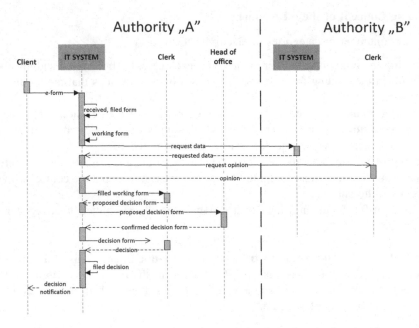

Fig. 3. Processing with forms in the example of two involved authorities.

4   An Architecture for the Electronic Forms-Based Processing in Hungary

In the course of the reform of the Hungarian public administration, numerous county level branch-offices of national authorities that previously worked independently, were reorganized on county (that is, territorial) base by into Government Offices [9]. The uniform operation of the county Government Offices can be enforced and supported by a single IT system. The previously built IT systems that supported the forehead county level branch-offices should be gradually incorporated in this new single overarching system. **We shall refer to this new system as the "unified integrated system".**

4.1   The Architectural Elements of the Unified Integrated System

In certain cases public administration systems have already used general purpose IT solutions (for instance the Hungarian family benefits disbursement system[2] uses an Enterprise Service Bus and workflow motor), but these solutions have often led to dependence on programmers and their connections with other IT systems in public administration is very limited. Therefore in order to implement the processing model described in Sect. 3, a set of optimized central services (called Regulated Electronic e-government Services /REeGS/) has to be set-up at its core [15]. These services are the

---

[2] http://www.kifu.gov.hu/kifu/en/projects/teba.

building blocks of a service oriented architecture. REeGS are defined and characterized in Act CCXXII of 2015 on electronic administration and the general rules of trust services in the Hungarian legal system.

There are a number of elements that are needed for the implementation of the unified integrated system that make it possible it to be quickly deployed and to co-exist with legacy systems. The main architectural elements are the following (see in Fig. 4).

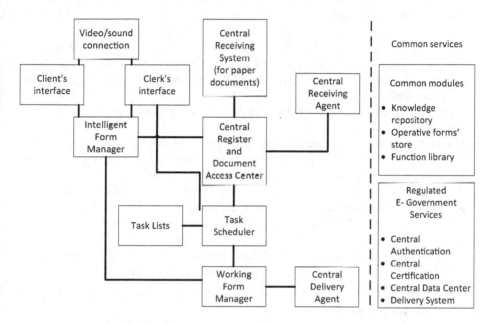

Fig. 4. Main architectural elements of the unified integrated system

- **Video/sound connection.** For both the clerks and clients the system provides a special chat connection with the specialist of the given procedure, allowing for not only the traditional chat and picture connection but also for the possibility of remote electronic transfer of the form being filled to the other party (for instance client to clerk and clerk to client after correction) providing direct assistance in the filling.
- **the Central Receiving System** is a REeGS which ensures that paper based documents are scanned centrally and provided with a structured electronic cover sheet.
- **the Central Receiving Agent** is a REeGS which is able to perform automatically the reception and filing tasks thanks to the structured electronic form.
- **Clerk's interface** is an interface surface optimized for the clerks, which displays the tasks and the document parts in the case of an ongoing processing, the allocated tasks than can or must be (if there is work-flow implemented) performed. The clerk is able to access legacy systems that are outside the scope of the unified integrated system (for example, the services of the register of the real estates in Hungary), he is also able to copy and paste data from a legacy system into other modules of the unified integrated system.

- **Client's interface**. The clients have access for self-service procedures from their home processing with a limited functionality that requires less skill and is simpler to use than that of the clerks.
- **the Intelligent Form Manager** is a system that supports the creation of parameterized electronic forms and the online filling of edited forms. The adjective "intelligent" describes that certain functions can be assigned to the fields of a form. For example, a form can automatically check or request data from other registers.
- **the Central Register and Document Access Center** is the REeGS component that keeps the registers of the location of e-documents through which the document can always be found. During the term of active processing (while legal remedy is available which usually means several months from the decision) the document resides in the operative forms' store. The central register records the actual location of the documents precisely.
- **Task lists** contain tasks allocated to individual clerks and their groups by the task scheduler.
- **the Task Scheduler** component of the system is responsible for the evaluation and timely (e.g. expired waiting period) distribution for execution of the tasks received by the system or created on the basis of clerk decisions or descriptions in the knowledge base. Note that the scheduler is more than a traditional workflow engine as it will able to handle rule-based task management.
- **the Working Form Manager** ensures that the information is processed in accordance with the rules.
- **the Central Delivery Agent** is a REeGS which is able to dispatch and transfer delivery documents automatically based on structured electronic forms.

There are common modules of the unified integrated system that can be used by the architectural elements as

- **the Knowledge Repository** which holds the "standard" description of all the procedures of public administration including form structures and work-flow descriptions, where relevant.
- **the Operative Forms' Store**. Contrary to the traditional model, where documents were moved between clerks, in the new model all documents (including forms and attachments) are to be stored in a central register (in the operative forms store) that contains the forms as well as their statuses. This approach eliminates the need for registering the filing statuses separately. Only a reference to the document in the operative forms store is passed between the organizations and when somebody needs some part of a document can retrieve it on the basis of the reference from the operative forms store.
- **The Function Library** that ensures that the system can reach the different specialized systems and that the processing is executed, characteristically providing them in the form of services registered as UDDI.

The below listed REeGS could and should also be used as building blocks of the unified integrated system as

- **the Central Authorization Service** manages the electronic authentication of the clients of public administration. Clients are allowed to use the services of different

Identity Provider. The task of this service is to hide away the complexity of using different identity providers [15];

- **the Central Certification Service** provides different ways of binding electronic documents to persons using a Public Key Infrastructure;
- **the Governmental Cloud** is a (dedicated) cloud facility provided for the Hungarian public administration organizations and
- **the Delivery System** is an electronic and hybrid delivery system used by the Hungarian public administration. In a hybrid system electronic documents are prepared but official paper equivalents are printed and delivered to the clients.

4.2 Processing in the Unified Integrated System

The simplified processing steps of a case in the unified integrated system are the following:

- The starting form is stored in the Central Register where a decision is made as to what kind of preliminary step is required to start the procedure. The Central Register will carry out the necessary the receiving and filing steps with the use of the Central Receiving Agent.
- Next the form is forwarded to the Task Scheduler which, based on a description in the Knowledge Repository, identifies the next processing step and the types of working forms needed, then it forwards the working forms to the Working Form Manager module. The Working Form Module prepares all the needed working forms by copying the necessary information into them. The Working Form Manager module also fills out fields that require data from other specialized systems at the same time (usually by calling web services).
- The Task Scheduler will allocate the cases (e-documents) to task lists of available clerks. The selected clerk (or where conceivable the computer) decides about how to proceed. If he finds that there is certain information that was not supplied then a supply of missing documents form will be forwarded to the client. Following the logics of the procedure there could be a repetition of these steps as described in the process description (that is, a new working form could be created on the basis of the previous, another request for transfer, etc.).
- The last step is the preparation of the decision form which records the decision based on the data taken from the working forms (and if the notification requires it, from any other form contained in the e-document) or the decision made by the clerk or by an algorithm. The decision form is processed by the Working Form Manager. It is important that both programmed and manual functions can be inserted into the decision making function, including the preparation and dispatch of the data transfer form. Note that often the decision refers to recording data in a register and so, the data have to be actually recorded in the register concerned. In this stage of processing it is important to allow the clerk to handle the task ignoring the automated solution, that is to ensure after each step in the form of exception management the possibility to act for the clerk (especially during the early stages of the implementation).

5 Conclusions

The mandatory structured format (the form) and the "dual" character of the electronic document, that is each form or document is in PDF format which can be displayed by a computer readable to the human eye and it can also be processed by computers due to the access to structured data in XM format, allows for the gradual implementation of the new model. Along with the systems ready to cooperate, the clerks also are able to accept and often even reply in the request for transfer forms using the simple filler function. The XML format is an intermediate element on which other applications can be built. This way of processing turns the form-filling bureaucracy into a modern data-driven workflow.

The main message of the paper is that the existing architectural elements, if pragmatically applied, can be utilized into a system able to support hybrid operations, that is, such a system where the contact with the client is partially based on paper.

References

1. Boyne, G.A.: Sources of public service improvement: a critical review and research agenda. J. Public Adm. Res. Theor. **13**(3), 367–394 (2003). doi:10.1093/jopart/mug027
2. Peters, B.G., Pierre, J.: Governance without government? Rethinking public administration. J. Public Adm. Res. Theor. **8**(2), 223–243 (1998)
3. Caiden, G.E.: Improving government performance. Public Adm. Rev. **66**, 139–142 (2006)
4. Kuipers, B.S., et al.: The management of change in public organizations: a literature review. Public Adm. **92**(1), 1–20 (2014)
5. Curry, D.: Trends for The Future of Public Sector Reform: A Critical Review of Future-Looking Research in Public Administration (2014). http://www.cocops.eu/wp-content/uploads/2014/04/TrendsForTheFutureOfPublicSectorReform.pdf
6. De Vries, M., Nemec, J.: Public sector reform: an overview of recent literature and research on NPM and alternative paths. Int. J. Public Sector Manag. **26**(1), 4–16 (2013). doi:10.1108/09513551311293408
7. OECD: OECD e-Government Studies: Hungary 2007. OECD Publishing, Paris (2007). doi: http://dx.doi.org/10.1787/9789264030527-en
8. Nemeslaki, A. (ed.): E-közszolgálatfejlesztés: Elméleti alapok és tudományos kutatási módszerek. Nemzeti Közszolgálati Egyetem, Budapest (2014). (in Hungarian)
9. OECD: Public Governance Reviews. Hungary: Towards a Strategic State Approach (2015). http://www.oecd.org/publications/hungary-towards-a-strategic-state-approach-9789264213555-en.htm
10. European Commission: eGovernment in Hungary, Edition 16.0 (2014). https://joinup.ec.europa.eu/elibrary/factsheet/egovernment-hungary-april-2014-v160
11. Hauder, M., Pigat, S., Matthes, F.: Research challenges in adaptive case management: a literature review. In: Proceedings of the 2014 IEEE 18th International Enterprise Distributed Object Computing Conference Workshops and Demonstrations, pp. 98–107 (2014)
12. Motahari-Nezhad, H.R., Swenson, K.D.: Adaptive case management: overview and research challenges. In: Proceedings of 2013 IEEE 15th Conference on Business Informatics, pp. 264–269 (2013). doi:10.1109/CBI.2013.44

13. Klischewski, R.: Information integration or process integration? How to achieve interoperability in administration. In: Traunmüller, R. (ed.) EGOV 2004. LNCS, vol. 3183, pp. 57–65. Springer, Heidelberg (2004). doi:10.1007/978-3-540-30078-6_10
14. PWC EU Services: Analysis of Structured e-Document Formats used in Trans-European Systems (2014). https://joinup.ec.europa.eu/sites/default/files/57/17/49/ISA%20Programme%20-%202014%20-%20Analysis%20of%20structured%20e-Document%20formats%20used%20in%20Trans-European%20Systems_v1.01.pdf
15. Kiss, J.K., Kiss, P.J., Klimkó, G.: Towards a model of client-driven access to public e-services. In: Kő, A., Francesconi, E. (eds.) EGOVIS 2015. LNCS, vol. 9265, pp. 117–131. Springer, Cham (2015). doi:10.1007/978-3-319-22389-6_9

E-Government, e-Governance and Urban Planning: Towards a Complete Digital Planning Process

Beatriz Santos[✉]

Department of Urban and Spatial Planning,
Government of Aragon, Zaragoza, Spain
bsantos@aragon.es

Abstract. Urban planning is changing in all its issues, especially with regard to transparency and citizen participation. The purpose of this paper is to provide a complete view of the planning process explaining the project implemented by Aragon's Government with the ultimate aim of digital switchover of all the stages. The project starts by ensuring urban information access through the use of web-based technology and Geographic Information Systems with a preliminary standardization work, continues with the development of an electronic processing system for urban planning instruments and finishes with the implementation of a new tool that will encourage citizen participation from the beginning of the process. The platform will allow the speed up of these procedures, facilitate the task of municipalities and achieve a greater coordination between administrations and also, as a transparency instrument, should enable the citizen to take an active part in the relationship with public administrations, in other words being involved in the decision-making process.

Keywords: Urban planning · Information access · Electronic processing · Participation · Web-based tools

1   Introduction

E-government and innovation can provide significant opportunities to transform public administration into an instrument of sustainable development. The UN Public Administration Program defines e-government as the use of ICT and its application by governments for the provision of information and public services to citizens and organizations (UNPAN 2014). Through innovation and e-government, public administrations can be more efficient, provide better services and respond to demands for transparency and accountability. Technologies can be used to manage data and information and enhance communication channels for engagement and empowerment of people.

Many authors focus on the potential of electronic government exploring different aspects contributing to citizens' participation and purposes of governance such us customer orientation (Schedler and Summermatter 2007), usability, functionality, security computer resource requirement, technical support provision (Hamilton et al. 2011; Venkatesh et al. 2012; Roman 2015). There is also a growing body of literature and research about the concept of e-Participation (Sandorf and Rose 2007; Sæbø et al.

© Springer International Publishing AG 2017
A. Kő and E. Francesconi (Eds.): EGOVIS 2017, LNCS 10441, pp. 32–45, 2017.
DOI: 10.1007/978-3-319-64248-2_4

2008; Medaglia 2012; Susha and Grönlund 2012) that confirms the interdisciplinarity of the field and refers to the use of ICT to support democratic decision-making. However, the potential of a digital state cannot be realized unless the rigid structures of contemporary bureaucratic state change along with the times in order to assimilate the integration of technology into government (Fountain 2001) and new procedures and activities have to be designed (Sanford and Rose 2008).

In recent years, cities are experiencing continual growth, and the challenge is to understand how we can use digital technologies and online resources to design livable cities and to engage citizens in urban planning. New digital tools and applications are developed to provide large quantities of data to better understand the reality of cities and visualization methods are increasing with varying degrees of technical complexity as communicate planning ideas is essential in participatory design (Al-Kodmany 2001). Also virtual reality environments are explored to help users interpret urban designs with new visualization options (Foth et al. 2009).

Urban planning and the methods for citizen participation in urban issues are also changing (Innes and Booher 2010) as digital tools invite people to experience urban space in new ways. Furthermore, there is an increasing effort to involve citizens from the beginning of the planning process and specific tools, such as Geographic Information Systems (GIS)-based services (Elwood 2001; Snellen 2001) and web-based technologies (Evans-Cowley and Hollander 2010; Ertiö 2015) play an important part in this challenge. But GIS could be difficult to use for citizens and user-friendlier tools such us Bottom-up GIS and map-based web applications, which enable citizens to create data on a map, have been developed (Talen 2000; Nuojua 2010; Adams 2013). In that sense, participatory planning becomes e-planning when participatory activities are expanded beyond face-to-face interaction to include ICT-mediated interaction.

The potential for e-government to enhance citizen participation makes it an enticing tool for planners and planning-related government entities (Conroy and Evans-Cowley 2006). E-planning, especially participatory e-planning, can be an important instrument of both e-democracy and e-governance (Conroy and Evans-Cowley 2004) although electronic tools has to be fit better into their context (Kubicek 2010) and digital methodologies have to be developed for widening public participation (Curwell et al. 2005). Some countries are taking advantage of the possibilities of e-planning to help the planning system deliver more efficient and accessible information and services (Horelli and Wallin 2010).

In Spain, Public Administrations are introducing important changes to improve the quality of services delivery bringing public issues closer to the citizen. That is also extended to urban planning, regional and local governments continue their efforts to promote the use of information and communication technologies, trying to simplify procedures, enhance transparency and strengthen citizen involvement. In order to achieve these goals, they have developed new instruments; both regulatory and ICT tools.

The Autonomous Community of Aragon has been developing for the past six years a complex and thorough project trying to achieve the *digital planning process,* starting with information access in order to ensure citizens access to urban planning information on a website. Thereafter, the project continues developing a platform as a transparency instrument, which also makes the electronic processing of urban planning possible. It will finish with the implementation of a new web-based tool that will encourage citizen participation from the beginning of the process. This approach tries to provide the necessary means to facilitate the work of municipalities, coordinate all different administrations and sectoral agencies that are involved in the planning process and improve services for citizens, not only to assist technicians but also to bring urban planning closer to citizens, in other words, providing information in a manner accessible for a non-specialist public.

This paper explains the project according to the different parts and stages of development. Part I analyses the necessary standardization process executed to achieve urban planning information gathering and dissemination. Part II refers to the electronic processing system, explaining the features and functionalities of the different IT tools designed and how it fits into the local authorities system since they are involved in urban planning procedure. Part III focus on e-governance advancing the upcoming developments aimed at developing an innovative web-based computer application to further improve urban planning participation.

2   Urban Planning Standardization Process and the Urban Information System

The region of Aragon has a large surface of 47.719 km^2, almost 10% of the extension of the Spanish territory, yet, its population, 1.346.293 inhabitants, supposes only 2,84% of the Spanish population. It has one of the lowest densities of Europe: 28,21 inhabitants/km^2, and several areas only have 3 inhabitants/km^2, so depopulation is one of the biggest problems here, especially in rural areas. The administrative structure consists of three provinces and 731 municipalities, but only 20 have more than 5,000 inhabitants, whereas 526 have less than 500 inhabitants.

The number and characteristics of the municipalities are decisive to define the type and degree of detail in urban planning information that could be gathered, since although there is a common regulation for all of them, the particular needs have led to the existence and development of several urban planning instruments (General Plans, Simplified Plans and Urban Land Restrictions) which have different level of detail and determinations. This, together with the distributions of competences among the regional government and local authorities, determine the type and level of urban information that regional administration can provide.

2.1   Urban Information Principles

One of the main objectives of e-Participation is to provide relevant information in an accessible and understandable way to the audience in order to enable more informed contributions (Macintosh 2004). In order to ensure urban planning information, the objectives and priorities were defined as follows:

a. Information shall be freely available on the Internet. Citizens may consult all the urban information of the region on a website: common access point (Urban System Information of Aragon, http://sitar.aragon.es/SIUa/).

b. Information has to be up to date and understandable. The existing planning instruments in each municipality, as well as their dates of approval and deadlines for entry into force, have to be shown the day after its publication.
c. Information should have legal certainty. Urban planning determinations have an important legal an economic impact so that documents available con the website must be related to the final ones, signed and stamped by the competent secretary. Citizens should be able to verify that documents correspond to originals (They must have digital signature and diligence).
d. Information has to be homogeneous. In order to ease of understanding urban planning documents by the citizen, a common language and criteria for the drafting and final presentation is needed.
e. The required information may not vary in level of detail from municipalities in order to provide a complete urban planning map.

2.2   The NOTEPA Project

To achieve the principle of simplification concerning urban planning activity, the Urban Planning Law of Aragon (2009) establishes the need to develop an Urban Planning Technical Rule (NOTEPA). This rule was approved in 2011 and serves the purpose of standardizing the urban planning instruments in order to facilitate and streamline their implementation and knowledge so it is set to become in the technical framework that simplifies the urban planning system in Aragon. Moreover, this technical rule is necessary to standardize criteria for the development of the urban planning documents, in other words, normalize the cartography, specific terminology and general urban concepts with the aim of reducing the degree of discretion in its interpretation and facilitating its integration into the Urban Information Systems, both regional and national. In that sense, the rule lays down the foundation for a common code ensuring that it does not reduce the initiative and creativity of the drafting teams.

We should focus on the role of the rule that has to contribute to the objective of urban planning information gathering and dissemination. That will be extended to all stages of the plans implementation, to all stakeholders involved in their processing and to all citizens as ultimate beneficiaries of urban activity. To that end, with the aim of homogenize and make easier the drafting of urban plans, the Urban Planning Department has undertaken the project called *NOTEPA*, in order to provide common criteria and the IT tools able to bring closer the contents and documents prepared by the technicians. The main objectives of the project are:

- To homogenize urban planning documentation.
- To provide greater legal certainty.
- To facilitate urban planning gathering and dissemination.
- To create a common code whilst preserving the creativity of the drafting teams.
- To provide a free software wool for the technicians.
- To make easier the understanding of technical urban planning documents.

This project is a major step forward towards the gathering and dissemination of urban planning information by further structuring and clarifying the urban planning documents. This ambitious project facilitates liaison and unification with the Urban Information System of Aragon where all the urban information about all the municipalities will be shown. It is made up of two parts: a Technical Rule, which is the heart of the project, and two software applications designed to help ensure compliance.

Urban Planning Technical Rule. This Rule constitutes the major part of NOTEPA's Project around which a set of tools is developed trying to get the maximum performance of urban planning homogeneity.

Before drafting the policy document, an exhaustive analysis about the situation and characteristics of urban planning in Aragon was done. General Urban Plans of representative municipalities were studied in order to draw the scheme of contents, required determinations, graphical models, etc. The conclusions of that study were reflected in an assessment that set out the need to define some criteria to clarify the information, both written and graphic, which any urban plan contains. In spite of the great diversity of cases and urban issue, there are some parameters that could be followed such us identification tags, color use in plots and shading, data sheets, layer structure or the list of contents that should enhance the quality of urban planning.

With all that information a draft of the policy document was prepared and in the hearing period sectoral agencies such us the different regional departments, the Environmental Agency, the Economic and Social Council, the Federation of Municipalities, the Urban Planning Regional Councils, the Official Schools of Architects, Engineers and Geographers made suggestions that were taken into account in the final version of the Rule. At the same time, the draft decree was published in the Official Gazette in order to offer citizens a two-month period to submit comments and requests.

The Urban Planning Technical Rule has the specifications and minimum characteristics that urban planning documents must have in Aragon. The main purpose of this rule is to define the quality, legality and standardization requirements that urban planning documentation must fulfill in order to integrate the structured information in the Spatial Data Infrastructure of Aragon at the conclusion of the administrative handling. To that effect, it contains:

- Definitions of the common concepts used in the area of urban planning, as well as abbreviations and acronyms for each of them.
- The type of cartography and reference scales that should be used as a basis for graphic documents.
- The guidelines and minimum requirements for the submission of documentation for each instrument.

Software Applications. NOTEPACAD is a free computer application developed by the Urban Planning Department that helps fulfilling the technical rule and makes easier the urban planning drafting. This specific software is a customization of the most widely used drawing application in Aragon, AutoCAD, and its installation process adds several toolbars to existing ones. With this method the technical author can continue drawing as usual, executing AutoCAD commands, and also translates information into urban planning concepts through specific graphic windows.

Using this application allows automatic metadata management, brings structure to information in different files, facilitates information being geo-referenced, increases the readability of graphical documents with shading, labels and layers automatic handle; involves a methodology which helps drafting teams and provides a real-time overview of the important numbers of urban planning, that is, zoning and surfaces.

In addition to NOTEPACAD, another software application known and hereinafter-called *L3* has been developed. It automates the urban data upload in the single data model from the files delivered by the technical authors (dwg, dxf and gml together with Excel sheets data) to the maximum extent possible.

To do this, depending on the file delivered, the user selects a gml file standardized from NOTEPACAD or one or more CAD files. If the process is done from the dwg files, as the technical author has respected and followed the layers structure, the application L3 can make a logical allocation of geometries. The input data are transformed into a vectorial format based on ESRI features in order to allow its visualization and management (shp file) and urban planning data are then added. That data are entered in two different ways: (i) Through Excel sheets and tables: General data can be entered at the time of the file upload and later it is possible to assign the specific data of each sector loading the tables. (ii) In a manual way: Geometry data could be modified at any time, either to introduce the missing data or to rectify any accuracy.

The tool allows the user to select the SDE environment to connect in order to get the data of the municipalities and update the layers of the model. Once the topologies are revised and the errors detected are corrected, a back-up copy is done and the tool makes the migration process of the new geometries to the appropriate database. This data base could be ArcSDE which has operated until now or PostGres - PostGIS which is scheduled to begin working in April 2017 when the corporate infrastructure change of IDEARAGON is completed. It also allows to save the transformation result of the drawing file both in dwg and shp formats and to generate the metadata file according to NOTEPA requirements.

2.3   Files Management Data Base

With the aim of storage all the documentation in a structured way and could search and retrieve any of the documents forming part of the urban planning file, a computer data base SAU BDD was created as well as two applications SAU-URBAN and SAU-GISWS. This database is the structural component that contains all the urban planning administrative records and links with the different applications and websites.

In the fist place, SAU-URBAN is a desktop application of the Urban Planning Department, based on Power Builder technology, which allows the urban planning files management. It enables the creation and development of different types of documents with several templates and also to attach files, drafted in advance, both in word and pdf format. The processed files are stored in *Documentum*, the document manager of Aragon's Government, from where they are checked and recover thereafter. In the second place, SAUGISWS is a web-based application developed with J2EE technology which publishes different web services to meaningfully integrate with other applications indicated below: SIUA, PUA and DDPW (Fig. 1).

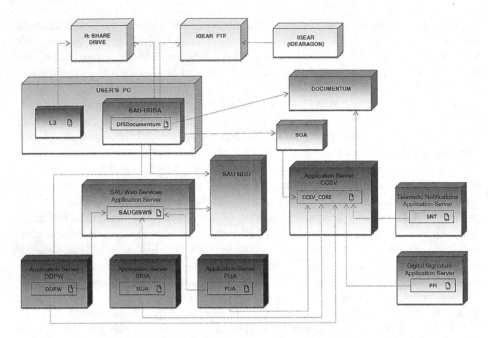

Fig. 1. Systems involved in urban planning process and management.

Therefore, the urban planning file data base, SAU BDD, can be accessed by both applications and it contains the tables and views filling by the application SAU-URBAN and after consulting by SAUGIS through its web services. Thus, all the approval agreements of urban planning instruments and the technical documents making up the files (memories, plans, regulations, data sheets, etc.) are stored in the data base and at the same time are shown for citizen consultation in two different web pages. If they are currently being processed, they will appear in the Urban Platform website (PUA) and if they are finally approved they will be available in the Urban Information System website (SIUA).

Moreover, the latest technological developments have been able to integrate SAU-URBAN application with the e-government services so that generated documents could be electronically signed through the Digital Signature Service of Aragon's Government, *Portafirmas*. At present, work is already under way to integrate with the Telematic Notifications Service in order to allow submitting notifications to citizens and local authorities through the application.

2.4   The Urban Information System

The Urban Information System of Aragon (SIUA) is a set of tools developed for the publication and dissemination of urban planning data and existing information in the Autonomous Community of Aragon. It has two main tools; the archive and the viewer, continuously updated and is a collaborative system that is co-ordinated with other information systems:

- National Urban Information System (SIU).
- Real Estate Cadastre.
- Spatial Data Infrastructure of Aragon (IDEARAGON).

Archive. The urban planning file ensures the telematic access to all information gathered about the urban planning instruments of Aragon municipalities. The information is organized by municipalities and enables citizens to acquaint themselves with the general and development urban planning instruments as well as their modifications. They could also consult and download the specific documents of each instrument, which have been previously scanned and classified for its diffusion through the use of web-based technology.

The archive is updated by scanning the documentation that has been finally approved. In this regard, the implementation of the Urban Planning Technical Rule is entirely related with the effective working and continued development of the archive, as it will provide a better understanding and dissemination of all urban planning information by setting common standards and instructions for drawing-up and submitting documentation in digital form. This update will be automatic and documents could be shown from the moment of its approval from the implementation and complete application of the Urban Planning Digital Diligence tool (DDPW), explained in point 3.2. This tool is already developed and tested and enables the digital signature and stamp of the technical documents and its sending through telematic means.

Viewer. The urban planning viewer is a geographic information visualization tool which makes accessible the urban planning information directly on the map and, moreover, it provide specific information and data related to current urban planning instruments such us land classification, types of land use, infrastructures and equipments, general urban data sheets, etc. A key feature of this tool is that it allows the user to overlay other geographic information layers which have a bearing in urban planning such us environmental and sectoral protections, transport infrastructures or land register. The viewer is updated annually after the vectorization and systematization process on the basis of the scanned documents. But, after the development and launch of the proposal preparation tool L3, it will be possible its automatic update from the files handed by the drafting teams, speeding up the process and avoiding manual works.

As mentioned above, the viewer is integrated with the Spatial Data Infrastructure of Aragon (IDEARAGON). This infrastructure is based on client/server architecture model using the OGC and ISO standards. The model allows the processing and answer of the client requests made via websites or specific softwares by means of transfer and communication languages that are standardized and interoperable. Interoperability enables data sharing and the possibility of information and knowledge exchange between different information systems that provides geographic information from many sources on the Internet. It consists of a set of servers able to manage the geographic information fully and properly from creation to publication enabling its control, register, organization, documentation, storage and later search and use by citizens. All these actions are achieved through different applications, services and data bases.

3 Electronic Processing System

Once the urban planning information improvement process has been completed, the second stage of the project starts. The main objective of this stage is to implement an electronic processing system of urban planning instruments that will allow the speed up of these procedures, facilitate the task of municipalities and achieve a greater coordination between administrations.

In view of the distribution of the population in Aragon, where more than eighty per cent of municipalities have mess than 1.000 inhabitants, the technical resources necessary for providing electronic processing services concerning urban planning are beyond the reach of local authorities. But information society is evolving continuously; citizens and businesses demand greater access and quality of services and Public Administrations have to face the new requirements through effective delivery of services. Moreover, the Electronic Access to Public Services Act establishes certain obligations that all public administrations must meet.

3.1 Urban Platform of Aragon

In order to make this happen, the Urban Planning Department has developed the Urban Platform of Aragon (PUA). It may be reinforced as a central service that incorporate the new technologies into all urban planning procedures, provide a web environment for the public reporting period and submission of reports, enable sending complete files and urban projects through telematic networks to the Provincial Council for their approval or report and promote a greater publicity of the urban planning instruments. In the end, this will encourage a more efficient public participation process and streamline procedures. The platform has three different modules that correspond to the user roles that could use this service in any stage of processing: municipal secretaries, sectoral agencies and citizens.

In the first place, municipal secretary's module includes several features which allow them to take the following actions: (i) sending the approval agreements to Aragon's official journal (BOA); (ii) requesting sectoral reports to all the sectoral agencies which have competences due to the specific conditions of the urban planning instrument as well as receive and download the content of the reports; (iii) receiving requests from citizens during the public reporting period and reply to those requests through the electronic notifications service.

In the second place, sectoral agencies' module allows the reception of requesting reports with link to the documentation of the urban planning instrument so that they can consult and download it on the website of PUA viewer. After that they can upload the report digitally signed or sign it with the application and finally send it through the platform. In that sense, it should be emphasized that due to the high number of agencies involved in urban planning, the collaboration between them is essential so that procedures could be speed up and improved by means of telematic services.

In the third place, citizens' module enables the dispatch of allegations during the public reporting period, after the initial approval of the instrument. To that end, the citizen can check all the documents, both written (memories, regulations, catalogues, annexes, etc.) and graphic (information and planning) in the viewer. The essential requirement is that the documentation must have the digital diligence so that citizens are assured of the validity of the documents. Therefore, PUA allows citizens to make representations to an urban planning instrument in the public reporting period that has been previously upload in the database and is shown through the viewer of the platform. For this, it is only necessary to have the electronic ID or another recognized certificate to access and then fill out the attached form.

The platform allows municipalities for sectoral reports request and sectoral agencies for referral the reports to the relevant municipality. To that end, e-government services enabling sending and receiving the notifications and documentation with the necessary legal security have been implemented. The application is completely integrated with the e-Government Aragon's Plan services:

- SRT: Telematic Register Service
- SNT: Telematic Notifications Service
- SIU: Users Identification Service
- SGA: Alert Management Service
- IBOA: Aragon's Official Gazette Application
- CCSV: Web-based application of the e-government service that integrates with the document manager, Documentum, providing web services.

But apart from e-government services, owing to the inter-administrative nature of the application, PUA is also integrated with the Documents Referral Service (SRD). This is a telematic service dedicated to the exchange of documents between the Local Administration Department of Aragon and the local authorities, which was launched in 2008. Through this service, local authorities send documentation relating to agreements, meeting records, resolutions and ordinances, budgets, tax regulations, inventories as well as the initiation agreements of proceedings that after will be deal with by the autonomous community. Until now, these documents were sent on paper by post, but since the introduction of SRD it has been replaced by electronic means with digital signature. Now, SRD includes two new links, one to the Urban Planning Digital Diligence (DDPW) and another one to the Urban Planning Platform (ETTPUA).

3.2 Urban Planning Digital Diligence

As previously mentioned, a fundamental requirement for launching the project is the digital diligence of the urban planning instruments. To date, after the approval agreement, the secretary in charge, depending on the type of instrument and stage of processing will be the secretary of the Town Council or the Provincial Council, executes the diligence act on paper documents, in other words, place their stamp with the date and signature. These documents are subsequently scanned in order to be accessible on the web of the Urban Information System but in order to achieve the telematic process, specially the public reporting period and consultations, there was a need to replace this stamp and signature with the corresponding digital.

To that end, the Urban Planning Department developed the Urban Planning Digital Diligence (DDPW), a web-based application that makes possible the digital diligence and it allows to attach the other administrative documentation (as certified copies) and to send them through telematic network to Documentum. After receiving all the documents telematically, SAUGIS' web services incorporate the documents to the data base SAU BDD and show them in PUA and SIUA websites.

The web application has been developed with the programme platform J2EE with JAVA programming language. The components of the architecture are data base Oracle 10 g and applications server Oracle Weblogic Server 12c (12.2.1). DDPW, like PUA, is integrated with SRD, which handle the Town Council Secretaries management, and with the Telematic Register Server that ensures the entry and reception of electronic documents. Therefore, the application is integrated with the following horizontal services of Aragon's Government:

- Document manager server: Documentum.
- CCSV: Web-based application of the e-government service that integrates with the document manager, Document, providing web services.
- SRT: Telematic Register Service.
- Signature Platform: @firma.

4   Participation: e-Government and e-Governance

In addition to fulfilling electronically the obligations on information and hearing procedures, the Urban Planning Department wants to encourage the addition of proposals or suggestions by citizens in the early stages of the urban planning instruments drafting. To do this, starting from the assessments of alternatives executed last year, the aim is to develop an innovative web-based computer application to further improve urban planning integrating new technologies, spatial analysis and citizen participation. The new tool shall be accessible from the Urban Platform of Aragon and may be integrated with the web portal Aragon Participates, a website developed by the Citizen Participation, Transparency and Cooperation Department to create greater involvement of citizens in the design and evaluation of public policies.

It will provide the possibility of designing and executing a participatory process during the drafting of an urban planning instrument to any municipality. During the study, different participation processes, both national and international, were analyzed in order to find the better option of a tool that can be applied in any municipality of Aragon. Due to the great diversity of urban areas and necessities, the key is that the application has to be scalable and flexible so that it can be used from a general urban plan for the whole city or town to an urban regeneration plan for a neighborhood. The chosen system is based on a number of guided-surveys developed and tested by the drafting team, which will be empowered in advance. A selection of questions, which could be used and amended, will be available for the technicians and could combine alphanumeric questions with "geographic" ones. In geographic questions, the framework, reference layers as well as the type of questions must be selected so that the citizen could choose geographical entities previously upload or draw freely points, lines or polygons.

Using geo-referenced questions will enable citizens to establish their needs and suggestions specifically and precisely on the map, for instance pedestrians' routes, dangerous sites, congestion problems, degraded areas, buildings need of retrofitting, green areas, equipments... Moreover, when the survey is completed, GIS allow detailed analyses, operation processing, visual representation and in-depth knowledge of the city situation identifying the critical areas and essential needs for inhabitants with.

Regarding the technical requirements, all external cartographic sources has to be included in the application according to Spatial Data Infrastructures. This means that they will be consulted through Web Map Services (WMS) that meet the standard OGC and be supplied by official bodies. All system information, both alphanumeric and geographical, should be stored in a database (Oracle 11g) that will have storage capacity of geographical objects.

5 Conclusions

In recent years, Public Administrations have been modernizing their services and, as a result of the possibilities of new technologies and digital media, new forms of relationship with citizens emerge. This includes not only enhancing proceedings' transparency and dissemination of information with several web pages but also platforms for user interaction and better coordination between different authorities.

Urban Planning Department of Aragon promotes the effective use of ICT in order to allow a greater spread and access to urban information, an increased transparency in planning process and citizens' participation. This includes moving towards an electronic processing system for urban planning instruments, but urban planning procedure is really complex due to the number of administrations and stakeholders involved in it, the several stages that have to be completed and the legal requirements that should be complied. Consequently new tools have been developed in order to facilitate the task of administrations and to make the entire decision-making process more transparent, from the preparatory stage to the final approval.

A database is the heart of the project which storages and manages all the urban planning data and documents through several web services that integrate with the other applications and services. The final result is the availability of reliable information in different websites for citizens' access to consult, use and download, including geographical viewers where visualization tools help to understand and analyze urban information and phenomena.

This project represented a costly technical challenge that has been gradually completed with the development and implementation of several computer tools that allow the execution of all the processes in digital form. But the key for the success of this initiative is the collaboration and participation of different administrations, sectoral agencies and also citizens at each stage of the process.

References

Adams, D.: Volunteered geographic information: potential implications for participatory planning. Plan. Pract. Res. **28**(4), 464–469 (2013)

Al-Kodmany, K.: Visualization tools and methods for participatory planning and design. J. Urban Technol. **8**(2), 1–37 (2001)

Conroy, M.M., Evans-Cowley, J.: Informing and interacting: the use of e-government for citizen participation in planning. J. E-Gov. **1**(3), 73–92 (2004)

Conroy, M.M., Evans-Cowley, J.: E-participation in planning: an analysis of cities adopting on-line citizen participation tools. Environ. Plan. C: Gov. Policy **24**, 371–384 (2006)

Curwell, S., Deakin, M., Cooper, I., Paskaleva-Shapira, K., Ravetz, J., Babicki, D.: Citizens' expectations of information cities: Implications for urban planning and design. Build. Res. Inf. **33**(1), 55–66 (2005)

Elwood, S.A.: GIS and collaborative urban governance: understanding their implications for community action and power. Urban Geogr. **22**(8), 737–759 (2001)

Ertiö, T.-P.: Participatory apps for urban planning—space for improvement. Plann. Pract. Res. **30**(3), 303–321 (2015)

Evans-Cowley, J., Hollander, J.: The new generation of public participation: internet-based participation tools. Plann. Pract. Res. **25**(3), 397–408 (2010)

Foth, M., Bajracharya, B., Brown, R., Hearn, G.: The second life of urban planning? Using NeoGeography tools for community engagement. J. Location Based Serv. **3**(2), 97–117 (2009)

Fountain, J.E.: Building the Virtual State: Information Technology and Institutional Change. Brookings Institution Press, Washington DC (2001)

Hamilton, F., Pavan, P., McHale, K.: Designing usable e-government services for the citizen – success within user centred design. Int. J. Public Inf. Syst. **3**, 159–167 (2011)

Horelli, L., Wallin, S.: The future-making assessment approach as a tool for e-planning and community development: the case of ubiquitous Helsinki. In: Silva, C. (ed.) Handbook of Research on E-Planning: ICTs for Urban Development and Monitoring, pp. 58–79. IGI Global, Hershey (2010)

Innes, J., Booher, D.: Planning with Complexity: An Introduction to Collaborative Rationality for Public Policy. Routledge, New York (2010). ISBN 9780415779326

Kubicek, H.: The potential of e-participation in urban planning: a European perspective. In: Silva, C.N. (ed.) Handbook of Research on E-Planning: ICTs for Urban Development and Monitoring, pp. 168–194. IGI Global, Hershey (2010)

Macintosh, A.: Characterizing e-participation in policy-making. In: Proceedings of the 37th Annual Hawaii International Conference on System Sciences, pp. 117–126 (2004)

Medaglia, R.: eParticipation research: moving characterization forward (2006–2011). Gov. Inf. Q. **29**, 346–360 (2012)

Nuojua, J.: WebMapMedia: a map-based Web application for facilitating participation in spatial planning. Multimedia Syst. **16**(1), 3–21 (2010)

Roman, A.V.: Delineating three dimension of e-government success: security, functionality and transformation. In: Information Resources Management Association (ed.) Public Affairs and Administration: Concepts, Methodologies, Tools, and Applications, pp. 135–157. IGI Global, Hershey (2015). doi:10.4018/978-1-4666-8358-7.ch007

Sandorf, C., Rose, J.: Characterizing e-participation. Int. J. Inf. Manage. **27**(6), 406–421 (2007)

Sanford, C., Rose, J.: Designing the e-participation artefact. Int. J. Electron. Bus. **6**, 572–589 (2008)

Schedler, K., Summermatter, L.: Customer orientation in electronic government: motives and effects. Gov. Inf. Q. **24**(2), 291–311 (2007)

Snellen, I.: ICTs, bureaucracies, and the future of democracy. Commun. ACM **44**(1), 45–48 (2001)

Susha, I., Grönlund, Å.: eParticipation research: systematizing the field. Gov. Inf. Q. **29**, 373–382 (2012)

Sæbø, Ø., Rose, J., Skiftenes Flak, L.: The shape of eParticipation: characterizing an emerging research area. Gov. Inf. Q. **25**(3), 400–428 (2008)

Talen, E.: Bottom-up GIS. A new tool for individual and group expression in participatory planning. APA J. **66**(3), 279–294 (2000)

UNPAN: UN e-Government Survey 2014. E-Government for the Future We Want. UNPAN, New York (2014). http://unpan3.un.org/egovkb/Portals/egovkb/Documents/un/2014-Survey/E-Gov_Complete_Survey-2014.pdf. Accessed 10 Jan 2017

Venkatesh, V., Chan, F.K.Y., Thong, J.Y.L.: Designing e-government services: key service attributes and citizens' preference structures. J. Oper. Manag. **30**(1–2), 116–133 (2012)

Open Data Ecosystem

Open Data Ecosystems

Introducing the Stimulator Function

Sébastien Martin[1,2] ⓘ, Slim Turki[1(✉)] ⓘ, and Samuel Renault[1] ⓘ

[1] Luxembourg Institute of Science and Technology, Esch-sur-Alzette,
Luxembourg
{sebastien.martin, slim.turki, samuel.renault}@list.lu
[2] Université de Paris 8, Saint-Denis, France

Abstract. The ecosystem perspective is widespread in open data research. First, some open data ecosystem models are discussed according to the roles identified. In these systems, we found room for a new role, at least a transversal role, consisting in stimulating the ecosystem. This role is specific in that it implies to understand the configuration, the mechanisms of the ecosystems and to define an influence strategy. Then, we show that strategic management has thoroughly analyzed the role of stimulator, or leader, that this discipline has built strong theoretical frameworks grounded in case studies. Therefore, we discuss the interest and the conditions to transpose these findings to an open data context and enrich the dimensions of stimulator's functions. Following several spearhead initiatives, we state that public procurement is the best vehicle for channeling stimulator interventions. We conclude by a diagram summarizing the stimulator's role that is intended to be instantiated in the frame of the BE-GOOD programme.

Keywords: Open data · Ecosystem · Stimulation

1 Introduction

Since the first data releases, open data generated many expectations in the economic or social domains. Most of these benefits remain however limited and their sustainability may be challenged. Open data initiatives have been warned against risks (Magalhães and Roseira 2016; Barry and Bannister 2014; Martin et al. 2013) and received several critics. In this paper, we try to explore the advantage of open data ecosystems, not only to improve the analysis of open data initiatives, but also to influence the ecosystems. In this frame, we present also an approach implemented in BE-GOOD, a European programme.

One stream criticizes open data initiatives as being too (data) supply-driven (Janssen et al. 2012). This way, the ecosystem perspective is a mean of decentring the analysis, since most of the current models concur on the need to identify interdependencies among the actors, thus on both sides. The assumption that publishing data is enough to get results has been criticized too, and maybe caricatured too strongly by the slogan "If you build it, they will come". The ecosystem concept bears complexity and

© Springer International Publishing AG 2017
A. Kő and E. Francesconi (Eds.): EGOVIS 2017, LNCS 10441, pp. 49–63, 2017.
DOI: 10.1007/978-3-319-64248-2_5

can be useful to bypass some naive assumptions about open data and value creation mechanisms even if, as stated by (Van Schalkwyk et al. 2016), this perspective itself remains a simplification, an ideal type, "to create order out of a complex, non-linear set of processes".

Among the arguments pleading for the adoption of an ecosystem perspective which would be considered as a lever to mitigate the risks, we propose essential elements to define a new function in the open data ecosystems, a stimulating function, from which a fundamental feature would be to prevent and mitigate the risks identified in an ecosystem. This document intends to examine theoretical foundations of a stimulator role and to summarize the first boundaries with elements extracted from several models of open data ecosystems. Some disciplinary domains have already integrated a similar function, this is the case of leadership in the frame of business ecosystems. Thus, we try also to acclimatize this role to narrow the stimulator function inside an open data ecosystem. In Sect. 1, we try to draw the main characteristics of an open data ecosystem and especially the diverse functions and the relationships occurring among them. In Sect. 2, we show the relevance to extrapolate some theoretical or empirical frameworks to be used in an open data context. In Sect. 3, we define the main features of a new function in the open data ecosystem that is stimulator. In Sect. 4, we discuss the benefits of exercising this function through public procurement actions. Section 5 exposes further research required and concludes this paper.

2   Open Data Ecosystems and Roles in the Ecosystems

2.1   Definition of an Open Data Ecosystem

(Harrison et al. 2012), building on Nardi and O'Day, provide a broad definition of what is an ecosystem, "a system of people, practices, values, and technologies in a particular local environment". More accurately, "ecosystems are comprised of interacting, relatively tightly connected components with substantial interdependencies. Specific components will vary from ecosystem to ecosystem." (Zuiderwijk et al. 2014) provide a state of the art of the open data ecosystem's definitions and point the possibility to consider open data ecosystem as a combination of various kinds of ecosystems.

Open data ecosystems have been analysed from different scales and perspectives: nationwide (Heimstädt et al. 2014), at a local scale (Dawes et al. 2016), according to their temporal evolution (Heimstädt et al. 2014). Ecosystems can be analysed too through the lens of the kinds of data and services created on them. Yet it is widely admitted that different kinds of data will lead to different kinds of services, that they do not bear the same economic value potential and thus can give rise to different kinds of ecosystem.

2.2   Functions in an Open Data Ecosystem

Some typologies already encompass close approaches in the field of open data, a helpful summary is provided in (EUDECO 2016). They are mentioned here for the record because they are similar to those used in studies devoted specifically to open data ecosystems. We can point however the EU Data Landscape framework, which differs from other models in that the authors refuse to draw the traditional distinction between users and re-users.

(Deloitte 2012) identified five archetypes: suppliers, aggregators, developers, enrichers, enablers. Interestingly, the authors' goal was not to describe the functions of an ecosystem, but rather to provide a typology of business models. To the best of our knowledge, it remains one of the most influential papers to describe the set of functions in the open data ecosystem literature. It is adopted for example by (Ponte 2015).

The figure below both summarizes the state of the art and our view of an open data ecosystem before its stimulation (Fig. 1).

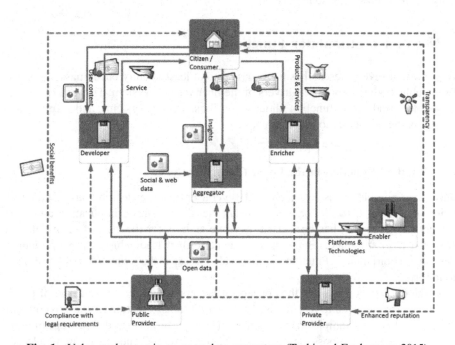

Fig. 1. Value exchanges in an open data ecosystem (Turki and Foulonneau 2015)

(Lindman and Kuk 2015) propose a quite similar framework by identifying five roles in the open data value network: data publisher, data extractor & transformer, data analyser, user experience provider and end users. For (Heimstädt et al. 2014), "minimal value chain within Open Data ecosystems consists of three elements: data suppliers, data intermediaries, and data consumers." (Immonen et al. 2014) distinguish between the **roles** (six main roles: data providers, service providers, application developers, application users, infrastructure and tool providers, data brokers, then refined in 22 sub-roles) and the **services** provided by the ecosystem (data provider support, data adaptation, tool support, diverse applications, contract-making, finding partners, finding services, finding information, finding markets, data validation, business models). (Dawes et al. 2016) identify roles too and characterize them by two main features:

goals, and practices. (Jetzek 2015) insists on the roles of the intermediaries for information aggregation, providing trust, facilitating and matching.

A key point in most contributions is their agreement on that roles in the ecosystem should not be devoted to one kind of actor, for example by restricting public institutions to the sole role of supplying datasets. The focus of these works is on the intermediaries' functions in that they enable or ease the work of other stakeholders of the ecosystem. As stated by (Van Schalkwyk et al. 2016) "keystone species are enablers, not necessarily drivers in the ecosystem; they can be useful but they are not essential to the sustained functioning of an ecosystem". To complement this approach, we wondered if the functions related to driving or leading the ecosystem could also be considered among these keystone species.

3   Need for a Stimulator Function

We show that several researches have early and at least latently encompassed the role of the public bodies as possible drivers of the open data ecosystem. Then we justify the re-use of a leadership function thought for business ecosystems and explain that strategy is the best common denominator.

3.1   A Latent Function in the Open Data Literature?

Among the eligible terms, we identified several options: leader obviously, architect, instigator, strategist, facilitator. Leader bears the idea of strong implication and commitment but, even if it has been used by some authors for the case of open data, we chose the term stimulator as being more generic than leadership and convenient to stress the coordination function. It may also escape the fears of public bodies' monopoly.

In the open data literature, the concept of leadership is used in the sense of public bodies' internal leadership and focuses on internal transformation of the government, see (Lee 2014) for example. (Heimstädt et al. 2014) do not use the concept of stimulation but mention the possible "government interventions" and argue that in addition to the supply side, these interventions must involve demand-side as well. The arguments of (Harrison et al. 2012) not only support the concept of leadership, but a leadership assumed by public bodies. These authors focus on intentionality, but in terms that remain close to those of stimulation: "[...] government organizations as central actors, taking the initiative within networked systems organized to achieve specific goals related to innovation and good government." (Dawes et al. 2016) recognize the government a role "to stimulate an ecosystem of data producers, innovators, and users" and claim the need for a better understanding of "the role of leadership" to "understand how and why influential stakeholders emerge and the roles they play in the design, health and, performance of OGD ecosystems".

Once admitted the need of this function, we intend to draw some concepts from other fields to fill its contents.

3.2 Relevance of Transposing Leadership's Concepts from Other Research Fields

Concepts derived from ecology in general have received an enthusiastic reception and have been widely disseminated in various disciplines. It seems fruitful to build on some models designed for platforms and business ecosystems as they consider the question of leadership. Beyond (O'Reilly 2011) who already suggested to consider government as a platform, across several publications, Jetzek has shown the possibility to describe the open data ecosystem as a case of multi-sided market.

Open Data as Multi-sided Markets
One important characteristic of the multi-sided markets according to (Jetzek 2015) is that they are "technologies, products, or services that create value primarily by enabling direct interactions between two or more customer or participant groups". The dynamics is described in terms of network effects which, according to (Gawer and Cusumano 2013), are "complementary innovations by tapping into the innovative capabilities of many external actors". As noted by (Jetzek 2015), network effects are one of the fundamental principles expected to build value from open data.

Multi-sided Markets as "Industry Platforms"
(Gawer and Cusumano 2013) add a requirement for that a multi-sided market may be considered as an industry platform that the authors aim to describe: it must "stimulate external innovation". An industry platform is composed of "products, services or technologies that are close to the former but provide the foundation upon which outside firms (organized as a 'business ecosystem') can develop their own complementary products, technologies, or services". Open data fits rather well with the case of external platforms, since data released are intended to be the foundations of new economic activities. There is no total agreement on the distinctions and the relationships between platform and ecosystem, but this does not prevent to extend the concept of leadership to the ecosystem provided that one recognizes ecosystem as a more generic concept.

3.3 Need for a Function Dealing with Strategy

It is thus relevant to import concepts designed for platforms and we focus then on leadership, the closest concept of what we mean by stimulation.

Hub Firm's Leadership
(Nambisan and Sawhney 2011) have designed two models of "hub firms", which can be considered as two models of leadership. An "innovation integrator primarily focuses on envisioning the core innovation and integrating partners' contributions to create the final product or offering, whereas a platform leader focuses on defining and developing the core innovation (platform) and facilitating partners' complementary innovations that expand its reach and range." If we try to draw an analogy with open data, the features of an open data leadership remain too fuzzy to fit strictly only one of these models, although the latter seems to be more adapted.

According to (Gawer and Cusumano 2012) a platform leader is a very close relative of the "keystone firm", "a firm that drives industrywide innovation for an evolving system of separately developed components". In this frame, the leader must "stimulate complementary innovations", we might also write drive the reuse, by other firms. A leader has to "develop a vision", "build a sufficiently open or modular architecture" and "manage ecosystem relationships". All these elements can be described in terms of strategic vision, consistently with (Harrison et al. 2012), who already introduced the concept of "strategic ecosystem thinking", "which means being guided by the goal of explicitly and purposefully constructing open government ecosystems".

The Main Feature of Stimulation is Strategy

By combining thoughts devoted to open data ecosystems and those to leadership in business ecosystems and platforms, we argue that the main specificity of the stimulator function is that it involves thinking about and influencing the ecosystem. The scale of this task and the framework of the ecosystem do not make excessive the use of the term 'strategy'. Some disciplines have built theories and practical frameworks to deal with strategy, we focus here on strategic management. Strategic management classically identifies three major stages of a strategy that could be a lens to analyse an ecosystem. **Strategic analysis** is the issue the best addressed in the open data literature. **Strategy formulation** is a more complex stage, on which we have currently few models and matter. Since the first open data initiatives, some public bodies were committed to publish their open data strategy, see for example the United-States or the United Kingdom. In the latter case, each department was committed to publish a strategy. However, a strategy of influence on the ecosystem requires to take into account a broader set of factors, both internal and external to these departments. We have even fewer insights on what could be a real **implementation strategy** specific to open data, though we do not lack partial information on a wide set of initiatives. There is also a lot of literature on guidance documents on very specific tasks (Open Data Institute) or best practices (e.g. Share-PSI 2.0).

We present in the next section a framework organizing the features of a strategic stimulation function, attempting to re-use the framework of orchestration processes.

4 Stimulator's Function in an Open Data Ecosystem

This section lays the foundations of a systematic framework aiming both to describe a stimulator's role and to be a tool for planning influence on the ecosystem. A final diagram intends to balance strategy design and concrete actions. We analyse the stimulator's function in three layers: analysis, developing a strategic vision and acting to influence the ecosystem.

4.1 Analysis of the Current Ecosystem and of the Relevant External Parts

Leadership implies **knowing the ecosystem** and most of the current thoughts on the concept of ecosystem can be related to this stage and to the strategic analysis defined above. Knowing the ecosystem means sketching the boundaries, the actors, their relationships, the contextual elements that influence the ecosystem. In some way, being a stimulator means reporting a state of the available resources.

(Dawes et al. 2016) list some of the features relevant to assess an open data ecosystem: climate for openness; climate for innovation; nature of the civil sector; nature of the private sector; characteristics and capability of the civic technology community. (Harrison et al. 2012) highlight four key points of the "ecosystem thinking": identifying actors, understanding the nature of transactions in the ecosystem, understanding the resources required by each, assess the health of the ecosystem. These are very close to the model of ecosystem analysis proposed by (Battistella et al. 2013), which develop a methodology for business ecosystems and to analyse them in four main stages: ecosystem perimeter, elements and relationships; ecosystem model representation and data validation (a less interesting step in the current stage, since open data ecosystems are still in their embryonic stage), ecosystem analysis (stage focused on value creation), ecosystem evolution (uncertainties, trends, scenarios).

To these points, we propose to add the evaluation of all other kinds of tangible or intangible aspects that might be included in the ecosystem or influence it. It seems for example relevant to include norms and values, as did (Dawes et al. 2016). It requires having some knowledge besides the current ecosystem to identify potential stakeholders who should be attracted in the ecosystem.

4.2 Developing a Strategic Vision

This stage addresses partially strategic analysis but also strategy formulation and implementation.

4.2.1 Definition of the Ecosystem's Goals

The range of objectives can be very large: direct and indirect job creations after the creation of new kind of economics activities, capacity building and strengthening of the economic framework emergence of services that private economic activity neglects, ease the spread of new approaches (e.g. data analytics) or of new technologies. Compared with the recommendations of the state of the art, we would insist on the necessity if not to adopt a prospective approach, at least the concern to set the ecosystem in a long-term perspective. A narrow issue is to watch the external evolutions that require an evolution of the ecosystem over time.

4.2.2 Shape and Functioning of the Ecosystem

The stimulator can influence the general architecture of the ecosystem, its place in this architecture and define the degree of influence it shall have on the other parts.

Place of the Stimulator in the Ecosystem
For a given actor, this role depends on the constraints, its resources its goals and its will to be implied in the network. It also depends on the internal alignment mechanisms to keep the congruence between the actor's internal organization and the whole ecosystem.

Influence the Boundaries, and Shape of the Ecosystem, the Nature and the Strength of the Relationships Between the Actors

As open data ecosystems are still underdeveloped, we argue that these aspects should be envisioned through the emergence mechanisms driving the rise of an ecosystem. This is consistent with (Gawer and Cusumano 2013) who point a limit on current research on platforms as "it takes for granted the existence of the market that transact through the platform". (Thomas 2013) engages an analysis of ecosystem emergence through the case of digital service ecosystems. The author distinguishes three stages of emergence: initiation, momentum, control and four main mechanisms: resource activities, technological activities, institutional activities and contextual activities.

We propose to integrate the influence on the ecosystem's goals and configuration in a broader model, which is the "orchestration process".

4.2.3   Orchestration Processes Serving a Strategic Vision

Orchestration process's model is developed by (Nambisan and Sawhney 2011). In this section, we intend to present its components and to discuss systematically the relevance of their transposition to the stimulation of an open data ecosystem. This concept implies to choose between two approaches. In an **integrator** model: "a hub firm defines the basic architecture for the core innovation and then invites network members to design and develop the different components that make up this core innovation". In a **platform leader** model the "hub firm defines and offers the basic innovation architecture, which then becomes the platform or the foundation for other network members to build on through their own complementary innovations." Although open data seem to fit better the model of the leader, some dimensions are more adapted to the prior model. Moreover, it matters from the degree of implication aimed by the stimulator. In consequence, both are envisioned here.

The orchestration process acts on two main dimensions: innovation design and network design. **Leveraging innovation** design consists in to act on the assets. Applied to open data, basic elements are data, whether raw or refined. One can also include aggregated data and all intangible dimensions - as knowledge - required to analyse and reuse these data. **Network design** means the arrangement of the relationships of the various entities inside the ecosystem. Three main levers of an orchestration process are: managing innovation leverage, managing innovation coherence, and managing innovation appropriability. The authors described these processes as the interplay of more basic mechanisms, five are discussed in the array below (Table 1):

Managing Innovation Leverage

It implies to envision both modularity and network openness to foster value creation capabilities and the attraction of new actors in the ecosystem. The means consist in "sharing or reuse of technologies, processes, intellectual property, and other innovation assets". There is a paradoxical and inverse relationship between innovation leverage and structural openness since open boundaries often give rise to an erosion of the links and conversely a need to concentrate all decision making, so there is a need of a "tiered decision-making structure whereby members that play more important roles in innovation leverage gain more say in such decisions".

Table 1. Main elements for inno. & network design and issues for an open data ecosystem.

Domain	Definition (Nambisan and Sawhney)	Potential application to open data
Modularity	"Degree to which the network's innovation architecture has been decomposed into independent or loosely coupled modules and the interfaces that connect those modules have been specified and standardized"	Open data ecosystems being still emergent, their components are naturally loosely coupled. The stimulator has to ease the emergence of interdependencies among the members to give rise to a (certain) tight coupling. Last part on interfaces = open API?
Structural embeddedness	"How well the network members are linked (directly or indirectly) to one another, that is, it captures the overall connectedness of the network structure"	Very weak connectivity since there is a lack of interdependencies
Cognitive embeddedness	"Degree of shared cognition among the network entities, that is, the extent to which members are connected to one another through shared vocabulary, common representation and interpretation schemes, and overlapping domains of knowledge"	Importance to adopt industry standards (formats, vocabularies...) already identified concerning the release of data
Structural openness	Permeable boundaries or not	Basically high openness for the data, more complex for the other products of the ecosystem
Decisional openness	"Degree to which the locus of innovation decision-making is diffused in the network"	Rather weak. Best practices advise to put in place a mechanism allowing to capture the data needs of the re-users

If we transpose this to an open data ecosystem, some elements were already given, as the necessity to know the ecosystem, but also the task to achieve subtle balances which will encourage the participants to share their assets. We notice equally that the paradox operates fully. At least concerning the asset that are public data already released, structural openness is the widest whereas the links between the components of the ecosystem are tenuous and even non-existent: these may help a stimulator to define priority interventions. The idea that those who invest the more their assets should be more influent in the decision-making process is interesting but if a public agency is the stimulator, it might rise some concerns about the fairness of the competition. However, the equal treatment principle is not bypassed if access to the data is equally granted for all the stakeholders. Even in the frame of public procurement, there are procedures, such as competitive dialog, which can be related to this idea.

Managing Innovation Coherence
There are two scales of innovation coherence to manage:

1. **Internal coherence** is the "alignment of the innovation tasks, components, and interactions of the members within the network". Risks of a lack of internal coherence ("process delays, design redundancies, technological incompatibilities, higher innovation costs, and inferior performance") seem to be a good representation of the current open data ecosystem. It is enough to look at the markets of applications reusing open data to find a large duplication. To increase internal consistency, the authors emphasize the role of modularity and particularly of functions such as communication and coordination, as can be workshops or hackathons.
2. **External coherence**, "coherence between a network's innovation goals and architecture and the external technological and market context", is less obvious in an open data context: it implies to keep attention on technical changes (including the standards), or to market changes.

Managing Innovation Appropriability
A wide range of studies focused on pricing as an incentive to increase participation in the ecosystem. Open data being accessible and re-usable for free, charging does not appear to be the main driver, but remains partially relevant since other assets - processes, knowledge, enriched data can still be charged and are supposed to be the basis of value creation and capture. The more generic concept of innovation appropriability appears to be better suited. Innovation appropriability refers to the "mechanisms available for partners to appropriate value from their innovative contributions". If the appropriability regime is unbalanced, the more assets a firm will have, the more it will be unwilling to participate in the ecosystem, or even if it participates, the more it will tend to show a conservative behaviour. The key element is to build a "trust-based environment", through mechanisms at the interplay between structural embeddedness and decisional openness, the first one to "minimize undue appropriation of value without sacrificing the intensity of knowledge sharing". Making room for other actors in the decision-making process is also a mean to increase trust in the ecosystem.

From the open data perspective, it echoes the idea that the use of open data should not be related to a requirement to share alike the products or services built from these data, to increase the ecosystem's attractiveness. If the stimulator envisions to go beyond the mere publication of data, for example through the funding of infrastructures or the development of specific services, it has to find a balance in terms of intellectual property rights: it requires at least a minimal openness of the products to allow the emergence of interdependencies and the leverage of assets by each other and in the other hand the need to manage a capture of the value large enough to keep the stakeholders inside the ecosystem.

We propose to go further in the interpretation to consider a trust related issue. (Heimstädt et al. 2014) present a potential risk of asymmetry between public bodies and other organizations. If public bodies choose to stop their open data initiatives, their central missions would not be directly jeopardized whereas other organizations who would have significantly invested in the re-use of the assets would see the ruins of their efforts and resources. This asymmetry weakens one of the basic dimensions of an ecosystem, the existence of interdependences between the components. What is considered as an interdependency by a central organization may be considered as an undue dependency and a risk by another actor. This is a risk of one-sided dependency that government should prevent. We think that sustainability could be considered here as a subset of trust and that a clear commitment to sustainability.

Conclusion: Limits for a Transposition of the Platform Leader Model
We acknowledge that the model has been tailored for firms whereas we try to use it for the intervention of public bodies, which have different resources, constraints, goals and commitments. Products and services at the heart of the platforms are far better defined than they are and maybe as they can be in the case of open data, where the focus is much more on data as a raw material. Some dimensions are not relevant and others require to be adapted to the open data context, but we think that this framework remains suitable to describe the influential levers available for a stimulator who would not act as platform leader but like a platform leader. We contend that a greater investment of a public body, for example through public procurement, would in turn increase the legitimacy of this framework.

4.3 Acting on the Ecosystem

To implement an influence strategy, our literature review allowed to identify several levers. Data publication is the first component of a stimulation strategy and it requires a strong internal leadership (Lee 2014). The obviousness of this remark shall not hide the success of the release of a large number of datasets since the first open data initiatives. The legal framework is fundamental too, but few public bodies have a real impact on its definition. Communication/dissemination, being direct or indirect, thematic workshops and apps competitions or hackathons are also helpful factors to influence the ecosystem. The evaluations of open data initiatives have shown that these actions are useful but that, in most cases, they were not sufficient. According to (Lee et al. 2016), lack of attention given to value capture is one cause of failure of civic apps competitions, consistently with the dimension of value appropriability that we propose to re-use.

4.3.1 Arguments for Public Bodies Acting as Stimulators

Leadership to promote open data inside the government is already accepted, at least to bypass the consequences of hierarchical organizations (Harrison et al. 2012). Envisioning public bodies as stimulators of the ecosystem may be a paradox since they have been broadly criticized. The question is meaningful as there cannot be a leadership if the actor aiming to endorse this function is not recognized as legitimate to do so by the other stakeholders (Thomas 2013). However, government is not the sole decision maker and being a stimulator does not automatically lead to an internal monopoly. Some actors like academics or non-for profit organizations like ODI can assist in the steering of the ecosystem. Government has already a central position as it defines the legal framework and as data provider, as stated by (Van Schalkwyk et al. 2016). This gives him the best place to act like a hub-firm and it in consequence the best suited to orchestrate the ecosystem.

4.3.2   Ecosystem's Stimulation by Public Procurement Lever

We could barely find an example of the kind of leadership described above in the current open data ecosystems and we contend that until a more mature network of firms could take the lead, leadership could be the responsibility of public agencies. This can be done through the implementation of new kinds of public-private partnerships. In the related domain of big data, (Lindman and Kuk 2015) mentioned that European Commission "would join with Europe's data industry to invest E2.5 billion to support research and innovation in exploiting big data from both open and private sources". One lever of this leadership could be the public procurement of services.

4.3.3   Current Practices

The idea to drive innovation through public procurement is not specific to open data and could be related to broader programs, since public procurement at large is recognised as a tool to influence economic activity, representing around 19% of GDP in the European Union[1]. Current legal framework recognizes strategic matters are of three kinds: social, environmental and innovation concerns. The latter is intended to be promoted by the new procedure of innovation partnership, although there is a lack of feedback from the practice. Moreover, the reformed EU directive focuses on "most advantageous economically tender", where lowest cost is only one weighted factor among others.

There is a wide range of initiatives intending to encompass the supply side, for example: Smart procurement in Finland; Paris[2], Barcelona[3], New York with "BigApps" (Dawes et al. 2016). We outlined (Turki et al. 2017) some pioneering initiatives that can be considered as the empirical roots of a stimulation function and showing the existence of a Zeitgeist which promotes a rise in the investment of public bodies in the reuse of their assets beyond punctual hackathons. However, several initiatives remain not or poorly documented, particularly concerning the choice of the challenges, the procurement procedures, the ways to engage re-users, the evaluation of the proposals, the assessment of the whole programs.

4.3.4   BE-GOOD

BE-GOOD[4] is a pioneering programme aiming to unlock, re-use and extract value from Public Sector Information (PSI) to develop innovative data-driven services in infrastructure and environment domains. The BE-GOOD approach is based on identifying "challenges" for public sector service delivery that could be addressed through better use of data. It will then source solutions from the marketplace. This approach is new for all partners involved in the programme, which mostly relied on long-term partnerships with solution providers, and only had local/national links with solution providers. By a novel demand-driven approach, starting with public service delivery challenges

---

[1] http://trade.ec.europa.eu/doclib/docs/2015/april/tradoc_153347.pdf.

[2] http://datacity.numa.co/paris/home.

[3] http://bcnopenchallenge.org.

[4] Building an Ecosystem to Generate Opportunities in Open Data; co-funded by the European Regional Development Fund Interreg North-West Europe; http://www.nweurope.eu/begood.

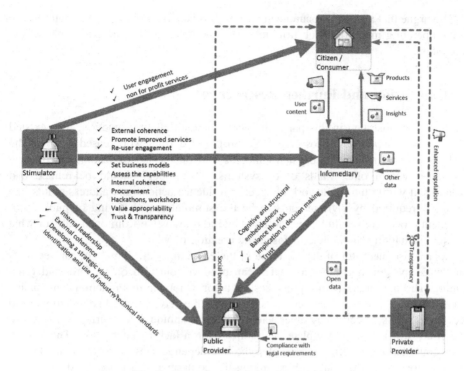

Fig. 2. Summary of stimulation function

common for public bodies across north-western Europe to unlock appropriate datasets and engage with the marketplace, BE-GOOD shows ambitions consistent with a strategic use of procurement (Fig. 2).

A stimulator can choose to attract re-user's attention and creativity on a given set of data, whether it considers that they are neglected or that their use could foster value creation. It may choose to engage with the re-users in a problem-solving approach, where the public body defines the problem. In both cases, civil servants will hardly have from the beginning a clear idea of what datasets or what problem they want to highlight to the re-user's community.

When a public body matures an idea intended to be submitted as problem to the re-users of open data, the civil servants will have to put themselves at the place of the potential re-users and make the experience of the problems they will face, e.g. data discoverability, data quality or other intellectual property concerns. A public body cannot be considered as a whole, the siloed data problem is encountered by the general public as well as by civil servants. Thus, public procurement can be a way to think as a re-user might do, and so to develop a better knowledge of the barriers and risks they face.

Public procurement seems especially suited to manage innovation appropriability. Public intervention in the creation of service can strengthen trust in the ecosystem. Above all, this role allows the stimulator to balance intellectual property rights in order to enable both appropriation of value and the sharing of intellectual property, thus the emergence of interdependencies and finally increasing strength of links inside the ecosystem.

We argue that a public procurement approach is suitable to bring a stimulator closer to the operating mode of a hub firm and that is a mean to ease the emergence of the ecosystem.

5 Conclusion and Further Researches

We have demonstrated in this paper the need for a stimulating function, who existed latently, in an open data ecosystem. We proposed a framework based both on the analysis of existing open ecosystems models and on the customization of concepts developed within other kinds of ecosystems. This model should be refined and instantiated within the framework of specific influence actions and address points like the skills required by civil servants to be the stimulators, what kind of public procurement procedure would be the most suitable to draw value from open data, or what are the evaluation criteria able to foster the creation of value.

As a conscious actor of the existence of the ecosystem, the stimulator can set goals for the ecosystem, not only on what it can produce, but also on its form and functioning. Through orchestration processes, an actor endorsing this function can manage risks in the ecosystem, not also the risks carried by the network, but also to mitigate and prevent the risks perceived by other actors. This role should foster current ecosystems, which are still fragile, incomplete, and suffer from a lack of integration. This framework could help to identify and develop the interdependencies, to increase the density and the strength of the relationships among the components of the ecosystem.

By mean of a public procurement designed in an ecosystem orchestration strategy, a stimulator can also impulse new dynamics: by enabling trust-related mechanisms, the stimulator can spread the weight of risk to make it bearable by the different actors, thus it contributes at once to set new interdependencies.

References

Barry, E., Bannister, F.: Barriers to open data release: a view from the top. Inf. Polity **19**, 129–152 (2014)

Battistella, C., Colucci, K., De Toni, A.F., Nonino, F.: Methodology of business ecosystems network analysis: a case study in Telecom Italia Future Centre. Tech. Forecast. Soc. Change **80**(6), 1194–1210 (2013)

Dawes, S.S., Vidiasova, L., Parkhimovich, O.: Planning and designing open government data programs: an ecosystem approach. Gov. Inf. Q. **33**, 15–27 (2016)

Deloitte: Open data driving growth, ingenuity and innovation. Deloitte analytics paper (2012). https://goo.gl/XrQR4S

EUDECO: Report on the socio-economic analysis. Modelling the European data economy (2016). https://goo.gl/nvgbdX

Gawer, A., Cusumano, M.A.: Industry platforms and ecosystem innovation. J. Product Innov. Manag. **31**(3), 417–433 (2014)

Harrison, T.M., Pardo, T.A., Cook, M.: Creating open government ecosystems: a research and development agenda. Future Internet **4**, 900–928 (2012)

Heimstädt, M., Saunderson, F., Heath, T.: From toddler to teen: growth of an open data ecosystem. JeDEM-eJournal eDemocracy Open Gov. **6**, 123–135 (2014)

Immonen, A., Palviainen, M., Ovaska, E.: Requirements of an open data based business ecosystem. IEEE Access **2**, 88–103 (2014)

Janssen, M., Charalabidis, Y., Zuiderwijk, A.: Benefits, adoption barriers and myths of open data and open government. Inf. Syst. Manag. **29**, 258–268 (2012)

Jetzek, T.: The Sustainable Value of Open Government Data: Uncovering the Generative Mechanisms of Open Data through a Mixed Methods Approach (2015)

Lee, D.: Building an open data ecosystem: an Irish experience. In: Proceedings of the 8th International Conference on Theory and Practice of Electronic Governance, pp. 351–360 (2014)

Lindman, J., Kuk, G.: From open access to open data markets: increasing the subtractability of open data. In: 48th Hawaii International Conference on System Sciences, pp. 1306–1313 (2015)

Magalhães, G., Roseira, C.: Exploring the barriers in the commercial use of open government data. In: 9th International Conference on Theory and Practice of Electronic Governance, pp. 211–214 (2016)

Martin, S., Foulonneau, M., Turki, S., Ihadjadene, M.: Open data: barriers, risks and opportunities. In: 13th European Conference on eGovernment, ECEG, pp. 301–309 (2013)

Nambisan, S., Sawhney, M.: Orchestration processes in network-centric innovation: evidence from the field. Acad. Manag. Perspect. **25**(3), 40–57 (2011)

O'Reilly, T.: Government as a platform. Innovations **6**(1), 13–40 (2011)

Ponte, D.: Enabling an open data ecosystem. In: ECIS 2015 (2015)

Thomas, L.: Ecosystem emergence: an investigation of the emergence processes of six digital service ecosystems. Ph.D thesis, Imperial College Business School (2013)

Turki, S., Martin, S., Renault, S.: How open data ecosystems are stimulated? In: Proceedings of EGOSE 2017, September 2017, St. Petersburg, Russian Federation (2017, to appear)

Turki, S., Foulonneau, M.: Valorisation des données ouvertes: acteurs, enjeux et modèles d'affaire. In: 5th Conference on DocSoc, 4–5 May 2015, Rabat, Marocco (2015)

Van Schalkwyk, F., Willmers, M., McNaughton, M.: Viscous open data: the roles of intermediaries in an open data ecosystem. Inf. Tech. Dev. **22**, 68–83 (2016)

Zuiderwijk, A., Janssen, M., Davis, C.: Innovation with open data: essential elements of open data ecosystems. Inf. Polity **19**, 17–33 (2014)

Enabling Spatial Queries in Open Government Data Portals

Pedro Arthur de Fernandes Vasconcelos, Wensttay de Sousa Alencar,
Victor Hugo da Silva Ribeiro, Natarajan Ferreira Rodrigues,
and Fabio de Gomes Andrade[✉]

Instituto Federal da Paraíba, Cajazeiras, Brazil
{pedro.arthur,wensttay.alencar,victor.ribeiro,
natarajan.rodrigues}@academico.ifpb.edu.br,
fabio@ifpb.edu.br

Abstract. Recently, many governments have developed open government data portals as a way to facilitate the finding and the access to datasets produced by their agencies. The development of these portals has facilitated the retrieval of this kind of data, but they still have significant limitations. One drawback of current portals concerns the resolution of queries with spatial constraints. Many portals solve spatial queries selecting the datasets that contain in their description the place name informed by the user, which can lead to queries with low recall and precision. Aiming to solve these limitations, we propose a new spatial search engine to improve information retrieval in open government data portals. The main contributions of this work are the development of a system that retrieves OGD at the level of resources and the proposition of a ranking metric that evaluates the relevance of each resource retrieved from a query. We validated the proposed search engine using real data provided by the Brazilian open government data portal. The results obtained from the initial experiments showed that our solution is viable as it can retrieve data with good accuracy for many spatial queries of different granularities.

Keywords: Geographical information systems · Information retrieval · Open government data

1 Introduction

Recently, Open Government Data (OGD) [1, 2] have gained increasing popularity throughout the world. The adoption of OGD provides significant advantages like the reuse of data produced by public agencies, the creation of new business opportunities, the enhancement of government transparency and the improvement of citizens engagement [3]. Currently, many governments have developed open government data portals, which represent a central point of retrieval and access to the data produced by their agencies. Examples of important current OGD portals include data.gov, in the United States, and data.gov.uk, in the United Kingdom. Initiatives for the development of OGD portals have also been developed in Brazil [4–6].

© Springer International Publishing AG 2017
A. Kő and E. Francesconi (Eds.): EGOVIS 2017, LNCS 10441, pp. 64–79, 2017.
DOI: 10.1007/978-3-319-64248-2_6

OGD portals are used by both data providers and clients. Providers, which are normally public agencies, use these portals to announce their data. For that, they register their datasets at the portal. During this process, they must provide a set of metadata about their datasets and their respective resources, which represent the files that the datasets are composed of. To make clients able to process the published data, agencies usually provide their resources using formats such as CSV, XLS, XML and JSON. On the other hand, clients use OGD portals to find out the data of their interest. For that, they pose a query describing the constraints that the data must satisfy. During the query resolution process, the portals match the constraints defined in the user's query against the metadata provided for each registered dataset. Then, they select and return to the client all the datasets whose metadata satisfy the search criteria.

Current OGD portals facilitate OGD retrieval, but they still have important limitations. One of these limitations concerns the solving of queries with spatial constraints. Usually, OGD portals perform this kind of query selecting the datasets that contain in their description the place name informed in the user's query. Such characteristic reduces the quality of the query result, since usually the spatial information described in metadata is too limited. For example, some metadata patterns provided by OGD portals do not have a specific field to describe the spatial extent covered by the resources provided in a dataset. On the other hand, other patterns have an attribute that represents the spatial extent of the dataset as a whole. Nevertheless, when we analyze the information provided by OGD portals more carefully, it is possible to notice that many times the description of the resource provides spatial information that is more precise than that one provided for its dataset. Furthermore, in many cases, the content of the resource enables us to extract spatial information even more accurate.

One other limitation of current portals is that they solve queries at the level of datasets. Thus, always a user performs a query they return the list of datasets that satisfy the search criteria. After that, the user still needs to evaluate the returned datasets and select the one of his interest. In the next step, he needs to identify, among all the resources provided by the selected dataset, the one that best fits his need. It is important to take in mind that this process can be quite tedious and time-consuming since a query can return a large number of datasets and each dataset can also provide a significant number of resources. Finally, another drawback is the lack of effective ranking metrics to evaluate the relevance of each dataset returned for a query. Such problem becomes even more important when we notice the vast quantity of datasets and resources provided by many OGD portals.

Aiming to solve these limitations, this paper proposes a new spatial search engine to improve geographic information retrieval in OGD portals. The contributions provided by this research are a model to perform geographic information retrieval at the level of resources and a ranking metric to evaluate the relevance of each selected resource. The search engine described in this paper was evaluated by using real data obtained from the Brazilian OGD portal. The initial results have shown that the approach used in this work is viable since it solves many queries with good rates of recall and precision.

The remaining of this paper is organized as follows. Section 2 discusses related work. Section 3 introduces the search engine proposed in this paper. Section 4 highlights the spatial geocoding process. Section 5 describes the information retrieval process. Section 6 discusses the experimental evaluation. Finally, Sect. 7 concludes the paper and presents further research.

2   Related Work

In the last years, open government data have become a hot research topic [7]. Some research works focus on linking OGD. Ding et al. [8] developed a portal for Linked Open Government Data that converts OGD to RDF triples. Their work has been applied to the data.gov portal and enables users to find out open data as well to explore the relationships that exist between these data. Flores and Ding [9] proposed techniques that automatically detect the relationships between data provided by OGD portals. Krataithong et al. [10] also developed a method that discovers relationships between OGD data. The developed method is based on semantic types and has been applied to data provided by the Thailand OGD portal. Relevant works about linking OGD were also proposed by [11, 12].

Some works have focused on the spatial facet of OGD. Dessi et al. [13] developed a solution called *ODMap*, which collects and geocodes data provided by an Italian OGD portal. The proposed solution geocodes and stores data in data marts and clients can visualize and explore these data using a map-based interface. On the other hand, Zhang and Yue [14] proposed a research work that maps and stores OGD in spatial grids of different granularities. The data stored in these grids can be mined and analyzed by the users. Consoli et al. [15] developed a similar work by using geospatial data from the municipality of Catania. In their work, geospatial data were converted to RDF triples, linked and related to concepts defined in ontologies. Leite et al. [16] implemented a software application that explores the spatial facet of OGD to provide a better visualization of these data. Their solution geocodes and stores data collected from some public agencies. Then, users can visualize the collected data on a map to identify public services offered in a locality. Although all these works are relevant, they do not solve spatial information retrieval in OGD portals, which is the research issue approached by this work.

Finally, some projects focus on OGD retrieval. Narducci et al. [17] proposed an information retrieval system called *CroSeR*, which finds links between e-gov services described in different languages. Their work discovers these links by using a semantic matching approach based on data from the Wikipedia. Rozell et al. [18] developed *IOGDS*, a system that performs information retrieval in datasets. Their solution relies on a catalog service that represents OGD as RDF triples and solves queries using SPARQL. Although these works can perform information retrieval in OGD portals, they do not explore the spatial facet of the data as the solution proposed in this paper.

3   The Spatial Search Engine

This section introduces the search engine we developed to enable spatial queries in OGD portals. The solution proposed in this paper is part of the *OurData* project, which is a research project that aims to develop a platform where clients can easily find and access data provided by an OGD portal. Before presenting our solution, we are going to discuss some requirements that our search engine should satisfy.

3.1 Requirements

Before presenting our solution, we are going to describe some requirements defined for our spatial search engine. Such discussion is necessary because these requirements influenced the decisions and choices we made during the development of this work.

- **Information retrieval at the level of resources (R_1):** current OGD portals usually solve queries by matching the constraints defined in the user's query against metadata that describe the dataset as a whole. After that, they return to the user a list containing all the datasets whose description satisfies those constraints. So, the user is charge of identifying, among all the resources offered by the returned datasets, the one he is interested in. To overcome such limitation, we defined that our spatial search engine should solve queries at the level of resources. Thus, the result for each query should be a list of all the resources that satisfy the search criteria;
- **Spatial extent represented as a bounding box (R_2):** to satisfy the requirement R_1, our search engine tries to identify the spatial coverage of each resource offered by the datasets registered in the OGD portal. For that, it firstly analyzes the metadata provided for each resource. After that, it processes the content of each resource, trying to identify the spatial extent of each one of its data lines. We decided to represent and store the data about the geometry of the spatial extents identified for each resource as a bounding box, which is the minimum rectangle that covers a given geometry entirely. We opted for using that kind of representation because it would enable our search engine to process geospatial data more quickly. Such characteristic is important because it reduces the time necessary to solve queries, which helps to keep the scalability of the proposed solution;
- **Ranking (R_3):** as defined in the requirement R_1, our solution should retrieve information at the level of resources instead of datasets. Since the number of resources is larger than the number of datasets (each dataset is composed of a set of resources), that requirement can lead to queries whose response has a vast quantity of resources. Thus, we defined that a ranking metric must be proposed to evaluate the relevance of each resource selected during the query resolution process. Such metric would make our search engine able to present more relevant resources firstly, enabling users to find out the data they are interested in more quickly;
- **Asymmetry (R_4):** we also defined that the ranking metric proposed for this work should be asymmetric. For a better understanding of this requirement, consider two bounding boxes A and B, where B covers A. If the user poses a query for data about the region A and the resource under evaluation covers the region B, then the resource it solves the query entirely. However, if the user requests for data about region B and the resource under evaluation covers only the region A, then it only answers the query partially. For that reason, in the latter case, the ranking value should be smaller than the value estimated for the former case.

3.2 Architecture

In this subsection, we present the architecture we used for implementing our spatial search engine. Such architecture is depicted in Fig. 1. The *Data Harvester* is the module that interacts with the OGD portal and retrieves the metadata about the datasets registered in the portal and their resources. During the harvesting process, the *Data Harvester* sends to the portal a query requesting for the metadata of the datasets registered in its database. Such requested is accomplished by using the web service API provided by the portal. The response returned by the portal is a JSON file containing the metadata about its datasets and their respective resources. The metadata describing a dataset usually contain information such as the id, the title, the name of the agency that published the dataset, a small text description, and timestamps describing when the metadata were created and modified. For each resource, the metadata normally describe features such as the id, the name, a small text description, the format and the URL from which users can download the resource. During this process, the *Data Harvester* filters just the resources offered as a CSV file. We initially opted for focus on this type of file because it offers the data by using a tabular form, which is a structure that enables a machine to easily process the content of the file.

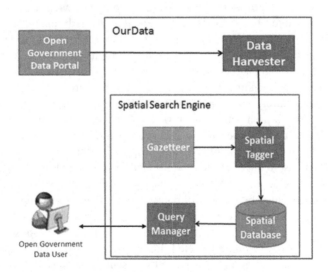

Fig. 1. The search engine architecture

The *Data Harvester* organizes the data obtained from the OGD portal and sends them to the *Spatial Tagger*, which is the module responsible for geocoding each identified resource. Firstly, it processes the metadata that describe the dataset and the resource to determine the spatial extent covered by the resource. After that, it downloads the resource and processes its content aiming to find more precise information about the spatial extent. It is important to highlight that the current version of this module is able to handle only OGD provided as a CSV file. During this entire process, the *Gazetteer* is used as the dictionary to identify spatial footprints from place names.

The results obtained from the spatial geocoding process are persisted in a database that can handle geospatial data. Finally, the *Query Manager* is the module responsible for solving the spatial queries received from the users. The query resolution process is performed by using the data obtained from the geocoding process.

3.3   The Data Schema

In this subsection, we describe the data schema we use for storing the data in the search engine database. The data schema is depicted in Fig. 2. The figure shows that our data schema is based on three entities: *Dataset, Resource* and *Resource Place*. It is important to highlight that our data schema is simple because we store only the data that are necessary for solving spatial queries and some attributes about the resources and their respective datasets. These attributes are stored because they can be showed to the user when the query result is presented. Nevertheless, for each resource retrieved for a query, the search engine provides a link to its respective page in the OGD portal. Then, users can use that link to see all the metadata provided for the selected resource and its dataset.

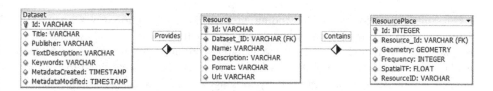

Fig. 2. The data schema

The entity *Dataset* is the abstraction that represents a dataset registered in the OGD portal. In an OGD portal, a dataset is a set of data produced and made available for one of the agencies that use the portal for sharing their data. For each dataset, we store the following attributes: *id, title, publisher name, text description, keywords,* and the timestamps describing the time of creation and modification of the metadata. In our schema, each dataset provides a set of resources, which are abstracted by the entity *Resource*. As stated before, the resource represents the granularity of the results returned by our search engine. The attributes stored for each resource are the *id, name, description, format* and the *URL* from which users can download the resource. To improve the quality of the information retrieval process as well to carry out the ranking process, we try to identify the spatial extents covered by each resource. Then, we process the content of each resource trying to determine the spatial extent covered by each one of its data lines. At the end of this process, each spatial extent identified for the resource is represented as an instance of the entity *Resource Place*. The attributes that describe that entity are: *id, geometry, frequency* and *spatialTf*. Next section provides a more detailed discussion about the geocoding process. On the other hand, Sect. 5 highlights the details about the meaning of the attributes defined to the entity *Resource Place*.

4 The Geocoding Process

As described in Sect. 3, our spatial search engine retrieves OGD at the level of resources. To make it able to perform that task, we try to determine the spatial extents covered by each resource registered in the OGD portal. Such process is called geocoding and is carried out in several stages, as it is depicted in Fig. 3. The process described in the figure is executed for each resource identified during the harvesting process. It takes as the input the metadata that describe the resource and its dataset. During the entire process, a gazetteer is used to convert place names to spatial footprints (in this case a bounding box). The gazetteer utilized in this work contains place names of Brazil at the level of country, regions, states and cities.

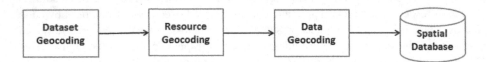

Fig. 3. Stages of the geocoding process

Our solution performs the geocoding process by using a top-down approach. Firstly, it tries to identify the spatial extent covered by the dataset as a whole. For that, the spatial tagger module processes the metadata provided for the dataset. As the metadata provided by the portal do not have a particular field to describe that information, the module tries to identify it by looking for place names in the title of the dataset. For that, it compares the value of that attribute to place names defined in the gazetteer. For example, consider the datasets *"Regiões Hidrográficas do Estado de Alagoas"*[1] and *"Quantidade de postos de atendimento na região Nordeste"*[2] registered in the OGD portal provided by the Brazilian government. Analyzing the titles of these two datasets, we can assume that the first dataset covers the state of Alagoas, while the other one covers the Northeast region of the Brazil. In cases where it is not possible to identify a place name from the title of the dataset, the module looks for place names in its text description. At the end of this process, the bounding box that covers all the places identified from the dataset metadata is considered to be the dataset spatial extent. Finally, if a place name still cannot be found, we assume that the coverage of the government that provides the OGD portal is the dataset spatial extent. The dataset spatial extent identified in this stage is utilized as a reference in the next stages of the geocoding process.

Once the spatial tagger determines the dataset spatial extent, it tries to determine the spatial extent covered by each resource. This task is necessary because many resources cover a spatial extent that is more precise than the one covered by its respective dataset. For example, a dataset that provides data about a region can supply resources about a specific state of that region. The spatial extent of a resource is identified by looking for

---

[1] http://dados.gov.br/dataset/regioes-hidrograficas-estado-de-alagoas.

[2] http://dados.gov.br/dataset/24895-quantidade-de-postos-de-atendimento-na-regiao-nordeste.

place names in its title and text description. The bounding box that covers the geometries of the place names selected for the resource is considered to be the resource spatial extent. If no places can be determined from resource metadata, the geocoding module considers that the resource spatial extent is the same of its dataset.

In the third stage of the geocoding process, the module downloads the resource being evaluated and processes its content aiming to find even more precise information about the resource spatial extent. At this stage, the module tries to extract the spatial extent covered by each data line contained in the resource. This step is important because it makes our search engine able to prioritize resources that have data related to locations that are closer to the region defined in the user's query. Initially, the spatial geocoding module accomplishes that task by looking for columns whose values represent a geographical data. We observed these cases when the agency supplies the resource by using a Web Feature Service (WFS), which provides a geometry column that is usually represented as a Well-Known Text (WKT) value. When the resource has a column that describes a geometry, we extract the bounding box of each value of this column and store it as a resource place of the resource.

If the resource does not have any column offered as a geographical data, the module looks for columns that describe the data spatial extent by using a place name. Examples of that kind of column include district, city, state, region, country and so on. To perform this task, we analyze the values of each column offered as a string, trying to verify if its values correspond to place names. For columns whose values represent place names, we also identify the granularity of their places (city, state, region or country). If the resource has more than one column describing place names (for example, one column describing the city and other informing the state), we choose the one with smaller granularity, since it provides more precise information about the spatial extents of the resource.

Finally, if the resource does not have a column that describes a geometry neither a column representing place names, the geocoding module generates a resource place related to the resource spatial extent and considers that each data line of the resource is related to such place. In the last stage of the geocoding process, all the information identified for the datasets and their resources are stored in a relation database that supports geospatial data, according to the schema presented in Sect. 3. After that, these data become available to be processed during the information retrieval process, which is discussed in next section.

5   The Information Retrieval Process

The search engine uses the information collected and identified during the harvesting and geocoding processes for solving spatial queries posed by its users. To perform a spatial query, the user needs firstly to inform the bounding box of the geographical region of his interested. The input for the query can be either a place name (a city, a state, a region or a country) or the coordinates of the bounding box of the desired area. If the user informs a place name, the search engine converts it to a bounding box, which represents the input to the information retrieval process. In the first stage of the query resolution process, the search engine selects all the resources that have at least one resource place that intersects the area defined in the query. Then, the selected resources are ranked by reusing techniques used in the classical information retrieval, by using an adaptation of the work developed by de Andrade et al. [19]. In our work, the ranking process is based on two metrics: the spatial overlap and the spatial relevance.

5.1   The Spatial Overlap

The spatial overlap is the main metric used for ranking the resources retrieved for a query. It enables our search engine to prioritize resources whose data cover spatial extents that are closer to the area defined in the query. For a better understanding of that metric, suppose a query where the user is looking for data about *Cajazeiras*, which is a city located in the state of *Paraíba*. Then, consider the three resources R_1, R_2 and R_3 depicted in Fig. 4.

R_1				R_2				R_3		
C1	C2	C3		C1	C2	C3		C1	C2	C3
X	X	Cajazeiras		X	X	Paraíba		X	X	Cajazeiras
X	X	São Paulo		X	X	São Paulo		X	X	João Pessoa
X	X	Belo Horizonte		X	X	Minas Gerais		X	X	Cajazeiras
X	X	Recife		X	X	Pernambuco		X	X	Recife
X	X	Rio de Janeiro		X	X	Rio de Janeiro		X	X	Cajazeiras

Fig. 4. Examples of resources

Figure 4 shows that the three resources have a column (C_3) that describes the spatial extent of each data line. The resources R_1 and R_3 provide such information informing a city, while the resource R_2 represents that information using a different granularity (state). In the first stage of the query resolution process, the search engine selects the three resources, since all of them contain data whose spatial extent intersects the region defined in the query. Nevertheless, it considers that the resources R_1 and R_3 are more relevant than R_2, as their spatial extents are closer to the one defined in the query.

To compute the spatial overlap for a resource, our spatial search engine firstly identifies the spatial extent of the resource under evaluation for the query. That task is necessary because the resource can have more than one resource place that intersects the region defined in the query. We assume that the spatial extent of the resource for the query is the bounding box that covers the spatial region of all its resource places that intersect the area defined for the query. Thus, let R be a resource under evaluation and $RP = \{RP_1, RP_2, \ldots, RP_N\}$ be the set of resource places of R that intersect the bounding box defined in the query. The spatial extent of R for the query (SE(R)) is the smallest rectangle that covers the spatial extent of all the RPs present in RP.

The spatial extent of a resource for the query is particularly important when the granularity of the spatial information provided by the resource is lower than the granularity requested in the query. For example, consider that the resource R_1 has resource places for all the cities of *Paraíba*. Then, if the user poses a query requesting for data about *Paraíba*, the spatial extent of R_1 will be the bounding box that covers all the cities of Paraiba, which generates a bounding box that is close to the one that covers the state. Moreover, such bounding box means that the resource under evaluation solves entirely (or almost entirely) the query performed by the user.

Once the spatial extent of the resource for the query is computed, the search engine computes the spatial overlap. The goal of this metric is to evaluate the similarity between the spatial extent of the resource for the query and the region requested by the user. We carry out such task by using an adaptation of the Tversky equation [20]. We opted for using that equation because it enables our search engine to prioritize resources whose spatial extent is closer to the region defined in the query. Moreover, it makes our solution able to satisfy the requirement about asymmetry described in Sect. 3. Thus, let Q be the bounding box defined in the user's query and R the bounding box of the spatial extent of the resource under evaluation, the spatial overlap between Q and R is calculated by using Eq. 1.

$$spatiaOverlap(Q, R) = \frac{|Q \cap R|}{|Q \cap R| + \alpha|Q - R| + (1 - \alpha)|R - Q|} \tag{1}$$

where:

- $|Q \cap R|$ represents the intersection area between Q and R;
- $|Q - R|$ represents the complement of Q, which is the area defined in the user's query that is not covered by the spatial extent of the resource;
- $|R - Q|$ represents the complement of R, which is area of the spatial extent of the resource that is not part of the area defined in the user's query;
- The constant α is used for determining the weight of each complement to the spatial overlap value. We have used the value 0.82 for that constant. This value was defined by using a technique called weighting [21].

5.2   The Spatial Relevance

The spatial relevance is the second metric we use for ranking the resources retrieved from a query. It is necessary because queries concerning place names that are present in many resources return a large number of results with the same value for the spatial overlap. The goal of that metric is to prioritize resources where the area defined in the query has a higher relevance. For example, suppose again a query requesting for data about *Cajazeiras*. If we observe the resources depicted in Fig. 4 again, it is possible to notice that the resources R_1 and R_3 will have the same value for the spatial overlap, since their data have the same granularity. However, in R_3, the area defined in the query is considered to be more relevant, since there are more data lines related to that area. The spatial relevance is an adaptation of the term frequency, which is a metric that is largely used in the classic information retrieval [22] for ranking documents.

In the classic information retrieval, search engines enable users to find out documents from a keyword (or a set of keywords). The query resolution process starts selecting the documents that contain the keyword defined in the query. Then, during the ranking process, documents whose the keyword defined in the query has more relevance are considered to be more relevant and are presented firstly to the user. Classic information retrieval systems use some metrics to evaluate the relevance of a keyword for a document. The main metrics used during this process are the *term frequency* (*tf*) and the *inverse document frequency* (*idf*). The *tf* is a metric that evaluates the relevance of the keyword for the document and is calculated by the ratio of the number of occurrences of the keyword in the document to the total of the terms of the document. On the other hand, the *idf* is the metric that evaluates the relevance of the keyword defined in the query for all the documents provided by the system and is calculated by the logarithm of the ratio of the number of documents of the system to the number of documents that contain the keyword defined in the query.

In our work, we use a metric *spatialTF* that computes the relevance of the area defined in the query to the resource under evaluation. The *saptialTF* is similar to the *tf* metric in the classic information retrieval. By making an analogy, the resource represents the document, while the data lines represent the terms the document is composed of. Thus, consider Q be the bounding box of the area defined in the query and R a resource under evaluation, the *spatialTF* is calculated by using Eq. 2.

$$spatialTF(Q, R) = \frac{freq(Q, R)}{length(R)} \tag{2}$$

where:

- *freq(Q,R)* represents the number of data lines of the resource whose spatial extent intersects Q;
- *length(R)* represents the number of the data lines of the resource.

It is important to highlight that we do not use in our work a metric similar to the inverse frequency. We opted for not using such metric for the sake of scalability. As it is not possible to precalculate the *spatialTF* for each spatial region that users can request, the search engine needs to calculate the value for that metric during the execution of the query. So, computing another metric during the query resolution process would increase the time necessary to answer queries.

5.3 The Spatial Ranking

In the last stage of the ranking process, the search engine combines the values obtained for the spatial overlap and the spatial relevance to obtain the spatial ranking for the resource, which is the metric used to sort the resources returned for the query. The spatial ranking is calculated by using a weighted sum. Thus, consider Q be the bounding box of the area defined in the query and R the resource under evaluation, the spatial ranking of R is calculated according to Eq. 3. In the equation, w_1 and w_2

represents the weight of each metric to the spatial ranking. We have used the values 0.8 and 0.2, respectively, for these weights.

$$spatialRanking(Q, R) = w_1 spatialOverlap(Q, R) + w_2 spatialTF(Q, R) \quad (3)$$

6 Implementation and Experimental Evaluation

Aiming to validate the viability of the solution proposed in this paper, we implemented a prototype of our spatial search engine. The search engine was fully implemented using the programming language java. To perform the collect of the metadata from the OGD portal we use the web service interface API provided by $CKAN^3$, which is a data management system used for the implementation of many important current OGD portals. All the metadata collected during the harvesting process, as well the information generated during the geocoding process, are stored in a relational database with support to geospatial data implemented using the *PostgreSQL* database system. Finally, the clients can interact with the search engine through a web interface implemented using the *Java Server Pages* technology.

To evaluate the performance of our search engine we use the data provided by dados.gov.br, which is OGD portal provided by the Brazilian government. Firstly, we collected the metadata of all the datasets and resources provided by the portal. At the time of the evaluation process, we retrieved metadata about 1123 datasets and 8994 resources. After that, we filtered the 1220 resources offered as a CSV file, which represented the set of resources selected for evaluation, and their metadata were used as the input to the geocoding process.

Before performing the evaluation, we generated a baseline. During this process, the metadata and the content of resources selected for evaluation were manually analyzed by graduation students. For each resource, the students identified the index of the column that provided the most precise information about the spatial extent covered by each data line present in the resource and, for spatial information provided as place names, its respective granularity (city, state, region or country). Whenever the resource did not have any spatial information provided in its content, the resource was annotated using information from its metadata. Based on that information, we processed the resources again and generated a new database. The data contained in that database were used as the reference database to evaluate the quality of each query performed during the validation process.

To validate our search engine, we performed several spatial queries requesting for places of Brazil, using as the input places of three granularities: region, state and city. During this process, we carried queries for 5 regions, 26 states and 35 cities defined randomly. Each query was executed in two stages. Firstly, we carried out the query using the reference database to determine a baseline containing the resources that must be retrieved for the query. After that, we performed the query using our search engine

---

[3] https://ckan.org/.

database. Then, the resources obtained from the search engine were compared to the resources contained in the baseline. The results of each query were analyzed by using four metrics: recall, precision, accuracy and f-measure. We opted for using these metrics because they are the main metrics used for evaluating the performance of information retrieval systems. Table 1 depicts the averages obtained for each one of the evaluation metrics, grouping the results by granularity. The data presented in that table show that the proposed search engine had good rates for queries of all the granularities. Nevertheless, we could notice that some mistakes generated during the geocoding process reduce the rates of these metrics.

Table 1. Experimental evaluation results

	Recall	Precision	Accuracy	F-measure
Region	92.79%	85.86%	84.44%	89.09%
State	93.62%	83.35%	81.00%	88.08%
City	83.21%	83.77%	83.20%	83.38%

Finally, Fig. 5 depicts the interface of our search engine. The page presented in the figure presents the results obtained from a query requesting for data *about Cajazeiras*. It is important to highlight that a query for that place in the current portal of dados.gov. br does not return any result.

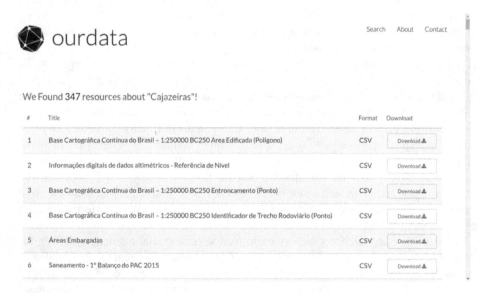

Fig. 5. Results for a query for Cajazeiras

7 Conclusions

Recently, open government data have gained increased popularity, enabling users to access and reuse data produced by public agencies. Currently, many governments have developed open government data portals to facilitate the retrieval and the access to these data. Nevertheless, OGD portals have improved the retrieval of open government data, they still have limitations that reduce the quality of that task. One of these limitations concerns the resolution of queries with spatial constraint. Many portals solve spatial queries by looking for resources that have in their metadata the place name defined in the query, which can lead to queries with low recall and precision.

Aiming to overcome that limitation, this paper proposed a new search engine that is able to solve spatial queries in OGD portals. The proposed search engine can retrieve open data at the level of resources, enabling users to find the data of their interest more quickly. Moreover, a ranking metric was proposed to estimate the relevance of each resource retrieved from a query. The search engine proposed in this paper was validated using real data offered by dados.gov.br. The first experimental evaluation showed that our approach is viable and can solve spatial queries with good rates of accuracy, recall and precision. Nevertheless, more experiments have to be done to get a deeper evaluation of the search engine. Firstly, experiments could be conducted to compare the performance of our search engine and the current OGD portal. Moreover, we plan to evaluate our solution with data provided by other current portals.

Further research can be developed to complement this work. One important future work consists of extending the solution proposed in this paper to support other file formats such as JSON, GEOJSON and XML, which will increase the quantity of resources managed by the search engine. Moreover, we are implementing new search engines to solve temporal and thematic queries. After that, we are going to integrate those engines for solving multifaceted queries. Moreover, future research can be performed for automatically detecting the relationships between the data located in different resources. Such research could help users to integrate data provided by different resources and obtain more information about the data. Finally, research can be executed to describe the data by using resources from the semantic web, which would make the semantic of the data understandable by both humans and machines.

References

1. Janssen, M., Charalabidis, Y., Zuiderwijk, A.: Benefits, adoption barriers and myths of open data and open government. IS Manag. **29**, 258–268 (2012)
2. Ubaldi, B.: Open government data: towards empirical analysis of open government data initiatives. OECD Work. Pap. Public Gov. **22**, 61 (2013)
3. Ding, L., Peristeras, V., Hausenblas, M.: Linked open government data. IEEE Intell. Syst. **27**, 11–15 (2012)
4. Breitman, K., Salas, P., Casanova, M.A., Saraiva, D., Gama, V., Viterbo Filho, J., Magalhães, R.P., Franzosi, E., Chaves, M.: Open government data in Brazil. Intell. Syst. IEEE. **27**, 45–49 (2012)

5. Matheus, R., Ribeiro, M.M., Vaz, J.C.: New perspectives for electronic government in Brazil: the adoption of open government data in national and subnational governments of Brazil. In: Proceedings of the 6th International Conference on Theory and Practice of Electronic Governance, ICEGOV 2012, pp. 22–29. ACM Press (2012)

6. Oliveira, M.I.S., de Oliveira, H.R., Oliveira, L.A., Lóscio, B.F.: Open government data portals analysis. In: Kim, Y., Liu, S.M. (eds.) Proceedings of the 17th International Digital Government Research, DG.O 2016, pp. 415–424. ACM Press, New York (2016)

7. Charalabidis, Y., Alexopoulos, C., Loukis, E.: A taxonomy of open government data research areas and topics. J. Org. Comput. E. Commer. **26**, 41–63 (2016)

8. Ding, L., Lebo, T., Erickson, J.S., DiFranzo, D., Williams, G., Li, X., Michaelis, J., Graves, A., Zheng, J.G., Shangguan, Z., Flores, J., McGuinness, D.L., Hendler, J.A.: TWC logd: a portal for linking open government data. Web Semant. Sci. Serv. Agents. World Wide Web. **9**, 325–333 (2011)

9. Flores, J.E., Ding, L.: Discovering the hidden cross-dataset links in data.gov. In: Proceedings of the 3rd International Conference on Web Science, WebSci 2011, pp. 14–17. ACM, New York (2011)

10. Krataithong, P., Buranarach, M., Hongwarittorrn, N., Supnithi, T.: A framework for linking RDF datasets for Thailand open government data based on semantic type detection. In: Morishima, A., Rauber, A., Liew, C.L. (eds.) ICADL 2016. LNCS, vol. 10075, pp. 257–268. Springer, Cham (2016). doi:10.1007/978-3-319-49304-6_31

11. Shadbolt, N., O'Hara, K., Berners-Lee, T., Gibbins, N., Glaser, H., Hall, W., Schraefel, M. C.: Linked open government data: lessons from data.gov.uk. IEEE Intell. Syst. **27**, 16–24 (2012)

12. Kalampokis, E., Tambouris, E., Tarabanis, K.: On publishing linked open government data. In: Proceedings of the 17th Panhellenic Conference on Informatics, PCI 2013, pp. 25–32. ACM Press, New York (2013)

13. Dessi, N., Garau, G., Recupero, D.R., Pes, B.: Increasing open government data transparency with spatial dimension. In: Reddy, S., Gaaloul, W. (eds.) Proceedings of 25th IEEE International Conference on Enabling Technologies: Infrastructure for Collaborative Enterprises, WETICE 2016, pp. 247–249. IEEE Computer Society (2016)

14. Zhang, C., Yue, P.: Spatial grid based open government data mining. In: 2016 IEEE International Geoscience and Remote Sensing Symposium (IGARSS), pp. 192–193. IEEE (2016)

15. Consoli, S., Gangemi, A., Nuzzolese, A.G., Peroni, S., Presutti, V., Recupero, D.R., Spampinato, D.: Geolinked open data for the municipality of Catania. In: Proceedings of the 4th International Conference on Web Intelligence, Mining and Semantics (WIMS14), WIMS 2014, pp. 1–8. ACM Press, New York (2014)

16. Leite, D.F.B., Rocha, J.H., de Souza Baptista, C., Falcão, A.G., de Figueiredo, H.F.: Geoprocessing applied to open government data. In: Ruckemann, C.-P. (ed.) GEOProcessing 2015 - The Seventh International Conference on Advanced Geographic Information Systems, Applications, and Services, pp. 100–105. IARIA (2015)

17. Narducci, F., Palmonari, M., Semeraro, G.: CroSeR: cross-language semantic retrieval of open government data. In: Rijke, M., Kenter, T., Vries, A.P., Zhai, C., Jong, F., Radinsky, K., Hofmann, K. (eds.) ECIR 2014. LNCS, vol. 8416, pp. 793–797. Springer, Cham (2014). doi:10.1007/978-3-319-06028-6_98

18. Rozell, E., Erickson, J., Hendler, J.: From international open government dataset search to discovery: a semantic web service approach. In: Ferriero, D., Pardo, T.A., Qian, H. (eds.) ACM International Conference Proceeding Series, pp. 480–481. ACM (2012)

19. de Andrade, F.G., de Souza Baptista, C., Davis Jr., C.A.: Improving geographic information retrieval in spatial data infrastructures. Geoinformatica **18**, 793–818 (2014)

20. Tversky, A.: Features of similarity. Psychol. Rev. **84**, 327–352 (1977)
21. Shaw, J.A., Fox, E.A.: Combination of multiple searches. In: Harman, D.K. (ed.) Proceedings of The Third Text REtrieval Conference, TREC 1994, Gaithersburg, Maryland, USA, 2–4 November 1994, pp. 105–108. National Institute of Standards and Technology (NIST) (1994)
22. Baeza-Yates, R., Ribeiro-Neto, B.: Modern Information Retrieval. Addison-Wesley, Boston (1999)

Practical Use Cases for Linked Open Data in eGovernment Demonstrated on the Czech Republic

Martin Nečaský[(⊠)], Jakub Klímek, and Petr Škoda

Faculty of Mathematics and Physics, Charles University,
Malostranské nám. 25, 118 00 Praha 1, Czech Republic
{necasky,klimek,skoda}@ksi.mff.cuni.cz

Abstract. The motivation for publishing data as Open Data and its benefits are already clear to many public authorities. However, most of open data is published as 3* data classified using the 5-star deployment scheme. When it comes to publishing data as 5* data, i.e. as Linked Open Data (LOD), for many authorities the benefits and motivation become abstract and unclear. In this paper, we introduce a playground which clarifies these benefits to public authorities in the Czech Republic using their own datasets. The playground consists of 73 real datasets transformed to LOD and two mature tools for LOD processing, visualization and analysis. We demonstrate the benefits on two concrete datasets provided by the Ministry of the Interior of the Czech Republic. We show how other public authorities may perform a similar demonstration on their own datasets. The paper is by no means limited to public authorities of the Czech Republic, as the same principles and processes are applicable everywhere else. Our example can be used to demonstrate the benefits of publishing 5* data on real datasets, and as a motivation and guidelines for building a similar playground for other countries.

Keywords: Linked open data · e-Government · Demonstration of benefits · Playground

1 Introduction

Recently, several Open Data initiatives have originated in different countries, publishing data on the highest level of openness according to the 5-star deployment scheme[1]. This level, denoted by 5* in the scheme, is called Linked Open Data (LOD). For example, the European Data Portal (EDP)[2], which collects metadata about datasets published as Open Data throughout the whole EU, publishes the metadata collection as LOD according to the European standard

---

This work was supported by the Czech Science Foundation (GAČR), grant number 16-09713S.

[1] http://5stardata.info.

[2] https://www.europeandataportal.eu/.

A. Kő and E. Francesconi (Eds.): EGOVIS 2017, LNCS 10441, pp. 80–96, 2017.
DOI: 10.1007/978-3-319-64248-2_7

for publishing dataset metadata called *DCAT Application profile for data portals in Europe (DCAT-AP)*[3]. Other examples include, but are not limited to, statistical offices publishing their data as LOD (e.g., Central Statistics Office of Ireland[4], UK Office of National Statistics[5], Swiss Federal Statistics Office[6] or Statistics Italy[7]) or environment agencies (e.g., European Environment Agency[8] or the Italian National Institute for Environmental Protection and Research[9]). However, most public authorities (European, national and local) still do not publish their data as LOD. According to our analysis, only 39 organizations out of the total 1856 organizations listed in EDP publish at least one dataset with a distribution in RDF. Recently, PwC made a study for Eurostat [8] which identifies the main blockers for publishing LOD. The blockers include: fear about the effort needed to deploy LOD, limited possibilities of reuse of LOD, lack of mature technologies or complexity of LOD. The often proclaimed benefits of LOD [3] like flexible data integration, better discoverability of LOD datasets and possibility to explore relationships between datasets have been demonstrated on various real scenarios in the literature (e.g., [5,7,9,10]). These benefits, however, are still too abstract for public authorities who decide about the target level of openness of their data. This shows a kind of the chicken-or-the-egg problem. Publishers ask why they should publish data as LOD and deal with all the blockers when the concrete benefits are not clear. On the other hand, it is very hard to demonstrate the benefits to them when there are only few real datasets available as LOD they could link to. In our work, we have built a playground which helps to solve this problem, at least in our country, the Czech Republic. The playground is a collection of 73 LOD datasets which we have created by transforming real datasets of several Czech public authorities. It consists of LOD datasets from various domains including public budgets and contracts, statistics, research data, medical data, environmental data or the code of law. It is cataloged in our CKAN catalog[10], in datahub.io[11] and present in the 2017 LOD Cloud diagram [1]. The contribution of this paper is a demonstration of how the playground can be used to illustrate the benefits of publishing two real datasets of the Ministry of the Interior of the Czech Republic (MICR) as LOD, while dealing with the blockers identified in [8]. Primarily, the paper targets employees of public authorities in the Czech Republic responsible for the agenda of open data in their organization and who want to validate the LOD benefits described in the literature using their own datasets. However, the audience is not restricted only to the Czech Republic. It is also relevant for open data publishers from other countries who

---

[3] https://joinup.ec.europa.eu/asset/dcat_application_profile/asset_release/dcat-ap-v11.

[4] http://data.cso.ie/query.html.

[5] http://statistics.data.gov.uk/sparql.

[6] http://data.admin.ch/sparql/.

[7] http://datiopen.istat.it/sparqlIstat.php.

[8] http://semantic.eea.europa.eu/sparql.

[9] http://dati.isprambiente.it/sparql.

[10] https://linked.opendata.cz.

[11] https://datahub.io/dataset?organization=opendata-cz.

want to see how to build such a playground with mature technologies to be able
to present the benefits of LOD in their own country. This paper is structured
as follows. In Sect. 2 we introduce the playground and principles of publishing
the dataset in the playground. In Sect. 3 we present the datasets of MICR and
concrete benefits we demonstrate to MICR with the playground. Sections 4–6 is
the demonstration itself. We conclude in Sect. 7.

2   Linked Open Data Playground

Our playground consists of 73 LOD datasets, which must follow the 4 LOD
principles introduced by Berners-Lee [2]. The principles require that (1) each
thing is uniquely identified by a URI, (2) this URI is an HTTP URI which can
be (3) accessed and dereferenced so that a client obtains data about the thing in
the RDF model which represents individual data values in a dataset as *triples* of
subject predicate and *object*. Moreover, the data may also be available through
a SPARQL endpoint. Finally, (4) URIs of related things from different datasets
are linked while links are also represented as RDF triples. The aim of LOD is to
create the global distributed linked data space which provides interlinked data
about entities in different data sets published by different providers. In addition,
each dataset in our playground must follow 4 general and 3 linking principles,
introduced in the rest of this section.

2.1   General Principles

1. A dataset D is represented by a resource R_D of type `dcat:Dataset`[12] where

$$R_D = \texttt{http://\{\$SUBDOM\}.opendata.cz/resource/dataset/\{\$DSID\}}$$

   `$SUBDOM` is a sub-domain which identifies one of our triple stores where the
   triples of D are stored and `$DSID` is a unique ID of D. If there are no specific
   needs, `$SUBDOM = linked` which identifies our default Virtuoso triple store[13].
2. The triples of D are stored in the triple store `$SUBDOM` in a graph named R_D.
   This enables a user to get the complete content of D by querying `$SUBDOM`
   for all triples in R_D.
3. The descriptive metadata of D (i.e., title, issuance date, etc.) are expressed
   using DCAT-AP and VoID [4] vocabularies. The triples with metadata are
   stored in a named graph $M_D = R_D$ `/metadata`.
4. D has a record C_D in our CKAN catalog. C_D is linked with R_D by property
   `dcat:landingPage`.

2.2   Linking Principles

There are three reference datasets any other dataset in the playground links to
whenever it is meaningful. Links may be direct or indirect (through other linked
datasests).

---

[12] `dcat` is a prefix for the DCAT vocabulary namespace http://www.w3.org/ns/dcat.
[13] http://linked.opendata.cz/sparql.

Registry of Territorial Identification, Addresses and Real Estate (RTIAR). RTIAR is run by the State Administration of Land Surveying and Cadastre (SALSC). It contains data about all buildings, plots, addresses, streets and geopolitical areas administered by local governments (e.g., villages, towns, cities or districts). RTIAR is originally published as a set of thousands of XML files (1 file for each town). We converted it to LOD representation according to the general principles described in Subsect. 2.1. It is represented by resource

R_{RTIAR} = http://ruian.linked.opendata.cz/resource/dataset/cz-ruian

where `ruian.linked` identifies a triple store dedicated to RTIAR[14] due to its size. RTIAR provides unique reference identifiers of geopolitical units. Principle 5 requires that references to geopolitical units in any dataset in our playground are represented as links to RTIAR.

Registry of Business Entities (RBE). RBE is run by the Ministry of Finance of the Czech Republic (MFCR). It contains data about economical subjects in the Czech Republic, including public authorities. RBE is originally published as a set of millions of XML files (1 file for each economical subject). We converted all public authorities and selected private organizations (those which are active in trading with public authorities) to LOD representation. RBE is represented by resource

R_{RBE} = http://linked.opendata.cz/resource/dataset/ares/basic

RBE provides a unique reference identifier for each economical subject. Principle 6 requires that references to business entities in any dataset in our playground are represented as links to RBE.

Legislation from the Code of Law of the Czech Republic (LEG). LEG is published by the Ministry of the Interior of the Czech Republic (MICR) as a collection of HTML pages[15]. It contains all legal acts. We converted this HTML representation to LOD representation. It is represented by resource

$$R_{LEG} =$$
http://linked.opendata.cz/resource/dataset/legislation/cz/uz

LEG provides a unique identifier for each legal act and each its section. Principle 7 requires that references to legal acts and their sections in any dataset in our playground are represented as links to R_{LEG}.

3 Demonstration for Ministry of Interior of the Czech Republic

In this section, we describe 2 datasets provided by the Ministry of the Interior of the Czech Republic (MICR), integrated into our playground to demonstrate

---

[14] http://ruian.linked.opendata.cz/sparql.
[15] http://portal.gov.cz/app/zakony/.

the benefits of LOD to MICR. The first dataset *Public Authorities List* provides basic data about all public authorities. The second dataset *Public Authorities Agenda* provides data about individual agendas performed by public authorities according to their duties defined by law. Both datasets are originally published as 3* data.

In particular, we wanted to demonstrate the following benefits:

B1 Users may explore datasets directly or indirectly (through other datasets) linked to the MICR datasets. For the exploration, no special service needs to be developed. It is only necessary that all datasets are published as LOD and with the 7 playground specific principles (Subsects. 2.1 and 2.2).

B2 Users may also explore concrete linking paths among datasets which helps them to specify analytical reports on public authorities combining various data aggregated from different datasets linked to the MICR datasets. The reports may be defined and computed using existing mature tools.

B3 An application which presents details about public authorities, their agendas and other related entities unknown in the design time of the application may be developed on top of the LOD datasets. Lay users without any knowledge of LOD principles and technologies, i.e. RDF, SPARQL, etc., are able to use it.

Table 1. Used vocabularies and their prefixes

Vocabulary	URI	Prefix
Schema.org	http://schema.org/	`s:`
Simple Knowledge Organization System (SKOS)	http://www.w3.org/2004/02/skos/core	`skos:`
Functional Requirements for Bibliographic Records (FRBR)	http://purl.org/vocab/frbr/core	`frbr:`
GoodRelations	vhttp://purl.org/goodrelations/v1	`gr:`
RTIAR vocabulary	http://ruian.linked.opendata.cz/ontology/	`rtiar:`
Public authorities vocabulary	http://linked.opendata.cz/ontology/domain/ seznam.gov.cz/ovm/	`ovm:`

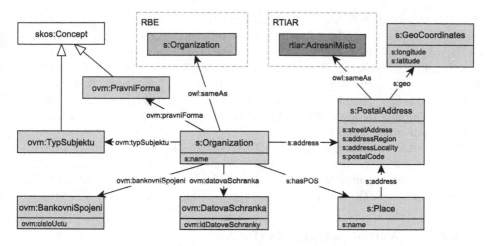

Fig. 1. Structure of R_{PA}

It was agreed in the discussions that these three benefits are seen as very hard to achieve when data is published as only 3* data. Now we describe how we represented the 2 datasets as LOD and how we integrated them to the playground. In the representation we try to reuse existing LOD vocabularies [11] as much as possible, their list is in Table 1. In some cases we introduce our own vocabulary, which is explained below.

3.1   Public Authorities List (PA)

The Public authorities list contains basic data about all ministries, other central government authorities and offices of local governments (districts and cities). For each authority, it contains the organization identifier, authority type, name, address, points of service and other basic data about each authority. According to the principles, PA is represented by a resource

R_{PA} = http://linked.opendata.cz/resource/dataset/seznam.gov.cz/ovm

The structure of the dataset is depicted in Fig. 1. Each public authority is represented as a resource of type s:Organization. It has a name (s:name), official address (s:address) and points of service (s:hasPOS). An address is a resource of type (s:PostalAddress). A point of service is a resource of type s:Place and has an associated address (s:address). The address of a point of service may be different from the official address. Both addresses and points of service have a structure conforming to the Schema.org vocabulary. In addition to Schema.org structures we also introduced proprietary classes and properties because no equivalent classes and properties exist in known vocabularies. Their names are in Czech because they are specific to the dataset of public authorities. Each public authority has a specification of its bank account (ovm:bankovniSpojeni) which is a resource of type ovm:BankovniSpojeni. It also has so called *data box* (ovm:datovaSchranka) which is a legally eligible electronic mailbox, intended for delivery of official documents and for communication with public authorities. Moreover, each public authority is classified in two classification systems. First (ovm:typSubjektu) is the type of the authority. Types of public authorities are instances of type ovm:TypSubjektu, a subclass of skos:Concept. Second (ovm:pravniForma) is the legal form of the public authority implied by law. Legal forms are instances of type ovm:PravniForma, a subclass of skos:Concept.

PA is linked to reference datasets RTIAR and RBE. Each resource representing a public authority in PA is linked (owl:sameAs) to the resource representing it in RBE. Each resource representing a postal address of a public authority PA is linked (owl:sameAs) to the resource representing the address in RTIAR.

3.2   Public Authorities Agenda (PAA)

This dataset contains basic data about agendas of public authorities. For each agenda, it provides its name, authorities or types of authorities which perform the agenda, references to legal acts which define it and activities performed by authorities as a part of the agenda. According to the principles, PAA is represented by a resource

$$R_{\text{PAA}} =$$
http://linked.opendata.cz/resource/dataset/seznam.gov.cz/agendy

The structure of the dataset is depicted in Fig. 2. Each agenda is represented as a resource of a proprietary type ovm:Agenda which is a subclass of skos:Concept. It has a name (skos:prefLabel) and code (skos:notation). An agenda is structured to activities which are performed by public authorities as a part of the agenda. An activity is represented as a resource of a proprietary type ovm:Cinnost which is a subclass of skos:Concept. Again, it has a name (skos:prefLabel) and code (skos:notation). An agenda is associated with its activities with a proprietary ovm:cinnost which is a subproperty of skos:narrower.   PAA is linked to LEG and RBE, each agenda is

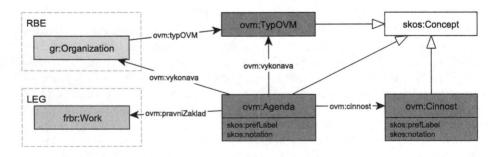

Fig. 2. Structure of R_{PAA}

defined by one or more legal acts. Each resource representing an agenda in PAA is therefore linked to resources representing corresponding legal acts in LEG (ovm:pravniZaklad). An agenda is performed by concrete public authorities and/or by all authorities of a given type such as all municipalities. In the former case, the resource representing the agenda in PAA is linked (ovm:vykonava) to resources representing corresponding authorities in RBE. In the other case, the resource representing the agenda is linked to a resource of a proprietary type ovm:TypOVM which is a subclass of skos:Concept using ovm:vykonava. This resource represents the respective type of authorities and it is linked to resources representing public authorities of that type in RBE (ovm:typOVM).

4   Use Case 1: Exploration of Linked Datasets

In this use case, we demonstrate the first expected benefit B1 introduced in Sect. 3. We show that even a user who is not familiar with the LOD principles may explore the playground to find out which datasets are linked with the MICR datasets. For this, we need to present the datasets and links between them in a graphical way. They form a graph structure which may be visualized and analyzed with existing software tools like Gephi[16] or GraphViz[17]. For our purposes we need an open source tool with a GUI for visualizing graph structures. Moreover, we needed a tool which supports importing the graph from an RDF or tabular (CSV) representation. This is because we plan to use SPARQL to extract the information about datasets and links among them, which produces RDF or tabular (CSV) output. Last but not least, we need the tool to support larger graphs with hundreds or thousands of nodes. We have chosen Gephi because it meets all the requirements mentioned above. We defined a set of SPARQL queries which extract the required graph structure of datasets and links between them and represent the result in CSV files with a structure required by Gephi. A node in the graph represents a set of instances of a given type in a given dataset. An edge in the graph represents links of a given type between instances of one type in one dataset to instances of another type in another dataset. Formally, we extract a graph $G = (N, E)$ where a node $n \in N$ is a pair (C, D) where C is a class, D is a dataset and C has some instances in D. A resource r is an instance of C in D if the triple $(r, \mathtt{rdf : type}, C) \in R_D$. Let us note that R_D denotes the named graph of all RDF triples of the dataset D. An edge $e \in E$ is a triple (n_s, n_t, p) between n_s and n_t labeled with a predicate p. The triple represents links between $n_s = (C_s, D_s)$ and $n_t = (C_t, D_t)$. It may be that $D_s = D_t$ and/or $C_s = C_t$. It informs us that there exists at least one triple $(r_s, p, r_t) \in R_{D_s}$ where r_s is an instance of C_s in D_s and r_t is an instance of C_t in D_t. D may be D_s, D_t or some other dataset which links D_s and D_t. The following SPARQL query is a basic query for extracting nodes of the graph described above from the datasets in our playground.

---

[16] https://gephi.org/.
[17] http://www.graphviz.org/.

```
SELECT DISTINCT ?Id ?Dataset ?Class
WHERE {
  GRAPH ?Dataset {
    [] a ?Class .
  }
  BIND(CONCAT(STR(?Dataset), "/", STR(?Class)) AS ?Id)
}
```

The following SPARQL query is a basic query for extracting edges.

```
SELECT DISTINCT ?Source ?Target ?Property
WHERE {
  GRAPH ?DatasetSource {
    ?ResourceSource a ?ClassSource ;
      ?Property ?ResourceTarget .
  }
  GRAPH ?DatasetTarget {
    ?ResourceTarget a ?ClassTarget .
  }
  BIND(LCASE(CONCAT(STR(?DatasetSource), "/",
      STR(?ClassSource))) AS ?Source)
  BIND(LCASE(CONCAT(STR(?DatasetTarget), "/",
      STR(?ClassTarget))) AS ?Target)
}
```

The second query for extracting edges timed out on both of our SPARQL endpoints, each running on a 4 core, 16 GB RAM virtual machine. As a solution we optimized the execution of the query with the LinkedPipes ETL tool (LP-ETL) [6]. It allows users to specify a complex RDF processing task as an ETL pipeline consisting of simpler steps. Moreover, the steps may be evaluated on the input data "per partes", which is suitable for SPARQL queries which otherwise cannot be evaluated due to the size of the data. This type of evaluation is called *chunking* in LP-ETL and "partes" are called *chunks*. The pipeline is depicted in Fig. 3. Step 1 gets the list of all datasets in the playground and prepares them as an input for Step 2 where nodes of the graph are extracted. The extraction in Step 2 works in chunks for individual datasets. In Step 3, the pipeline stores the nodes in a CSV file with a structure required by Gephi. Steps 4 and 5 extract edges of the graph. Step 4 works in chunks for individual nodes extracted in Step 2. For each node (C, D), it gets a list of resources which are instances of C in D. Step 5 then extracts edges with (C, D) as a source node from this list of resources. Step 5 works in chunks for individual resources. To get the best result, we need Step 4 to get all resources which are instances of C in D. However, it would be time consuming to inspect all resources in Step 5. To optimize Step 5, we get only 100 pseudo-randomly selected resources for each chunk, i.e. for each (C, D), in Step 4. This optimization would not work in case of heterogeneous structure of resources of type C in D. In our case, it works because the datasets in our playground are quite homogeneous. Finally, Step 6 stores the edges in CSV file

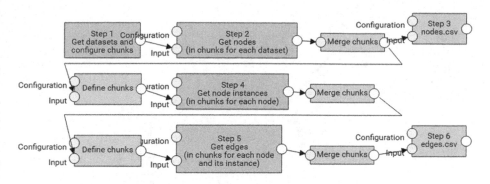

Fig. 3. ETL pipeline for constructing graph with structure of datasets in the playground

with a structure required by Gephi. We loaded the CSV files defining the graph to Gephi and we used the Radial Axis Layout algorithm to layout it. The result is displayed in Fig. 4. The algorithm groups nodes by a given feature, in our case we group nodes by the datasets they belong to. The groups are displayed as individual axes. Gephi provides several analytical features which can be used for exploration of linked datasets. We do not provide an overview of all the features, which can be found in the documentation. Instead, we demonstrate the features on concrete tasks described below. First, MICR wants to know how are its LOD datasets enriched with other existing LOD datasets. For example, what is linked, directly or through other nodes, to agendas in the PAA dataset. This can be easily previewed in Gephi using the heat map feature. The user may find the required node, i.e. the node representing resources of type ovm:Agenda in PAA, and apply the feature on this node. Gephi highlights all nodes reachable from the selected one as shown in Fig. 5. The result enables one to analyze which datasets and instances of which types are reachable from ovm:Agenda. However, it does not show the path connecting ovm:Agenda to another selected node. To analyze paths between two nodes, Gephi provides the shortest path feature between two nodes selected by the user. For example, using the heatmap feature, we may find out that rtiar:Obec in RTIAR, which is a class of all towns in the Czech Republic, is reachable from ovm:Agenda in PAA. Using the shortest path feature, we may easily find out the concrete path connecting both nodes. The path is displayed in Fig. 6. The left-hand side shows the shortest path displayed in the original layout. The two larger red nodes are the two selected by the user. The other red nodes are the other nodes on the discovered shortest path. The right-hand side shows the same path but only the nodes on the path are displayed. This view was created by copying the nodes on the shortest path to another Gephi workspace and layouting these nodes only, which provides a clearer view for the user. This exploration may be done for other datasets which are added to our playground according to the principles. It is only required that new datasets are available in our SPARQL endpoint **linked**. The optimized LP-ETL pipeline can then be executed and its result can be directly imported to Gephi. The

Fig. 4. Visualization of the schema of Czech LOD

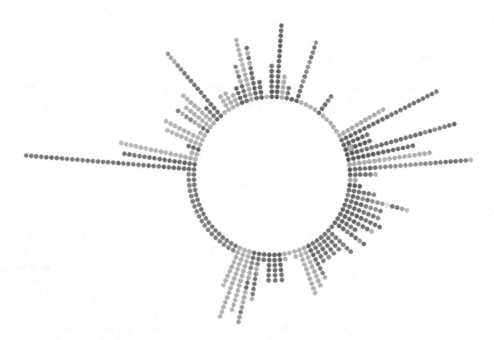

Fig. 5. Heatmap preview showing nodes (in red) reachable from `ovm:Agenda` in `PAA` (in green) (Color figure online)

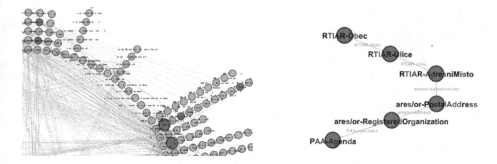

Fig. 6. Shortest path between `ovm:Agenda` from `PAA` and `rtiar:Obec` from `RTIAR`

only step which has to be ensured by a LOD expert is the transformation of data to the LOD representation. The exploration itself is abstracted from the LOD details and can be done by an analyst who is not familiar with technical details of LOD in Gephi. Therefore, we proved that benefit B1 can be achieved in practice.

5   Use Case 2: Analytical Reports

In this use case, we demonstrate the benefit B2 by showing that the output from the previous use case simplifies definition of complex analysis on top of linked datasets and that the analysis, when defined as a SPARQL query, may be computed in a reasonable time. We will demonstrate the simplification on a concrete problem of MICR which needs to compare efficiency and effectiveness of public authorities. It makes sense to compare only similar authorities. However, it is not straightforward to define the similarity of two public authorities and it is certainly not possible to define the similarity only based on the similarity of their simple classifications presented in Subsect. 3.1. For simplicity, let us consider only one specific type of public authorities which are so called *municipalities with extended power (MEPs)*. These are cities which manage an area geographically consisting of several smaller cities and villages. There are approximately 200 MEPs in the Czech Republic. When defining similarity of two MEPs, it is necessary to take into account the complexity of the area managed by each MEP. The complexity of the area may be defined in many ways but it is clear that it must consist of multiple indicators. These indicators include

- complexity of the geopolitical region in terms of numbers of streets, addresses, plots and buildings
- demography in terms of numbers of inhabitants in economically active age groups
- business community in terms of numbers of entities registered in the MEP area.

We do not list all indicators as that is not the purpose of this paper. We only show that publishing data as LOD helps to compute them. The list of indicators above was discussed with MICR as possibly interesting. The data about complexity of geopolitical regions is available in the RTIAR dataset. The demography data is in datasets published by the Czech Statistical Office, available as LOD in our playground. Information about business entities is in the RBE dataset. The first question is whether these datasets are linked to the PA dataset and how. This can be answered with the techniques demonstrated in Sect. 4 which allows us to check whether the datasets are linked to PA and discover the linking paths. Figure 7 shows the discovered paths. The path on the left connects an MEP, an instance of s:Organization in the PA dataset, with the managed geographical area, an instance of rtiar:Orp. The path in the middle connects a geographical area managed by an MEP with all its plots, instances of rtiar:Parcela in the RTIAR dataset. The path on the right connects a geographical area managed by an MEP with demography observations of the area in various age groups. The report which consists of two indicators, the number of plots and demography statistics, can be therefore computed with two SPARQL queries. One query uses the left and middle path from Fig. 7. One query uses the left and right path from Fig. 7. However, the data processed by both queries is large and our SPARQL endpoint timed out on these two queries.   To solve this problem, we again

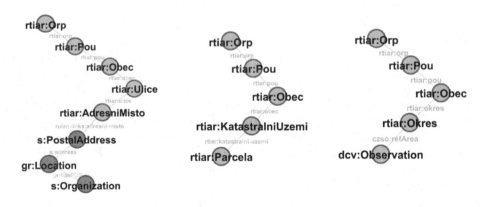

Fig. 7. Paths for analytical SPARQL queries (Color figure online)

used the LinkedPipes ETL tool and its chunking feature to optimize the queries. The resulting ETL pipeline is displayed at Fig. 8. Step 1 selects all MEPs and addresses of their points of service from the linked triple store. It uses the orange part of the left path in Fig. 7 for navigation. Step 2 selects geopolitical areas manged by MEPs from the ruian.linked triple store. It uses the grey part of the left path in Fig. 7 for navigation. It works with chunks of 100 MEPs from Step 1. Next, the pipeline is split to two branches. The first branch consists of Step 3 which selects the numbers of plots in the geopolitical areas of MEPs from the ruian.linked triple store. It works with chunks of 1 MEP and its geopolitical

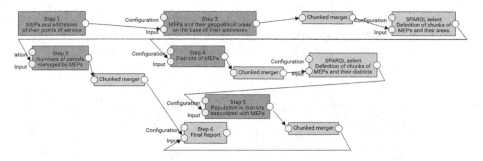

Fig. 8. ETL pipeline which optimizes the computation of analytical report of MEPs (number of plots)

area from Step 2. It uses the middle path in Fig. 7 for navigation. The second branch consists of Steps 4 and 5. It computes the demography for each MEP. Step 4 gets a district for each MEP. A district is a territorial unit associated with a MEP used by the Czech Statistical Office to measure demography. It works with chunks of 100 MEPs from Step 2. Step 5 computes the demography in districts associated with the MEPs. It works with chunks of 1 MEP and its district. Finally, Step 6 combines the indicators computed for each MEP and computes the final report as CSV file which is available for download. This optimized ETL pipeline computes the analytical report of MEPs in 14 s. This is a significant improvement in comparison to executing the original non-optimized SPARQL queries. According to our measures, the original SPARQL query which computes demography for all MEPs was evaluated in 970 ms. Therefore, optimizations are not necessary for this query. However, the original SPARQL query which computes numbers of plots for all MEPs cannot be measured on our SPARQL endpoint since it has timed out. Let us note that both the original SPARQL queries as well as the SPARQL queries in the optimized ETL pipeline were executed on the same SPARQL endpoints (`linked` and `ruian.linked`). As we have shown, it is possible to define and execute complex analysis on real LOD datasets. First, the complexity of LOD may be reduced by the way of presenting the structure of datasets and links between them in the visualization created in the previous use case. This visualization can be used even by an analyst who is not familiar with the details of LOD principles and technologies. He may use it to identify the paths which will then be used by a SPARQL expert to define the queries for computing the analysis. We also showed how the SPARQL expert may use LinkedPipes ETL tool to optimize his queries. Therefore, we proved that the benefit B2 can be achieved by existing tools which work in practice.

6 Use Case 3: Presentation of Selected Entities

In this use case we show an application presenting public authorities, their agendas and related entities which are unknown in the design time. The application demonstrates the benefit B3. We have developed a simple application called

Public Authorities Agenda Browser[18].. It is available in Czech only, because we do not have English labels. We only translated the labels needed for the screen shots presented below. The application enables a user to search for a particular

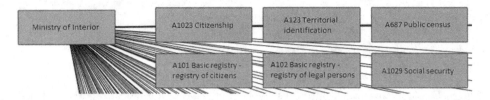

Fig. 9. Sample application screenshot - agendas of the ministry of interior of Czech Republic

public authority by its identification number and agendas by their codes. For a public authority it displays a list of its agendas. A sample screen with the detail of MICR is displayed in Fig. 9. The user may click on a selected agenda and get its detail. For an agenda it displays the activities belonging to the agenda and other related entities. For example, these entities may be legal acts which define the agenda and its activities. The entities are displayed around the agenda on the screen. The activities belonging to the agenda are displayed inside the agenda. The user may click on a chosen public authority and get its detail. Therefore, the user may easily browse related public authorities and agendas. A sample screen with the detail of the agenda *A893 Drug prevention policy* is displayed in Fig. 10. The application is a web application running in a web browser, writ-

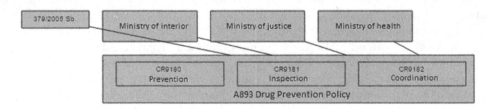

Fig. 10. Sample application screenshot - detail of agenda A893 drug prevention policy

ten in JavaScript. It queries the `linked` SPARQL endpoint using HTTP POST requests. It requests JSON-LD output which is then processed in the JavaScript code in a standard way of processing JSON data. The logic of selecting necessary data is encoded in SPARQL endpoints. For the required extensibility, it is just necessary to extend the SPARQL query for extracting additional entities related to a chosen agenda and their relevant data. The rest of the code of the application does not need to be updated as it just displays all entities related to the

---

[18] http://opendata.cz/agendový-prohlížeč

agenda obtained in the resulting JSON-LD data. The application code consists of 346 lines of code. It shows that no additional code is necessary in comparison to applications consuming 3* datasets and regular programming languages and libraries can be used to present the data. The programmer, when supplied with necessary SPARQL queries, may even consume the result of the SPARQL queries formatted in JSON and does not need to know the details of LOD principles and technologies. Our presented application enables lay users to browse public authorities, their agenda and linked entities. It was not intended for direct reuse with other kinds of entities. However, its architecture can be reused for other types of entities by changing the SPARQL queries and necessary changes in the layout of particular types of entities.

7 Conclusions

We presented a LOD playground which gives public authorities a possibility to verify the benefits of publishing data as LOD using their own datasets. We demonstrated how concrete benefits can be verified on two datasets of the Ministry of the Interior of the Czech Republic (MICR). We also showed how other public authorities may repeat this demonstration using their own datasets. We showed that our kind of demonstration deals with the often mentioned blockers of publishing data as LOD [8]. In particular, we decreased the effort needed to deploy LOD at least for experimental verification. We also showed possibilities of LOD reuse in data exploration and complex data analysis and in regular applications for lay users. Moreover, we demonstrated ways of reducing the complexity of LOD, and showed that mature tools already exist for LOD exploration, querying and application development. The presented results may be directly applied by or for other public authorities in the Czech Republic as well as authorities from other countries. They may use the results either as examples to demonstrate benefits of LOD or as guidelines to demonstrate benefits on their own datasets. Currently, the Ministry of Interior of the Czech Republic provides employees of public organizations with Linked Open Data training. They use the outputs presented in this paper, i.e. the playground as well as the demonstrations, as a training material. Since the beginning of 2017 they trained 20 employees from 5 governmental organizations and 1 municipality.

References

1. Abele, A., McCrae, J.P., Buitelaar, P., Jentzsch, A., Cyganiak, R.: Linking Open Data cloud diagram (2017). http://lod-cloud.net/
2. Berners-Lee, T.: Linked Data - Design Issues (2009). https://www.w3.org/DesignIssues/LinkedData.html
3. Bizer, C., Heath, T., Berners-Lee, T.: Linked data - the story so far. Int. J. Semant. Web Inf. Syst. **5**(3), 1–22 (2009). cited By 2013
4. Böhm, C., Lorey, J., Naumann, F.: Creating void descriptions for web-scale data. Web Semant.: Sci. Serv. Agents World Wide Web **9**(3), 339–345 (2011)

5. Höffner, K., Martin, M., Lehmann, J.: LinkedSpending: openspending becomes linked open data. Semant. Web **7**(1), 95–104 (2016)
6. Klímek, J., Škoda, P., Nečaský, M.: LinkedPipes ETL: evolved linked data preparation. In: Sack, H., Rizzo, G., Steinmetz, N., Mladenić, D., Auer, S., Lange, C. (eds.) ESWC 2016. LNCS, vol. 9989, pp. 95–100. Springer, Cham (2016). doi:10. 1007/978-3-319-47602-5_20
7. Latif, A., Scherp, A., Tochtermann, K.: LOD for library science: benefits of applying linked open data in the digital library setting. KI-Künstliche Intell. **2**(30), 149–157 (2016)
8. Loutas, N.: Study on LOD requirement-main findings and proofs of concept. In: ESS Workshop on Dissemination of Official Statistics as Open Data, 18–19 January 2017, Malta (2017)
9. Prongué, N., Ricci, F., Schneider, R., Schurte, R.: Art and design as linked data: the LODZ project (linked open data zurich). Libellarium: J. Res. Writ. Books Cult. Heritage Inst. **9**(2) (2017)
10. Roller, R., Roes, J., Verbree, E.: Benefits of linked data for interoperability during crisis management. ISPRS Int. Arch. Photogram. Remote Sens. Spat. Inf. Sci. **XL–3/W3**, 211–218 (2015)
11. Vandenbussche, P.-Y., Atemezing, G.A., Poveda-Villalón, M., Vatant, B.: Linked open vocabularies (LOV): a gateway to reusable semantic vocabularies on the web. Semant. Web **8**(3), 437–452 (2017)

Intelligent Systems in E-Government

Ontological Models of Legal Contents and Users' Activities for EU e-Participation Services

P. Schmitz[1], E. Francesconi[1,2(✉)], B. Batouche[1], S.P. Landercy[1], and V. Touly[1]

[1] Publications Office of the European Union, Luxembourg, Luxembourg
enrico.francesconi@publications.europa.eu, francesconi@ittig.cnr.it
[2] Institute of Legal Information Theory and Techniques of CNR (ITTIG-CNR),
Florence, Italy

Abstract. This paper presents a modular knowledge organization system within a pilot project for e-Participation in the EU law-making process. The ontological approach here presented is the ground of a web platform allowing citizens and other stakeholders to actively participate in public consultations. Citizens can provide comments and amendments, as well expressing sentiments on pre-legislative documents. The modeling approach follows a pure RDF(S)/OWL implementation for all the produced contributions (documents, comments, amendments, statistics), with the aim to made them available as Linked Open Data.

Keywords: Legal knowledge modeling · Linked open data · e-Participation

1 Introduction

The direct participation of citizens in decision-making can be highly promoted by the use of the social dimension of Internet, in particular by social networks, able to create communities of stakeholders, to convey the interest of lobbies or to promote the debate among citizens on specific matters under discussion in institutional assemblies. On the other hand the tendency to improve openness and accessibility of public sector information (as legislation) by the semantic web technologies promotes the possibility for citizens to open debates and provide opinions on specific topics and legislative text fragments under discussion.

The pilot project "Promoting Linked Open Data (LOD), Free Software and Civil Society Participation in Law-Making throughout the EU", in short "LOD and e-Participation" launched by the European Parliament and developed by the Publications Office of the European Union (OP), actually aims to engage citizens all over Europe in the democratic game, empowering them to play a more active role in public services and decision-making. The key technical aspect of this project is to make all the information produced available as Linked Open Data

---

E. Francesconi is author of Sects. 3, 4, 5, 6; P. Schmitz, B. Batouche, S.P. Landercy, V. Touly are authors of Sects. 1, 2, 7.

A. Kő and E. Francesconi (Eds.): EGOVIS 2017, LNCS 10441, pp. 99–114, 2017.
DOI: 10.1007/978-3-319-64248-2_8

(LOD). Essential pre-condition to achieve this objective is to model information according to a proper knowledge organization system able to represent legal contents under debates (basically pre-legislation) and social activities linked to the debate (as agreement or disagreement on specific matters or texts, amendments on specific fragment of pre-legislative documents, etc.).

In this paper we present the modular knowledge organization system the project is based on, as well as the functionalities of the system prototype. In Sect. 2 the main prototype services and use-cases are illustrated. In Sects. 3 and 4 the legal documents organization within the OP resources, as well as the document modeling adopted are respectively described. In Sect. 5 the way how amendments to legal texts proposed by the users are represented. In Sect. 6 the approach for representing users' social activities for e-Participation are illustrated. Finally, in Sect. 7 some conclusions and future developments are briefly discussed.

2   Services and Main Use-Cases

The system prototype is able to retrieve pre-legislative documents in all the EU official languages from relevant authentic sources, in particular from CELLAR [1, 2], the document and metadata repository of the OP, and make them accessible via semantic search facilities. On such documents users can formulates comments and amendments at different granularity levels (entire document, paragraphs, and sentences), as well as express sentiments and ratings on legislative proposals and comments, becoming followers of or being followed by other users, creating groups, provide social tagging and sharing comments. In order to address the European multilingual context, translations of the users' comments in all the 24 EU official languages are provided through MT@EC[1], the automatic translation API service provided by the Directorate-General for Translation (DGT) of the European Commission. Choosing a language for a legal text under discussion, the users choose also the language in which comments are shown.

On the other hand different graphical representations of the document are available, in order to visualize the full text, the parts that received the highest number of comments and amendments, the parts on which more positive or negative feedback were received. Such graphical representations are organized either to respect the sequential order of the articles, or as bubble-chart able to highlight the different activities on a document in terms of nodes representing document fragments, the number of comments/amendments submitted, as well as links between them.

Users' activities are selectively registered and pave the way to the elaboration of statistics on the system. In particular statistics by nationality, by group of interest the users belong to, by language, as well as by document fragments and document topics, are given. Such statistics are shown as associated to each

---

[1] https://ec.europa.eu/info/resources-partners/machine-translation-public-administrations-mtec_en.

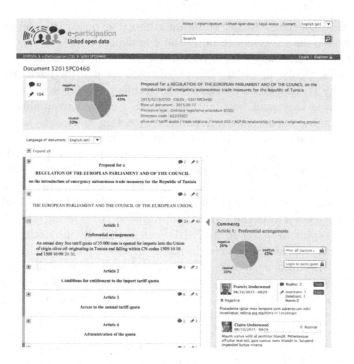

Fig. 1. The visualization of a document and the related statistics on users' activities

document and document fragments as illustrated in Fig. 1. Users' activities and statistics are shown also using timeline views or they are geolocalized in a map.

An essential pre-condition to provide such services is the availability of documents in structured format, and modeling users' e-Participation activities. In the next sections the knowledge organization system of the e-Participation platform, including pre-legislative documents within the OP resources taxonomy, as well as metadata models for the representation of content amendments and users' e-Participation activities, are illustrated.

3   Resources Taxonomy and FRBR

As discussed pre-legislative acts are retrieved from CELLAR, which is based on a Fedora digital objects repository[2], organized in two logical units: the Common Content Repository (CCR), including documents in 24 languages, and the Common Metadata Repository (CMR) including metadata in as many languages described according to semantic web technologies, resulting in about 1100 million triples, stored in an RDF triple store. Currently CELLAR receives about 5 million requests per day, providing information results through the EUR-Lex

---

[2] http://www.fedora-commons.org.

service and through the SPARQL endpoint recently exposed in order to complement linked open data services to potential consumers.

Pre-legislative documents are retrieved as far as metadata and content are concerned. In particular metadata from CELLAR are provided according to the CDM[3] ontology [1] developed by the OP for bibliographic resources. In particular, the Eurovoc thesaurus, available in SKOS[4], is used to qualify legislative documents by subject, therefore a document browsing service, as well as search and retrieval facilities, are provided based on the Eurovoc taxonomy.

In the LOD and e-Participation project, documents are organized in terms of the FRBR[5] model [3], following the approach described in [2] which is aimed to keep a distinction between the taxonomy of the bibliographic resources and the FRBR model itself. This approach has been tailored for the LOD and e-Participation project within the `lodep`:[6] namespace, considering a pre-legislative act as a bibliographic *Resource* in the ISBD[7] sense, namely *"an entity, tangible or intangible, that comprises intellectual and/or artistic content and is conceived, produced and/or issued as a unit, forming the basis of a single bibliographic description"*. This basically means that resources are actually not equivalent to, or sub-class of, any individual FRBR classes [4]. As pointed out in [5] each FRBR classes *reflects* one aspect of a resource, seen as a bibliographic entity at different levels of abstraction.

A *Resource* (in the ISBD sense) has the same intention as the combined attributes of the FRBR model [5], therefore it can be considered as the disjoint union of the Work, Expression, Manifestation and Item levels in FRBR model, as expressed by (1):

$$Resource = Work + Expression + Manifestation + Item \qquad (1)$$

where the disjoint union is represented by the '+' operator.

The relationship between the two domains (resources taxonomy and FRBR model) is therefore of *part-of/aspect*. In this context, every FRBR level is an *aspect* of a current resource and can be considered as collector of the metadata able to describe a resource at that level.

Therefore, a bibliographic resource and its FRBR model can be viewed as aspects of the same reality in two perspectives [4]:

1. The "web of data" perspective
2. The "bibliographic data" perspective

A *Resource* identified by a specific URI represents an entity of the "web of data". The resources published by the OP, including pre-legislative acts of interest for the LOD and e-Participation project, are basically bibliographic entities. As such they can be described according to the FRBR model. Works,

---

[3] Common Data Model.

[4] https://www.w3.org/2004/02/skos/.

[5] Functional Requirements for Bibliographic Records.

[6] xmlns:lodep = "http://publications.europa.eu/eparticipation".

[7] International Standard Bibliographic Description.

Expressions, Manifestations and Items of the FRBR model are also type of entities of the web of data, but they can also be viewed as specific aspects of a bibliographic resource, therefore viewed in the "bibliographic data" perspective.

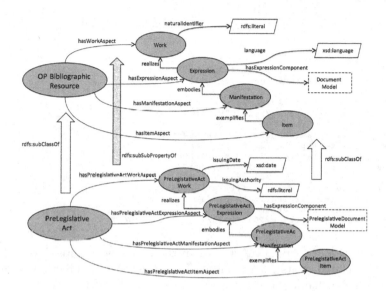

Fig. 2. Taxonomy of the resources and FRBR model

In Fig. 2 a sketch of the OP resource taxonomy (limited, for simplicity, to the root and the sub-class of pre-legislative acts of interest for the project), as well as its relationships with the FRBR model at each taxonomy level, is represented. In particular, the generic class of OPBibliographicResource is linked with hasWorkAspect, hasExpressionAspect, hasManifestationAspect, hasItemAspect to the corresponding classes of the FRBR model. Sub classes in the bibliographic resource taxonomy (like PrelegislativeAct) are linked to the corresponding sub classes of the FRBR model (like for example PrelegislativeActWork) with specific properties (hasPrelegislativeActWorkAspect, hasPrelegislativeActExpressionAspect, etc.). Such "aspect" properties are organized in pure taxonomic relationships too (rdfs:subPropertyOf) at each level of the FRBR model (for example hasPreleg- islativeActWorkAspect is a sub property of hasWorkAspect, and so on).

The FRBR classes are collectors of metadata at their specific taxonomy level: for example (see Fig. 2) at Work level a resource will have naturalIdentifier as generic metadata, described by object or datatype properties, shared by all the OP bibliographic resources. Similarly at PreLegislativeActWork level, specific metadata shared by all the pre-legislative acts are given (or inherited), as for example issuingDate and issuingAuthority of a legal measure. The same holds for the other FRBR classes at each level of the OP resource taxonomy.

Specific identifiers are foreseen for the instances of the resource taxonomy classes and the FRBR instances, according to the organization shown in Fig. 2:

- identifiers of the instances of resource taxonomy classes are derived from CELLAR and built as follows: `cellar-record:[hash-value]`[8].
- identifiers of the instances of the FRBR classes follow the ELI[9] standard [6] within the `eli:`[10] namespace.

The following RDF snippet depicts the usage of these URIs:

```
<rdf:Description rdf:about=
"&cellar-record;58da3a99-a91d-11e4-8e01-01aa75ed71a1">
 <rdf:type rdf:resource="&lodep;PreLegislativeAct"/>

 <lodep:hasPreLegislativeActWorkAspect
  rdf:resource="&eli;preleg/2016/0593"/>

 <lodep:hasPreLegislativeActExpressionAspect
  rdf:resource="&eli;preleg/2016/0593/eng"/>
 <lodep:hasPreLegislativeActExpressionAspect
  rdf:resource="&eli;preleg/2016/0593/fra"/>

 <lodep:hasPreLegislativeActManifestationAspect
  rdf:resource="&eli;preleg/2016/0593/eng/file.pdf"/>
 <lodep:hasPreLegislativeActManifestationAspect
  rdf:resource="&eli;preleg/2016/0593/eng/file.xml"/>
</rdf:Description>
```

Moreover, the PreLegislativeAct class in the previous example has metadata (properties) related to its corresponding FRBR aspects, or inherited from corresponding higher hierarchical levels. An excerpt of the metadata at Work level is the following:

```
<rdf:Description rdf:about="&eli;preleg/2016/0593">
 <rdf:type rdf:resource="&lodep;PreLegislativeAct"/>
 <lodep:naturalIdentifier>
    L 26/1
 </lodep:naturalIdentifier>
 <lodep:issuingDate rdf:datatype="&xsd;dateTime">
    2016-01-26T00:00:00
 </lodep:issuingDate>
 <lodep:issuingAuthority>
    Council of the European Union
 </lodep:issuingAuthority>
</rdf:Description>
```

The main benefit of this modeling approach is the possibility to access the metadata of a resource through SPARQL queries directly at each FRBR level and independently of the resource type. In fact, with the inheritance mechanism on classes and properties, it is sufficient to express queries at the top level of the hierarchy to access metadata at all the levels of the hierarchy, thus simplifying the query framework. For example, let `?resource` contain a URI of a pre-legislative resource, the following query on the hasWorkAspect top property

```
SELECT ?work WHERE { ?resource lodep:hasWorkAspect ?work }
```

---

[8] where `cellar-record:` represents the namespace. http://publications.europa.eu/resource/cellar-record/.

[9] European Legislation Identifier.

[10] xmlns:eli = "http://publications.europa.eu/eli/".

is able to provide access to all the metadata of a PreLegislativeAct at Work level (the ones associated to the class PreLegislativeActWork and the ones inherited from the class Work). This is also useful in case of extensions of the document types actually managed by the e-Participation platform.

4   The Document Model

To the aim of linking users activities (as comments, amendments, sentiments) to each document fragment, a model able to describe legal acts in terms of fragments as articles, paragraphs, etc., is needed.

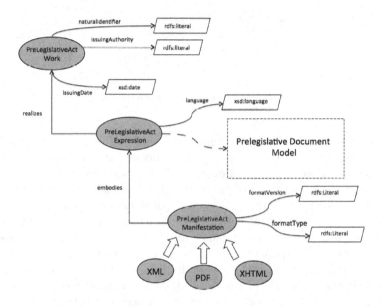

Fig. 3. The document model in the FRBR hierarchy

A legal act, viewed at Work level, can have different internal organizations in different languages or versions described at Expression level (for example two different versions of an act generated by amendments), therefore a document model describing its content is associated to the FRBR Expression level (see Fig. 3).

In this project the document model for EU pre-legislation follows the CEN-Metalex model [7], also used by specific XML standards like AkomaNtoso [8], NormeInRete, CHLexML, etc. In view of implementing a Linked Open Data service, the document model is an ontology, able to represent metadata and document subdivisions which a legislative document is made of, as well as subdivisions relationships and content datatypes. An excerpt of the adopted document model is reported in Fig. 4.

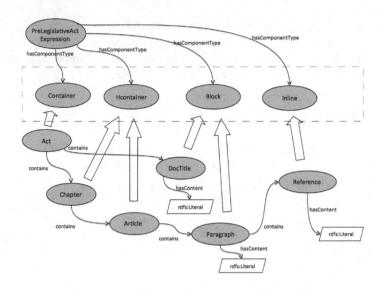

Fig. 4. An excerpt of the document model

According to CEN-Metalex, a legal act is made of components of different types or *patterns*, the main ones are: Block for document components containing text, Container containing a list of other elements, Hcontainer (hierarchical container) containing a hierarchy of components, Inline for inline elements within a Block (see [7] for more details). Specific legal document components are subclasses of such types, like Chapter and Article which are sub-classes of Hcontainer, or Paragraph which is sub-class of Block, and Reference, sub-class of Inline.

Each document component is identified by an extension of the ELI standard. In particular articles and paragraphs are identified by the prefix /eli/ [doctype]/[year]/[natural_number]/, followed respectively by [article_number]/[lang] and [article_number]/[paragraph_number]/[lang]. The values of the [article_number] and [paragraph_number], as well as of the other subdivisions at deeper levels, follow the hierarchy and the IDs naming convention of the subdivisions defined in Formex[11], the XML standard used by OP: for example the ID "art1.par2" is related to article 1 paragraph 2.

The approach of defining the document model as an ontology has different benefits: first of all it allows to represent document contents in RDF and to store them as fragments in a native RDF triple store for providing LOD services for documents content and metadata; moreover it allows to generate different representation of a document in different XML formats, as AkomaNtoso, Formex 5, as well as PDF and XHTML formats, as possible Manifestation exemplars (Fig. 3); finally this approach provides all the benefits of using RDF as standard format,

---

[11] http://formex.publications.europa.eu.

as for example implementing reasoning facilities for document subdivisions and metadata, using existing reasoners (like Pellet[12] or HermiT[13]).

An excerpt of RDF representation of a document subdivision is the following:

```
<rdf:Description
   rdf:about="&eli;preleg/2016/0593/eng/art1">
  <rdf:type rdf:resource="&lodep;Article"/>
  <lodep:is_contained
     rdf:resource="&eli;preleg/2015/0154/eng/titI"/>
  <lodep:content rdf:parseType="Literal">
       <i>Subject matter and scope</i>
  </lodep:content>
</rdf:Description>

<rdf:Description
   rdf:about="&eli;preleg/2016/0593/eng/art1.par1">
  <rdf:type rdf:resource="&lodep;Paragraph"/>
  <lodep:is_contained
     rdf:resource="&eli;preleg/2015/0154/eng/art1"/>
  <lodep:content rdf:parseType="Literal">
  This Directive lays down rules which aim at further harmonising the Union
  law applicable to copyright and related rights in the framework  of the
  internal market, taking into account in particular digital and cross-border
  uses of protected content. It also lays down rules on exceptions and
  limitations, on the facilitation of licences as well as rules aiming at
  ensuring a well-functioning marketplace for the exploitation of works and
  other subject-matter.
  </lodep:content>
</rdf:Description>
```

When shown on a Web page, documents are transformed in a qualified XHTML format using XSLT technologies. A representation of the previously RDF document excerpt, transformed in a qualified XHTML format is the following:

```
<div class="article"id="art1">
  <div class="article_title">
       <i>Subject matter and scope</i></div>
  <p class="paragraph"id="art1.par1">
     <div class="num">1.</div>
     This Directive lays down rules which aim at further harmonising the Union
     law applicable to copyright and related rights in the framework  of the
     internal market, taking into account in particular digital and cross-border
     uses of protected content. It also lays down rules on exceptions and
     limitations, on the facilitation of licences as well as rules aiming at
     ensuring a well-functioning marketplace for the exploitation of works and
     other subject-matter.
  </p>
</div>
```

5   The Amendments Model

As described in Sect. 2, registered users of the LOD and e-Participation platform have the possibility to provide amendments to the original version of a pre-legislative text.

A wide literature exists about amendments representation in the Semantic Web. Pioneer works in this field have been produced by Arnold Moore for

---

[12] http://clarkparsia.com.

[13] http://hermit-reasoner.com.

the Tasmanian legislation [9,10], while more recent initiatives are related to the description of amendments using XML standards [11], including the semi-automatic extraction of the textual amending actions [12,13]. Currently, in the LOD and e-Participation platform amendments can be provided at the level of articles. Once the user is registered and logged-in, he can select a text partition to comment and, in case, to amend. In order to provide amendments, the text of the selected partition becomes editable in an embedded editing instance of CKEditor[14]: such editor provides the possibility to show documents in a qualified XHTML format and to edit the text by well-established XHTML editing technology, so that changes can be provided and shown in a familiar track-change mode.

In order to describe amendments, a proper implementation of the Provision Model [14] has been developed. According to the Provision Model, the semantics of legislative texts is composed by provision instances, usually conveyed by paragraphs (Fig. 5) and organized into two main groups: Rules (introducing entities or expressing deontic concepts) and RulesOnRules (different kinds of amendments). As for RulesOnRules, they can be distinguished into:

- Content amendments, modifying literally the content of a norm;
- Temporal amendments, modifying the times of a norm (come-into-force and efficacy times);
- Extension amendments, extending/reducing the cases on which the norm operates.

In the LOD and e-Participation platform the users are supposed to provide "content amendments". In the EU legislative process such changes are usually provided through specific acts including amendment provisions (mainly content amendments) that express word by word the actions how to modify the content of a norm on a target document. Such actions are basically insertions, substitutions and repeals of text portions. Changes provided by the users of the LOD and e-Participation platform can be therefore considered as a result of virtual content amending provisions. Such changes are described by the Provision Model in terms of classes and related properties.

Under the prv: namespace of the Provision Model, content amendments are described by the top-class ContentAmendment which subsumes all the types of possible textual changes (Fig. 5). Any ContentAmendment provides information on the begin position (property begin_position) of the text to insert, repeal or substitute, in terms of number of characters from the beginning of the original text portion to be amended (the begin_position property range is therefore xsd:nonNegativeInteger).

The ContentAmendment class has two subclasses: Insertion and Repeal. They inherit begin_position property from the ContentAmendment class, thus representing: for the Insertion the begin position of the new text to be inserted; for the Repeal the begin position of the text to be repealed, respectively. Moreover, the Insertion provides a new content to be inserted by the property new_content

---

[14] http://ckeditor.com.

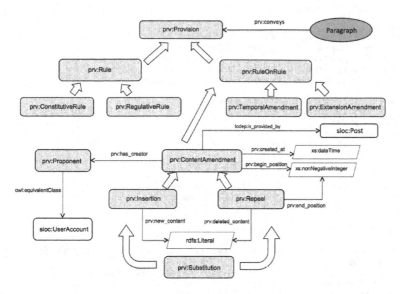

Fig. 5. Model for content amendments in the provision model

as literal, while the Repeal provides the end position of the text to be deleted (property end_position having a xsd:nonNegativeInteger range). Finally, substitutions are types of amendments including the characteristics of both insertions and repeals, for this reason the class Substitution can be modeled either as composition of the classes Insertion and Repeal, or as intersection of these two classes, thus considering Substitution as subclass of both Insertion and Repeal. We have chosen to model Substitution as intersection of both Insertion and Repeal because it is optimal from an instantiation point of view. However in the inferred model, a query on the number of insertions or repeals will provide also the number of substitutions. This problem can be solved at the level of queries, therefore for retrieving the number of insertions, repeals or substitutions only, the queries will not consider the inferred model and are respectively the followings:

```
SELECT ?insertion WHERE { ?insertion a prv:Insertion }
SELECT ?repeal WHERE { ?repeal a prv:Repeal }
SELECT ?substitution WHERE { ?substitution a prv:Substitution }
```

On the other hand, in order to have the whole set of amendments, the following query in the inferred model, can be performed:

```
DEFINE input:inference"lodep_rule_set"
SELECT ?amd WHERE { ?amd a prv:ContentAmendment }
```

where **lodep_rule_set** is the inference rule set created within the triple store.

Examples of content amendment instances, providing amending actions (Insertion, Substitution and Repeal) for a specific article (article 1, paragraph 1) of the English version of a legislative proposal identified by a given ELI, are the following (the URIs of posts and proponents are reported in terms of placeholder):

```
<rdf:RDF
xmlns:xs="http://www.w3.org/2001/XMLSchema#"
xmlns:rdf="http://www.w3.org/1999/02/22-rdf-syntax-ns#"
xmlns:rdfs="http://www.w3.org/2000/01/rdf-schema#"
xmlns:lodep="http://publications.europa.eu/eparticipation/"
xmlns:prv="http://publications.europa.eu/ProvisionModel/">

<rdf:Description rdf:about="[URI-amend1]">
 <rdf:type rdf:resource="&prv;Repeal"/>
 <prv:modifies rdf:resource="&eli;preleg/2016/0593/eng/art1.par1"/>
 <lodep:is_provided_by rdf:resource="[URI-post1]"/>
 <prv:begin_position rdf:datatype="&xs;nonNegativeInteger">
         209</prv:begin_position>
 <prv:end_position rdf:datatype="&xs;nonNegativeInteger">
         222</prv:end_position>
 <prv:created_at>2016-10-21T09:34:06</prv:created_at>
 <prv:has_creator rdf:resource="[URI-proponent]">
</rdf:Description>

<rdf:Description rdf:about="[URI-amend2]">
 <rdf:type rdf:resource="&prv;Insertion"/>
 <prv:modifies rdf:resource="&eli;preleg/2016/0593/eng/art1.par1"/>
 <lodep:is_provided_by rdf:resource="[URI-post1]"/>
 <prv:begin_position rdf:datatype="&xs;nonNegativeInteger">
         93</prv:begin_position>
 <prv:created_at>2016-10-21T09:36:01</prv:created_at>
 <prv:new_content xml:lang="eng">European </prv:new_content>
 <prv:has_creator rdf:resource="[URI-proponent]">
</rdf:Description>

<rdf:Description rdf:about="[URI-amend3]">
 <rdf:type rdf:resource="&prv;Substitution"/>
 <prv:modifies rdf:resource="&prv;preleg/2016/0593/eng/art1.par1"/>
 <lodep:is_provided_by rdf:resource="[URI-post1]"/>
 <prv:begin_position rdf:datatype="&xs;nonNegativeInteger">
         154</prv:begin_position>
 <prv:end_position rdf:datatype="&xs;nonNegativeInteger">
         162</prv:end_position>
 <prv:new_content xml:lang="eng">context</prv:new_content>
 <prv:created_at>2016-10-21T09:38:10</prv:created_at>
 <prv:has_creator rdf:resource="[URI-proponent]">
</rdf:Description>
</rdf:RDF>
```

They represent three different amending actions, whose creator (prv:has_creator property) is the user [URI-proponent] (instance of the class prv:Proponent), at a certain timestamp (prv:created_at property). The three amending actions are submitted by a proponent along with (lodep:is_provided_by property) a post [URI-post1] derived from the SIOC ontology (see Sect. 6). Such amendments modify (prv:modifies property) the English version of the article 1 paragraph 2 of a legislative text identified by the ELI identifier /eli/preleg/2016/0593. Note that the properties prv:begin_position and prv:end_position are automatically set by editing the legislative text using CKEditor, therefore all the amending markup elements in the partition (if any) are included when identifying the characterwise positions of the amending actions. Such amendments are the results of the following amending actions represented by the <ins>...</ins> and <del>...</del> XHTML elements shown in track-change mode on the browser

```
<p class="parag"id="art1.par1>
 <div class="num">1.</div>
 This Directive lays down rules which aim at further harmonising the
 <ins>European</ins> Union law applicable to copyright and related rights
 in the <del>framework</del><ins>context</ins> of the internal market, taking
 into account <del>in particular</del> digital and cross-border uses of
 protected content. It also lays down rules on exceptions and limitations,
 on the facilitation of licences as well as rules aiming at ensuring a well-
 functioning marketplace for the exploitation of works and other
 subject-matter.</p>
```

The amendment of formal partitions as a whole, as for example the deletion of articles, follows a similar approach: in this case the IDs of the partitions are sufficient to identify the textual elements to be amended.

In our opinion one of the benefits of an RDF description of the amendments, with respect to an XML-based description, is that amending actions can be stored in an RDF triple store and be reused for different purposes (document consolidation, LOD services, etc.). Similarly, the approach relies on qualified XHTML document visualization, therefore XHTML editors (like CKEditor) can be used to visualize and amend document fragments. Moreover, since the whole ontology approach results in the OWL-DL computational profile, the system can benefit of existing DL reasoners for inferences and advanced reasoning.

6   The Users' e-Participation Activities Model

Social activities in the LOD and e-Participation platform are represented as extension of two main ontologies typically used for describing users' interactions in social networks, in particular the SIOC[15] ontology for information from online communities and the FOAF[16] ontology for people and social groups, as well as to link people and information.

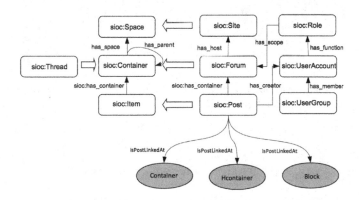

Fig. 6. SIOC and its relations with FOAF and the document model

---

[15] http://rdfs.org/sioc/spec/.
[16] http://www.foaf-project.org.

The basic social activities are implemented: in particular the possibility to post comments on legislative text fragments, to express sentiments associated to comments, as well as rating and voting a specific text version or comment. Comments are identified by http URIs, linked to legal text fragments identified by ELI-URIs. As shown in Fig. 6, users' comments, represented by instances of a sioc:Post, are linked to components of type Block or Hcontainer: in our case they can be paragraphs or articles. Users are described using the FOAF ontology able to specify several aspects of their profiles, including for example name, family name, nationality, language, the avatar, the group of interest they belong to, etc.

Statistics about users participation are also possible. In this respect specific properties are added to the different SIOC items and containers, so to consider the number of comments received by document fragments or by the whole document, as well as the number of positive, neutral or negative comments a text fragment has received. The amount of comments each fragment has received is graphically highlighted in terms of a circle packing document graph: each circle represents a document fragment, its size is proportional to the number of received comments, the color (gradients of green, gray and red) indicates the prevailing sentiment (positive, neutral or negative) expressed on it (Fig. 7). Other statistics by users' nationality or interest groups are available too.

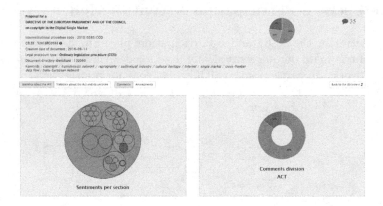

Fig. 7. Circle packaging about comments on different sections and comments percentage on the whole act. (Color figure online)

7   Conclusions and Future Developments

The LOD and e-Participation web platform prototype is implemented as Java-based open-source software, published in JoinUp[17], the service of the European Commission to help e-Government professionals share experiences and implement interoperability solutions.

---

[17] https://joinup.ec.europa.eu/software/e_participation/home.

In this paper we have described the knowledge organization system which the project is based on. The main advantage is to provide Linked Open Data services for all the data actually managed (documents, metadata, as well as users' social activities and statistics), thanks to the use of a pure ontological modeling based on RDF(S)/OWL technologies. In order to prevent possible misuse of the system (like spamming, hate speech, hacking), a governance of the platform based on a self-moderation mechanism is under study, combined with a traditional back-office moderation. A self-moderation mechanism will be based on users' reputation and privileges. In such governance mechanism the more reputation you earn, the more privileges you gain. Reputation is earned by posting good questions and useful answers (voted by the community), while specific privileges are granted according to the level of reputation earned, allowing selected users to manage accounts and comments (including filtering/summarizing comments).

References

1. Francesconi, E., Küster, M.W., Gratz, P., Thelen, S.: The ontology-based approach of the publications office of the EU for document accessibility and open data services. In: Kö, A., Francesconi, E. (eds.) EGOVIS 2015. LNCS, vol. 9265, pp. 29–39. Springer, Cham (2015). doi:10.1007/978-3-319-22389-6_3
2. Francesconi, E., Küster, M.W., Gratz, P., Thelen, S.: Semantic modeling of the EU multilingual resources. In: Schweighofer, E., Galindo, F., Serbena, C. (eds.) Proceedings of the Multilingual Workshop on Artificial Intelligence and Law, Vienna, Austria, pp. 65–74. Austrian Computer Society (2015). ISBN 978-3-903035-02-7
3. Study group on IFLA: Functional requirements for bibliographic records. Technical report, International Federation of Library Associations and Institutions (1998). http://www.ifla.org/VII/s13/frbr/frbr.pdf
4. Bianchini, C., Willer, M.: ISBD resource and its description in the context of the semantic web. Cat. Classif. Q. **52**, 869–887 (2014)
5. Dunsire, G.: Resource and work, expression, manifestation, item. Amended 6 October 2013, following comments by Patrick Le Boeuf and discussion at IFLA 2013, 28 July 2013
6. Council of European Union: Council conclusions inviting the introduction of the european legislation identifier (ELI). Technical report (2012/C 325/02) OJ C 325, Council of the European Union, October 2012
7. Boer, A., Hoekstra, R., de Maat, E., Hupkes, E., Vitali, F., Palmirani, M.: Cen workshop agreement 'open xml interchange format for legal and legislative resources'. Technical report CWA 15710:2010 E, CEN European Committee for Standardization (2010)
8. Palmirani, M., Cervone, L., Vitali, F.: A legal document ontology: the missing layer in legal document modelling. In: Sartor, G., Casanovas, P., Biasiotti, M., Fernández-Barrera, M. (eds.) Approaches to Legal Ontologies. Theories, Domains, Methodologies, pp. 167–178. Springer, Heidelberg (2011)
9. Arnold-Moore, T.: Automatic generation of amendment legislation. In: Proceedings of the International Conference of Artificial Intelligence and Law, pp. 56–62. ACM, New York (1997)
10. Arnold-Moore, T., Clemes, J., Tadd, M.: Connected to the law: tasmanian legislation using enact. Technical report, TeraText (2002)

11. Palmirani, M.: Legislative change management with Akoma-Ntoso. In: Sartor, G., Palmirani, M., Francesconi, E., Biasiotti, M.A. (eds.) Legislative XML for the Semantic Web: Principles, Models, Standards for Document Management. Law, Governance and Technology Series, vol. 4, pp. 101–130. Springer, Heidelberg (2011). Chap. 7
12. Spinosa, P., Giardiello, G., Cherubini, M., Marchi, S., Venturi, G., Montemagni, S.: NLP-based metadata extraction for legal text consolidation. In: Proceedings of the International Conference of Artificial Intelligence and Law, pp. 40–49 (2009)
13. Garofalakis, J., Plessas, K., Plessas, A.: Automatic identification, extraction and application of textual amendments in Greek legislative texts. In: Proceedings of the Jurix Conference: Legal Knowledge and Information System, pp. 187–190. ACM, New York (2016)
14. Francesconi, E.: A description logic framework for advanced accessing and reasoning over normative provisions. Int. J. Artif. Intell. Law **22**(3), 291–311 (2014)

Complexity Based Analysis of eGov Ontologies

Jean Vincent Fonou-Dombeu[1](✉) and Yannick Kazela Kazadi[2]

[1] Department of Software Studies, Vaal University of Technology, Private Bag X021,
Andries Potgieter Blvd, Vanderbijlpark 1900, South Africa
fonoudombeu@gmail.com
[2] Department of ICT, Vaal University of Technology, Private Bag X021,
Andries Potgieter Blvd, Vanderbijlpark 1900, South Africa
yan.kazadi@gmail.com

Abstract. The analysis of complexity of ontologies in a domain reveals their underlying characteristics and support their selection, reuse and maintenance. This study performs the analysis of e-government ontologies in the oeGov repository based on their complexity. The complexity metrics of oeGov ontologies are computed and analysed. Results revealed that only the top level ontologies in the oeGov architecture have classes, properties and instances; the majority of the constituents of the oeGov repository are instances or datasets of the top level ontologies. Results further revealed important facts on the distribution of relations and instances in the oeGov ontologies and portrayed that the government (gov) and geopolitical ontologies are the more complex ontologies in the oeGov repository.

Keywords: E-Government · Ontology · Ontology complexity metrics · oeGov · Ontology repository

1 Introduction

Ontology is a formal, explicit specification of a shared conceptualization of a domain of knowledge [1]. It represents knowledge as a set of concepts within a domain and the relations between them. An ontology defines the basic terms and relations comprising the vocabulary of a topic area as well as the rules for combining terms [2]. The emergence of the Semantic Web has resulted in the need for the use and development of ontologies. Therefore, as the ontologies of a given domain (medicine, geology, biomedical, e-government, e-science, etc.) grow in number and size, it is important to evaluate their complexity to facilitate their understanding by Semantic Web developers for the purpose of reuse, integration and maintainance [3].

The evaluation of complexity of existing ontologies would reveal their underlying characteristics and provide relevant information for improving their quality for better reuse as well as estimating the cost and time for their future maintenance [4]. It is argued that a quantitative measurement of the complexity of

© Springer International Publishing AG 2017
A. Kő and E. Francesconi (Eds.): EGOVIS 2017, LNCS 10441, pp. 115–128, 2017.
DOI: 10.1007/978-3-319-64248-2_9

ontology improves the understanding of its structure and enables a better evaluation of its design as well as the control of its development process [3].

One of the active areas of ontology development to date is the e-government domain where ontologies are being developed to describe and specify government services and processes [5–7]. Due to the challenges encountered in building ontologies *de novo*, existing e-government ontologies on the Semantic Web need to be shared and reused to promote the adoption of semantic technologies in e-government. To this end, TopGuadrant has launched the oeGov ontology repository to store and share a number of e-government ontologies of the US government [8].

This paper determines and analyses the advanced complexity features of e-government ontologies stored in the oeGov repository. These advanced complexity features are determined using the basic semantic features of the ontologies and appropriate programming constructs and algorithms. Currently, the oeGov repository includes 28 e-government ontologies. However, the interface of the oeGov repository [8] does not provide any facilities for getting quantitative information on the ontologies. This hinder the understanding of the underlying structures of the oeGov ontologies from the Semantic Web community in general and the e-government community in particular.

To the best of our knowledge, this is the first study that has focused on determining the complexity features of oeGov ontologies. Both primitive and advanced complexity metrics are calculated to analyze the complexity of oeGov ontologies. The primitive complexity metrics are the basic characteristics of ontology including the number of classes, properties and instances. They are utilized to compute the advanced complexity metrics of ontologies, namely, the depth of inheritance tree (DIT), size of the vocabulary (SOV), entropy of ontology graphs (EOG), average part length (APL) and average number of paths per class (ANP), tree impurity (TIP), relationship richness (RR) and class richness (CR). The analysis of the primitive complexity metrics of oeGov ontologies revealed that only the top level ontologies in the oeGov architecture [8] have classes, properties and instances; the majority of the constituents of the oeGov repository are instances or datasets of the top level ontologies. The primitive complexity metrics further revealed that the bigger ontology in the oeGov repository is the government ontology (gov) with 151 classes, 72 properties and 24 instances, follows by the geopolitical ontology (geopolitical) with 11 classes, 101 properties and 312 instances. The analysis of the advanced complexity metrics of the top level oeGov ontologies portrays that the gov and geopolitical ontologies have higher values for the SOV, TIP, ANP and DIT; this suggests that they are the more complex ontologies in the oeGov repository. Furthermore, the analysis of the distribution of relations in the oeGov ontologies reveals that (1) the government core (gc) ontology has little or no inheritance relationships, as denoted by the high ANP and RR values, (2) the RR is almost equal for gov and US government (usgov) ontologies and lower than that of gc and geopolitical ontologies; this is an indication that they include more subclass relations among their concepts, (3) all the classes of the gc ontology have instances, and hence its CR value is high,

(4) some classes in the usgov and geopolitical ontologies don't have instances due to their smaller CR and (5) the gov ontology displays the lowest CR, revealing that many of its classes don't have instances.

The rest of the paper is organized as follows. Section 2 discusses related works. The Materials and Methods utilized in the study are presented in Sect. 3. Section 4 conducts the experiments and discusses the experimental results. The conclusion and future direction of research are drawn in the last section.

2   Related Works

Many studies have demonstrated that the level of complexity of a software artefact determines its quality [10–12]. In the Object-Oriented field, this has led to the proposal of several metrics for measuring software quality including the cyclomatic complexity [10], coupling [11], Chidamber and Kemerer Object-Oriented [12] and Object Oriented Design (MOOD) metrics [13]. Similarly, many researches have proposed metrics that can be used to determine the complexity of ontology. The calculation of these metrics depends on the basic characteristics or primitive metrics of ontology including the number of classes, properties and instances [13,14].

In [13], sets of eight and three metrics for measuring the structural complexity and size of ontology, are proposed, respectively. Inspired by [13], authors in [9] proposed a method that consists in weighting class dependence graphs to represent ontology; they further presented a structured complexity measure of ontology based on entropy distance. This consists in assigning a value to each of the ontology classes and relations through an algorithm and applying these values to the Shannon's entropy function.

Another study in [15] proposed three metrics for measuring the cohesiveness of an ontology, namely, number of root classes, number of leaf classes, and average depth of inheritance. This study was inspired by the principle of cohesiveness in Object-Oriented design [13]. The concept of software metrics is used to propose a suite of ontology metrics to measure the design complexity of ontologies in [3]. Another suite of metrics that examine the quantity, ratio and correlativity of concepts and relationships of ontologies is proposed in [4].

In the biomedical domain, a tool that enables users to select suitable bio-medical ontologies for use when building applications that integrate clinical and biological data is proposed [14]. Although some ontology metrics such as the scope, granular density and integration are tackled [14], the focus was not on the analysis and discussion of the complexity features of biomedical ontologies.

3   Materials and Methods

In this section, the primitive and advanced complexity metrics of ontology are defined as well as the methods for calculating these metrics.

3.1 Primitive Complexity Metrics of Ontology

The primitive metrics that determine the basic characteristics of ontology include the:

- Number of classes ($|C|$) - Total number of classes or concepts of an ontology [16].
- Number of properties ($|P|$) - Total number of properties of an ontology [3,4].
- Number of instances ($|I|$) - Total number of instances or individuals of an ontology [9,16].

3.2 Advanced Complexity Metrics of Ontology

The advanced complexity metrics of ontology include:

Size of Vocabulary (SOV) - this metric defines the total number of named classes and instances, and properties in the ontology; it is defined as in Eq. 1.

$$SOV = |C| + |P| + |I| \tag{1}$$

where $|P|$ represents the number of properties of the ontology, and $|C|$ and $|I|$, the number of classes and instances, respectively [17]. A higher SOV implies that the ontology is big in size and would require a lot of time and effort to build it [3].

Depth of Inheritance of Ontology (DIT) - it is the average number of subclasses per class in the ontology [16]. An ontology with a low DIT may indicate a specific kind of information, whereas, a high DIT may represent a wide variety of information in the ontology. The DIT of an ontology is defined as in Eq. 2.

$$DIT = \frac{\sum_{c_i \in C} NS_{C_i}}{|C|} \tag{2}$$

where C is the set of classes in the ontology and NS_{C_i} the number of subclasses of the class C_i belonging to C.

Average Number of Paths per Concept (ANP) - it indicates the average connectivity degree of a concept to the root concept in the ontology inheritance hierarchy [4]. A higher ANP indicates the existence of a high number of inheritance relationships in the ontology; it also shows that there is a high number of interconnections between classes in the ontology. This metric is defined as in Eq. 3:

$$ANP = \frac{\sum_{i=1}^{m} p_i}{|C|} \tag{3}$$

where p_i is the number of paths of a given concept. The value ANP for any ontology must be greater or equal to 1; a $ANP = 1$ indicates that an ontology inheritance hierarchy is a tree.

Tree Impurity (TIP) - this metric is used to measure how far an ontology inheritance hierarchy deviates from a tree; the TIP is defined as in Eq. 4:

$$TIP = |R'| - |C'| + 1 \tag{4}$$

where R' and C', represent the sets of relations and concepts in the inheritance hierarchy, respectively. The rational of the TIP is that a well-structured ontology is composed of classes organized through inheritance relationships. A TIP = 0 means that the inheritance hierarchy is a tree. The greater the TIP, the more the ontology inheritance hierarchy deviates from the tree and the greater its complexity is.

Average Path Length of an Ontology (APL) - this metric indicates the average number of concepts in a path in the ontology. An ontology with a bigger APL indicates that there are too many inheritance relationships in the ontology; as a consequence, the management and manipulation of concepts in such ontology could be a complex task [4]. It is defined as in Eq. 5:

$$APL = \frac{\sum_{i=1}^{m} \sum_{k=1}^{p_i} pl_{i,k}}{\sum_{i=1}^{m} p_i} \tag{5}$$

where $pl_{i,k}$ and p_i represent the length of the kth path and the number of paths for the ith concept of the ontology, respectively. The APL is the ratio of the sum of the path lengths $pl_{i,k}$ of each of the m concepts in the ontology over the sum of the number of paths p_i of concepts.

Entropy of Ontology Graph (EOG) - this metric is the application of the logarithm function to a probability distribution over the ontology graph in order to provide a numerical value that can be used as an indicator of the graph complexity [3]. It is defined as in Eq. 6:

$$EOG = -\sum_{i=1}^{n} p(i) \log_2(p(i)) \tag{6}$$

where $p(i)$ is the probability for a concept to have i relations. The minimum value of EOG corresponds to $EOG = 0$, it is obtained when concepts have the same distribution of relations in the ontology, that is, all the nodes of the ontology sub-graphs have the same number of edges. Therefore, an ontology with a smaller EOG can be considered as less complex in terms of relations distribution [3].

Relationship Richness (RR) - it explains the distribution of relations in an ontology. It is the ratio of the total number of relations over the sum of the number of subclass relations and the number of relations in the ontology [16]. It is defined in Eq. 7:

$$RR = \frac{|R|}{|SC| + |R|} \tag{7}$$

where, $|R|$ and $|SC|$ represent the number of relations between classes and the number of subclass relations in the ontology, respectively. A RR value close to one indicates that most of the relations between concepts in the ontology are not subclass relations, while a RR close to zero specifies that the subclass relations are predominant amongst the concepts of the ontology [18].

Class Richness (CR) - the value of this metric explains the distribution of individuals or instances in the ontology [16]. It is the ratio of the total number of classes having at least one instance ($|C'|$) over the total number of classes ($|C|$) in the ontology. Its definition is provided in Eq. 8.

$$CR = \frac{|C'|}{|C|} \tag{8}$$

According to Tartir et al. [16], a CR close to one indicates that most of the ontology classes have instances.

3.3 Calculation of Advanced Complexity Metrics

For each ontology in the dataset, the advanced complexity metrics in Eqs. 1 to 8 are computed in Java Jena Application Programming Interface (API) [19]. A Jena Model is built for each ontology. Thereafter, the Jena Model is processed to compute the relevant primitive ontology metrics which are then used to calculate the advanced complexity metrics. The processing of the Jena Model requires the design and use of various Java constructs including Arrays, Queues, Lists and Iterators as well as the design and implementation of appropriate algorithms.

4   Experiments

4.1   Dataset

The dataset is constituted of 28 ontologies downloaded from the oeGov repository [8]. These ontologies are listed in Table 1 and are the semantic modelling of the US government and its branches, agencies, departments, offices and state governments. They include the:

- US government ontologies - These are the top level ontologies in the oeGov hierarchy including government core (gc) ontology (O_1), government (gov) ontology (O_3) and US government (usgov) ontology (O_6).
- US government department ontologies - These include the ontologies of various US government departments such as the: Department of Homeland Security (dhs) ontology (O_9), Department of Interior (doi) ontology (O_{12}), Department of Transportation (dot) ontology (O_{16}), Department of Housing and Urban Development (hud) ontology (O_{21}), and so forth.

Table 1. List of e-Government ontologies in the oeGov repository

Index	oeGov Ontologies
O_1	Government core ontology
O_2	Creative commons ontology
O_3	Government ontology 1
O_4	Geopolitical ontology
O_5	Government ontology 2
O_6	U.S. government ontology 1
O_7	U.S. government ontology 2
O_8	U.S. constitution ontology
O_9	Department of Homeland Security ontology
O_{10}	Department of Commerce ontology
O_{11}	Department of Energy ontology
O_{12}	Department of Interior ontology
O_{13}	Department of Justice ontology
O_{14}	Department of Labour ontology
O_{15}	Department of State ontology
O_{16}	Department of Transportation ontology
O_{17}	Education Department ontology
O_{18}	Environment Protection Agency ontology
O_{19}	General Service Administration ontology
O_{20}	Department of Health and Human Services ontology
O_{21}	Department of Housing and Urban Development ontology
O_{22}	National Archives Administration ontology
O_{23}	National Aeronautics and Space Administration ontology
O_{24}	National Oceanic and Atmospheric Administration ontology
O_{25}	Treasury ontology
O_{26}	United States Department of Agriculture ontology
O_{27}	U.S. Department of Veterans Affairs ontology
O_{28}	White House ontology

- Creative common ontology (O_2) - It is an extension of the Resource Description Framework (RDF) description of copyright licenses; all oeGov ontologies have dependencies with this ontology.
- Geopolitical ontology (O_4) - This ontology does not have any dependency with other oeGov ontologies; its semantic descriptions serve two purposes: provide a standardized way for data exchange and sharing among systems and handling of information concerning countries and/or regions.

- US government agency ontologies - ontologies in this category are: National Archives Administration (nara) ontology (O_{22}), National Aeronautics and Space Administration (nasa) ontology (O_{23}), National Oceanic and Atmospheric Administration (noaa) ontology (O_{24}), Treasury (treasury) ontology (O_{25}), and White House (wh) ontology (O_{28}).

4.2   Computer and Software Environment

The experiments were carried out on a computer with the following characteristics: 64-bit Genuine Intel (R) Celeron (R) CPU 847, Windows 8 release preview, 2 GB RAM and 300 GB hard drive. The algorithms for computing the complexity metrics were implemented in Java Jena API [19] configured in Eclipse Integrated Development Environment (IDE) Version 4.2.

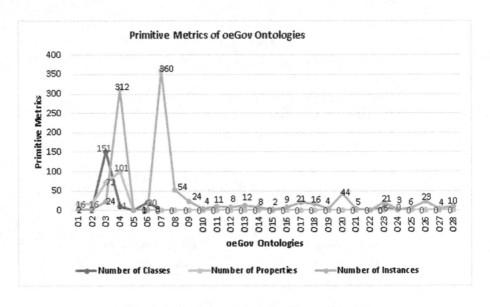

Fig. 1. Primitive metrics of oeGov ontologies

4.3   Analysis of Primitive Metrics of oeGov Ontologies

In order to compute the advanced complexity metrics for all the ontologies in the dataset, it was necessary to determine the basic semantic characteristics or primitive metrics of these ontologies such as the number of classes, properties and instances. This was done through the processing of the Jena Model for each of the ontology as mentioned earlier in Subsect. 3.3. Figure 1 displays the primitive metrics of oeGov ontologies.

The results in Fig. 1 depicts that only the top level ontologies in the oeGov architecture including gc (O_1), gov (O_3), usgov (O_6) have classes, properties and instances; the majority of the constituents of the oeGov are instances or dataset of the top level ontologies. It is shown in Fig. 1 that the bigger top level ontology in the oeGov is the gov ontology with 151 classes, 72 properties and 24 instances. The second larger ontology in the oeGov repository is the geopolitical ontology (O_4) constituted of 11 classes, 101 properties and 312 instances. The results in Fig. 1 portray that the majority of oeGov ontologies do not have classes nor properties, they are instances or datasets of the top level ontologies.

4.4   Analysis of Advanced Complexity Metrics of oeGov Ontologies

The advanced complexity metrics defined in Eqs. 1 to 8 applied to ontology graphs, i.e., complete ontologies with classes, properties/relations and instances. However, the discussion of the primitive metrics of oeGov ontologies in Subsect. 4.3 portrayed that only four ontologies in the oeGov repository including gc, gov, usgov and geopolitical are complete ontologies (Fig. 1). Therefore, in this subsection, the discussion of the advanced complexity metrics is limited to these four oeGov ontologies.

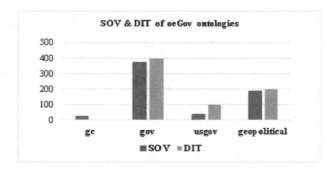

Fig. 2. Size of vocabulary and depth of inheritance of oeGov ontologies

Size of the Vocabulary and Depth of Inheritance. The size of vocabulary (SOV) and depth of inheritance (DIT) of oeGov ontologies including gc, gov, usgov and geopolitical ontologies are displayed in Fig. 2. It is shown that the gov ontology has the bigger SOV, followed by the geopolitical ontology. The usgov and gc have smaller SOV. The SOV indicates the degree or level of complexity of an ontology. Therefore, an ontology with a higher SOV is highly complex and would require more effort to maintain it [3]. From Fig. 2, it is shown that the gov ontology is the more complex oeGov ontology followed by the geopolitical ontology. These two ontologies with large SOV would be difficult to maintain. The gc and usgov ontologies have smaller SOV and would be easy to maintain.

With regard to the DIT, it is shown once again in Fig. 2 that the gov ontology has the bigger DIT followed by the geopolitical ontology and the usgov, respectively. The gc ontology has zero DIT; this is an indication that there is no inheritance relationship in the gc ontology at all. The gov ontology has the higher DIT, this is an indication of its higher complexity compared to other oeGov ontologies. This finding was also reached with the analysis of the SOV.

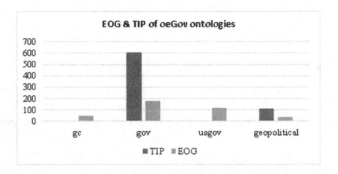

Fig. 3. Entropy of ontology graph and tree impurity of oeGov ontologies

Entropy of Ontology Graph and Tree Impurity. Figure 3 represents the EOG and TIP of the oeGov ontologies. The EOG represents the distribution of relations in an ontology; an ontology with smaller EOG indicates a uniform distribution of relation within the ontology sub-graphs [3]. On the other hand, a higher EOG indicates an irregular pattern of relations within the ontology. Figure 3 shows that the gc and geopolitical ontologies have smaller values for EOG; this is an indication that the distribution of relations in these ontologies is nearly uniform. The gov ontology has the higher EOG; this indicates an irregular distribution of relations within the gov sub-graphs and a high level of complexity compared to other oeGov ontologies.

Similarly, Fig. 3 represents the TIP of oeGov ontologies. The TIP represents how far the inheritance hierarchy of an ontology deviate from a tree. An ontology with a TIP close to zero indicates that its graph is structured as a tree. Therefore, a higher TIP indicates that the ontology graph is not a tree.

Figure 3 depicts that the TIP for the gc and usgov ontologies are nearly zero, therefore these ontologies' graphs are structured like trees. The gov and geopolitical ontologies shows high TIP values, this indicates that their graphs are irregular and more complex.

Average Number of Paths and Average Path Length. Let's recall that the ANP indicates the degree of connectivity of concepts to the root concept in the ontology inheritance hierarchy. Figure 4 provides a joint analysis of the ANP and APL. It is shown that the gov ontology have a high ANP; this reveals that there is a high number of inheritance relationships in the gov ontology and expresses the intensity of interconnection between the classes. Figure 4 also depicts that the geopolitical ontology has a low ANP; this is an indication of a low level of inheritance relationships and interconnection between its classes. The ANP for gc and usgov is zero; this tells that these two ontologies have either little or no inheritance relationships among their classes.

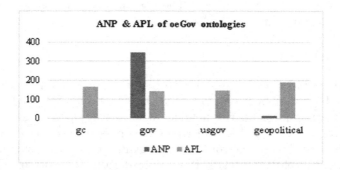

Fig. 4. Average number of paths and average path length of oeGov ontologies

The APL of an ontology expresses the average number of concepts in a path. Figure 4 shows that the gc and geopolitical ontologies have high APL; this is due to the fact that they have high number of paths per concepts and low number of classes. The APL for the gov and usgov ontologies are almost the same and lower than the APL for gc and geopolitical ontologies; this is justified by their relatively high number of classes.

Relationship Richness and Class Richness. The RR explains the distribution of relations in an ontology. Figure 5 depicts the RR and CR for the oeGov ontologies. It is shown that the RR is higher for the gc and geopolitical ontologies; this reveals that there is a low number of subclass relations in these ontologies. The RR is almost equal for gov and usgov and lower than that of gc and geopolitical ontologies; this is an indication that they include more subclass relations among their concepts than the gc and geopolitical ontology.

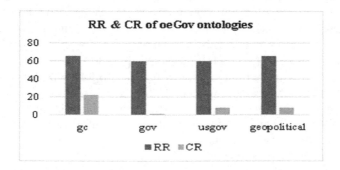

Fig. 5. Relationship and class richness of oeGov ontologies

The CR explains the distribution of individuals or instances in the ontology. Figure 5 shows that the gc ontology have the higher CR; this tells that all its classes have instances. The usgov and geopolitical ontologies have the same CR that is low compared to that of the gc ontology; this tells that some classes in these ontologies don't have instances. The gov ontology displays the lowest CR revealing that many of its classes don't have instances.

5   Conclusion

This study determined and analyzed both the primitive and advanced complexity features of e-government ontologies in the oeGov repository. The primitive complexity metrics included the number of classes, properties and instances, whereas, the advanced complexity metrics encompassed the depth of inheritance tree, size of the vocabulary, entropy of ontology graphs, average part length and average number of paths per class, the tree impurity, relationship richness and class richness. The analysis of the primitive complexity metrics of oeGov ontologies revealed that only the 3 top level ontologies in the oeGov architecture have classes, properties and instances; the majority of the constituents of the oeGov are instances or datasets of the top level ontologies. The primitive complexity metrics further revealed that the bigger ontology in the oeGov is the government ontology (gov) with 151 classes, 72 properties and 24 instances, follows by the geopolitical ontology (geopolitical) with 11 classes, 101 properties and 312 instances. The analysis of the advanced complexity metrics of the top level oeGov ontologies portrays that the government (gov) and geopolitical ontologies have higher values for the SOV, TIP, ANP and DIT; this suggested that they are the more complex ontologies in the oeGov repository.

Furthermore, the analysis of the distribution of relations in the oeGov ontologies reveals that (1) the government core (gc) ontology has little or no inheritance relationships, as denoted by the high ANP and RR values, (2) the RR is almost equal for gov and US government (usgov) ontologies and lower than that of gc and geopolitical ontologies; this indicated that they include more subclass relations among their concepts, (3) all the classes of the gc ontology have instances, and hence its CR value is high, (4) some classes in the usgov and geopolitical ontologies don't have instances due to their smaller CR and (5) the gov ontology displays the lowest CR revealing that many of its classes don't have instances. These findings may be useful for the reuse and sharing of these ontologies in the e-government. The reuse may consist in using (1) parts of existing oeGov ontologies to build new ones or (2) the full ontologies in new applications [20]. In fact, ontology reuse (1) reduces human efforts required to formalized new ontologies from scratch, (2) increases the quality of the resulting ontologies because the reused ontologies have already been tested, (3) simplifies the mapping between ontologies built using shared components of existing ontologies, and (4) improves the efficiency of ontology maintenance [20].

In future, it would be interesting to expand the study to other e-government ontologies that are not part of oeGov ontologies and develop a framework for classifying e-government ontologies based on their level of complexity.

References

1. Gruber, T.R.: Toward principles for the design of ontologies used for knowledge sharing. Int. J. Hum.-Comput. Stud. **43**, 907–928 (1993)
2. Neches, R., Fikes, R.E., Finin, T., Gruber, T.R., Senator, T., Swartout, W.R.: Enabling technology for knowledge sharing. AI Mag. **12**, 36–56 (1990)
3. Zhang, H., Li, Y.F., Tan, H.B.K.: Measuring design complexity of semantic web ontologies. Syst. Softw. **83**, 803–814 (2010)
4. Yang, Z., Zhang, D., Ye, C.: Evaluation metrics for ontology complexity and evolution analysis. In: IEEE International Conference e-Business Engineering, pp. 162–170 (2006)
5. Sabucedo, L.M.A., Rifon, L.E.A., Corradini, F., Polzonetti, A., Re, B.: Knowledge-based platform for e-government agents: a web-based solution using semantic technologies. J. Expert Syst. Appl. **37**, 3647–3656 (2010)
6. Xiao, Y., Xioa, M., Zhao, H.: An ontology for e-government knowledge modelling and interoperability. In: IEEE International Conference on Wireless Communications, Networking and Mobile Computing (WiCOM 2007), Shanghai, China, pp. 3600–3603 (2007)
7. Jarrar, M., Deik, A., Farraj, B.: Ontology-based data process governance framework - the case of e-government interoperability in palestine. In: IFIP International Symposium on Data-Driven Process Discovery and Analysis (SIMPDA 2011), Campione, Italy, pp. 83–98 (2011)
8. oeGov: Ontologies for e-Government. http://www.oegov.us/
9. Kang, D., Xu, B., Lu, J., Chu, W.C.: A complexity measure for ontology based on UML. In: 10th IEEE International Workshop on Future Trends of Distributed Computing Systems, pp. 222–228 (2004)
10. Fenton, N., Melton, A.: Deriving structurally based software measures. J. Syst. Softw. **12**, 177–187 (1990)
11. Chidamber, S., Kemerer, C.: A metrics suite for object oriented design. IEEE Trans. Softw. Eng. **20**, 476–493 (1994)
12. Brito, E., Abreu, F., Melo, W.: Evaluating the impact of object-oriented design on software quality. In: 3rd International Metric Symposium, pp. 90–99 (1996)
13. Manso, M., Genero, M., Piattini, M.: Non-redundant metrics for UML class diagram structural complexity. In: 15th International Conference Advanced Information Systems Engineering, pp. 50–65 (2003)
14. Maiga, G., Ddembe, W.: Flexible biomedical ontology selection tool. Int. J. Comput. ICT Res. Spec. Issue **3**, 53–66 (2009)
15. Yao, H., Orme, A., Etzkorn, L.: Cohesion metrics for ontology design and application. J. Comput. Sci. **1**, 107–113 (2005)
16. Tartir, S., Arpinar, B., Moore, M., Sheth, A., Aleman-meza, B.: OntoQA: metric-based ontology quality analysis. In: IEEE Workshop on Knowledge Acquisition from Distributed, Autonomous, Semantically Heterogeneous Data and Knowledge Sources, pp. 45–53 (2005)
17. Mallea, A., Arenas, M., Hogan, A., Polleres, A.: On blank nodes. In: Aroyo, L., Welty, C., Alani, H., Taylor, J., Bernstein, A., Kagal, L., Noy, N., Blomqvist, E. (eds.) ISWC 2011. LNCS, vol. 7031, pp. 421–437. Springer, Heidelberg (2011). doi:10.1007/978-3-642-25073-6_27
18. Sugumaran, V., Gula, J.T.: Applied Semantic Web Technologies. Tailor & Francis Group, LLC, Abingdon (2012)

19. Jena, M.B.: Implementing the RDF model and syntax specification. In: 2nd International Workshop on the Semantic Web - SemWeb 2001, pp. 308–320 (2001)
20. Ding, Y., Lonsdale, D., Embley, D.W., Hepp, M., Xu, L.: Generating ontologies via language components and ontology reuse. In: Kedad, Z., Lammari, N., Métais, E., Meziane, F., Rezgui, Y. (eds.) NLDB 2007. LNCS, vol. 4592, pp. 131–142. Springer, Heidelberg (2007). doi:10.1007/978-3-540-73351-5_12

Process-Based Query Tool to Rationalize Document Bases

Katalin Ternai[(✉)] and Ildikó Szabó

Department of Information Systems, Corvinus University of Budapest,
Fővám tér 13-15, Budapest 1093, Hungary
katalin.ternai@uni-corvinus.hu,
iszabo@informatika.uni-corvinus.hu

Abstract. Organizational activities require and produce documents like policies, transactional documents, business reports, audit reports. These documents are usually stored in document bases belonging to their hosting IT systems that makes difficult to search them. However they are connected to their generating, modifying and utilizing activities in process models which can be transformed into process ontologies. Process ontologies can be served as a basis for transforming process models into workflows, and interpreting or searching documents released during the runtime of processes. An application presented in this paper uses process model transformation, process-based text mining and semantic technologies for processing documents and querying them.

Keywords: Semantic searching · Business process management · Document base

1 Introduction

European Commission declared the need of making data, information and knowledge settled in isolated systems more accessible in order to enhance collaboration[1]. Four main areas have been pointed out to improve: information retrieval and delivery, knowledge sharing and cooperative collaboration, data usage for better policy-making, and organizational culture of knowledge sharing and learning. The first and third directions aim at organizing document and databases in more flexible way.

Data, information and knowledge are stored and organized sometimes along different terminologies and format requirements in integrated systems, data warehouses, repositories, databases across the European Union. The following action points were determined to make them searchable, easily retrievable and as widely available as possible

"Develop the capability to search easily across different systems in order to find and retrieve all the relevant information held by the Commission, irrespective of where that information is stored or the underlying technology.
Where appropriate information will be made more easily accessible, sensitive and classified information needs, however, to be protected. Restrictions on such information will be strictly enforced and, where necessary, security will be improved.

---

[1] C(2016)6626/F1 Communication.

© Springer International Publishing AG 2017
A. Kő and E. Francesconi (Eds.): EGOVIS 2017, LNCS 10441, pp. 129–139, 2017.
DOI: 10.1007/978-3-319-64248-2_10

Finding and combining information and delivering it to where it is needed will be made easier by introducing standards for corporate data and metadata management, e.g. for the description of content in information systems. As a first step, ongoing projects to create common metadata in specific areas and policies on metadata management will be reviewed, in order to identify gaps and set priorities by the end of 2016.

To facilitate the exchange of data and information new information systems need to be user-centric and interoperable by design. All new systems should be designed targeting reusability of the provided services and data. A plan will be put in place by the end of 2016 identifying IT systems that need to be made more user-centric and interoperable, including a timeline to achieve this" [1].

European Commission emphasized the need for developing a system extracting information from different systems easily. A semantic searching layer above these systems are applicable for solving this problem, because semantic technologies like ontologies provide opportunities to transform information derived from different sources into common, conceptualized, and explicit format. But mostly domain ontologies and not process ontologies are used for constructing a semantic searching layer. For example the SemSearch is a search engine, which pays special attention to these issues by providing several means to hide the complexity of semantic search from end users and thus make it easy to use and effective [2]. Due to the Linked Open Data initiative different websites in RDF format appear on the Web and becoming querying by SPARQL endpoints. DBpedia is one good example of this initiative which aims at "extracting structured information from Wikipedia and making this information available on the Web. DBpedia allows you to ask sophisticated queries against Wikipedia, and to link the different data sets on the Web to Wikipedia data. These are realized by domain ontologies" [3].

Process ontologies, in contrast of domain ontologies, are capable of preserving organizational processes being responsible for creating, reusing, transforming, modifying the information stored in documents. Hence documents are connected to not just responsible persons but also to the relevant activities, hereby these documents become searchable via these activities and not just through the metadata stored in domain ontologies. This paper presents a process-based semantic layer on document bases in order to organize and search documents easily by using process models in design-time and to process the documents in run-time. Semantic business process management deals with analyzing semantics of business processes both in design-time and run-time and get process ontologies involved in executing these tasks. Section 2 presents the theoretical background. Section 3 shows an application combining process model transformation, process-based text mining and semantic technologies for creating a semantic layer to execute queries on it and process document if it is needed. Conclusions and future work are summarized in Sect. 4.

2   Theoretical Background

2.1   From Business Process Management to Process Ontology

Business process modeling was coined in the 1960s and by now it has a very large literature. In the 1990s, the term "process" became a new productivity paradigm.

Companies were encouraged to think in processes instead of functions or procedures. Business process modeling has emerged as a practical solution for obtaining a preferable understanding of business processes with an approach similar to that used for representing physical control systems. Nevertheless, there are different views, concepts and misconceptions in this area [4].

While process modeling is a traditional and well established topic, the various possible motivations for modeling a process, the various sources of models, and the resulting variety of requirements on the formalisms used for representing processes are often not considered.

Business process management (BPM) includes process engineering (design and modeling), execution, monitoring, optimizing and re-engineering. Process engineering includes the illustration of business processes by the aid of instruments like reference models, benchmarking and simulation. Various methods for optimizing, evaluating and ensuring the quality of the processes are available. A complex management toolset integrates BPR concepts, quality management approaches, change and project management methods and IT related tools and methods. Generally, processes are engineered at the type level. Reference models, which can be developed on the basis of real-world situations as best practices, or theoretically. Reference models document process know-how that can be utilized for further modeling. In dynamic simulations, the dynamic behavior of alternative processes are studied.

BPM includes modeling and analyzing the current process, through redesign and optimization resulting a new process. The methods, such as process analysis, model comparison or simulation, can be employed for process improvement.

In the early phase of the BPM lifecycle a business analyst creates an analytical process model with help of a modeling tool by specifying the tasks and their sequence (s) within the business process. The modeling tool typically supports a graph-based modeling approach adopting a popular process modeling notation. In addition to predefined graphical notations, business analysts have normally the possibility to specify some additional information in natural language for each element in a process model, such as what the tasks in the process are supposed to do and by whom they are expected to be performed. Process models created in the modeling phase are usually too high level to be executed by a process engine due to the lack of technical information such as binding of IT services and data formats for each task. Therefore, an analytical process model must be transformed to an executable process model, which is the focus of the process implementation phase.

In the process implementation phase a process model created in the process modeling phase is transformed and enriched by IT engineers into a process model, which can be executed in a process engine. The standard language for describing executable processes in the context of Service-Oriented Architecture (SOA) and Web services is the Business Process Execution Language (BPEL). The executable process model can only be partly generated from the analytical process model. The web services that are needed to execute the process model have to be manually and statically assigned. The resulting executable process model can be deployed into a process engine for execution.

From the managerial point of view BPM is the appropriate approach of managing the execution of IT supported business operations. BPM should provide a uniform representation of a process at a semantic level, as well. The semantics would available intelligent queries or compliance checks [6]. It is expected, that BPM notation should cover every aspect of the processes available at the managerial level, too.

Fensel and his colleagues propose to combine Web services and BPM, and yield a consolidated technology, which they call semantic business process management (SBPM) [5]. Ontologies have key role in SBPM as well as semantic web [7]. Ontology is responsible for domain conceptualization, structuring knowledge embedded in business processes. It describes not only data, but also the regularity of connection among data. The goal is to be able to apply machine reasoning for the translation, in particular for the discovery of processes, process fragments and for process composition [8]. The use of ontologies is a key concept that distinguishes SBPM from conventional BPM. Via the semantic description of the data, business process analysis can be semantically enhanced since the meaning of the data is preserved during all phases of the process lifecycle [9].

Ontologies, as general but formalized representation can be used for describing the concepts behind a business process. Process ontology can be referred as a conceptual description framework of processes [10]. In this interpretation process ontologies are abstract and general. Task ontologies determine a smaller subset of the process space, the sequence of activities in a given process [11].

Ontology definition can be the key element of turning process models into working software, providing a visual and textual representation of the processes, data, information, resources, collaborations and other measurements. The approach is identified as a semi-automatic generation of BPM defined ontologies. Semi-automatic generation of new business processes allows redeploying processes in a flexible manner whenever business requirements change [9].

The process ontology is used to reconcile the heterogeneous semantics of process modeling constructs, i.e. meta-model semantics existing in different process modeling languages. It indicates that process ontology should include a set of meta-concepts that are able to describe the semantics of process models.

3   Process-Based Document Processing and Querying

Organizations work along business processes which are represented in business process models. Process model transformations create process ontologies from the models, in order to explore the embedded semantics, and as a result the process models will be more searchable, analyzable with the help of process ontologies. There are two important remarks (Fig. 1):

First, in the process modeling tool what we use (ADONIS) it is difficult to add new attributes and data types to the model elements in the, therefore a script is required to transform the descriptions of the model elements into the attributes of the relevant classes in the process ontologies. Having prepared the process ontologies in this way, the locations of documents handled by the activities must be connected to the classes of the newly created process ontologies.

Second, process ontologies can be used as meta-models in the preliminary phase, meaning that documents are just templates and contain only metadata, which will be

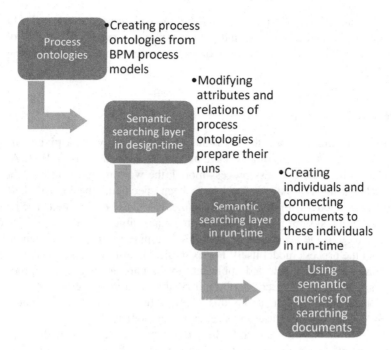

Fig. 1. Background processes

individualized only in run-time. The meta-model of the semantic searching layer is ready to be connected to the individualized documents that can be realized in two ways:

1. Transforming process ontologies into workflows, and automatic executions of them will connect to the individualized documents with the corresponding activities (process steps). We applied this method to improve application development in a collaboration framework (eBest project) [12]. The focus was given to the automatic and reusable generation of workflows based on ontologies derived from business process models [10].
2. Using any other application for executing processes, but the locations of documents will be connected manually to the individuals of the meta-classes.

Having assigned the individualized documents or their locations to their responsible activities (process steps), the semantic searching layer is applicable for running semantic queries on it.

The operation of this application is presented by the following use case.

4 The 'Erasmus Mobility' Use Case

Internationalization of higher education is fueled in large extent by the EU Erasmus mobility actions. Erasmus mobility enables students to follow courses in a foreign institutions if their performance would be acknowledged by the home institution. The procedure is known as credit transfer, and the corresponding document the Learning Agreement, in which the course(s) and grade(s) officially registered. In the following use case we highlight the advantages of our solutions through the processing of Learning Agreement.

4.1   Process Engineering

In the process modeling phase the 'Erasmus student mobility' **at a given university** use case, the business process models have been implemented by using BOC ADONIS modeling platform. The business process model, the working environment, the document model and the IT system model have been specified. The logical shell of the business process model with the core objects (e.g. task) has been created. The input and output data, the IT system information and the responsible role from the organogram have been linked to the activities. In the modelling phase semantic annotation can be embedded in the process model itself. For example, "Learning Agreement" was linked to the "Announcement of selected applicants to the partner institutions" process step the. In this solution the "description" field of the "Learning Agreement" document element contains information about this element (e.g. the features of courses like component code, ECTS credit etc.) as semantic annotation (Fig. 2).

The meta-level mapping converts the Adonis model elements to the appropriate ontology elements. This conversion has been performed by means of XSL Extensible Style sheet Language (XSL) translation. The model transformation preserves the semantics of the business model. OWL was used as the language for representing ontologies, due to its wide-spread acceptance. In the use case Portégé-OWL application supports ontology building (Fig. 3).

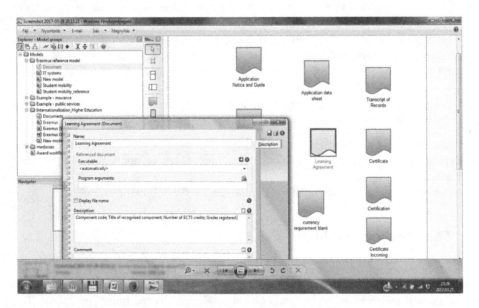

Fig. 2. The "Learning Agreement" data

Fig. 3. The "Learning Agreement" data in the process ontology in Protégé 5

The process ontology is created in RDF format, hence an API using ontology building library can be used to transform the descriptions (Fig. 3) into the attributes of the Learning Agreement class (Fig. 4). (Not all metadata of a Learning Agreement was presented in the process model.)

During the Erasmus application process, the Learning Agreement of an applicant will be filled out and a process ontology-based workflow is capable of storing this information into a process ontology. Recently applicants upload the Learning Agreements in pdf format on the Erasmus project website (e.g. (http://www.euroinka.eu/apply) that makes easy the processing.

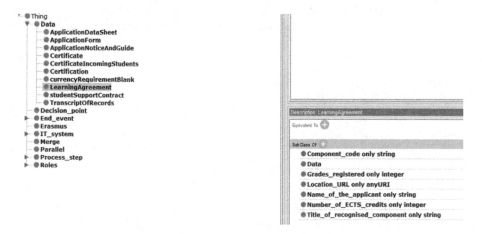

Fig. 4. Extended process ontology in Protégé 5

A text processing script is required to process the text documents converted from pdf files and insert an individual of the Learning Agreement with its data into the process ontology (Fig. 5).

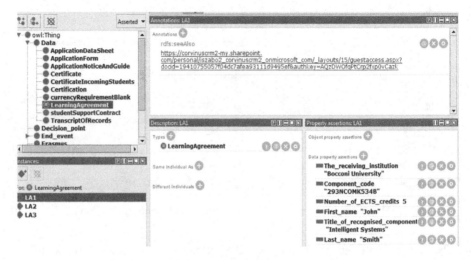

Fig. 5. An individual of the Learning Agreement class

Having processed Learning Agreements of all the applicants, the document base becomes applicable for semantic queries.

DL query is only capable of presenting instances and subclasses, and not attributes of any instance or subclass. We can just identify which Learning Agreements are used as input of a given activity. For example, in the Announcement Of Selected Applicants To The Partner Institutions process step we have to inform one of our partner institutions about the selected applicant(s). The following DL Query (Fig. 6) presents the Learning Agreements that must be checked before transferring them to a given partner. The query does not show the URLs or access paths in the information systems.

Fig. 6. DL query in Protégé 5

The SPARQL query language is more expressive than the DL Query, because it collects the locations of all the above-mentioned Learning Agreements (Fig. 7).

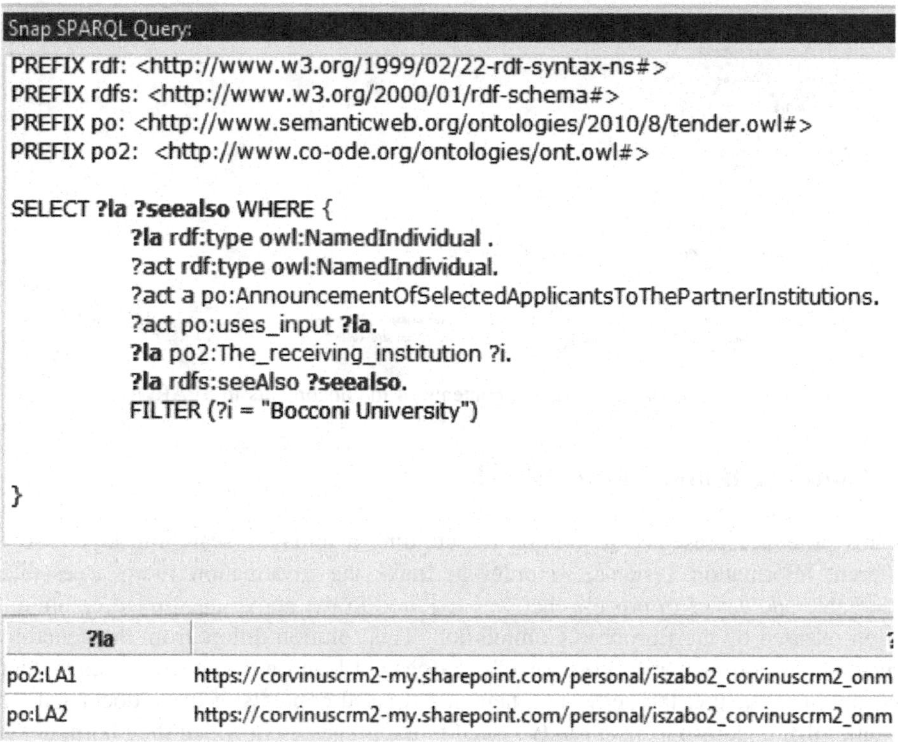

```
Snap SPARQL Query:
PREFIX rdf: <http://www.w3.org/1999/02/22-rdf-syntax-ns#>
PREFIX rdfs: <http://www.w3.org/2000/01/rdf-schema#>
PREFIX po: <http://www.semanticweb.org/ontologies/2010/8/tender.owl#>
PREFIX po2: <http://www.co-ode.org/ontologies/ont.owl#>

SELECT ?la ?seealso WHERE {
        ?la rdf:type owl:NamedIndividual .
        ?act rdf:type owl:NamedIndividual.
        ?act a po:AnnouncementOfSelectedApplicantsToThePartnerInstitutions.
        ?act po:uses_input ?la.
        ?la po2:The_receiving_institution ?i.
        ?la rdfs:seeAlso ?seealso.
        FILTER (?i = "Bocconi University")


}
```

?la	
po2:LA1	https://corvinuscrm2-my.sharepoint.com/personal/iszabo2_corvinuscrm2_onm
po:LA2	https://corvinuscrm2-my.sharepoint.com/personal/iszabo2_corvinuscrm2_onm

Fig. 7. SPARQL query in Protégé 5

Learning Agreements are verified at the end of the scholarships. Courses are administered in the student administration system, grades obtained in the courses are taken from the authentic information system and transferred to the Learning Agreement. A Java script using Apache Poi library and OWL API is capable of extracting student names and grades, and stores them into the appropriate process ontology reflecting the mobility evaluation process. SPARQL query can collect students who get a grade and who did not. The following query (Fig. 8) discovers students failed in a course, mentioned in either the Learning Agreement, and the transcript of record. The query points the location of the transcript out as well.

In conclusion, process ontologies extend the repository of semantic queries due to the fact that they preserve the structure of the process models. Connection between the documents and the activities can be automatized by workflows. The location of documents can be determined by URL provided by on-premise systems and paths provided by on-demand systems. The determination of these paths are dependent on the system structure, hence it is difficult to state general rules about them. An other paper provides enough place to discuss this question.

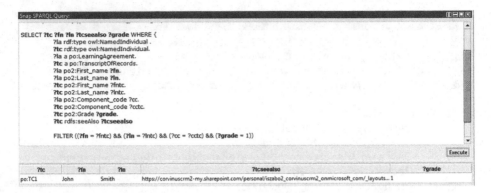

Fig. 8. Comparing semantic contents of the documents in SPARQL

5 Conclusion and Future Work

In this paper we presented a solution for building a semantic searching layer above different information systems, in order to make the information more accessible, searchable and easier to process that was required in the above-mentioned communication released by the European Commission. This solution differs from the generally accepted procedures like full text search. It does not lean on the semantics embedded into the file structure, the keywords, tags or extracted contents of these documents. It assumes that documents are strongly linked to the processes in which they born, hence these documents become searchable via these processes.

The application uses process ontologies transformed from process models providing backbone of semantic searching layer. In contrast of other solutions that using domain ontologies, our suggested solution provides opportunities for searching documents according organizational process elements and not only through metadata. Moreover, semantic searching layer is applicable not only query the document base, but compare semantically contents of the documents. The development of the application continues, it requires different scripts written in Java, including OWL API, Apache Poi library and Snap SPARQL extensions, as well. Our future work is to develop a user-friendly interface, creating workflows connecting documents to the process steps in the easiest way, applying process-based text mining method to extract content from the documents and insert them into the appropriate process ontology.

Acknowledgement. The authors would like to acknowledge the valuable contributions of Dr. András Gábor, associate professor of the Corvinus Unversity of Budapest, as lector of this paper.

References

1. Data, information and knowledge management at the european commission. The European Commission, Brussels (2016). http://ec.europa.eu/transparency/regdoc/rep/3/2016/EN/C-2016-6626-F1-EN-MAIN.PDF. Accessed 26 Mar 2017

2. Lei, Y., Uren, V., Motta, E.: Semsearch: a search engine for the semantic web. In: Staab, S., Svátek, V. (eds.) EKAW 2006. LNCS, vol. 4248, pp. 238–245. Springer, Heidelberg (2006). doi:10.1007/11891451_22
3. About—DBpedia. http://wiki.dbpedia.org/about. Accessed 26 Mar 2017
4. Gábor, A., Szabó, Z.: Semantic technologies in business process management. In: Fathi, M. (ed.) Integration of Practice-Oriented Knowledge Technology: Trends and Prospectives, pp. 17–28. Springer, Heidelberg (2013). doi:10.1007/978-3-642-34471-8_2
5. Weber, R.: Ontological Foundations of Information Systems. Coopers & Lybrand Research Methodology Monograph, vol. 4. Coopers & Lybrand and the Accounting Association, London (1997)
6. Berners-Lee, T., Hendler, J., Lassila, O.: The semantic web. Sci. Am. 284(5), 28–37 (2001)
7. Hepp, M., Cardoso, J., Lytras, M.D.: The Semantic Web: Real-World Applications from Industry. Springer, Heidelberg (2007)
8. Karastoyanova, D., Lessen, T., Leymann, F., Ma, Z., Nitzsche, J., Wetzstein, B., Bhiri, S., Hauswirth, M., Zaremba, M.: A reference architecture for semantic business process management systems. In: Multikonferenz Wirtschaftsinformatik. GITO-Verlag, Berlin (2008)
9. Török, M.: Ontology based workflow architecture implementation for SMEs - case study. In: Cunningham, P., Cunningham, M. (eds.) eChallenges e-2011 Conference Proceedings IIMC International Information Management Corporation (2011)
10. Ternai, K., Török, M.: Business process modelling and implementation in collaborating environments. J. E-Bus. Dev. 2(4), 2225–7411 (2012)
11. Herborn, T., Wimmer, M.: Process ontologies facilitating interoperability in egovernment, a methodological framework. In: Workshop on Semantics for Business Process Management, the 3rd Semantic Web Conference, Montenegro (2006)
12. eBEST-empowering business ecosystems of small service enterprises to face the economic crisis. The project co-funded by the European Commission, FP7-SME-2008-2 no. 243554

E-Government Research and Intelligent System

Proposal for Application of Data Science Methods in E-Government

A Case-Study About the Application of Available Techniques for Performance Measurement with the Help of Data Science

Bálint Molnár[(⊠)] [iD]

Faculty of Informatics, ELTE, Eötvös Loránd University,
Pázmány Péter sétány 1/C, Budapest 1117, Hungary
molnarba@inf.elte.hu

Abstract. The business processes and workflows of Public Administration within the Hungarian Government are transformed profoundly in the past years. As more and more tasks of public administration are carried out by the assistance of electronic solutions, the tracking and monitoring of activities became possible whereby data in electronic form are available for data processing. In enterprises, the performance measurement, strategic enterprise management and similar approaches turn out to be fashionable; moreover, the techniques and methods out of data science provides the opportunities for data analytics on the collected data. As the e-public administration develops and significant amount of data will be accessible for data processing it will give the chance to apply data science for the wide spectrum of activities within public administration. There is project that is planned and dedicated to the before-mentioned task. Firstly, a data warehouse will be built that will collect and load the data from disparate sources in a data schemes within the data warehouse that will suit data analytics. We will analyze the E-government architecture, public administration processes and the available techniques of data science that will provide useful services for the senior public officers.

Keywords: E-Government · Public administration · Data science · Data analytics · Enterprise architecture · Business processes · Workflow

1 Introduction

There is a transformation process of public administration in Hungary that aims at creating one-stop shops for citizens in country wide. These one-stop shops are called One-Stop-Government and organized into a hierarchy under the Prime Minister's Office moreover, there is a middle level management organization in each county called *Office of Public Administration*. One-Stop-Government represents a kind of centralization of Citizen Relationship Management, i.e. the majority of business with public administration can be commenced by citizens at this service points. The public officers at One-Stop-Government can handle a wide spectrum of problems and cases that occur

© Springer International Publishing AG 2017
A. Kő and E. Francesconi (Eds.): EGOVIS 2017, LNCS 10441, pp. 143–157, 2017.
DOI: 10.1007/978-3-319-64248-2_11

for citizens and belong to various sectors of public administration. The public officers can access and use electronic information systems of disparate branches of government. One-Stop-Government Portal or Government Gateway is available for citizens for certain tasks as e.g. personal income statement, requesting for 'European health insurance card', etc. However, some cases being highly complex need the assistance of public officers or the nature of the specific case requires appearance in person (as e.g. request for credentials) therefore there is a need for One-Stop-Government points (there are more than 240 places in the country). The distributed service points of citizen relationship management for specific sectors within the public administration are gradually united physically and geographically at certain places. Consequently, the business processes and workflows went through profound transformation so that the electronic services provided by the information systems of the various sectors supported continuously the public officers at One-Stop-Government points. This makeover modified deeply the underlying Enterprise Architecture and its essential component the Business Process View with each related perspective. The objective of this transformation was to improve the relationships with the citizens and constituents. The reason for the alteration of business processes is that senior management of the public administration is aware that the public administration plays a crucial role how the government exercise its role within society. In general, the citizens have more interactions with public officers than with their representatives that they voted for. The citizens feel the policies and politics, the organization of government through their contacts with public administration, e.g. law enforcement or other organizations for public services. The local service points of the public administration as the One-Stop-Government shops are the tools for mutual trust building between citizen and government. The private service sector has had it developed approaches and solutions for Customer Relationship Management (CRM) [5, 6]. The everyday experiences of citizens as customers had an impact on the expectations on relationship management by public administration. We can describe electronic public administration and electronic government as the application of information and communication technologies (ICT) to buttress business processes within public administration and make available the services of government in electronic format for citizens [7]. ICT removes several barriers for accessing services by citizens in the sense of constraints as time, spatial and even hierarchy. The modern citizen relationship management has two facets: (1) the effectiveness and efficiency of the *business processes* within the One-Stop-Government shops and the information systems of the sectors involved in the specific case, (2) the *services* that are yielded directly for citizens electronically and by human actors. The collaborative citizen relationship management concentrates on channels as One-Stop-Government shops and the services desks, Internet/Web, Call centers, and the spectrum of mobile devices. There is a plan that the business processes and workflows will be integrated in the back and front offices as well. The financial management is crucial issue for One-Stop-Government shops and for their supervising, directing and coordinating authorities. The information system dedicated to accounting and controlling, moreover the human resource management systems operate as an integral part of the back office. The plan is that business processes of public administration and the financial management will be linked together in any case when any financial related activity will be carried out. In such an integrated environment, the data originated from business processes and citizens can be analyzed using the available technologies as data warehouses, on-line analytical processing (OLAP), data mining and more generally data analytics.

For comparison of our proposal and other authors, we may look at Morabito [11] who proposes an innovation model of public administration but the description lacks a detailed architecture and set of concrete algorithms that can be used in real-life project as guidance. Chen and Hsieh [12] analyses the impact of Big Data on public administration in a global perspective, and primarily from a management viewpoint. It proposes big data strategy but it remains short of description of the architecture and combination of algorithms that can be employed successfully. Rogge et al. [13] provides a survey on issues of performance management of public organizations and suggests a research agenda, however it does not contain any architecture and artifacts for information systems that may yield some clues for an implementation.

2 Citizen Relationship Management and Public Administration Architecture

The operation and structure of e-government and e-public administration can be grasped from the viewpoint of Enterprise Architecture and Service Science [8–10]. The basic philosophy of Citizen Relationship Management concentrates on the maintenance and enhancement of relationships towards to citizens because of objectives originated from politics, the aim of the citizen friendliness of public administration and the concept of government as a service provider. The Customer Relationships Management (CRM) in a competitive environment can be classified into collaborative, operative and analytical type. The *collaborative CRM* concentrates on the communication channels to provide a coherent customer/citizen experience. In the e-government context as well, the electronic channel is very appealing as it offers the opportunity for self-servicing, beside it the telephone, the functions of mobile devices can offer a kind of communication channel with similar comfortability. The *operational CRM* is in fact an application integration solution as it connects typically together the enterprise resource planning system (ERP), typically modules for accounting, invoicing, and management of financial transactions, modules for assistance in problem solving and management of citizens' issues, problems and cases, and modules for knowledge management systems [3]. The *analytical CRM* focus on the elucidation of data about partners/citizens and the performance of public officers. The technology level architecture for an analytical Citizen Relationship Management System consists of a Business Process and Workflow Management System, Content and Document Management, date and performance data collection and logging, database management and data warehouse along with data and text analytics system [4]. On understanding of the structure of processes and their relationships with specific attention on Citizen Relationship Management, the Zachman framework [8], the underlying theory of Service Oriented Architecture, Web services and the application integration yields a helping hand.

As there are lots of legacy systems that are responsible for data processing within certain sectors of Public Administration that should communicate with public officers placed into One-Stop-Government shop so that this situation creates a complex interrelationships environment even with a workflow that is dedicated to certain tasks and public officers. To make order from chaos, the Service Systems and Management [10], the Web services and service centric organization of processes within Public Administration provide a theoretical and semi-formal framework [1, 2]. To understand the ecosystem of Public Administration Activities, we can exploit the Zachman framework and the mapping the theory of service orientation onto the Zachman framework (Table 1).

Table 1. A mutual mapping between Zachman framework and business activities and fact handling of public administration (PA)

Views of stakeholders	Overarching models (perspectives)						
	1.what	2.how	3.where	4.who	5.when	6.why	Models of views
1.Contextual	Fact, data PA	PA service	Chain of PA processes, workflows	PA legal entity, function	Chain of PA processes, workflows	PA goal	*Scope*
2. Conceptual	Underlying conceptual data model	Service	Service composition	Actor, role	PA process model	PA objective	*Enterprise model*
3. Logical	Class hierarchy, logical data model	Service component	Hierarchy of service component	User role, service component	BPEL, BPMN, orchestration	PA rule	*System model*
4. Physical	Object hierarchy, data model	Service component	Hierarchy of service component	Component, object	Choreography	Rule design	*Technical model*
5. Detail	Data in DBMS	Service component	Hierarchy of service component	Component, object	Choreography, security architecture	Rule specification	*Components*
6. Functioning enterprise	Data	Function	Network	Organization	Schedule	Strategy	*ITIL*[a]

[a]*Information Technology Infrastructure Library*, [14].

We can perceive the Citizen Relationship Management as service oriented system at organization level with an IT support that owns a structure, i.e. it consists of:

- Organization culture. Processes of Public Administration for managing issues, life events and problems, moreover the overarching arrangement of activities into workflows (see first row in Table 1);
- The fourth column (*who*) in the table along with the first and second row describes the organizational structure (organigram) and responsibilities of administration units, roles, actors together and their consequences in the form of access rights, identification, authentication and authorization rules;
- The models of third column deals with networked governance and collaboration with specific sectors of public administration in the first row then a series of refinement steps concludes with a physical network architecture and with a communication infrastructure among information systems of various administrative domains;
- The interactions between participants of Public Administration can be presented by the perspectives of "*who*" and "*how*", i.e. the column four and two contain the adequate models;

- The assortment of administrative services that are delivered by the One-Stop-Government shops can be represented by models of columns the two, the four and the six.
- The application of Data Science in the form of Data Analytics brings forth *insights* of activities at One-Stop-Government shops for managers of Public Administration. As Data Analytics consist of complex processes at both management and data processing level, the comprehensive model that describes the preparation, cleaning, analysis, visualization and interpretation of data is composed of the models appearing in the column one, two, five, six and partly four.

Beside the information analysis, the task of Data Analytics is to provide a reasonable partitioning of information domain, segmentation of data by personal needs and interaction patterns of citizens, customization of administrative services and information interchange for citizens; moreover, measurements of performance and quality of services, the measuring the indicators that reflect the realization of strategy objectives of central and local governments that require a citizen centric culture and approach are essential components of Citizen Management System both conceptual and management level. We have discussed the concept of Citizen Relationship Management for the reason that it can be perceived as either a management concept or a complex information system thereby a theory or a theoretical framework can be elaborated that helps depict the effects on activities of Public Administration and create an environment for performance measurement, control, monitoring through exploitation of Data Analytics. The Citizen Relationship Management as a complex application system is still an emerging area that is a subject of research, development, academic discussion and conceptualizing of business/administrative requirements. As we have seen previously one of the major aims of a Citizen Relationship Management system is to improve the quality of relationships with citizens and incorporate their requirements and opinions into a comprehensive system instead the demands of citizens would be embodied into processes of certain sectors of public administration and into their data processing function of legacy systems. Another aim is to create a Performance Management and Measurement System for the One-Stop-Government shops, or more generally for Public Administration. The data about cases, issues, problems and activities of citizens are valuable sources of information that can be used for service planning and service delivering. An effective and efficient Citizen Relationship Management system that appears as responsive, easily accessible and citizen-friendly, furthermore it provides chances for participation and inclusion can foster a trustful relationship with citizens whereby it supports democracy at the same time.

2.1 Technology Architecture for Citizen Relationship Management and Data Analytics

The application and technology architecture of Citizen Relationship Management empower public managers and officers to react in a quick, correct and proper way to citizens' requests. On the one hand, public officers can retrieve the necessary and authorized data of citizen profiles; on the other hand, the case management activities of public officers can be logged and the data about of their deeds can be collected in a database then loaded into a data warehouse. During the case management, the public officers can use a knowledge store that contains semi-structured textual information on the procedural activities codified in legal rules for public administration. The channels between citizens and public administration can be classified as channel for *information*, *communication*, *transaction* like services (tax statement), *face-to-face*/one-stop-government services, telephone, Web self-service (downloading official documents, initiating case, automated e-mail and kiosks. The administrators can develop and enhance of the available databases, data marts and data warehouse to get them aligned with future requisites. On the one side, the data about cases, life events of citizens that trigger the official business processes can be analyzed to build up personalized information, dedicated services of public administration, and perhaps emerging problems can be forecasted and recognized. On the other side, by investigating the citizens', public officers' *profiles* that are linked to business process and to the usage of services provided by public administration can be analyzed the same way as performance data of corporations. That analysis can offer insights of actual processes and offer the chances to improve processes and policy. The before-mentioned data analysis can be established as a business process that is integral part of the activities of public administration at One-Stop-Government shops and the Government's Offices that supervises them. This means that the data analysis will be executed in a cycle manner similarly to other functions of organizations thereby the data analysis as a business process will promote innovation for public administration.

2.2   Data About Citizens, Public Officers and Services of One-Stop-Government

The citizen data can be grouped into profile data (typically demographic data as name, address, digital accessibility, birth date, education level), administrative procedure data (i.e. life events, business issues, complaints, suggestions, inquiries, trigger for commencing official procedures), contact data (contact person at One-Stop-Government shop, date and time of contact), and service data (type of service demanded from public administration, usage time, allocated costs). The data of public officers can be grouped in a similar way, i.e. the data can be clustered into profile data, official procedures of public administration in which the public officer is involved, and data about the provided services. The services that are provided by One-Stop-Government shops in the form of business processes can be measured by their completion rate. As it can be seen in the Fig. 1) there are several channels through which the citizens may communicate with the One-Stop-Government shops so that the completion rate of transactions – either digitals or personal assisted – can be defined as the percentage of transactions that citizens complete and of all transactions that citizens commence. In the future, the measure of satisfaction will be planned. The tool for that purpose could be a citizen survey, primarily aiming at citizens using digital channels. The other source could be a feedback site within the Hungarian Government Gateway or within the electronic business processes that would be set up as an in-service feedback page. This site can be the subject of text mining and sentiment analysis.

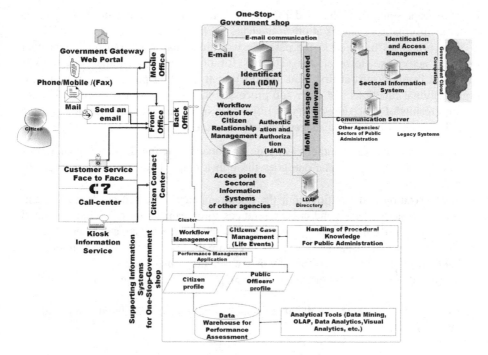

Fig. 1. Data analytics architecture for performance management at One-Stop-Government shop

2.3 Business Process and Workflow Modeling

There is an on-going project whose main objective is that to create an integrated business process management environment within which the business processes of One-Stop-Government can be formulated and arranged into workflows. The planned framework can handle the documents in electronic format that are related to business processes starting from the registration of document arrival to the final resolution that are bundled into cases linked to citizen or a group of citizens involved in the case. In the table (Table 1), the first and second row contains the architectural building blocks that are connected to the *Business Process Architecture.* As it can be seen form the table the Business Process Architecture can be perceived as a hierarchical structure of models that describe disparate views of stakeholders. The models start with high level process maps that can be interpreted rather as process chains, then roles and actors as business units and functions, and finally strategic level business objectives and moti-vations. These models are refined into detailed process flow descriptions depicting specific tasks and their relationships to roles, actors, data, document and information systems. We can suppose that the business processes within public administration should deal with electronic document because e-government services are defined and operational for transforming of documents in the case of paper-bound documents into electronic format and vice versa if it were necessary for the adequate communication channel designated by citizens who are involved in the case. The documents can be formally represented and handled by business processes in the workflows and the sectoral information systems at other agencies [15].

The processes included in the passable workflows can carry out document management activities. However, the activities for document management seem to be separated from citizens at first blink the document handling processes can be part of organizational functions and other sub-processes that are connected to citizens' cases and the results of procedures strongly influences of citizens' experience and satisfaction. The major document management activities are as follows:

- Receiving documents: either electronic or paper-based the document that will be transformed into electronic one goes through a preparation phase for further processing and registering.
- Categorization and identification: the document meta-data are catalogued; identification code is created and cross-references to other relevant cases are generated.
- Storing of documents: the documents and related meta-data are inserted into a suitable database management system to ensure the accessibility and availability for later use, and references to the adequate cases are constructed.
- Retrieval of documents: meta-data and categories enable the enquiring, searching and retrieving of documents.
- Displaying documents: the documents should be visually exhibited or printed in a human-readable format.

2.4   Achievable Goal-Centric Data Analytics

The steadily changing internal and external environment, and the varying data that are related to the processes of public administration makes necessary a flexible approach of Data Analytics (Fig. 2). In an iterative way, three stages for enabling of processes for Data Analytics should be defined. The objective of Data Analytics procedure is (1) to

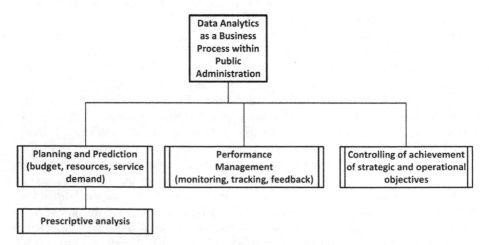

Fig. 2. Overarching data analytics within public administration at One-Stop-Government shops

acquire knowledge out of collected data through discovering associations and relationships. Some data will be in numeric or structured format, nevertheless some data will be in unstructured and semi-structured format as we have discussed previously the document management and surveys' information on citizens' satisfaction.

However, the technology is available (2) to analyze data in any format with or without hypotheses. The Data Analytics steps beyond the prepared reports that exploit information stored in Data Warehouse, nonetheless (3) the communication towards the decision makers is important task. The procedures of Data Analytics require a meticulous and thorough preparation of data that may happen in a Data Warehouse environment. The structured and quantitative data are apt to organize them into *multidimensional models* as data cubes, e.g. citizens' transactions at counties, regions and citizens' contact points, time series. This kind of data structure is suitable for the so called exploratory data analysis that a traditional list-centric reporting mechanism cannot yield. The influence factors on the indicators can be investigated out of various viewpoints of stakeholders; quantitative and qualitative measures can be formulated on the inferred facts. Using the combination of Data Warehouse and OLAP technologies, it makes possible that the senior management concentrates on the core issues thereby they avert of information overburden. The core analysis should bring the key performance indicators – as e.g. successfully completed transactions of citizens' cases, the processed cases at One-Stop-Government shop weekly, monthly etc. – and parameters of processes being executed into relations; whereby the senior management may discover very quickly the deviations from the presupposed ones or serious problems. The consequence of this approach is that the time that is allocated for analysis sharply reduced and at the same time the quality of analysis is increased.

2.5   Process Data Mining by Exploiting Data Analytics and Workflow Management

One-Stop-Government shops will have a fully-fledged Data Warehouse and Workflow Management System beside the online connections to sectoral Information Systems at agencies in the near future (Fig. 3). The parameters of transactions and event logs of sectoral Information Systems, furthermore the indicators, the calculated and quantified factors originating out of the Workflow Management System can be exploited for Process Mining [16]. The system building for a Data Warehouse and an Integrated Workflow Management System has a collateral objective, namely that the system may be used for extraction data from transaction data, event logs and citizens' feedbacks. The requirement against a Workflow and Business Process Management System to be used for process mining are as follows: (1) the event should be linked to a *task* within a process; (2) the event should denote a *case* (i.e. a particular instance of a process that is bundled together a set of documents and data relevant to the citizens' issue); (3) the event should have a *role* or *actor* who executes the human side and triggers the automated side of the process; (4) the events have time and date stamp when they occurred.

The combination of Data Warehouse and Workflow technology in an integrated system provides the opportunity for the in-depth analysis of processes and tasks of

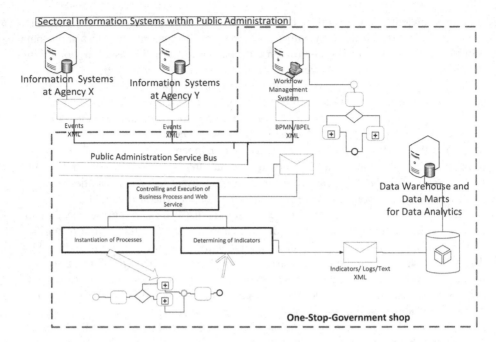

Fig. 3. Data collection of indicators through XML interface for processes

day-to-day operation. The relevant data can be generated in various forms, structured data, semi-structured documents and feedbacks from citizens. The analysts come across an assortment of structured, semi-structured and unstructured data, we may call this collection of data as poly-structured data. The traditional database technology is not suitable for poly-structured data that do not conform to a stringent scheme requirements.

The NoSQL database management systems loosen the demand for strict data structure for the interests of more efficient distribution of data processing tasks and higher performance of data retrieval [17]. The present-day NoSQL database management systems are appropriate for parallelizing data processing and analysis tasks. In the Data Analytics domain, these type of data stores can be exploited for pre-processing semi-structured and unstructured data. The NoSQL data stores and the traditional Data Warehouse would provide a good compromise. Although, the NoSQL database management systems do not guarantee the consistency of the underlying database (the ACID properties – as atomic, consistent, isolation and durability). The consequence of the aforementioned properties is that the NoSQL databases are suitable for storing poly-structured data. An interface as e.g. a database connector between NoSQL database management systems and relational DBMS and the strongly coupled Data Warehouse can be exploited for the seamless data extraction of the required data. The NoSQL databases can be utilized as analytics platforms for particular analysis tasks, in such a case the results should be passed back to the data warehouse. The relational DBMS and the data warehousing environment can be applied for analysis of combination of structured data and poly-structured data (extracted and then loaded from

NoSQL databases) the data processing may employ amalgam of SQL like queries and analytic functions aimed at poly-structured data.

2.6   Combination of Data Processing and Data Warehouse Technologies

The core promise of application of data warehouse technology is to provide answers for relevant business issues. The tenet that is lay the foundation for that purpose is the data integration. The data warehouse technology yields the tool to reconcile the data that are extracted out of multiple data sources and various information systems (Fig. 4). The system analysis and design methods that are used are as follows: data modeling, entity-relationship modeling, designing interfaces for ETL (extract, transform, load), methods, techniques and tools for data-cleansing, and creating semantic description that can partly be interpreted by machines and perceived by humans. Within the realm of predictive analytics, a set of techniques can be used that belong primarily to classification techniques as e.g.: decision tree analysis, statistical analysis, neural networks, case-based reasoning, Bayesian classifiers, genetic algorithms, rough sets (Fig. 5).

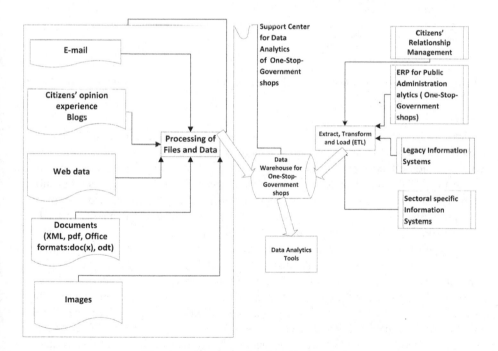

Fig. 4. Information flow into data analytics

2.7   Problems in Public Administration Addressed by Data Analytics

As we have seen previously, the public administration comes across business problems that are similar to enterprises as e.g. business process efficiency and effectiveness,

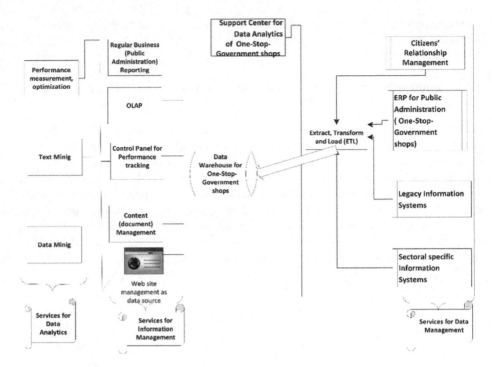

Fig. 5. Conceptual information architecture for support center dedicated to On-Stop-Government-shop

budget and cost reduction, satisfying citizens' needs and augmenting their "user experience". The data analytics offers numerous advantages for public administration and as a side-effect it can promote a gradual turn from paper-based document and filling-in to electronical documents, as the enhanced integration level among public administration entities lead to requirements for elimination of paper-based documents. The On-Stop-Government shops provide services to fulfill local demands instead of local governments or supporting service of local governments. There is an interest for application of innovative solutions for gathering citizens' opinions and customize the spectrum of services to the citizens' needs. The digital citizens may have the advantage that data analytics can help public administration to assemble a detailed and precise profiles of citizens using the electronic channel with government in an environment that is legally controlled and complies with the laws whereby the public services can be tailored to the requirements and needs of the citizens. The performance measurements of public officers in relation to case management may include such features as quality and citizen-friendliness of services. Incorporating these aspects of non-functional requirements into the performance assessment of government services, it improves the lawfulness of performance measurement, furthermore the transparency and account-ability of public administration towards peoples.

The data analytics can turn out to be a new source of information for public administration for chasing efficiency and effectiveness in their operations. In a public administration environment to find out the efficiency and effectiveness can be considered as hard problem. The critical issue is to identify objective measure or figures that can describe the quality and quantity of outcomes of public administration. The data warehouse, the analysis of poly-structured data and generally the data analytics can provide more adequate evaluation parameters exploiting the technologies for the business process modeling and realization.

The operative use of data can enhance the efficiency of business processes by reducing the amount of the required input data that are needed to provide the actual service levels. The output of the data analysis can be used to promote employees, to give rewards and to create differentiated salaries. The Human Resource Management can be assisted by data analytics to locate and to attract talented people within and outside of public administration. The HR departments and the line managers can use a variety of information (data on working conditions, satisfactions of public officers and their productivity) and therefore the responsible managers can assign tasks to persons more optimally. The distribution of tasks among public officers and their departments, section can be improved that results in better work conditions, in enhancing employee satisfaction and productivity. The data analytics can help to move the focus from internal performance assessment to citizens-oriented evaluation of services. A control panel or dashboard that can be established based on the data warehouse and data analytics technologies and that can contain lots of operational and financial data. The managers can make use of data on the dashboard to evaluate and compare efficiency of departments, sections within the overall organizations for One-Stop-Government shop.

3 Conclusion

This paper discussed the application of data analytics along with sophisticated business process modeling. The impact of these technologies has been investigated on public administration organization that is responsible for operating One-Stop-Government shops. We started our analysis on Citizens' Relationship Management, Business Process and Workflow modeling in relationship to performance measurement, furthermore opportunities for service provision that deal with citizens as digitally competent and having awareness of their rights. Adoption of data analytics has several challenges considering data ownership, data quality, privacy, civil rights, equality and the public administration's ability to bring able employees that are expert at data analytics.

We have outlined organization, information and technology architecture that can be implemented in public administration on a complex environment where the combined tools of data science were not applied before. Namely, we proposed a combination of data warehouse techniques and methods of data science that can be exploited for two-pronged strategy as establishing a fair performance management and measurement for public officers and enhancing of user experience and satisfaction for citizens.

The paper contains the major elements of integrated information systems and a project that can be realized and pursued for One-Stop-Government. The proposed approach is feasible and viable regarding the most recently available information technologies and may achieve the planned and required outcomes for both the public officers and citizens. For this analysis, we have used a Case-Study approach on an on-going project to demonstrate the strength and relevancy of the proposed approach.

Acknowledgement. This paper has been written with the support of the National University of Public Service in the framework of the priority project KÖFOP-2.1.2-VEKOP-15-2016-00001 titled "Public Service Development for Establishing Good Governance" - Ludovika Digital Governance Research Group.

References

1. Molnár, B.: IT Security in Hungarian public administration, Models of Information Security Architecture in Practice. In: Nedkov, P., Mastronardi, G., Schgör, P. (eds.) Associazione Italiana per l'informatica ed il Calcolo Automatico, AICA, IT Star, Milan, Italy, pp. 28–44 (2016)
2. Molnár, B., Benczúr, A., Béleczki, A.: Formal approach to modelling of modern information systems. Int. J. Inf. Syst. Proj. Manag. 69–89 (2016). doi:10.12821/ijispm040404
3. Molnár, B., Béleczki, A., Benczúr, A.: Application of legal ontologies based approaches for procedural side of public administration. In: Kő, A., Francesconi, E. (eds.) EGOVIS 2016. LNCS, vol. 9831, pp. 135–149. Springer, Cham (2016). doi:10.1007/978-3-319-44159-7_10
4. Molnár, B., Tarcsi, A.: Architecture and system design issues of contemporary web-based information systems. In: 5th International Conference on Software, Knowledge Information, Industrial Management and Applications (SKIMA), pp. 1–8. IEEE (2011). doi:10.1109/SKIMA.2011.6089978
5. Bretthauer, K.M.: Service management. Decis. Sci. **35**, 325–332 (2004). doi:10.1111/j.0011-7315.2004.35031.x
6. Laing, A.: Marketing in the public sector: towards a typology of public services. Mark. Theory **3**(4), 427–445 (2003). doi:10.1177/1470593103042005
7. Heeks, R.: Implementing and Managing Egovernment: an International Text. Sage, Thousand Oaks (2005). ISBN 1446230066, 9781446230060
8. Zachman, J.: The Zachman framework for enterprise architecture. Zachman Int. **79** (2002)
9. Haren, V.: TOGAF Version 9.1. Van Haren Publishing, Zaltbommel (2011)
10. Cardoso, J., Fromm, H., Nickel, S., Satzger, G., Studer, R., Weinhardt, C.: Fundamentals of Service Systems. Springer, Heidelberg (2015). doi:10.1007/978-3-319-23195-2
11. Morabito, V.: Big data and analytics for government innovation. In: Morabito, V. (ed.) Big data and analytics, pp. 23–45. Springer International Publishing, Switzerland (2015). doi:10.1007/978-3-319-10665-6_2
12. Chen, Y.C., Hsieh, T.C.: Big data for digital government: opportunities, challenges, and strategies. In: Politics and Social Activism: Concepts, Methodologies, Tools, and Applications, pp. 1394–1407. IGI Global (2016). doi:10.4018/978-1-4666-9461-3.ch072
13. Rogge, N., Agasisti, T., De Witte, K.: Big data and the measurement of public organizations' performance and efficiency: the state-of-the-art. Public Policy Adm. (2016). doi:10.1177/0952076716687355
14. Barafort, B., Renzo, B., Merlan, O.: Benefits resulting from the combined use of ISO/IEC 15504 with the Information Technology Infrastructure Library (ITIL). In: Oivo, M., Komi-Sirviö, S. (eds.) PROFES 2002. LNCS, vol. 2559, pp. 314–325. Springer, Heidelberg (2002). doi:10.1007/3-540-36209-6_27

15. Molnár, B., Benczúr, A.: A document centric approach for analysis and design of e-government systems. In: Kő, A., Francesconi, E. (eds.) EGOVIS 2015. LNCS, vol. 9265, pp. 319–333. Springer, Cham (2015). doi:10.1007/978-3-319-22389-6_23

16. Agrawal, R., Gunopulos, D., Leymann, F.: Mining process models from workflow logs. In: Sixth International Conference on Extending Database Technology, pp. 469–483 (1998)

17. Strauch, C.: NoSQL databases (2011). http://www.christof-strauch.de/nosqldbs. Accessed 19 Mar 2017

A System Architecture for a Transnational Data Infrastructure Supporting Maritime Spatial Planning

Henning Sten Hansen(✉), Ida Maria Reiter, and Lise Schrøder

Aalborg University Copenhagen,
A.C. Meyers Vaenge 15, 2450 Copenhagen, Denmark
hsh@plan.aau.dk

Abstract. The use of the seas and oceans is overall regulated by the United Nations through the UN Convention on the Law of the Sea, which defines the rights and responsibilities. However, with the rapidly increasing use of the sea and oceans it is inevitable that conflicts may arise. Accordingly, there has been an increasing international recognition of the need to manage human activities that influence the marine environment and its ecosystems in an integrated, cross-sectoral manner. Recently, Maritime Spatial Planning (MSP) has gained significant attention as a new paradigm aiming at minimising the conflicts among different sea uses through involving various stakeholders and sectors while aiming for sustainable growth. The aim of this research is to build a conceptual model for a Data Infrastructure to support marine space in a transnational context addressing the challenges related to the increasing use of marine areas and resources. The work was carried out in a close cooperation between several public authorities and research institutes in the Baltic Sea Region.

Keywords: Maritime spatial planning · Spatial data infrastructure · Distributed systems · Marine governance · Open data

1 Introduction

The seas have always been used by human beings but mainly for fisheries and transport of goods and people. In recent decades, the use of marine space is being enhanced through new marine uses like off-shore oil and gas production as well as wind energy. Aquaculture along the coasts and in fjords is also becoming a major industry, which currently accounts for half of the global fishery production [1]. Also, marine mineral resources, and marine biotechnology are among the rapidly evolving use of seas and oceans. Furthermore, coastal and cruise tourism are among the activities competing for marine space, and the importance of this industry was emphasised by the EU Strategy for more growth and jobs in coastal and maritime tourism [2].

The current and potential use of the seas and oceans is often called the 'Blue Economy', and recently the European Commission has launched Blue Growth Strategy on the opportunities for marine and maritime sustainable growth [3]. From the European Commission's point of view, the so-called Blue Growth is a long-term strategy in the marine and maritime sectors with great potential for innovation and economic growth.

© Springer International Publishing AG 2017
A. Kő and E. Francesconi (Eds.): EGOVIS 2017, LNCS 10441, pp. 158–172, 2017.
DOI: 10.1007/978-3-319-64248-2_12

The use of the seas and oceans is overall regulated by the United Nations through the UN Convention on the Law of the Sea – the so-called UNCLOS Convention [4], which defines the rights and responsibilities. UNCLOS provides full jurisdiction over the territorial waters up to 12 nautical miles from the coast line for the coastal states. In addition, the coastal states have the rights to establish an exclusive economic zone (EEZ) up to 200 nautical miles [4]. Within EEZ the coastal state has sovereign for exploring and exploiting, conserving and managing the natural resources [4]. However, with the rapidly increasing use of the sea and oceans it is inevitable that conflicts may arise. Accordingly, there has been an increasing international recognition of the need to manage human activities that influence the marine environment and its ecosystems in an integrated, cross-sectoral manner to promote the sustainable development of oceans and seas and their resources.

Recently, Maritime Spatial Planning (MSP) has gained significant attention as a new paradigm aiming at minimising the conflicts among different sea uses through involving various stakeholders and sectors while aiming for sustainable growth [5]. MSP is a framework, which has embraced the new blue growth discourse, being broader and more economic in scope than the preserving strategies. Specific methods of zoning and marine protected areas (MPAs) are incorporated into the broader framework of MSP [6], which demands for future-oriented, adaptable processes that take temporal changes and new knowledge into consideration [7]. To create the best possible data and knowledge foundation for MSP, a well-functioning Geographic Information System (GIS) with comprehensive, detailed and regularly updated data is needed [7]. Not only the data inputs and the technical platforms are important for implementing MSP. The entire spatial data infrastructure (SDI) needs to be thoroughly considered. An SDI takes into considerations the access networks for accessing data, interoperability, knowledge sharing, and the experiences of the people accessing and using the data, as well as the legal fundament for acquiring and distributing knowledge and data, considering open source options [8].

Therefore, the aim of this research is *to build a conceptual model for a Spatial Data Infrastructure to support Maritime spatial Planning in a transnational context addressing the challenges related to the increasing use of marine areas and resources and the challenges related to coordination difficulties and technical limitations.* The conceptual design is currently tested in the Baltic Sea Region as a prototype for the new data portal for The Helsinki Commission (HELCOM)[1].

2   Background and Theory

Creating a data infrastructure supporting maritime spatial planning requires a basic understanding of the underlying principles regarding the legal framework for planning and managing the sea, as well as the existing agreements for establishing transnational data infrastructures in Europe. The following paragraphs describe the principles and

---

[1] http://helcom.fi.

frameworks for maritime spatial planning, and for spatial data infrastructures and their European implementations.

2.1 Maritime Spatial Planning

Maritime Spatial Planning (MSP) is a new, ambitious planning framework that does not only consider conservation [5]. MSP takes a cross-sectoral, ecosystem based approach to maritime management, aiming at meeting the possibilities inherent in new commercial use of marine space, while at the same time paying attention to the increasing concern for marine ecosystems, and aiming at sustainable growth [5].

Since the beginning of this century, the European Union has embraced MSP as a political ambition. By using the term 'maritime' instead of 'marine' in the EU Integrated Maritime Policy (IMP), the European Commission stresses the economic dimension more than the conservation-related aspect of the concept [6]. However, only one of the two pillars behind the IMP is economic; the Lisbon Strategy, launched in 2000. The other pillar, which is more environmental than economic, is the Marine Strategy Framework Directive [9] that aims at improving the marine environmental conditions of Europe by 2020. As Backer states [7], it can be problematic, if the two pillars are not given equal consideration. Whereas human activities cause economic growth, they also influence environmental degradation [7]. Despite this challenge involving MSP in practice, MSP is currently the best strategy that reflects the realities of the global needs for marine management and the complexity of the task [10]. The two pillars of IMP together with stakeholder involvement and other important legislation such as the Habitats Directive of 1992, the Common Fisheries Policy of 2002, and the Water Framework Directive of 2000 have been important strategies to put MSP on the agenda within EU [6]. Finally, in 2014, the EU Maritime Spatial Planning Directive [11] was introduced, building on the earlier marine legislation and highlighting the importance of MSP. It demands by law that the 23 EU coastal states by 2021 have implemented marine plans based on an ecosystem based approach [10]. While there is no single internationally agreed-upon ecosystem based approach, the concept is generally understood to encompass the management of human activities, based on the best understanding of the ecological interactions and processes to ensure that ecosystem services are sustained for the benefit of present and future generations. Ecosystem services are defined as functions and processes through which ecosystems, and the species that they support, sustain and fulfil human life [6].

For the EU member states to implement MSP as part of national integrated maritime policies, the EU maritime spatial planning roadmap from 2008 provides ten guidelines to implement IMP [5]. The principles are: MSP should be place-based; it should address the seabed, the water column, and the sea surface; that MSP should build on future-oriented, long-term, and operational objectives; its processes should be transparent, also for the public; all relevant stakeholders and knowledge from local people should be included; MSP should recognise the importance of cross-border cooperation; MSP should be adaptable to changing knowledge; and MSP should imply coherent terrestrial and marine spatial planning. Last, but not least, it is important to have a strong and detailed data foundation behind the MSP [5], for which reason a spatial data infrastructure is an important prerequisite for maritime spatial planning.

2.2   Spatial Data Infrastructures

A Spatial Data Infrastructure is about facilitation and coordination of the exchange and sharing of spatial data. It is described as the underlying infrastructure, often in the form of policies, standards and access networks that allows data to be shared between people within organisations, states or countries. The fundamental interaction between people and data is governed by the technological components of SDI represented by the access network, policies and standards [12]. The dynamic nature of the spatial data infrastructure is attributed to the rate of technological advancement and changing user needs. People and data are the key elements in SDI, and a spatial data infrastructure at any level whether local, regional, national or even global involves an array of stakeholders both within and across organisations including different levels of government, the private sector, and a multitude of users. In order to design and implement a spatial data infrastructure, the stakeholders need to be identified together with the business processes and functions of the organisations involved. Besides, one must know the data required or provided by the functions – and the flow of data between various functions. In this respect data sharing, exchange, security, accuracy, and access as well as rights, restrictions, and responsibilities must be managed.

Thus, it is evident that SDIs represent very complex systems and several researchers have utilised various theoretical foundations to understand the complex and dynamic nature of SDI. Onsrud and Pinto [13] use diffusion of innovation theory to understand the spread and adoption of SDI, whereas Rajabifard et al. [12] developed a hierarchical concept which is very useful in describing the complex vertical and horizontal relationships between the political and administrative levels of SDI. Each layer of the organisational structure has distinct information requirements and therefore need support from a specific SDI level. Thus, it is important regarding data management to classify different levels of an SDI hierarchy according to their roles played within different administrative levels.

2.3   EU Directives Supporting Access to Information

The legal framework including data related EU directives is important to ensure SDI's within Europe. Recognising the importance of a wider usage of public sector information (PSI) in the social and economic development of the European community, the European Union has implemented several directives to support the sharing and reuse of PSI, and below we mention the three most important directives. First, Regulation 1367/2006 [14] on public access to environmental information has contributed significantly to the notion of easier access and sharing of public sector information. Second, the PSI Directive [15] was implemented in July 2005 with the aim of regulating and stimulating the reuse of public sector information (PSI). The initial intention of the European Commission was to make all public-sector information in the Member States available for re-use. Nevertheless, the PSI directive has gained high impact for example on the creation of European geoportals. Third, the INSPIRE Directive was adopted by the European Council and Parliament in Spring 2007 and entered into force May 2007 [16]. Overall, the INSPIRE Directive is considered as a major step forward towards a pan-European spatial data infrastructure.

A key objective of INSPIRE is to make more and better spatial information available for EU policy-making and implementation in a wide range of sectors. Initially, it focused on information needed to monitor and improve the state of the environment - including air, water, soil, and natural landscape - but is now extended to cover spatial information broadly. One of the results of a better European framework for data management and data sharing, is the existence of European geoportals. However, as the next subsection underlines, improvements are still to be made.

2.4   Existing Data Portals for Maritime Spatial Planning

Geoportals are web-based, often public access points, containing networks of geographic data with the purpose of allowing portal users to find existing geodata. Within marine spatial planning, marine geoportals are important tools for easing access to existing marine data, creating collaboration projects between different shareholders owning marine data, and improving interoperability between technical platforms of different data users and data owners by using internationally recognised standards.

Various geoportals containing marine data already exist around the world, and the geographic areas they cover vary in scope. To examine the qualities and flaws in existing marine geoportals, Canada, Australia, and Ireland are important countries to consider, since they have geoportals developed early dating back to at least 2004. Seip and Bill [17] point out that all three countries are successful in using international standards and open source to improve interoperability, gathering data from many different shareholders, and presenting many core datasets. However, they also point out that the portals from Canada and Australia lack a single entry, and that all three countries have separate metadata portals instead of including the metadata search as part of the geoportal, which would link the information better together [17]. Kocur-Bera and Dudzińska [18] examined geoportals of interest for the Baltic Sea region, and they similarly conclude that current environmental data unfortunately are not available from one single entry and that the resolution of the data is sometimes inadequate for marine planning. Two of their examples are the INSPIRE geoportal, which links the user to terrestrial and marine environmental data at various European institutions' homepages, and HELCOM Data & Map Service, which hosts many marine datasets from the Baltic Sea region [18].

When examining the mentioned geoportals, it becomes apparent that the setup, interfaces, and abilities of the platforms vary. Some of the geoportals have only a small map viewer (e.g. the INSPIRE geoportal), while other portals have a big map viewer (e.g. HELCOM Data & Map Service). Some portals have few or no data search options (e.g. the INSPIRE portal & and HELCOM Data & Map Service), while others have many data search options. In general, it is difficult to gain an overview over the data download options. The IMOS portal has a very nice stepwise and intuitive interface with big buttons providing a fine overview over the structure of the portal. All portals include metadata to some extent. For the European portals, the metadata is in the INSPIRE standard, but it is difficult to gain an overview over all the data provided and the date of origin of the data. Furthermore, not all data are downloadable, and the degree to which the portals include data from private companies appear to be limited.

2.5   Interoperability and Data Exchange Formats

In regards to managing data and geoportals, interoperability is an important concept. The recent introduced EU e-Government Action Plan 2016–2020[2] underlines the importance of reusability of data and technologies and refers to the European Interoperability Framework (EIF), which is the core document defining interoperability seen from a common European perspective [19]. Interoperability means reusability of data and technologies, which is cost-saving in regards to time and economy [19]. Interoperability within EU has since 1995 been closely linked to a public-sector agenda through various programmes. The focus has moved away from being on technical interoperability within single sectors to include semantic, legal, and organisational interoperability aspects working not only within sectors, but also across sectors [19]. With the ISA (Interoperability Solutions for Public Administrations) and later ISA[2] programmes, the EU leaders agreed to align their national interoperability frameworks with the EIF. The whole interoperability process also has links to INSPIRE, since INSPIRE urges member states to share environmental data, and since INSPIRE has implemented a metadata standardization for the whole of EU (EU e-Government Action Plan 2016–2020).

The four types of interoperability refer respectively to linking data and technologies through formats and standards (technical), preserving the meaning of semantic concepts when sharing data and information (semantic), introducing legislation for data and technology reuse (legal), and coordinating information-based processes between different organisations with mutually beneficial goals (organisational) [19].

International recognised standards and the concept of SDI are very much related to ensuring technical, legal, and organisational interoperability. When diving into technological standards enabling technical interoperability and expanding options for data sharing, web services are important to put to the fore. Web services are applications that use the Internet to make themselves accessible for other applications. They can put the concept of service-oriented architectures (SOA) into practice [20]. SOA describes architectures that are involved with providing, searching for, and using services over a network, thus embracing the new era of many Internet-based distributed information systems [20]. Web services use the hypertext transfer protocol (HTTP) and sometimes the simple object access protocol (SOAP) to communicate with servers over the internet. The web service description language (WSDL), based on the Extensible Markup Language (XML), is used to describe the specific abilities of web services [20]. The Open Geospatial Consortium (OGC), which is an international, non-profit organisation including members from government, companies, universities, and NGOs, have defined some of the most used web mapping services. The web map service (WMS) enables sharing of images, the web feature service (WFS) enables sharing of feature data with attributes, the web coverage service (WCS) enables sharing of raster data, and the web processing service (WPS) enables sharing of algorithms to perform on data, for example coded in Python [21]. All these OGC web services have later been adopted by ISO.

While many articles and reports focus on technical and legal interoperability by highlighting the importance of applying widely approved and used technical standards

---

[2] https://ec.europa.eu/digital-single-market/en/european-egovernment-action-plan-2016-2020.

(e.g. [22, 23]), the importance of ensuring semantic interoperability is often overlooked in SDIs [24]. According to van den Brink et al. [24], increasing semantic interoperability could advantageously be seen as a complex, but important ongoing process enabling domain modellers to gradually discover and analyse overlaps between concepts and models and to provide metadata that describes the found meaning overlaps.

2.6   Defining Requirements for a System Design

To exemplify the implementation of MSP in practice, the Baltic Sea area provides an interesting case. In 2003, MSP was introduced to the Baltic Sea area by a joint statement of HELCOM and OSPAR[3] on adopting an ecosystem based approach to marine spatial planning. The HELCOM Baltic Sea Action Plan took the step further by aiming at improving the Baltic Sea marine environment by 2021 [7]. Today, the HELCOMs data portal for the Baltic Sea Region can be further improved based on the conceptual model of a data infrastructure presented in the next chapter.

Summing up this background chapter, it is important for a geoportal to be founded in national marine SDIs and to ensure long-term strategies for data sharing from a maritime planning perspective by for example improving the interaction of different data layers. The portal should include many different ways of downloading and accessing data, but at the same time provide the user with an easy overview over the options. Technical, organisational, legal, and semantic interoperability need to be considered. A clear overview should be provided of all data and download options available, and a clear strategy should be developed for how the data is published and updated.

3   Systems Design

Based on the experiences gained from earlier projects and the requirements from a rather diverse and transnational user community we have defined a systems architecture based on modern principles, and developed a prototype to test it in a practical context. Based on an ongoing project and as part of the BalticLines project[4], HELCOMs data portal for the Baltic Sea Region will be further developed to meet the data and information requirements for marine governance and maritime spatial planning. Below, we first describe the user communities, and then the systems architecture and prototype.

3.1   The User Community and Their Needs

The users of the system represent a wide range of stakeholders working within or being interested in marine and maritime affairs, but the main target group is the national authorities, which are responsible for managing the marine space. Other professional

---

[3] https://www.ospar.org.

[4] http://www.vasab.org/index.php/balticlines-eu.

users are various NGO's working within sectors like the environment, fishery, energy, shipping, etc. The Baltic Sea Region has been a pioneer in developing MSP in Europe originated in the late 1990 s and developed by pilot projects based on collaboration among national stakeholders in the region and VASAB and HELCOM. VASAB is an intergovernmental multilateral co-operation of 11 countries of the Baltic Sea Region in spatial planning and development, guided by the Conference of Ministers responsible for spatial planning and development[5]. HELCOM was established in 1992 to protect the marine environment of the Baltic Sea from all sources of pollution through inter-governmental cooperation, and HELCOM is the governing body of the Convention on the Protection of the Marine Environment of the Baltic Sea Area, known as the Helsinki Convention. The Contracting Parties are Denmark, Estonia, the European Union, Finland, Germany, Latvia, Lithuania, Poland, Russia, and Sweden. During the previous 25 years, the HELCOM organisation has collected a huge amount of infor-mation for the Baltic Sea Region with emphasis on the marine environment, but due to the development of new technologies and methods for storing and distributing infor-mation, there is a need for redesigning the system from a pure centralised system into a new system based on distributed principles.

Common for all the users is a requirement for easy, transparent, and open access to up-to-date information. Despite that the scope of maritime spatial planning is mainly national, several marine entities like pollution, fish, and sea mammals do not care about national sea borders. Likewise, cables, pipes and shipping routes go across national sea borders. Thus, there is a need for information about the environmental state and eco-nomic activities in at least the neighbouring countries.

As part of the INTERREG projects Baltic Scope and BalticLines, surveys and interviews among planners have been carried out in order to be able to specify the more specific needs they are facing, when dealing with cross-border issues. Both MSP projects focus among other things on raising awareness of the processes and challenges referring to the Blue growth strategies, sustainability and the ecosystems approach as well as on putting collaborative issues to attention in order to increase corporation across borders. Concerning the marine data infrastructure, an important challenge is to support usability and focus on actual needs concerning data and functionality, and how to get access to data that fits the purpose.

In the BalticLines project the focus is on cross-border issues on shipping and energy lines, leading to a specific need for information on linear structures. The importance of paying attention to other important cross-border issues like the envi-ronment is also emphasised by the planners. The MSP process timeframes between countries vary, military areas are difficult to include in planning, because data is restricted. Furthermore, some national borders at sea are not defined, Natura 2000 network and blue corridors are not coherent, and monitoring fisheries is a challenge. Background data is important concerning other aspects: marine protected areas, fish-eries, hotspots of ecological features (nursery areas, etc.). For example, in regards to aquaculture, relevant background data could advantageously contribute to assessing options for co-location.

---

[5] www.vasap.org.

Interviews among MSP planners illustrate the big differences among the countries concerning the planning and governance processes as well as concerning data requirement and availability. A specific challenge is how to deal with the issues of harmonisation issues. In general, the approach will be pragmatic and aiming at solutions fit for the purpose. Detailed datasets are needed, when doing complex analysis, though a lot of cross-border planning cases can be handled based on simple harmonised images. Likewise, the planners have pointed out the importance of focussing on semantics and the attributes needed. Some planners also emphasised how shared GIS expertise to perform more complex analysis would support the planning procedures.

3.2 A Conceptual Systems Architecture

Many countries are now developing national Spatial Data Infrastructures for marine and maritime information. These national nodes will serve as base components in a transnational data infrastructure in accordance with the INSPIRE principles [16]; that 'data should be collected once and maintained at the level where this can be done most effectively', and that 'it should be possible to combine seamlessly spatial information from different sources across Europe and share it between different users'. The conceptual model, presented in Fig. 1, describes how a geospatial geoportal can be designed, building on the SDI principles and on the needs highlighted through interviews with maritime spatial planners in the Baltic Sea Region.

Data are most often stored in spatial relational databases like Oracle, SQL Server, and PostGIS. The ISO 19125 standard defines a data model for simple features (2D features) with a hierarchy of geometry classes from points over lines to polygons. Besides, the distributed national data servers, it is most often necessary to have a dedicated central data server containing data, that are not general available from the official data servers. These data comprise research data, voluntary geographic information, and other non-operational data sets.

The central node should in principle only be an access point - a data portal - where the different users can search for data through a Catalogue and Discovery service, visualise the data through a Portrayal service, transform the data through a Processing service, and finally getting access to the data through download or via web services.

Data Discovery

A catalogue service enables you to search for geographical data sets and geoservices based on the corresponding metadata. In Europe, the INSPIRE Directive sets the rules for metadata used to describe the spatial data sets and services as listed in the directive. The Member States within the EU are obliged to describe their data by metadata and setting up local catalogue services. The metadata elements follow the ISO 19115 for data and services. The Metadata XML schema implementation is defined by ISO 19139.

Data Visualisation

The Portrayal service allows data to be presented interactively through services such as WMS (Web Map Service) and WFS (Web Feature Service) using a standard interface over the internet. The ISO 19117 standard defines a schema to create graphic output for data provided through the ISO 19110 group of standards. The ISO 19117

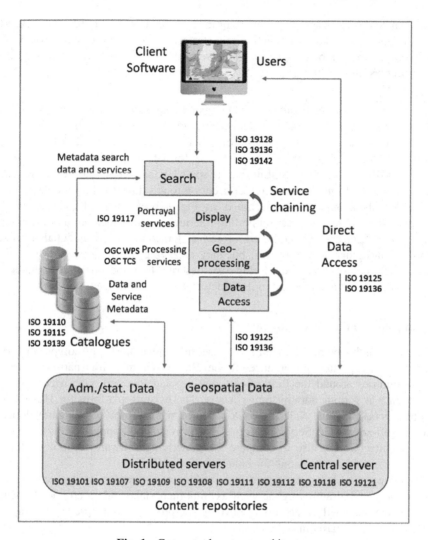

Fig. 1. Conceptual systems architecture

standard does not contain standardisation of cartographic symbols, which are kept separate from the data. Thus, the cartographic representation of an object is stored in a portrayal catalogue.

<u>Data Processing</u>

The processing services allows spatial data to be processed by using Web Processing.

Service (WPS), which is an OGC implementation [21]. Web Coordinate Transformation Service (WCTS), Routing Service or Analysis and Topologic Overlay Service are other examples on web based processing. The WPS standard defines how a request send by the client can initiate the execution of a process, and how the output from the process is afterwards handled. The data required by the Web Processing

Service can be delivered across a network or they can be available at the server. A WPS process is normally a singular function that performs a specific geospatial operation, but a WPS process can be designed to call a sequence of web services including other WPS processes, thus acting as the service chaining engine.

Data Access

These services are needed to access raw geo-spatial data (not maps in case of Web services) by downloading static data files through FTP or via Web Services using common file formats such as XML, GML, NetCDF, GeoTIFF, and ASCII. Access though FTP most often uses proprietary file formats like ESRI's Shape file, or MapInfo's MIF file. Recently, SQLite and its spatial extension SpatiaLite[6] have gained increasing popularity in file based direct access through downloading the data.

The described architecture illustrated in Fig. 1 provide a robust platform for developing data infrastructures supporting marine e-governance in a transnational context. Most data are still collected, stored and maintained by national agencies, authorities, and other data providers, but they are being distributed by web-services based on international standards. Below, we describe how the proposed architecture can be used to build a spatial data infrastructure for the Baltic Sea.

3.3 Implementation of Prototype

Based on the architecture described above, we have developed a prototype for a data infrastructure supporting governance of the Baltic Sea in a transnational context. Several countries around the Baltic Sea today provide free and open access to government data at various administrative levels. The existing platform for HELCOM's data portal is based on the ArcGIS Server platform, while prototype being developed is based on well-known GeoServer platform. This provide good opportunities not only to test the architecture but also to compare the underlying software technology for the system. There are pros and cons for both software platforms.

The prototype is being developed in a step-by-step approach in close cooperation between the national authorities as well as important stakeholders around the Baltic Sea. The next steps will be to further develop the prototype with processing capabilities, and with data harmonisations tools.

4   Discussion

The overall architecture of the prototype is compliant with the model described in Fig. 1, but several obstacles need to be overcome. Below, we discuss the challenges and possible solutions.

Challenges

1. The data required by the maritime authorities are not available under similar conditions among the countries surrounding the Baltic Sea. Some countries like

---

[6] http://www.gaia-gis.it/gaia-sins/.

Denmark and Finland have implemented the principle of Open Government Data, while other countries have various degrees of restrictions. Data may in principle be open, but sometimes one must pay for the data, and at other times the data may be available free of charge while being confidential due to military or other security reasons.

2. The data are only available in formats, which are not interoperable and compliant with the architecture of Fig. 1. If the data is open and freely available, they can in most cases be downloaded in shape file or GML formats, while the accessibility to the data via web services are less frequent. This is particularly the case for the highly valuable data in GML format provided through WFS (Web Feature Service). Trying to get access to free Danish data through web feature services, will require a special permission by the mapping authority, and in that case, only for a limited amount of data. This is due to the heavy processing power and network bandwidth needed to process and transfer the data.

3. Most of the information referred to above is available through the public authorities and are required to follow the INSPIRE Directive. However, information on shipping traffic is provided through the so-called AIS-system standardised by the S57 and S100. Through the national AIS centres one can be granted access to data by a (low cost) annual subscription.

4. Finally, the fact that each of the nine countries around the Baltic Sea has its own language is a challenge, since this creates difficulties combining data sets from different countries.

Solutions

- Ad. 1. Luckily, several data are imposed by regulations according to the INSPIRE Directive, and are at least in some degree available. Although some data still have limited accessibility we believe that this will change in a rather short term, also due to the recent Open Government Data initiatives. We even expect, that data which today are not general available will become accessible during the project period.

- Ad. 2. The INSPIRE Directive defines the data specifications for several data sets included in the data requirements list, and this latter list is the guideline behind the implementation of this prototype. Data available through web services are used directly in our data infrastructure and hereby follow the main road in the distributed systems architecture of Fig. 1. Data that are not available through web services are stored in a central database, until they eventually become available by web services. Thus, the systems architecture in the prototype is a mixture between a pure centralised solution and a decentralised solution. We use the term hybrid systems architecture for our prototype. The advantage of this approach is that we are not excluding data sets, which do not support a pure decentralised solution through web services, but instead adapt the system gradually over time, when more data will be available through web services.

- Ad. 3. This challenge is less problematic, because the HELCOM portal already provides access to shipping traffic and allows its members to access generalised historical shipping traffic data, but if raw shipping data are required, they cannot be provided through our data portal.

- Ad. 4. The language issue is solved through a translation table for the layer names in the map services from the different countries around the Baltic Sea. The layer names in our system are in English, but before sending a request for a data layer, the name of the data set is converted to the local name for that data layer. This, principle can later be extended enabling users in the individual countries to use their native languages when requesting data from the different countries.

The prototype is being developed in a step-by-step approach in close cooperation between the national authorities as well as important stakeholders around the Baltic Sea. The next steps will be to further develop the prototype with processing capabilities, and with data harmonisations tools.

5   Conclusion

The seas and oceans provide resources for transport, fishery, oil and gas production, mineral extraction, and tourism. In addition, the seas are being used for renewable energy production by off-shore wind farms, and wave energy. At the same time, the ecosystems of the seas and oceans are coming under increasing pressure, leading to the need for management. Furthermore, because the seas are often 'shared' between several countries, an international or transnational approach is required. Overall, the use of seas and oceans are regulated internationally by UN through the UNCLOS law, but more detailed management of the seas requires maritime spatial planning, and this was facilitated by the adoption of an EU Directive on Maritime Spatial Planning strengthening the ecosystem based approach as well as transnational cooperation. To be efficient and trustworthy, the marine management needs to be knowledge based through information systems, but due to the development of new technologies and methods for storing and distributing information, there is a need for redesigning the original HELCOM system from a pure centralised system into a new system based on distributed principles. The current BalticLines project will contribute to this process by developing a prototype based on a distributed systems design.

Using state-of-the-art principles regarding organisational issues, as well as current systems architecture standards, we have developed a new proposal for a data infrastructure supporting marine governance in a transnational context. In a close cooperation with the primary user groups and other stakeholders, a prototype is developed. However, several challenges exist, including accessibility to data, their formats, and the multi-language environment we are working in. The challenges were met in a pragmatic way through a step-by-step approach, implementing strategies to the extent of what is currently possible, while keeping the ambitions of the overall systems architecture at the longer-term perspective. After having developed the visualisation and download tool we have turned our attention to defining needed and appropriate processing tools together with the authorities around the Baltic Sea Region.

Acknowledgement. This research is carried out as part of the BalticLines project co-funded by the European Union through the INTERREG Baltic Sea Region 2014–2020 programme. Also, many thanks to the HELCOM Secretariat for valuable input to the current paper.

References

1. FAO: The State of World Fisheries and Aquaculture. Food and Agriculture Organization of the United Nations, Rome (2010)
2. European Commission: A European Strategy for more Growth and Jobs in Coastal and Maritime Tourism. Communication from the Commission to the European Parliament, The Council, the European Economic and Social Committee and the Committee of the Regions. European Commission (2014)
3. European Commission: Blue Growth Strategy on the opportunities for marine and maritime sustainable growth. Communication from the Commission to the European Parliament, The Council, the European Economic and Social Committee and the Committee of the Regions. European Commission (2012)
4. United Nations: Convention on the Law of the Sea. New York, 10 December 1982
5. Schaefer, N., Barale, V.: Maritime spatial planning: opportunities & challenges in the framework of the EU integrated maritime policy. J. Coast. Conserv. **15**, 237–245 (2011)
6. Santo, E.: Environmental justice implications of maritime spatial planning in the European Union. Mar. Policy **35**, 34–38 (2011)
7. Backer, H.: Transboundary maritime spatial planning: a Baltic Sea perspective. J. Coast. Conserv. **15**(2), 279–289 (2011). doi:10.1007/s11852-011-0156-1
8. Strain, L., Rajabifard, A., Williamson, I.: Marine administration and spatial data infrastructure. Mar. Policy **30**, 431–441 (2006)
9. European Commission: Directive 2008/56/EC of the European Parliament and of the Council of 17 June 2008 establishing a framework for community action in the field of marine environmental policy (Marine Strategy Framework Directive). Off. J. Eur. Union **L164**, 19 (2008)
10. Fairgrieve, R.: Maritime Spatial Planning – "ad utilitatem omnium". Plan. Theory Pract. **17**, 140–143 (2016)
11. European Commission: Directive 2014/89/EU of the European Parliament and of the Council of 23 July 2014 establishing a framework for maritime spatial planning. Off. J. Eur. Union **L257**, 135 (2014)
12. Rajabifard, A., Feeney, M.-E.F., Williamson, I.: Spatial data infrastructures: concept, nature and SDI hierarchy. In: Williamson, I.P., Rajabifard, A., Feeney, M.-E.F. (eds.) Developing Spatial Data Infrastructures: From Concept to Reality, pp. 17–40. Taylor and Francis, London, New York (2003)
13. Onsrud, H.J., Pinto, J.K.: Diffusion of geographic information innovations. Int. J. Geogr. Inf. Syst. **5**, 447–467 (1991)
14. European Commission: Regulation (EC) No 1367/2006 of the European Parliament and of the Council of 6 September 2006 on the application of the provisions of the Aarhus Convention on Access to Information, Public Participation in Decision-making and Access to Justice in Environmental Matters to Community institutions and bodies. Off. J. Eur. Union **L264**, 13 (2006)
15. European Commission: The reuse of public sector information, Directive 2003/98/EC of the European Parliament and of the Council. Off. J. Eur. Union **L345**, 90–96 (2003)
16. European Commission: Directive 2007/2/EC of the European Parliament and of the Council of 14 March 2007 establishing an Infrastructure for Spatial Information in the European Community (INSPIRE). Off. J. Eur. Union **L108**, 1–14 (2007)
17. Seip, C., Bill, R.: A framework for the evaluation of marine spatial data infrastructures – accompanied by international case studies. Geosci. Eng. **62**, 27–43 (2016)

18. Kocur-Bera, K., Dudzińska, M.: Information and database range used for maritime spatial planning and for integrated management of the coastal zone – case study in Poland, Baltic Sea. Acta Adriat. **55**, 179–194 (2014)
19. Bovalis, K., Peristeras, V., Abecasis, M., Abril-Jimenoz, R.-M., Rodríguez, M., Gattegno, C., Karalopoulos, A., Szekacs, I., Wigard, S.: Promoting interoperability in Europe's e-government. Computer **47**, 25–33 (2014)
20. Treiblmayr, M., Scheider, S., Krüger, A., von der Linden, M.: Integrating GI with non-GI services – showcasing interoperability in a heterogenous service-oriented architecture. GeoInformatica **16**, 207–220 (2012)
21. OGC: OpenGIS Web Processing Service. Open Geospatial Consortium (2007)
22. D'Ancra, A., Conte, L., Nassisi, P., Palazzo, C., Lecci, R., Creti, S., Coppini, G.: A multi-service data management platform for scientific oceanographic products. Nat. Hazards Earth Syst. Sci. **17**, 171–184 (2017)
23. Hahn, A., Bolles, A., Fränzle, M., Fröschle, S., Park, J.: Requirements for e-navigation architectures. Int. J. e-Navig. Marit. Econ. **5**, 1–20 (2016)
24. van den Brink, L., Janssen, P., Quak, W., Stoter, J.: Towards a high level of semantic harmonisation in the geospatial domain. Comput. Environ. Urban Syst. **62**, 233–242 (2017)

mGovernment and Inclusion

Exploring Usability and Acceptance Factors of m-Government Systems for Elderly

Tamás Molnár[1(✉)], Andrea Kő[2], and Bálint Mátyus[2]

[1] Humboldt-Universität zu Berlin, Berlin, Germany
tamas.molnar@cms.hu-berlin.de
[2] Corvinus University Budapest, Budapest, Hungary

Abstract. Mobile penetration rate is high, so m-government services have a huge potential to spread. Our research aims to investigate how elderly users profit from m-government. Europe is now and will be in 2060 the oldest continent in the world, so elderly is an important target group for future m-government services. There are several m-government initiatives and projects offering various government services, like information sharing, alerting and mHealth services, which provide mobile remote patient monitoring in order to measure vital signs, bio-signals of patients outside hospital environments. Such systems can strongly benefit from improved acceptance by elderly users; therefore, investigation of social and psychological aspects of mobile adoption is an emerging field of research. The goal of our research is to find a way to map the needs of the elderly and set guidelines for the design of m-government systems. We apply IGUAN framework [11] for usability investigation, which we developed, in our earlier research as a guideline for improving the usability of e-government systems. We constructed a scenario in usability investigation, a search for medical treatment. Our research follows a user-driven method and uses the data acquired on usability of m-government by the elderly from Germany and Hungary. The main contribution of this paper is the assessment of the requirements for m-government systems' development for elderly, by investigating the factors, which lead to a low acceptance of m-government by this group.

Keywords: m-government for elderly · Usability · IGUAN usability framework

1 Introduction

E-government has to be accessible by every member of the population makes usability for governmental systems a key component and warrants research projects with the goal of creating solutions for higher usability and making stationary or mobile government services easily accessible for the whole population.

E-government systems facilitate governments in theory to reach the ultimate efficiency in internal processes and enable an effective access to governmental services for citizens and businesses. Mobile systems, which are targeted by our research are specialised part of these and are defined as "the government that provides information and services to citizens and firms using wireless user infrastructure, service software application and mobile devices" [1]. It includes government services and applications

© Springer International Publishing AG 2017
A. Kő and E. Francesconi (Eds.): EGOVIS 2017, LNCS 10441, pp. 175–188, 2017.
DOI: 10.1007/978-3-319-64248-2_13

(Apps) through mobile technology such as tablets, smartphones, etc. [1] as defined by Ibrahim Kushchu from Japan who was one of the first researcher of the aspects of m-government [2]. Apart from efficiency, a second aspect of electronic government, and in particularly m-government, which needs a new approach, is the user-friendliness.

The interface of a system determines the overall complexity by either masking or increasing the complexity of the task behind the system. E-government system are for this aspect unlike any other interactive services, as these systems should be offered so that the "digital divide" [3] is narrowed to a minimum. The challenge in this is the incorporation of the complex task into a simple interface, which is usable by the whole population. We can measure this by taking a user group with the least experience, the elderly, who will also become increasingly important users for these systems in the future.

European population is aging fast; it is now and will be in 2060 the oldest continent in the world. Old-age dependency ratio (the ratio of over 65 years old to the working age population), is estimated to be about 49% [4], one inactive elderly will eventually be supported by two active people from 2060 [5]. At the same time, mobile devices like smart phones, mobile phones, tablets and e-book readers are more and more popular amongst the elderly as well. Mobile penetration rate is high, by the end of 2016, two thirds of the world's population owned a mobile subscription [6]. GSMA report estimates that by 2020, almost three quarters of the world's population (5.7 billion people) will subscribe to mobile services. Regional penetration rates are forecasted to range from 50% in Sub-Saharan Africa to 87% in Europe. These numbers draw attention for the m-government services as well, especially in remote areas where internet services are limited. Using mobile devices in government services has several advantages like the mobility of telecommunications and the supporting of many communication services content. There are several m-government initiatives and projects offering various government services, like information sharing, alerting and mHealth services provide mobile remote patient monitoring in order to measure vital signs, bio-signals of patients outside hospital environments [7]. Khan collected typical m-government applications, like transportation systems, education systems, health and urban policy information [8]. He analysed the m-government challenges and determined that the security concern and the weak ICT infrastructure are decisive. Such systems can strongly benefit from improved acceptance by elderly users, therefore investigation of social and psychological aspects of mobile adoption is an emerging field of research. Younger people have clear social and psychological motivations towards the use of the mobile services, while in the group of the elderly there is no such a commitment [9]. We have found in our previous research project [10] when investigating the acceptance of stationary e-government systems by the elderly, that users started to favour mobile devices (tablet computers) from 2013 onwards. E-government research primarily focused on non-m-government services, but the importance of these services are increasing, according to the previously mentioned factors. According to the above-mentioned issues and our own results, we concluded that it would be reasonable to perform a dedicated follow up project with m-government systems.

This decision is further supported by the fact that the development of less expensive mobile devices in last 5–6 years offer users the easy to use opportunity to access electronic services who would never have used stationary computers or laptops because of the complexity or costs of the systems. These premises made it apparent that the utility of mobile e-government for the ageing population warrants a deeper research project, which should focus on this essential population group. As shown by other research projects the use of e-government can be promoted to elderly if the interface of the system is in accordance with the needs of them [10, 11]. Al-Hubaishi and his co-authors developed a comprehensive framework of mobile government service quality [12]. They identified twenty mobile government service quality sub-dimensions classified within six dimensions (source was the literature on m-government). Additionally, papers also describe the strong correlation between usability and acceptance for elderly [13]. Hung et al. [14] analysed the factors that determine user acceptance of the m-government services using the theory of planned behaviour. They had a sample of 331 users from Taiwan (all users had m-government experiences). Their research model included nine external variables and they investigated twelve hypotheses. Their conclusion was that perceived usefulness, perceived ease of use, trust, interactivity, external influence, interpersonal influence, self-efficacy, and facilitating conditions are critical factors in improving user acceptance of m-government services. However their study did not deal with those users who are older than 40.

Our research is investigating the following questions:

- How do elderly users profit from m-government?
- Which are the decisive factors in usability and acceptance of m-government services for elderly?
- Is it possible to create m-government systems in accordance with the needs of the elderly?

We mapped these questions into a research project with the goal to discover the acceptance of m-government systems by the elderly. The project is built upon a user-driven approach and uses in the first phase of the research the data acquired in our earlier studies on usability of e-government by the elderly [10].

This method enables us to compare our findings with the data from stationary e-government systems, and prove the notion that elderly users favour touch screen devices when using e-government systems.

This paper will be structured as follows:

First, in the introduction section, some decisive problems and challenges in m-government are detailed; then research methodology is discussed. The following part presents the methodology, the research phases and the IGUAN framework, which we applied for usability investigation. Next, we detail our approach understanding the target group. Discussion part presents some preliminary results. Finally, conclusion part summarizes strengths and weaknesses of IGUAN with further improvement directions.

2 The Methodology

The examined case grounds on the previously developed IGUAN framework (Fig. 1) [10], which serves for improving usability of e-government systems. The selected guideline helps to design applications and services in agreement with the target group needs and provides elderly users easy access too. According to previous research results, the framework proved to increase the acceptance of the system measurably [10]. Multiple studies [15–17] show that elderly can benefit from certain improvements of the user interface.

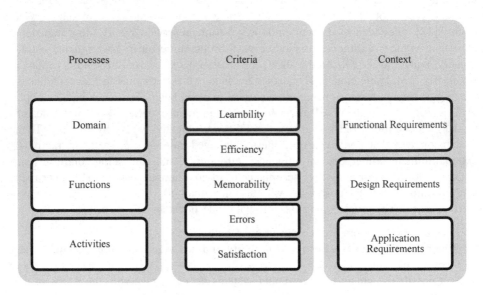

Fig. 1. Structure of the IGUAN framework

With proper optimization, the elderly may have better user experience, easily accept the system as a valid alternative compared to uncomfortable, and time consuming offline services. We applied the methodology previously in one of our projects, which opens the possibility to compare acquired data, ensuring a good evidence that mobile government systems are favored over traditional systems by the target group.

The guideline is built along three main aspects, which are constructed upon the general usability improvement methods of Richter and Flückinger [18]. The framework defines three interlinked aspects, each forming a dimension of the usability of the system. By integrating the core requirements of the application design with user requests, internal and external aspects of the improvement process are incorporated into the base structure of the guide. Later this is broken down into easily executable functions.

The functional requirements incorporate general guidance aspects and configuration requirements, which are specified by the objective of the application. These are immutable, as the requirements describe the internal functions and processes of the e-government service. Derived from the Technology Acceptance Modell [19], the design requirements include as focus the perceptions and attitudes towards the system. These have to be declared in relation to the targeted user group. The needs characterizing for the connection of the target group and the system are included in the application requirements. Trustworthiness, representing citizens' impression of the credibility of the application is an aspect of e-government systems. The second aspect describes criteria controlling the usability of an application. The mentioned criteria have been chosen in accordance with the experience from comparable studies in general software usability assessment [20–22], and represent a link to the ISO/IEC 25010:2011 [23, 24] (previously ISO/IEC 9126). In the early phases of our research five core factors by Fisk et al. [13] determining acceptability of a system were also used to construct the interviews, which enabled an overview of the user requirements.

The actual best-practices for the IGUAN framework are provided by the process aspect, which can be split up into the domains, functions and activities. The domains describe the improvement process by describing the redesign cycle with four domains:

- Interview and Understand
- Analyze and Specify
- Design
- Evaluate and Effect

These domains are aligned with the contextual design and the usability improvement sequence cited earlier for the better understanding of system requirements of the elderly. The hybrid flow-model based on the ISO 9241-110/ISO 9241-210 was refined to create the domain model of the IGUAN.

Activities resulting in usability improvements are called functions. These specify what is to be done to achieve a better acceptance of the application. The steps guiding the improvement process are modelled with 23 distinct steps.

The direct actions required to achieve a measurable usability improvement can be seen as the execution of the more general functions and allow for a wide customization of the guidelines for the particular application. These activities contain the actual methodology of the functions enabling to use the sophisticated toolset required by the actual usability improvement. The functions are grouped by the domains, each domain representing a key component in the usability improvement process.

This method enables creating a procedure, which is proved to provide profound data, but also offers the possibility to directly compare findings of previous research on e-government systems. During the procedure development, the findings of several analogous research projects [17, 25] were taken into account. The integration of inspection methods and interface tests are the most comprehensive methodology for usability assessment, which is supported by multiple authors [13, 26] as the only method which results in a comprehensive overview of the system. Heuristics, cognitive walkthroughs and action analysis are used as inspection methods, which are for pre-implementation general usability assessment by developers.

We applied these theories and concepts in our integrated usability improvement research method. This framework serves as a basis for an iterative usability improvement process created along the hypothesis that heuristics in combination with dedicated user input will not only result an improved system as postulated by multiple authors, but also lead to a solution, which can be used to create a generalized guideline. The process can be seen in Fig. 2.

As described above, and seen on the schematics of the research, the initial premise was that currently offered m-government systems offer low usability and have measurable problems motivating elderly users. This idea was further developed into the theory that systems should work for the user, and be aligned with the tasks, which are

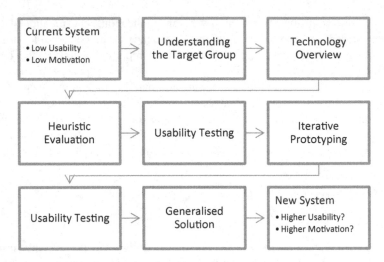

Fig. 2. Integrated usability improvement process – broad schematics of the research

considered significant by the target group. The general framework of the project was therefore built upon three phases, which include multiple proven principles of human factors approaches:

- Understanding the target group (interview) and technology overview
- Heuristic evaluation and usability testing
- Development of a solution.

We finished the first phase of the research; this paper is summarizing the corresponding process and results.

3   Understanding the Target Group

The first phase forms the basis of our investigation, and is used to understand whether elderly users favor and profit from mobile government systems. It was designed to give an overview about the requirements and the fundamental issues of the target group. The data gathering for this is based on deep interviews and standardized questionnaires. This step also includes a technology overview, which was fundamentally a generalized expert analysis of the currently offered electronic government systems in Germany and Hungary. We have tested the scenario with 30 test participants between the age of 60 and 90; they were recruited in Germany and Hungary. The summative median age was 74 years.

In this phase of our research we reuse the qualitative data acquired for our previous study on the impact of e-government system on the elderly as a basis for a comparison between stationary e-government systems and mobile government and create through this an opportunity to directly compare the theoretical acceptance of stationary and mobile systems.

The approach for the interviews in this step have been created on a purely theoretical basis. This decision was essential, as any application or functional system might influence the test group with actual and real problems, which consequently would create falsified data based on a single system. This makes an analogous approach in both countries (Germany and Hungary) possible and centered the scenario on a theoretical system, which would give the elderly several advantages through improved service quality and efficiency. This procedure has been successfully demonstrated in earlier research [10] and has produces reliable data about the theoretical acceptance of the user group.

As for the scenario we selected a theoretical system, which would have a strong usefulness for the target group: "searching for medical treatment". The selections were based on information acquired from local government officials in both countries.

We identified maturity levels for this service as well, which helps to create a model for the assessment of m-government application. Data was acquired by the means of a standardized questionnaire, which included multiple questions about the acceptability of the targeted system. Next part summarizes the scenario and the maturity levels.

3.1   The Scenario: Searching Medical Treatment

The local government of Belváros-Lipótváros in Budapest operates a health center (BLESZ) for ambulatory patients living in the 5th district. The facility provides health care services through twenty-one different medical areas. Having some kind of health issue, several questions may be raised by the patient: Which physician should I choose? How may I contact my physician and make an appointment? When is my medical expert available or have consulting hours?

Level 0: To answer above questions potential patient may turn for help to BLESZ costumer service in person or by phone. Beyond these communication forms there exists no other option to gain information (e.g.: website, mobile application).

Level 1: Some static information is available online on the official website, however, it is not updated regularly. The system contains details about physicians at a specific medical area. Online forms or other interactive interfaces are not available.

Level 2: In addition to the previous levels, patients may be informed by the website/mobile application providing opportunity to schedule an appointment with the selected medical expert. Reading other patients' previous experiences one can make a better decision of choosing professional help.

Level 3: Additionally to the previous levels, patients may ask their questions on forums and online (video) chat to their medical expert. Organizing online consultations with medical record transfer is also possible.

The choice of Hungary as a comparable test environment to Germany was made on multiple premises: e-government distribution, the Internet penetration rate and the demographic structure. The centralized approach to e-government in contrast to the federal system of Germany enabled an evaluation of multiple governmental procedures in a similar environment. A further question when dealing with e-government services is the complexity of the integrated electronic components. The maturity model for e-government systems created by the European Commission can illustrate this increasing complexity and development of e-government solutions. We used this maturity level based model for the different systems, enabling the easy and proven assessment of electronic services, thereby creating a framework for the research and an option to compare systems with different components and goals.

This approach guarantees that users are confronted step-by-step with more and more electronic components and were not overwhelmed by new concepts, which might create refusal or other sudden and uncontrolled changes in the attitude of the test candidates. The results from the previous research [10] support the theory, that there is a threshold in the acceptance of electronic government by the elderly. We have seen that younger elderly (under 65) approves electronic government systems which offer electronic components up to level 3. Older citizens might not accept present systems beyond level 2; interactive systems seem to encourage a fear of new technology and fuel disapproval in about 50% of the tested participants.

The acceptance of the levels is measured with a standardized questionnaire, consisting of standard questions of the ASQ method, based on the research by Lewis [27] at IBM. We have modified the method for the use with the scenario, as the basic framework places its emphasis on multiple choice grading. This was modified to grading scheme with four possible levels, from very satisfied to very unsatisfied.

In addition, the standard ASQ questions, described in the next chapter, were accompanied with supplementary queries, needed for a deeper understanding of attributes unique to e-government.

The three main aspects of the ISO 9241-210 – efficiency, utility and effectiveness – link the standard with the ASQ. Before the questionnaire, the participants are familiarized with the scenario by a short verbal introduction consisting of the narrative overview. This is followed by the relevant questionnaire. This is repeated for each maturity level with the relevant narrative part and then the questionnaire. The standard questions are asked for each maturity level. The supplementary questions are asked at the relevant maturity levels, thereby creating a deeper understanding of the user experience of highly advanced systems. This is followed by the socio-demographic questions, consisting of age, gender, housing, schooling and previous experience with e-services.

The filled in questionnaires are analyzed and evaluated in order to understand and visualize the theoretical acceptance of e-services for elderly users. As for the earlier, comparable research, the theoretical acceptance is calculated from the three ASQ questions by assigning one or zero for positive or negative answers. The theoretical system is considered as accepted if the three scores were positive for the user. The earlier research with standard e-government systems concluded that there is a threshold in the acceptance of e-government and probably other types of e-services for different cohorts.

The earlier results support the theory that younger elderly approve e-government systems, which offer electronic components up to level 2. Level 3/4 systems were somewhat more controversial, but even such systems were acceptable for about 50% of the younger test participants in both countries. Older elderly might however not accept present systems beyond level 1. Interactive systems seem to encourage a fear of new technology and disapproval in about 50% of the tested participants. Further research was therefore concentrated on this issue, as these cohorts could profit the most from new offerings. Level 3 and 4 electronic applications could offer the most for this age group, as it would enable easy and comfortable G2C communication and could support the efficiency of ambient assisted living through a communication platform with the government.

4   Discussion

The acceptance of the levels was measured with a standardised questionnaire, consisting of standard questions based on the ASQ method, shown in the previous section, based on the research by Lewis [27] at IBM. In addition, the standard ASQ questions were accompanied with supplementary queries, needed for a deeper understanding of attributes unique to e-government. The three main aspects of the ISO 9241-110mentioned and described earlier – efficiency, utility and effectiveness – link the standard with the ASQ, leading to comprehensive and reproducible results. Utility in the ASQ is consistent with utility in the ISO 9241-210. Ease of use is consistent with effectiveness and time gain is consistent with efficiency.

Before the questionnaire, the participants were familiarised with the scenario by a short verbal introduction consisting of the narrative overview. This was followed by the relevant questionnaire. This was repeated for each maturity level with the relevant narrative part and then the questionnaire. The standard questions were asked for each maturity level. The supplementary questions were asked at the relevant maturity levels, thereby creating a deeper understanding of the user experience of highly advanced systems. This was followed by the socio-demographic questions, consisting of age, gender, housing, schooling and previous experience with e-services. The answered questionnaires were analysed and evaluated in order to visualise the theoretical acceptance of e-services for elderly users. The theoretical acceptance was calculated from the three ASQ questions by assigning one or zero for positive or negative answers. The theoretical system was considered as accepted if the three scores were positive for the user.

The results from the different levels analysed in accordance with the maturity model of the European Commission seems to support the hypothesis that there is a threshold in the acceptance of mobile government and probably other types of e-services for different cohorts. This threshold can be observed in Fig. 3. The results demonstrate a distinct drop in acceptance for the elderly at level 2. Simulated approaches rejected by at least one-third of the participants should be considered as not accepted and such applications will probably suffer from general acceptance problems if offered to the population in their current design.

The results support the theory that younger elderly approve e-government systems which offer electronic components up to level 2. Level 3/4 systems were somewhat more controversial, but even such systems were acceptable by approximately one-third of the test participants in both countries. This validates our hypothesis that mobile government systems can be useful for the elderly and will be accepted if created with the users in mind. This warrant therefore further research in order to analyse the requirements of such systems and find a generalised solution, which will help to

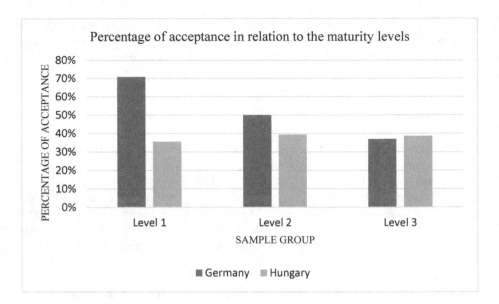

Fig. 3. Comparison of the acceptance of the scenario levels by the elderly users in Hungary and Germany, 2017

alleviate the acceptance threshold. As a next step in our research we moved to the second function of the IGUAN: Analyse and Specify.

M-government services are the next evolutionary step of e-government systems and are built on the premise of combining the advantages of traditional e-government systems with the possibilities of the app-based ecosystem on mobile devices. M-Government systems might be a solution to improve the effectiveness of governmental services for the population, as traditional e-government has reached its limit in user acceptance, in particularly for the peripheral user groups, as the elderly [10]. The popularity and ubiquity of mobile devices and applications can strongly contribute to an inherently better acceptance by building on the previous experience of the users with such systems. This can be seen on the example of interactive applications which can be compared or even surpass the complexity of level 4 e-government systems and are readily accepted by elderly users on mobile devices [27].

Multiple factors contribute to this higher acceptance:

- The perceived usability of touchscreen devices is measurably higher for elderly users. This is caused by the direct control of the interaction without the representation of interaction through a mouse controlled pointer. As shown by other researchers, this can directly influence the acceptance of applications when compared to identical tasks with mouse and keyboard based input [28].
- The development of mobile services has caused a high penetration of mobile devices in all cohorts of the population. Elderly users, who have not necessarily access to a standard computer, have a smartphone and/or a tablet, which they use for multiple tasks on daily basis.

- The ubiquity of mobile devices has led to a higher general acceptance of mobile applications by elderly users. Users have also gained experience with mobile applications through practice, and these factors cause a higher perceived usefulness for such devices.

The higher perceived usefulness and the perceived ease of use are critical features in acceptance of systems. This combined with more experience with the underlying mechanics of touchscreen applications offers a better basis for acceptance of e-government systems on this platform, than traditional systems. This stems from the factors, which influence the perceived usability of applications:

- "The perceived complexity of the interface, which is created by the complexity of the task to be done and the design of the user interface..." [30]. The task itself should be considered a constant; therefore, the only way to decrease this factor is the improvement of the interface.
- "The previously acquired general experience of Internet applications..." [31]. In our case, interactive mobile e-services. This experience gives the user the edge when trying to solve a problem presented by the unfamiliar task and/or interface, thereby helping to overcome the perceived difficulties of the system.
- Additionally, in case of e-government systems the perceived security and privacy is a decisive factor for the users when assessing the usability of the system. In particularly for elderly users, who are influenced by security problems heralded by the media, the trust in the application could be critical.

Other authors have also described these factors. Alharbi and his colleagues investigated which factors are decisive in m-government services in Saudi Arabia. Their research applied TAM model (technology acceptance model), which is widely used to measure the acceptance of new technology [32]. Authors identified five main potential factors in Saudi context and ten sub factors that may influence the adoption of m-government. These main factors are the following: perceived trustworthiness, usage experience, enjoyment, awareness and security. This conclusion can be projected onto our user group, the elderly.

As described earlier the experience of the users with mobile applications is inheritably higher as for standard e-government applications, as users are familiar with touchscreen interfaces. This means that the perceived usability of the system will governed mainly through the perceived complexity and the perceived security of the application.

As shown earlier, the first step of our research was the analysis of the theoretical service acceptance, which will give us insight into the accepted maturity level of the m-government services. This has to be followed by a general assessment of m-government systems for the elderly by testing an existing system along the premises of the IGUAN guideline.

The main objective of the tests in the second phase will be to gather data about the usability of systems in an everyday environment with the users of the selected cohort. The tests will therefore be not only based on the proven scenarios, but also backed-up by methodology designed for the assessment of the user experience and verified by analogous studies. To completely understand the users' previous familiarity with comparable systems, an analysis of the experience on an individual level is needed [31]. This is based on the CLS (Computer Literacy Scale) developed at the Chair of Engineering-Psychology at the Humboldt-University Berlin [33]. This model can assess the computer literacy of the user precisely through a series of questions, creating a matrix from typical tasks on a computer.

We conduct the actual tests using the data gathered in the 1st phase, and make up the main part of the user tests. They will be performed with a "thinking-aloud" method to document the accomplishment of the tasks. The touch movements on the screen will be captured by screen-capture technology. In addition, the required mental effort will be measured by the application of the RSME (Rating Scale Mental Effort) developed by Zijstra [34]. During the scenarios, the quantity of assistance required by the test participants will be recorded and categorized according to their impact. The significance of the problem was characterized by the frequency (F), the impact (I) on the successful competition of the task and the persistence (P) between individuals. The score (S) of a problem is calculated by a function (1) based on Nielsen and Loranger [20].

$$S = (F * I * \sqrt{P})/\sqrt{10} \tag{1}$$

The impact of the problems is classified on a scale of three, with minor issues as one and problems with critical outcome for the success of the task with three. Additional data is acquired by the after scenario questionnaire (ASQ) which was adapted for the user tests in our previous research. The three questions, which the ASQ is based on, were modified according to the results from the 1st phase, thereby contributing to the comparability of the results. The ASQ itself was based on the work of Lewis [27].

- "I am satisfied with the ease of completing the tasks in this scenario."
- "I am satisfied with the information and consider this system useful."
- "I am satisfied with the amount of time it took to complete this scenario."

The answers are provided through five intervals from strongly disagree (1) to strongly agree (5).

5   Conclusion

M-government services are combining the advantages of traditional e-government systems with the possibilities of the app-based ecosystem on mobile devices. They might be a solution to improve the effectiveness of governmental services for the population, in particularly for the elderly.

The results from the first phase and our previous research have shown that elderly are interested in e-government applications and the theoretical acceptance of such systems can be improved with a structured approach. Data from similar research projects also show that mobile systems have a higher acceptance by the elderly compared to traditional electronic service. The next phase of our research will be the development of the m-government service related to the scenario detailed above, which will offer insight into the acceptance of actual systems by the target, and enable us to gather information about the particular requirements of elderly users. This system will then be modified in accordance with the acquired data from the second step and tested again with the identical methodology to create a system with a higher acceptance and usability.

Acknowledgement. "This paper has been written with the support of the National University of Public Service in the framework of the priority project KÖFOP-2.1.2-VEKOP-15-2016-00001 titled "Public Service Development for Establishing Good Governance" - Ludovika Digital Governance Research Group".

References

1. Wang, C., Feng, Y., Fang, R., Lu, Z.: Model for value creation in mobile government: an integrated theory perspective. Int. J. Adv. Comput. Technol. **4**(2), 16–23 (2012)
2. Kushchu, I., Kuscu, H.: From E-government to M-government: facing the inevitable. In: Proceeding of European conference on E-Governemnt (ECEG 2003) (2003)
3. Mehra, B.: Virtual Communities on the Internet: Social Interactions Across the Digital Divide. Univerisity of Kansas, Lawrence (2004)
4. European Commission: The 2015 Ageing Report (2015)
5. Abadie, F., Codagnone, C., van Lieshout, M., Pascu, C., Baum, P., Hoikkanen, A., Valverde, J., Maghiros, I.: Strategic Intelligence Monitor on Personal Health Systems (SIMPHS) Market Structure and Innovation Dynamics, European Commission Joint Research Centre, Institute for Prospective Technological Studies (2011)
6. GSMA association: "the mobile economy", GSMA (2017)
7. Kő, A., Gábor, A., Szabó, Z.: Innovative ehealth services – PISCES solution. In: Kő, A., Francesconi, E. (eds.) EGOVIS 2015. LNCS, vol. 9265, pp. 206–219. Springer, Cham (2015). doi:10.1007/978-3-319-22389-6_15
8. Khan, M.A.: Exploring the push and pull drivers in M-government framework that influence acceptance of services on mobile devices. Int. J. Comput. Sci. Netw. Secur. **16**(2), 23–26 (2016)
9. Conci, M., Pianesi, F., Zancanaro, M.: Useful, social and enjoyable: mobile phone adoption by older people. In: Gross, T., Gulliksen, J., Kotzé, P., Oestreicher, L., Palanque, P., Prates, R.O., Winckler, M. (eds.) INTERACT 2009. LNCS, vol. 5726, pp. 63–76. Springer, Heidelberg (2009). doi:10.1007/978-3-642-03655-2_7
10. Molnar, T.: Improved Usability of Electronic Government Services for the Ageing Population. HU, Berlin (2014)
11. Righi, V., Sayago, S., Blat, J.: Towards understanding e-government with older people and designing an inclusive platform with them. Int. J. Public Inf. Syst. **3**, 131–142 (2011)
12. Al-Hubaishi, H.S., Ahmad, S.Z., Hussain, M.: Exploring mobile government from the service quality perspective. J Enterp. Inf. Manag. **30**, 4–16 (2014)
13. Fisk, A.D., Rogers, W.A., Charness, N., Czaja, S.J., Sharit, J.: Designing for Older Adults. CRC Press, Boca Raton (2009)
14. Hung, S.Y., Chang, C.M., Kuo, S.R.: User acceptance of mobile e-government services: an empirical study. Gov. Inf. Q. **30**(1), 33–44 (2013)
15. Hipp, C.: Elderly Friendly HMI: Graphical User Interface for Ambient Assisted Living. Fraunhofer IAO, Stuttgart (2009)
16. Robinet, A., Picking, R., Grout, V.: A Framework for Improving User Experience in Ambient Assisted Living. University of Plymouth, Plymouth (2008)

17. Bruder, C.: Gestaltungsprinzipien für das Training älterer Benutzer elektronischer Geräte. Technische Universität Berlin, Berlin (2008)
18. Richter, M., Flückinger, M.: "Die 7 ± 2 Wichtigsten Usability-Methoden", in Usability Engineering Kompakt, pp. 21–76. Spektrum Verlag, Heidelberg (2010). doi:10.1007/978-3-8274-2329-0_3
19. Davis, F.D.: Perceived usefulness, perceived ease of use, and user acceptance of information technology. MIS Q. 13(3), 319–339 (1989)
20. Nielsen, J., Loranger, H.: Prioritizing Web usability. The University of Michigan: New Riders, Ann Arbor (2006)
21. Park, K.S., Lim, C.H.: A structured methodology for comparative evaluation of user interface designs using usability criteria and measures. Int. J. Ind. Ergonomics 23, 379–389 (1999)
22. Nokelainen, P.: (2004). http://www.uta.fi/laitokset/aktk/papers/tech_ped_usability/edmedia2004_pn.pdf. Accessed 5 Dec 2011
23. ISO: ISO/IEC 9126-1:2001 software engineering - product quality - Part 1: quality model, ISO (2001)
24. ISO: ISO/IEC 25010:2011 systems and software engineering - systems and software quality requirements and evaluation, ISO (2011)
25. Sayago, S., Sloan, D., Blat, J.: Everyday use of computer-mediated communication tools and its evaluation over time: an ethnogrpahical study with older people. Interact. Comput. 23, 543–554 (2011)
26. Nielsen, J.: Usability Engineering. Academic Press, San Diego (1993)
27. Lewis, C.H.: Using the "Thinking Aloud" Method in Cognitive Interface Design. IBM, New York (1982)
28. Choudrie, J., Pheeraphuttharangkoon, S., Zamani, E., Giaglis, G.: Investigating the adoption and use of smartphones in the UK: a silver-surfers perspective. University of Herfordshire (2014)
29. Kobayashi, M., Hiyama, A., Miura, T., Asakawa, C., Hirose, M., Ifukube, T.: Elderly user evaluation of mobile touchscreen interactions. In: Campos, P., Graham, N., Jorge, J., Nunes, N., Palanque, P., Winckler, M. (eds.) INTERACT 2011. LNCS, vol. 6946, pp. 83–99. Springer, Heidelberg (2011). doi:10.1007/978-3-642-23774-4_9
30. Jung, R.: Formale Bewertung der Benutzerkomplexität bildschirmgeschützter Informations- und Unterhaltungssysteme im Kraftfahrzeug. ZMMS Spektrum, vol. 15, no. VDI (2002)
31. Maeda, J.: Simplicity - Die zehn Gesetze der Einfachheit. Spektrum, München (2007)
32. Alharbi, S., Drew, S.: Using the technology acceptance model in understanding academics' behavioural intention to use learning management systems. IJACSA, Int. J. Adv. Comput. Sci. Appl. 1, 143–155 (2014)
33. Sengpiel, M., Dittberner, D.: The computer literacy scale (CLS) for older adults - development and validation. In: Mensch & Computer, pp. 7–16 (2008)
34. Zijstra, F.R.H.: Efficency in Work Behaviour. A Design Approach for Modern Tools. Delft University of Technology, Delft (1993)

Designing Human Behavior Through Social Influence in Mobile Crowdsourcing with Micro-communities

Mizuki Sakamoto, Kota Gushima, Todorka Alexandrova,
and Tatsuo Nakajima[✉]

Department of Computer Science and Engineering,
Waseda University, Tokyo, Japan
{mizuki, gushi, toty, tatsuo}@dcl.cs.waseda.ac.jp

Abstract. This paper proposes a new mobile social media infrastructure for motivating collective people to participate in flourishing our society. For motivating them, designing human behavior through social influence within communities is one of the most important issues to make their lifestyle better, but it is not easy to promote the entire collective people's activities towards achieving a common goal. Our proposal is to use a layered approach where an entire community consists of many micro-communities; if each independent community is encouraged to contribute to its society, the entire community will be finally motivated to achieve a flourishing society. Our approach adopts a virtual currency and a crowdfunding concept to encourage members in a micro-community; we analyze the effect of social influence on human behavior from the experiment-based analysis. The analysis shows that the proposed approach might work well within a community of well-known people. We finally suggest a possible solution to overcome potential limitations as a future direction.

Keywords: Human behavior · Social influence · Mobile crowdsourcing · Micro-level crowdfunding

1 Introduction

Achieving a flourishing society is one of the most important issues in a modern society [22]. Ubiquitous computing technologies are considered useful tools that reduce energy and recycle resources to achieve a sustainable society to make our daily life smarter [16]. However, technical advances alone cannot solve most of the essential social problems. People need to be aware of the importance of their contribution to solving these problems. Ubiquitous computing technologies can also help people become aware of this importance and alter their behavior toward a more sustainable and flourishing society [4]. Psychological techniques to alter people's attitude and behavior have become popular, and findings in social psychology have been widely adopted to shape behavior through public policies [24]. If these design patterns can be immersively incorporated into our daily environments by using ubiquitous computing technologies, they will increase the opportunity to improve our lifestyle in a more flourishing manner.

A. Kő and E. Francesconi (Eds.): EGOVIS 2017, LNCS 10441, pp. 189–205, 2017.
DOI: 10.1007/978-3-319-64248-2_14

Our solution is to use a mobile crowdsourcing concept as a mobile infrastructure to encourage collective people to achieve a flourishing society. *Amazon Mechanical Turk*[1] is currently the best-known commercial crowdsourcing service and uses monetary rewards to encourage people to undertake micro-tasks. The system, then, uses only economic incentives. However, for achieving a flourishing society, we need to empower the social relationship in each community to improve people's daily lifestyle; the most important factor is to design human behavior through social influence for enhancing the social relationship in the community and for making people's daily life more meaningful through the positivity in the relationship [22].

In this paper, we focus on designing human behavior through social influence to motivate collective people. However, the effect of social influence may not work well if the number of community members is increased [17]. Our approach suggests that an entire community consists of many micro-communities, and each micro-community independently achieves a common goal of the entire community from the bottom-up. This means that we take the approach of *"changing the entire world by changing the small world around us."* This paper introduces a new mobile social media infrastructure, named *micro-crowdfunding* that adopts the above idea.

The purpose of this paper is to describe our explorations into how to facilitate collective actions through social influence. People need to perform activities towards a flourishing society to make our daily life better. For realizing the society, designing human behavior through social influence is essential because as shown in [17], most people do not perform desirable activities even if the activities are important. In our approach, we use virtual currency and a crowdfunding concept for designing human behavior through social influence to motivate people to enhance their social relationship through their activities, and analyze the effect of social influence on human behavior through the experiment-based analysis. The analysis shows that the proposed approach might work well within a community of well-known people. We finally suggest a possible solution to overcome possible limitations as a future direction. The analyzed insights described in the paper are useful to design human behavior through social influence in micro-communities.

2 Related Work

Tinytask is a design research project whose aim is to design objects for the good and flourishing life [20].[2] When starting to use the service, a user receives an envelope with six key chain coins. Each coin represents a lightweight mission. The back of the coin depicts a marker. The user can read the instruction for the mission on his or her profile page on the *Tinytask* web site with that marker. The user chooses one coin to commit to, and attaches it to his or her key chain. It should stay there until the mission has been completed. Once completed, the user can confirm this on the web site, and make notes in his or her personal diary. When five out of the six missions are completed, the user

---

[1] https://www.mturk.com/mturk/welcome.

[2] https://vimeo.com/35682922/.

will automatically receive a new set of coins. Users can collect the coins as rewards and subtle reminders of their achievement. However, this approach has the following drawbacks. The first one is that it is hard to scale the approach to be used in a larger community. The second one is that the effect of social influence used in the approach is not powerful enough to activate collective human behavior.

Some research has already investigated existing crowdfunding infrastructures like *Kickstarter*[3] [8], but very little research has been devoted toward the design and experience of building new crowdfunding infrastructures. In [15], an experiment in enterprise crowdfunding is presented as a useful example. Employees allocated money for employee-initiated proposals in an enterprise Intranet site, including a medium-scaled trial of the system in a large multinational company. The results showed that communities in a large company propose ideas, participate and collaborate and that their activities can be encouraged through crowdfunding. The approach details a new collaboration opportunity and shows that crowdfunding is a promising method for increasing activity within communities.

Amazon Mechanical Turk is a commercial crowdsourcing service based on monetary rewards. However, as shown in [1], monetary rewards are not always the best strategy for motivating people to perform micro-tasks. Instead, contributors appreciate many intangible factors, such as community cooperation, exposure to new ideas and entertainment. The results of the research investigating human motivation in crowdsourcing show that not only monetary rewards but also intrinsic motivation, such as eudaimonic pleasure, autonomy, and various skills required to complete tasks, are important for the continuation of micro-task engagement [10, 19].

There is some promising previous related work focusing on the effect of social influence that has already been published by our research group. The location-based, real-time, question-answering service *MoboQ* is built on a micro-blogging platform through which people help each other with minimal effort [13]. Using *MoboQ*, end users can ask location- and time-sensitive questions, such as whether a restaurant is crowded, whether a bank has a long waiting line, or whether any tickets remain for an upcoming movie at the local cinema—i.e., questions that are difficult to answer with ordinary Q&A services. The insights of the work show that the effect of social influence is an important design factor to guide collective human behavior, but they did not discuss how to design human behavior through social influence if the number of community members is increased.

3   Strengthening the Effect of Social Influence for Making Our Society Flourish

In this section, we show the basic design strategies of *micro-crowdfunding*. We define the goal of *micro-crowdfunding* as achieving a flourishing society. Free resources that are shared by a number of people, such as public toilets or the natural environment tend to be overused as a consequence of the *tragedy of the commons* [9]. This problem

---

[3] http://www.kickstarter.com/.

occurs because each individual derives a personal benefit from using the resource, whereas any costs are shared among all of the users; this circumstance leads to use that is inconsiderate toward others. An example of this behavior is the wasteful use of free plastic shopping bags, which are filling landfills. A common strategy to address the tragedy of commons is to impose a tax on the use of the resource. An environmental tax can be widely adopted to cover the cost of maintaining the resource. However, for taxpayers, it is not clear how the tax is used to maintain each common resource that is shared by the members of the community. People must experience a feeling of having contributed to the sustainability of the resource to be motivated to pay the necessary cost. In this paper, after presenting an overview of *micro-crowdfunding*, we focus on how human behavior through social influence can be designed for guiding collective human behavior because designing human behavior through social influence is the most necessary factor to achieve the goal. The paper does not address the issue whether our approach can achieve a flourishing society: the feasibility of this aspect will remain as a future direction.

The most important design strategy involves using a micro-community to encourage more crowdsourcing activities through social influence among community members. The design strategy of a community-based social approach is to adopt altruism as a social mechanic [14], but altruism alone is not strong enough to motivate participants within the micro-community, and other temptations usually obstruct people's altruistic behavior, especially, in a modern society, people need to make essential decisions without considering the importance deeply [11]. Thus, we must maintain the number of community members small for making the effect of social influence among them significant. If each micro-community consists of a small number of members, the possibility of a free ride is decreased [17]. This design is essential for crowdsourcing for collective action because the existence of a large number of free riders significantly decreases the motivation of active participants. This approach is also important to increase participants' curiosity because community members who know each other can propose a new activity that may be of interest to members within the same community. In the current version of micro-crowdfunding, we focus on the following three factors regarding the influence on human behavior: *reciprocity, commitment and consistency*, and *social proof* [2] to strengthen the effect of social influence among community members. *Micro-crowdfunding* assumes that the number of community's members in a micro-community is about 10–20 people to, which decreases the possibility of members being strangers to each other and strengthens their reciprocity. Also, the virtual currency mechanism incorporated in crowdsourcing activities is to strengthen commitment and consistency, and social proof.

The crowdsourcing activities in micro-crowdfunding are designed to make community members more flourished. As shown in positive psychology literatures, human activities to remind everyday occurrences that make people happy are the key to flourish their daily life [12]. *Micro-crowdfunding* encourages community members to propose crowdsourcing activities to make the members perform the activities with as much as possible positivity. If most of the community members are willing to perform these activities while helping their communities, they are aware of their internal positive power and the positive power makes them happier [22]. Thus, as a consequence, the entire community flourishes more and also the sustainability of the community is increased.

4 Guiding Collective Actions

4.1 Micro-missions in Micro-crowdfunding

In *micro-crowdfunding*, we aim to provide an opportunity to everyone who wishes to contribute and take part in improving our world. The project in this service is called a *micro-mission* because it requires only a small amount of time to be completed and because it attempts to achieve the sustainability of a small, common resource in a person's spare time with minimal effort.

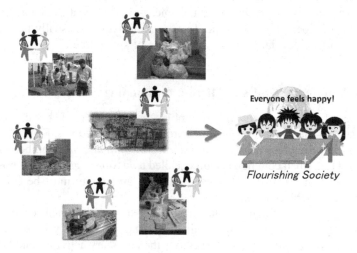

Fig. 1. A layered community-based approach

Technological advances alone are not sufficient to achieve the goal of a better future [24]. People must alter their behaviors and attitudes. In [6], designing activism is an important direction for solving various serious social issues. It aims to alter human behavior and attitude through design. Governments embed persuasive strategies in public policies; however, this method has limits, particularly because setting public policy is a long process [24]. Persuasive technologies are promising and effective approaches to altering human behavior and attitudes [7]. This preliminary research suggests the possibility of an information infrastructure to effectively alter human behavior and attitudes toward a desirable, sustainable and flourishing society. Of course, today, social media, such as *Facebook*[4] and *Twitter*[5], have very strong influences on human behavior and attitudes; however, current social technologies do not explicitly guide collective people's behavior and attitudes. In *micro-crowdfunding* to direct collective human behavior and attitudes, a micro-mission to steer people toward a goal should be a central abstraction. Additionally, to involve more people, these micro-missions should be designed by a variety of stakeholders in a micro-community who contribute social issues based on participatory design [5].

---

[4] https://www.facebook.com/.

[5] https://www.twitter.com/.

A layered community-based approach shown in Fig. 1 overcomes the issue described in the previous section. With this approach, a community member can propose a micro-mission for maintaining the community's sustainability, and other members of the community can then complete the mission. However, members usually do not have enough time to contribute to a micro-mission. In particular, people who live in urban areas are busy and have many commitments. Therefore, they usually forget the importance of sustainability in our society. In our daily environments, we have numerous small, common resources that are costly to maintain if maintained by the government, nonprofit organizations or individual companies. However, maintaining these resources typically necessitates micro-missions that can be achieved with minimal effort in a person's spare time. In our urban lives, we usually have plenty of opportunities to take advantage of small amounts of spare time.

4.2   Crowdfunding Activities in Micro-crowdfunding

The basic idea of *micro-crowdfunding* resembles that of traditional crowdfunding, such as *Kickstarter*, but the goal is to maintain shared common resources. Figure 2 shows an overview of crowdfunding activities in *micro-crowdfunding*. A member of a community related to a small common resource, called a *mission organizer*, proposes a new micro-mission when he or she becomes aware that an activity must be completed to maintain the sustainability of the resource.

Typical examples of these common resources are a public sink on a floor of a building or a public shelf used by a university laboratory. The proposal includes a summary of the micro-mission, which specifies the necessary activities and the price of achieving the micro-mission.

When specifying micro-missions, a *mission organizer* needs to take into account activities to make us flourish as shown in Table 1 presented in [12]; the list was proposed by Lyubomirsky to make our daily life more flourish by increasing our positive attitude in our daily life. For example, when proposing to clean up a public sink, a *mission organizer* also asks participants in his/her community to forgive people who have not cleaned up the sink (10th activity in Table 1). In another example, a *mission organizer* asks participants to organize a shared bookshelf and to remember when they can enjoy some books in the bookshelf (7th activity in Table 1). A micro-mission proposal is published to all other participants by touching a common resource with a *mission organizer*'s mobile phone and sending a photograph showing the current status of the common resource. Micro-missions in *micro-crowdfunding* are basically related to organizing common resources in participants' everyday life much better.

When other members, called *mission investors*, receive a request to fund the micro-mission, they decide whether they want to do so based on the delivered photograph representing the micro-mission. Members wishing to fund the micro-mission simply click on the requests on their phones to notify the *mission organizer*. The micro-mission can be performed by any member who can access to the resource in his or her spare time once the total contributed value satisfies him or her. This member is called a *mission performer*. The micro-mission is usually a simple task, such as cleaning a public sink or putting a shelf in order. After completion, the *mission performer* takes a photograph of the

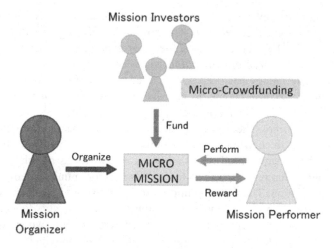

Fig. 2. Overview of micro-crowdfunding

Table 1. A list of activities that make people more flourish [12]

Activities making us flourished
I. Counting your blessings
II. Cultivating optimism
III. Avoiding overthinking and social comparison
IV. Practicing acts of kindness
V. Nurturing relationships
VI. Doing more activities that truly engage you
VII. Replaying and savoring life's joys
VIII. Committing to your goals
IX. Developing strategies for coping
X. Learning to forgive
XI. Practicing religion and spirituality
XII. Taking care of your body

resource to show that the micro-mission has been completed and sends it to the *mission organizer*. Finally, the *mission organizer* verifies the quality of the achievement, and notification of the completion of the micro-mission containing a photograph of the resource is delivered to all the members who funded the micro-mission.

4.3 Virtual Currency in Micro-crowdfunding

An economic incentive is a tangible reward that users consider to be valuable; however, the reward is not necessarily actual money or goods. Instead of using real money, *micro-crowdfunding* adopts a special mechanism, called a local currency [23], from an economic perspective. A local currency is a currency that is not backed by a national government and is intended to be traded only in a small geographic area. As a tool of fiscal localism, local money can raise awareness of the local economy. One of the most important aspects of local currency is the possibility of adopting different money models, which cannot be used as legal tender. For example, the aging money model [23] that is adopted in *micro-crowdfunding* has been a popular example of the local currency idea. Aging money has been widely used to encourage monetary circulation within a community because people do not want to save their money for their future. Thus, the aging money is effective in increasing a community's economic activity. In the aging money concept, the value of money gradually decreases with time, and people naturally want to contribute to micro-missions before the value of the money is degraded; thus, they want to fund micro-missions as quickly as possible.

Also, the aging money allows us to increase a community member's money without causing inflation. The aspect is important when using virtual currency because each member needs to have initial money for joining *micro-crowdfunding* activities. To encourage community members to contribute to a micro-mission, we set the rule that the value does not degrade when a person funds a micro-mission with his or her money. When a micro-mission is completed, half of the money provided by a participant is returned as a reward to him or her. This arrangement provides an incentive for participants to fund more micro-missions. Because the proposed *micro-crowdfunding* concept uses virtual currency, all of the transactions occur electronically.

4.4 Implementation Overview

We have developed a *micro-crowdfunding* prototype system to demonstrate the effectiveness of our idea. The prototype system has three components. The first is an Android phone that possesses an NFC reader as shown in Fig. 3.

The second is an embedded computer that is connected to a server—named *Resource Management Server*—integrated in a small, common resource based on IoT-based technologies. *Resource Management Server* embedded in a small, common resource and storing information about a community that manages the resource. A user registers a new micro-mission to a public resource that is managed by its *Resource*

Showing a micro-mission's details.

Touching on an NFC Card Embedded in a Tiny Resource

Fig. 3. Micro-crowdfunding prototype system

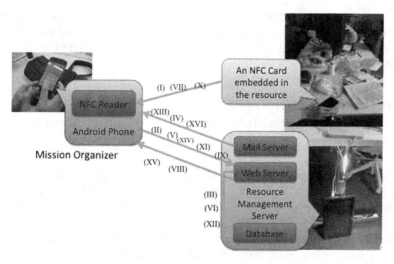

Fig. 4. Interaction between components

Management Server through his/her Android phone. The server manages all micro-missions related to the public resource, and currently funded virtual currency for the micro-mission. The last component is a server that stores various information related to the *micro-crowdfunding* activities in a database. This server is named *micro-crowdfunding Server*, which knows all *Resource Management Servers*. The server also contains all information about each user in *micro-crowdfunding*, and notifies a user about public resources related to him/her. The system has been implemented as an HTML5[6] web application. Thus, the participants can easily begin using the *micro-crowdfunding* service with minimal effort by using their mobile phones.

Figure 4 shows the interaction between an Android phone and a *Resource Management Server*. When a *mission organizer* touches the NFC card embedded in a *Resource Management Server* managing the small, common resource by containing an IoT-based device with his Android phone, a camera in his Android phone starts, with which he or she takes a picture of the small, common resource (I). When he or she inputs some information about the micro-mission and clicks the button, an event is delivered to the *Resource Management Server* for the small common resource (II). Then, the information, including a photo that shows the resource's current status, is stored in a database in the server (III). Afterward, *mission investors* receive emails that contain URLs (IV). In the retrieved forms, they specify the amount of the micro-mission's funds by controlling a seek bar on their phones and this information is also stored in the database (V, VI). By touching a *mission performer*'s Android phone on the NFC card contained in a common resource (VII), its *Resource Management Server* returns information about currently available micro-missions (VIII), and he or she knows the micro-missions. Then, he/she chooses the micro-missions that he or she may want to perform (IX). After completing a selected micro-mission, the *mission performer* touches the NFC card contained in the common resource (X), and registers a

---

[6] http://www.w3.org/TR/html5/.

photo that shows the completed status (XI, XII), which is also delivered to the *mission organizer* via an email (XIII). After the *mission organizer*'s confirmation (XIV, XV), *mission investors* can see the success of their investment by clicking the URLs in the emails they receive (XVI).

5   Experimenting Micro-crowdfunding Based on the Analysis of the Effect of Social Influence on Community Members' Activities

In this section, we present the results of some experiments with the *micro-crowd-funding* prototype system. The goal of this section is to discuss some psychological factors that influence human attitude and behavior in the *micro-crowdfunding* prototype system, referencing the results of the user studies and the experiments with the prototype system. If the effect of social influence is sufficient, a community' members are encouraged to perform more *micro-crowdfunding* activities, they perform micro-missions that make them more flourish. Thus, we consider that strengthening the effect of social influence is a key factor to make people flourish in *micro-crowdfunding*.

Eleven people including eight males and three females participated in the experiments, and their ages ranged from 20 to 39. Each participant was presented with the following two scenarios. We designed the micro-missions in the experiment based on the role-playing game-based method [18] with the prototype system. The experiment identifies potential pitfalls before starting a large scaled field study. In the experiment, the authors defined several possible micro-missions before the experiment. Each participant in the experiment was assigned a role of *mission organizer, mission investor* or *mission performer*. When assigned the role of the *mission organizer*, a participant chose one of the predefined micro-missions, and several participants whose roles were *mission investors* appropriated their contribution to the proposed micro-mission. The *mission performer* explained to the other participants how he or she performed the micro-mission to the other participants. The role of each participant changed during each turn, and we carried out several iterations so that all participants would understand the purpose of the approach. The approach was effective for understanding how the participants used the prototype.

In the first scenario, a participant played the role of a member of a community whose members were all well known to each other. We called this community consisting only of close friends *Friendly Community*. In contrast, in the second scenario, *Stranger Community*, consisted of members who did not know each other, and each participant played the role of a member of *Stranger Community*. The participants answered a questionnaire under the conditions of the above two scenarios; we then conducted semi-structured interview sessions with all the participants.

In *micro-crowdfunding*, the influence of *reciprocity* among participants depends on the relationships among community members. We first investigate the differences in this influence between *Friendly Community* and *Stranger Community* in the experiments. In the case of *Friendly Community*, the influence works well in the scenario without an extra mechanism to enhance the influence, and each member actively participates in micro-missions.

As mentioned above, the influence of *commitment and consistency* is defined such that if people make a small effort to achieve a more difficult goal, the likelihood of reaching the goal sooner tends to increase. Applying this influence to *micro-crowd-funding*, a small effort is investing funds in a micro-mission as a *mission investor*, and the *mission investor* will contribute to more *micro-crowdfunding* activities as either a *mission organizer* or a *mission performer* in the near future. We also investigate whether a member who has supported a micro-mission as a *mission investor* in the past tends to participate in other micro-missions as either a *mission organizer* or a *mission performer* in the same community.

In *micro-crowdfunding,* the influence of *social proof* may increase among *mission investors* who invest funds in the same micro-mission; almost all participants answered that other people's funds affected their decisions of how much to invest in a micro-mission; as a result, we assume that many participants' investing in a micro-mission increases other people's participation. We finally investigate whether others activities have this influence in both *Friendly Community* and *Stranger Community*.

5.1   The Influence of Reciprocity

We asked the following questions to each participant when belonging to *Friendly Community*.

RA1:   Aiko, who is one of your close friends, identifies a problem and organizes a micro-mission to solve it. You currently have fifteen minutes of spare time. Can you cooperate with the micro-mission organized by Aiko as either a mission performer or a mission investor? You must take ten minutes to perform the micro-mission as a mission performer. Please select your answer from "Cooperate", "Cooperate under some conditions" or "Do not cooperate".

RA2:   Please answer this question if your answer in RA1 is "Cooperate". Do you want to participate as a mission investor or a mission performer? Additionally, please state the reason for your choice.

RA3:   Please answer this question if your answer in RA1 is "Cooperate under some conditions". What type of condition does your cooperation require?

Additionally, the following questions were asked when participants belonged to *Stranger Community*.

RB1:   Hiroshi, who is a stranger to you, identifies a problem and organizes a micro-mission to solve it. You currently have fifteen minutes of spare time. Can you cooperate with the micro-mission organized by Hiroshi as either a mission performer or a mission investor? You must take ten minutes to perform the micro-mission. Please select your answer from "Cooperate", "Cooperate under some conditions" or "Do not cooperate".

RB2:   Please answer this question if your answer in RB1 is "Cooperate". Do you want to participate as a mission investor or a mission performer? Additionally, please state the reason for your choice.

RB3:   Please answer this question if your answer in RB1 is "Cooperate with some conditions". What type of condition does your cooperation require?

In RA1, eight of eleven participants answered "*Cooperate*", and three answered, "*Cooperate under some conditions*". Additionally, the results show that most participants wanted to be *mission performers* when the *mission organizer* was their friend in RA2. Some of the reasons given included "*I want to contribute to help my friends as much as possible*" and "*I show my good faith through my activity*". These results indicate that the influence of *reciprocity* works well within a close community regardless of a mission's goal. In contrast, in RB1 and RB2, only two participants answered "*Cooperate*" in the case of *Stranger Community*, and all of them wanted to participate in the micro-mission as *mission investors*. Reasons given in RB3 included "*I will help provided that the mission organizer has cooperated with my micro-mission*" and "*If he/she can help me when I need some help, [then I will participate in the micro-mission]*". These results show that people are conscious of the influence of *reciprocity* when they focus on the relationships and the benefits to themselves, indicating that a stranger may become a friend if approached with kindness.

There are clear differences among participants' consciousness of the use of the economic incentive. In interviews, participants stated "*I want to apply the monetary reward in Stranger Community, but I do not want to do so in Friendly Community*", "*I am resistant to the employer-employee relationship among friends*" and "*I do not like a clear mechanism to show the amount of debt*". Although visualizing information about a community is one of the merits of using information technology, it is not always the best method of motivating participants. When designing a social information infrastructure, the social influence of *reciprocity* should not be introduced as a support tool, and it should be designed as a process to alter human attitudes and behavior. However, introducing this mechanism is not easy. For example, a participant stated "*I cannot feel others' feelings of gratitude if there is an easy mechanism to represent 'thanks' to others.*" An easy mechanism, such as "*Like!*" on *Facebook*, is useful to show one's interest but seems superficial in representing gratitude. Finally, when the economic incentive is effective, we must carefully address monetary rewards to show the participants' achievement.

From the results of the experiments, we suppose that extrinsic motivational mechanisms, such as monetary rewards, points and badges, become less important when participants are all close friends. The mechanisms that make participants feel that others are real friends are more effective than the extrinsic motivational mechanisms.

5.2   The Influence of Commitment and Consistency

For the experiment on the social influence of *commitment and consistency*, the following scenario was provided to the participants: "*So far, Friendly Community's members have performed some micro-missions, and you have also participated in a micro-mission as a mission investor. All the community members except you actively participate as mission organizers and mission performers. You know generally that these micro-missions are good for environmental sustainability in your community but do not understand their importance."*

Additionally, the participants were asked the following question:

RC1:   *Under the conditions of the above scenario, will you become either a mission organizer or a mission performer at some time? Please choose among "Become a mission organizer or performer", "Become a mission organizer or performer under some conditions" and "Do not become either". Additionally, please state the reasons for your answer.*

Most of the participants answered that they wanted to become either *mission organizers* or *mission performers* provided that their friends made efforts to perform micro-missions and had participated in some past micro-missions as *mission investors*. The reasons for participation in the experiments are classified into the following two types: curiosity-oriented and cooperativeness-oriented. One cited reason supporting the former type was *"I want to experience the activity that my friends are really into"*, and one supporting the latter type was *"We need cooperativeness for a community's sustainability"*. In the scenario, we did not inform participants of the micro-mission's clear goal; however, these answers show an influence of *commitment and consistency*. Understanding the clear goal of a micro-mission is not important in the first step of participating in the micro-mission. However, to maintain desirable activities, the goal of the micro-mission appears to become more important. Two of the eleven participants answered, *"I will not become a mission organizer or a mission performer because the presented mission's goal is not clear"*. Another participant answered, *"I will try the mission because I may understand its importance"*. If the participants understand the goal of a micro-mission with a small effort, then the participants are more likely to commit to contributing to the micro-mission.

In the interviews, participants also discussed the risk of the *bystander effect*[7] (*Social loafing*). Some stated *"I ask others to contribute to a micro-mission if they perform it better"* and *"I feel that I must do it by myself when a community is small"*. Although the visualization of the reward or achievement does not always work well as noted earlier, visualizing participants' contributions as social achievements is effective.

5.3   The Influence of Social Proof

To gauge the social influence of *social proof*, participants are asked the following questions:

RD1:   *Assume that you often hang out at Ikebukuro with Friendly Community's friends. The members of the community start a micro-mission to clean Ikebukuro. One of the friends in the community is a mission organizer, and the other three members serve as mission investors. Each mission investor funds 200 units of the virtual currency used in micro-crowdfunding to support the*

---

[7] http://psychology.about.com/od/socialpsychology/a/bystandereffect.htm.

> *micro-mission. You now have 1000 units of the virtual currency. How much do you want to contribute to this micro-mission?*
>
> RD2: *Some members of Stranger Community start a micro-mission to clean an area, which is unknown to them. One community member is a mission organizer, and the other three serve as mission investors. Each mission investor funds 200 units of the virtual currency to support the micro-mission. You now have 1000 units of the virtual currency. How much do you want to contribute to this micro-mission?*

Although the goals of the micro-missions were not clear, all the participants wanted to fund over 200 units of the virtual currency in RD1. The influence of *social proof* provided by close friends, then, has a strong influence on people's activity. However, the amount of funds differed among participants in RD2. Regarding RD2, one participant stated *"It depends on the purpose of the micro-mission"*. The goal of the mission becomes more important than other members' behavior in this case. However, we found an anchoring effect [11] in both *Friendly Community* and *Stranger Community* because almost all the participants decided the amount of funds they would contribute based on 200 units of the virtual currency, which is the amount funded by others specified in the questions. The anchoring effect is effective in steering participants to more desirable situations. Controlling the anchoring point seems natural to motivate participants to fund the appropriate amount of the virtual currency. For example, a member even in *Stranger Community* may offer an anchoring effect to advance a micro-mission. If the member funds the specific amount as an anchoring point and disclose the information to other community members, it induces the participant to fund a similar amount.

We suppose that the influence of *social proof* among participants will work well when a participant easily finds information on other participants' contributions in every place. If participants feel more reality with this information, the trustworthiness of the information increases the power of *social proof*. The information strengths the bonds within a community. Also, increasing the trust relationship among community members enhances the influence.

5.4   Design Implication

The results of these experiments show that the influences of *reciprocity, commitment and consistency*, and *social proof* have strong impact on participants within a community whose members are close friends. We suppose that the trust within a community is one reason for the results. Additionally, introducing virtuality can encourage *micro-crowdfunding* activities; if strangers are replaced with empathetic virtual humans, the effect of social influence weakened via the strangeness among community members is recovered using empathetic virtual human. This is a promising approach to making other participants feel like close friends and to strengthen the bonds among friends, which increases participants' intrinsic motivation to cooperate. Similarly, if some personal detailed profiles of strangers are explicitly presented, the trust relationship may be established, in particular, when people find some similarities in strangers' profiles. Exchanging gifts between people is another approach to strengthen the effect of social influence [14]. For example, if potential *mission performers* or *mission investors* receive virtual gifts before contributing to the *micro-crowdfunding* activities, the possibility of their activities will be increased. However, the realness of the introduced virtuality is an important factor in encouraging the activities [21].

Understanding the importance of the goal of a micro-mission is essential for appreciating the value of reaching the goal in the future. When people are sure that there will be value for them in achieving the goal, they actively perform micro-missions to do so. The value is not always offered as extrinsic motivation like monetary reward, points and visible achievements. It can instead offer intrinsic motivation, such as close bonds through friendship, honor and life satisfaction. Additionally, the discussion presented in this section shows that the social influences of *reciprocity, commitment and consistency,* and *social proof* may be strong even in a community consisting only of strangers if the community members can feel closer to each other through virtuality.

Finally, we present our findings to gamify information/social services to encourage participation in them. As noted above, *gamification* is one of the most popular topics in building future information/social services [3]. Of course, games offer pleasure, and embedding game elements into the services to encourage participants seems promising. However, our experience shows that the *gamification-based approach* does not work well if the underlying infrastructure service is not well designed. First, we found it is essential to identify the major psychological factors, rather than system factors such as key performance indicators (KPI), to increase participants' motivation. Then, service designers must identify when the psychological factors have pitfalls that obstruct the service operation and remove those pitfalls through *gamification.* An underlying infrastructure service should therefore work well in some cases. *Gamification* does not compensate for bad design of an underlying infrastructure service.

Micro-crowdfunding uses several types of techniques to spur activism, and the basic scenario works well when participants belong to the same community. Additionally, we identify several psychological factors, such as *reciprocity, social proof,* and *commitment and consistency.* Then, we can adopt a *gamification-based approach* to enhance the strength of these psychological and social concepts to motivate participants who do not belong to the same community. The role of *gamification* is therefore to push people from behind to encourage certain behavior such that they believe that the idea to change their behavior was their own in this case. One of basic principles of design is that it is desirable to explicitly identify psychological or social factors that can be measured and discuss how the concepts can work well.

Like the influence of *commitment and consistency,* attracting participants to micro-missions through virtuality initially and conveying the importance of the missions through fictionality to commit to reaching the goal at a later stage is also effective. The reason for this is the fact that people may not alter their behavior without intrinsic motivation because the value of the extrinsic motivation can be reduced when their situations are suddenly changed. As shown in [21], incorporating ideological messages is essential to increasing human intrinsic motivation and altering people's behavior, and attitudes toward a flourishing lifestyle because participants can understand the meaning of the goal with minimal effort. One essential element in increasing human intrinsic motivation is encouraging users to create their own stories while participating in the activities. Perhaps the success of *gamification* depends on whether a user can create his/her own story with the *gamification* elements; they feel that the elements are meaningful through the story. While incorporated fictional stories help a user create his/her own story, some people can create their own stories from even a few game elements, such as when playing a board game or working on a puzzle. We think that the question of whether *gamification* is effective depends on users' ability to create their own stories. We believe that fictionality helps to create a user's story in order to enhance his/her intrinsic motivation.

Transmedia storytelling is a promising way to present information representing through fictionality in various places to encourage human behavior [21]. In particular, ambient and ubiquitous visual expressions of the information are useful techniques to offer information with a low mental load [16]. We will be able to investigate how the transmedia storytelling approach can be incorporated in *micro-crowdfunding* activities as one of future promising directions.

6   Conclusion

The paper claims that designing human behavior through social influence is essential to motivate collective people to achieve a flourishing society by encouraging more activities to make them flourish. We discuss how human behavior through social influence can be designed based on *micro-crowdfunding*, which adopts a crowd-sourcing concept to motivate collective people. Our analysis of the effect of social influence in *micro-crowdfunding* shows some pitfalls; we also show that a generalization of the basic concept can solve the issue and offer a new possibility to design human behavior through social influence.

As shown in [21], values can be used to increase the meaningfulness of human activities, thus they can be used to make micro-missions more meaningful. The approach is to incorporate virtuality into *micro-crowdfunding* activities. In this approach, each *mission investor* adds virtual items or creatures as additional values. The micro-mission becomes more attractive through the added values.

References

1. Antikainen, M., Väätäjä, H.: Rewarding in open innovation communities – how to motivate members? Int. J. Entrep. Innov. Manag. 11(4), 440–456 (2010)
2. Cialdini, R.B.: Influence: The Psychology of Persuasion, Revised edn. HarperBusiness, New York (2006)
3. Deterding, S., Dixon, D., Khaled, R., Nacke, N.: From game design elements to gamefulness: defining "ramification". In: Proceedings of 15th International Academic MindTrek Conference: Envisioning Future Media Environments, pp. 9–15 (2011)
4. DiSalvo, C., Sengers, P., Brynjarsdóttir, H.: Mapping the landscape of sustainable HCI. In: Proceedings of 28th International Conference on Human Factors in Computing Systems (2010)

5. Ehn, P.: Scandinavian design: on participation and skill. In: Schuler, D., Namioka, A. (eds.) Participatory Design: Principles and Practices, pp. 41–77. Lawrence Erlbaum, Hillsdale (1993)

6. Fuad-Luka, A.: Design Activism – Beautiful Strangeness for a Sustainable World. Earthscan, London (2009)

7. Fogg, B.J.: Persuasive Technology: Using to Change What We Think and Do. Morgan Kaufmann, Burlington (2002)

8. Gerber, E.M., Hui, J.S., Kuo, P.-Y.: Crowdfunding: why people are motivated to post and fund projects on crowdfunding platforms. In: Proceedings of International Workshop on Design, Influence, and Social Technologies: Techniques, Impacts and Ethics (2012)

9. Hardin, G.: The tragedy of the commons. Science **162**, 1243–1248 (1968)

10. Kaufmann, N., Schulze, T.: Worker motivation in crowdsourcing and human computation. In: Proceedings of AAAI Workshop on Human Computation (HCOMP) (2011)

11. Kahnemann, D.: Thinking, Fast and Slow. Penguin, London (2012)

12. Layous, K., Lyubomirsky, S.: The how, why, what, when, and who of happiness: mechanisms underlying the success of positive activity interventions. In: Gruber, J., Moskowitz, J. (eds.) Positive Emotion: Integrating the Light Sides and Dark Sides. University Press, Oxford (2014)

13. Liu, Y., Alexandrova, T., Nakajima, T.: Using stranger as sensors: temporal and geo-sensitive question answering via social media. In: Proceedings of 22nd International Conference on World Wide Web, pp. 803–814 (2013)

14. McGonigal, K.: The Willpower Instinct: How Self-control Works, Why it Matters, and What You Can Do to Get More of It. Avery Trade, London (2013)

15. Muller, M., Geyer, W., Soule, T., Daniel, S.A., Cheng, L.-T.: Crowdfunding inside the enterprise: employee-initiatives for innovation and collaboration. In: Proceedings of 31st International Conference on Human Factors in Computing Systems (2013)

16. Nakajima, T., Lehdonvirta, V.: Designing motivation using persuasive ambient mirrors. Pers. Ubiquitous Comput. **17**(1), 107–126 (2013)

17. Olson, M.: The Logic of Collective Action. Public Goods and the Theory of Group, Harvard University Press, Cambridge (1975)

18. Powell, J.: The Community Currency Role Play. http://www.complementarycurrency.org/ccLibrary/asia/thailand/ccroleplay.html. Accessed 13 May 2017

19. Ryan, R.M., Deci, E.D.: Intrinsic and extrinsic motivations: closer definitions and new directions. Contemp. Educ. Psychol. **25**(1), 54–67 (2000)

20. Ruitenberg, H.P., Desmet, P.M.A.: Design thinking in positive psychology: the development of a product-service combination that stimulates happiness-enhancing activities. In: Proceedings of 8th International Conference on Design and Emotion (2012)

21. Sakamoto, M., Nakajima, T., Alexandrova, T.: Enhancing values through virtuality for intelligent artifacts that influence human attitude and behavior. Multimedia Tools Appl. **74**(24), 11537 (2015)

22. Seligman, M.E.P.: Flourish: A Visionary New Understanding of Happiness and Well-being. Free Press, New York (2011)

23. Silvio, G.: The Natural Economic Order, Revised edn. Peter Owen, London (1958)

24. Wolfe, A.K., Malone, E.L., Heerwagen, J., Dion, J.: Behavioral change and building performance: strategies for significant, persistent, and measurable institutional change. US Department of Energy (2014)

Cast as Intended Verifiability for Mixed Array Ballots

Víctor Mateu[1,2(✉)] and Magda Valls[1]

[1] Department of Mathematics, Universitat de Lleida,
Jaume II, 69, 25001 Lleida, Spain
{vmateu,magda.valls}@matematica.udl.cat
[2] Scytl Secure Electronic Voting, Plaça Galla Placídia 1-3, 08006 Barcelona, Spain

Abstract. Nowadays, remote electronic voting has to deal with the fact that any computer can be a voting client for its voters, and these computers may be running malicious software on it. For this reason, cast as intended verifiability must be provided in any secure remote electronic voting scheme. However, existing cast as intended solutions for homomorphic tallying paradigm require the use of modular operations which cannot be performed by an average voter. Therefore, these solutions rely on the assumptions that a voter have access to a second device running a verification software and that the attacker cannot attack both. In this paper, we present a voting protocol under homomorphic tallying paradigm which provides a usable cast as intended verifiability solution using short codes without any extra device requirement.

Keywords: Electronic voting · Verifiability · Cryptography · Cast as intended

1 Introduction

The benefits of remote electronic voting over traditional voting are widely known. In an election, remote voting gives participants a chance to cast their votes from anywhere they have access to an Internet connection. Moreover, the votes can be tallied automatically, reducing the economic cost while improving the speed and accuracy of the process.

The security requirements remain the same for traditional and remote electronic elections. These requirements are privacy and integrity. The first one ensures that the relation between the vote content and the caster of the vote can not be obtained. The second guarantees that the voting protocol provides authentication, unicity and fairness.

The use of cryptographic tools to preserve privacy and integrity is mandatory when the voting information is sent using a channel such as Internet. Remote voting solutions are classified into three main paradigms: *blind signature based*, *mix-type* and *homomorphic tallying*.

In the *blind signature based* paradigm [1,2], voters compose their ballots and ask an authentication server to provide blind signatures of their ballots. If it is

© Springer International Publishing AG 2017
A. Kő and E. Francesconi (Eds.): EGOVIS 2017, LNCS 10441, pp. 206–218, 2017.
DOI: 10.1007/978-3-319-64248-2_15

an eligible voter and, it blindly signs ands sends it back to the voter. Finally, voters may cast their ballots through an anonymous channel. The polling station only accepts ballots that have been digitally signed by the authentication server. At the end of the voting period, the received ballots are decrypted and tallied.

The *mix-type* paradigm [3–5] resembles a traditional voting process. Here, voters generate their ballots, encrypt, and digitally sign them. The ballots are sent to the polling station which validates digital signatures and stores the ballots. Once the voting period has ended, the ballots are shuffled and re-encrypted (mixed) in order to break the relation between each ballot and its caster. Finally, the mixed ballots are decrypted and tallied.

In *homomorphic tallying* [6–8] paradigm, participants generate their votes and encrypt them under a public key cryptosystem with a homomorphic property. When the voting period ends, the polling station aggregates all the ballots generating a new ciphertext. The resulting ciphertext is decrypted and the election results are obtained.

The last two paradigms can provide proofs to ensure the integrity of the voting protocol. For this reason, they are suitable for elections where verifiability of the electoral process is mandatory. Nevertheless, these proofs affect the performance of the voting scheme in different ways. It is well known that mix-type paradigm can easily accomodate several types of election with a small impact on its computational cost. Homomorphic tallying paradigm, on the contrary, is heavily affected by the addition of voting options to the election. However, the performance of homomorphic tallying voting schemes is outstanding for elections with a small amount of candidates.

1.1 Motivation

Traditional elections provide different tools allowing auditors to verify correctness of the voting process. In electronic voting, verifiability has been mandatory since the first proposals [3,9]. Voting protocols must publish cryptographical proofs guaranteeing integrity of the election. These proofs ensure that all the ballots came from eligible voters, that no voter voted twice, and that ballots were not modified during the election. This way, electronic elections offer:

- *Recorded as cast verifiability:* in order to guarantee that ballots received by the polling station are exactly the ones cast by voters.
- *Counted as recorded verifiability:* ensuring that ballots tallied are the valid votes received by the polling station.

Previously, the voting client from which a voter casts her ballot was assumed to be trusted. However, this assumption can not be made in real environments where web browsers and even operating systems have demonstrated to be vulnerable. For this reason, new proposals must provide end to end verifiability to prevent voting clients from modifying voters choices. In practice, this means that, apart from *recorded as cast* and *counted as recorded* verifiability, a new property ensuring that the ballot cast contains the intended voting choice must be provided. This property is called *cast as intended* verifiability.

Nowadays, there exist few solutions offering *cast as intended* verifiability. Most of these proposals are suitable for mix-type electronic voting but some of them can also be adapted for homomorphic tallying. One of the first approaches was the Benaloh's challenge used in Helios 2.0 [7]. This solution, which can be used in homomorphic tallying paradigm, gives voters the option to decide if they want to cast their ballots or check its correctness. This way, a voter may audit a ballot generated by the voting client and, therefore, check that the voting client is not tricking her. However, if the voting client is missbehaving, it could also cheat with the validation. As a consequence, another trusted device is required to run the verification operations.

A different solution was proposed by Joaquim in [8]. Here, the vote is generated in a way that allows the voting client to generate a code that can be used to validate the option encrypted to be the one intended to be. The problem remains the same, voters need a trusted device to verify their votes because the cryptographic operations are too complicated to be computed by them.

1.2 Contribution

Our proposal uses return codes for providing cast as intended verifiability. The first electronic voting solution using return codes was originated due to the e-voting project in Norway [10,11] held in 2011. A variation of that system, focused on reducing the number of required independent entities during the voting phase, was implemented for the Swiss Canton of Neuchtel [12] and has been used for their elections since 2015.

Our solution consists of an improvement over an already secure homomorphic tallying voting scheme [13]. The improvement relies on offering voters an easy and usable way to prove their ballots, cast from their voting clients, to contain the voting options they have chosen. In order to do that, each voter receives a voting card with the correspondence between voting options and return codes. Once a ballot is cast, its voter receives a return code associated with her voting option which can be easily verified by just checking the voting card. This way, voters do not need any additional device to cast their ballots in a secure way.

The original proposal [13] provided recorded as cast and counted as recorded verifiability. Our modifications transforms it into an end to end verifiable voting scheme under homomorphic tallying paradigm.

2   Preliminaries

In this section we are going to introduce the cryptography basics required to understand our proposal and also the notation used. We start with the cryptosystem used in our online voting protocol and, after that, we show the zero knowledge proofs that will be used in the protocol and provide the notation for them.

2.1 Elliptic Curve ElGamal Cryptosystem

In this paper, we use an analogue of the ElGamal cryptosystem [14] using elliptic curves to improve its performance, the Elliptic Curve ElGamal (EC-ElGamal). For simplicity, only elliptic curves defined over a prime order finite field are considered.

Setup and Key Generation: The setup of the cryptosystem requires choosing a prime p, which defines a finite field $\mathbb{F}_p$, and two parameters a and b defining an elliptic curve E over $\mathbb{F}_p$. We also need an order m point $P \in E(\mathbb{F}_p)$, such that m is a large prime.

A private key is created by taking a random integer $d \in \{1, \ldots, m-1\}$. The corresponding public key is $Q = dP$.

Encryption: A point $V \in E(\mathbb{F}_p)$ is encrypted under public key Q as follows:

$$\mathrm{Enc}_Q(V) = C = (A, B) = (rP, V + rQ),$$

where r is a random integer in $\{1, \ldots, m-1\}$. When the value r is given as an input we denote the encryption as $\mathrm{Enc}_Q(V, r)$.

Decryption: A ciphertext $C = (A, B)$ can be decrypted when the private key d is known. The cleartext V is recovered by computing:

$$\mathrm{Dec}_d(C) = B - dA = V.$$

2.2 Zero Knowledge Proofs (ZKP)

A zero-knowledge proof [15] is a method by which a prover can prove to a verifier that a given statement is true, without conveying any additional information apart from the fact that the statement is indeed true. Most mixing protocols provide zero knowledge proofs [5,16] of correctness of a shuffle.

Equality of Discrete Logarithm: In order to provide cast as intended verifiability, the use of a ZKP of equality of discrete logarithms is required. Proving two points Y', Z' to have the same discrete logarithm s with two different bases Y, Z can be done in zero knowledge using the algorithm in [17]. We denote this proof as:

$$\mathrm{ECDLE}_s(Y, Y', Z, Z').$$

The ECDLE algorithm can be easily extended to work with EC-ElGamal ciphertexts instead of just points of the curve. We use the notation EECDLE (Elliptic ElGamal Ciphertext Discrete Logarithm Equality) to diferentiate when we are working with these ciphertexts:

$$\mathrm{EECDLE}_s(Y, Y', C, C').$$

where C and C' are EC-ElGamal ciphertext.

Correct Decryption: Given an EC-ElGamal ciphertext $C = \text{Enc}_Q(V) = (A, B)$ a decrypter may prove, in zero knowledge, the value V to be obtanied from the decryption of C by using $\text{ECDLE}_d(P, Q, A, B - V)$. In our proposal, when we use this construction we will use the following notation representing correct decryption proof:

$$\text{CDec}_d(C, P, Q).$$

Plaintext Equality: Proving two ciphertexts to be encryptions of the same plaintext can also be done using ECDLE. Given 2 EC-ElGamal ciphertexts $C = (A, B)$, $C' = (A, B')$ such that $C = \text{Enc}_Q(V, r)$ and $C' = \text{Enc}_{Q'}(V, r)$. A prover can compute $\text{ECDLE}_r(P, A, Q - Q', B - B')$ to demonstrate both C and C' to be encrypting the same value. We denote this proof as

$$\text{PTE}_r(C, C').$$

3   Our Proposal

In this section, we present an end to end verifiable voting protocol based on a previous proposal [13] of a vector-based homomorphic tallying remote voting system using a ZKP of correct mixing to prove ballot correctness. Our protocol uses return codes to allow voters to verify that the ballot generated by the voter's device contains a vote for the intended candidate. The main parts of the voting scheme remain the same but we added new steps in each phase to accomodate return codes without leaking compromising information.

3.1   Participating Roles

Our proposal includes a new entity (RCA) that was not present in the original voting scheme [13]. This entity is required to generate the information for the cast as intended verification. The new voting scheme involves the following entities:

- *Registrar:* It publishes the electoral roll on the bulletin board.
- *Talliers:* They are in charge of the private key of the election. They will perform a verifiable decryption when required.
- *Voters:* They choose a candidate and cast a ballot containing a vote for this candidate.
- *Polling Station (PS):* It collects the ballots cast by eligible voters. Checks the correctness of these ballots and publishes on the bulletin board all the public information of the election.
- *Return Code Authority (RCA):* This entity is in charge of generating return codes and retrieving them to the voters during the election.

We assume there exists a publicly readable bulletin board on which data such as the received ballots are published so that external entities can verify the correctness of the process. Only the Registrar, the Talliers and the PS can write on it.

3.2   System Description

This proposal provides individual cast as intended verifiability to the homomorphic tallying voting scheme presented in [13]. We kept the same three stages to mantain the workflow of the voting protocol but added some new computations in order to provide end to end verifiability using return codes. The stages composing the new voting protocol are detailed below.

Setup Stage. The first stage of the election is devoted to initialize and publish all the information required to run the protocol: the list of candidates, the electoral roll, and the cryptographic keys.

In order to do that the Talliers:

- Choose and publish an elliptic curve $E(\mathbb{F}_p)$ whose cardinality is divisible by a prime number m.
- Choose a point $P \in E(\mathbb{F}_p)$ of order m.
- Choose a private key d and publish the public key $Q = dP$.

The Talliers store the private key d in a secure way. For the sake of simplicity, we are going to use one secret key d and assume Talliers to be trusted. The original protocol distributes the key into a set of entities to avoid trust requirements.

Apart from that, the Registrar publishes:

- The electoral roll containing all the eligible voters $\{v_1, \ldots, v_n\}$ with their public keys $\{pk_1, \ldots, pk_n\}$.
- The list of candidates $L = \{L_1, \ldots, L_k\}$.

Any voter v_i may check pk_i to be the public key associated with her private key sk_i.

After that, the PS:

- Publishes a point $V \in E(\mathbb{F}_p)$ generated as $V = rP$ for a random r.
- Generates and publishes a vector of ciphertexts $C = (C_1, C_2, \ldots, C_k)$ where:

$$C_1 = \mathrm{Enc}_Q(V, 1),$$

and

$$C_j = \mathrm{Enc}_Q(\mathcal{O}, 1) \quad \text{for } j = 2, \ldots, k.$$

Once all the public information has been generated and published, the RCA generates the voting cards for each voter. A voting card [11] consists of a document containing the following information:

- *Voter key:* a key required to cast a ballot.
- *Voter commitment:* a point associated with the voter key.
- *Return codes:* A set of pairs (candidate, code), where code is an alphanumeric of length 6, and candidate represents a voting option.
- *Confirmation code:* A random value used to confirm that everything is ok.

The process to generate the voting cards requires a one-way function f which receives as input a point of the elliptic curve, and outputs a random 6 digit integer. Once the function is defined, the RCA may generate the voting cards as follows:

- The RCA chooses d' at random in $\{1 \ldots, m-1\}$ and publishes $Q' = d'P$.
- For each voter v_i:
  - Chooses ℓ_i at random in $\{1, \ldots, m-1\}$.
  - Chooses a random 16 characters alpha numeric value z_i.
  - Computes $w_i = \ell_i \cdot d'$.
  - Computes the list $w_i V, 2w_i V, \ldots, k\, w_i V$ (as many values as candidates).
  - Computes $rc_j = f(jw_i V)$ for $j = 1, \ldots, k$.
  - Prints a voting card containing ℓ_i as a voter key, the voter commitment $U_i = \ell_i P$, the return codes as pairs

$$((L_1, rc_1)), \ldots, (L_k, rc_k)),$$

  and the confirmation code z_i.
- Sends each printed voting card to its corresponding voter.
- Publishes the set $\{\mathcal{H}(U_1, z_1), \ldots, \mathcal{H}(U_n, z_n)\}$ in the bulletin board.

Each voter will require the information in the voting card to cast her ballot. Although the voting card could be sent in other ways, we have chosen a paper voting card because it does not require any other device to check it.

Vote Casting Stage. Once the setup phase has ended, each voter v_i may cast her ballot. As in the original proposal [13], a ballot will consists of a vector of ciphertexts $(C_{i1}, \ldots, C_{ik})$ in which, if v_i is voting for candidate L_s then C_{is} will be an encryption of V under the public key of the election Q. The rest of ciphertexts C_{ij} will be an encryption of $\mathcal{O}$ for $j \neq s$.

More in detail, to generate her ballot, a voter v_i would proceed as follows:

1. Checks that $C = (C_1, \ldots, C_k)$ are encrypted using 1 as a random value. She should obtain V for $j = 1$, and $\mathcal{O}$ for $1 < j \leq k$.
2. Generates at random $\{r_{ij}\}_{1 \leq j \leq k}$ where $r_{ij} \in \{1, \ldots, m-1\}$.
3. Creates a permutation π of k elements such that $\pi(s) = 1$.
4. Permutes C into $C'_{v_i} = (C'_{i1}, \ldots, C'_{ik})$ such that $C'_{ij} = C_{\pi(j)}$. Hence, $C'_{is} = C_1$.
5. Computes $C_{ij} = C'_{ij} + \text{Enc}_Q(\mathcal{O}, r_{ij})$. Obtaining the resulting vector $C_{v_i} = (C_{i1}, \ldots, C_{ik})$.
6. Generates a zero-knowledge proof α_i of correctness of a shuffle that guarantees C_{v_i} to be the result of shuffling C.

Once the ballot C_{v_i} is generated, the voter generates the values and proofs which will allow to verify the ballot to be cast as intended. In order to do that, the voter v_i:

1. Computes the homomorphic aggregation $T'_i = \sum_{j=1}^{k} jC_{ij}$.

2. Computes the random value $r_i = \sum_{j=1}^{k} j \cdot r_{ij}$.
3. Generates the ciphertext $T_i = \text{Enc}_{Q'}(sV, r_i)$, where L_s is her voting choice.
4. Multiplies using her voter key $X_i = \ell_i T_i$.
5. Proves correctness of the process by computing

$$\beta_i = \text{EECDLE}_{\ell_i}(P, U_i, T_i, X_i),$$

$$\delta_i = \text{PTE}_{r_i}(T_i, T_i').$$

Finally, the voter generates her digital signature $\text{Sig}_{sk_i}(C_{v_i}, T_i, X_i, \alpha_i, \beta_i, \delta_i)$ using her private key sk_i and sends:

$$C_{v_i}, T_i, X_i, \alpha_i, \beta_i, \delta_i, \text{Sig}_{sk_i}(C_{v_i}, T_i, X_i, \alpha_i, \beta_i, \delta_i), pk_i$$

to the PS.

When the PS receives all this information, it proceeds as follows:

1. Checks if pk_i is published on the electoral roll.
2. Checks that the voter has not voted before.
3. Validates the signature using pk_i.
4. Checks that vector C_{v_i} do not contain ciphertexts that appear in any previously received ballot.
5. Verifies the zero-knowledge proof of mixing α_i.
6. If all the checkings are satisfied, it sends the following information to the RCA:

$$C_{v_i}, T_i, X_i, \beta_i, \delta_i.$$

When the RCA receives these values, it starts a protocol to find the corresponding return code. The RCA proceeds as follows:

1. Computes the homomorphic aggregation $T_i' = \sum_{j=1}^{k} j C_{ij}$.
2. Verifies β_i and δ_i.
3. Computes $W_i = d' X_i$.
4. Generates the ZKP $\gamma_i = \text{EECDLE}_{d'}(P, Q', X_i, W_i)$.
5. Decrypts W_i to find the original value from which the return code was generated $\text{Dec}_{d'}(W_i) = s\,w_i V$.
6. Generates the ZKP $\mu_i = \text{CDec}_{d'}(W_i, P, Q')$.
7. Securely stores the proof μ_i to allow private audits. This is done to prevent RCA from generating fake return codes.
8. Computes the digital signature $\text{Sig}_{d'}(f(s\,w_i V), W_i, \gamma_i)$ and sends

$$f(s\,w_i V), W_i, \gamma_i, \text{Sig}_{d'}(f(s\,w_i V), W_i, \gamma_i)$$

to the PS which publishes the information on the bulletin board.

Once the PS receives the information from the RCA, it first sends the return code $f(s\,w_i V)$ to the voter and waits for a response. The voter checks if the return code corresponds to her voting choice and, if this is the case, she sends the confirmation code z_i to the PS. The PS checks if it is the correct confirmation code by computing $\mathcal{H}(U_i, z_i)$ and checking if there is a match in the table that was previously published in the bulletin board. If it finds the same value on the table then the PS publishes

$$C_{v_i}, T_i, X_i, W_i, \alpha_i, \beta_i, \delta_i, \gamma_i,$$

and the digital signatures, from the voter and from the RCA, on the bulletin board.

Once a ballot is published on the bulletin board, a private auditor may ask RCA to send him μ_i and verify that the voter has not been deceived by the RCA. Notice that this information cannot be provided before sending the appropriate confirmation code because the auditor could collude with the voting client and would be able to compute valid return codes for the voter v_i.

Tallying Stage. The last stage takes place when the established voting period concludes. In this stage the election results are obtained and published in the bulletin board. The tallying process remains the same from the original paper, and can be summarised in three steps:

1. Homomorphically aggregate all the ciphertexts in the same position of each vector.
2. Verifiably decrypt each resulting ciphertext, one for each possible candidate of the election.
3. Find the elliptic curve discrete logarithm with base V of the point resulting from the decryptions of the previous step. This discrete logarithm has n possible solutions and can be easily precomputed or just computed during the decryption.

Finally, the resulting values are published in the bulletin board as the amount of votes for each candidate. Apart from that, the proofs of correct decryption are also published so that the election integrity becomes universally verifiable.

4 Security

The original proposal already provided a security analysis focusing on privacy and integrity. In this section, we discuss how security of the proposal remains unaffected with the additions we have made to the protocol. Moreover, we will also proof that our protocol is end to end verifiable.

The security of our protocol is based on the following assumptions:

- The elliptic curve discrete logarithm problem (ECDLP) can not be solved with a polynomial algorithm.
- The RCA does not leak any information about the generated return codes or the value r.
- The Talliers do not decrypt ballots, only the aggregated ciphertext.

4.1   Integrity

Election integrity must guarantee the voting protocol not to allow election results modification. Given that our solution does not modify the original ballot and does not add any information to be tallied, integrity of our protocol relies on the integrity of the original voting scheme [13] which has been proven.

It is easy to negligiblehas not been modified in our contribution. Hence, the chances to modify the election results without being noticed are neglible.

Moreover, guaranteeing voters eligibility and unicity is done by means of the digital signature of each ballot, and the ZKP of correct composition as detailed in [13]. This protocol was proven to be secure and we have not changed this.

4.2   Privacy

An election provides privacy if nobody is able to find the relation between a voter and her voting choice. As it is proven in [13], the original voting protocol already offers privacy against external attackers. Here, we prove the newly generated information to keep preserving privacy.

Given that, the published information from the original voting scheme provides privacy, we focus on the additional data which is published in our proposal:

$$T_i, X_i, \beta_i, \delta_i, f(s\,w_iV), W_i, \gamma_i.$$

By definition, the ZKPs β_i, δ_i, and γ_i do not leak any information apart from the fact that their statements are true. Additionally, T_i is an EC-ElGamal ciphertext. Since EC-ElGamal is IND-CPA secure, no information about the cleartext is leaked. Moreover, the points X_i and W_i are obtained from a scalar point multiplication. The only way to find the secret values ℓ_i and d_i' is by solving the ECDLP which we assumed unfeasible in the security assumptions. Finally, $f(s\,w_iV)$ is the result of the one way function f. The value itself does not give any information and to find the point sw_iV would require to break the one-way property. Hence, privacy is preserved in our proposal.

Notice that, the RCA has all the information of the voting choices. To prevent that, we could distribute the voting card generation so that the link between w_iV and ℓ_i remains secret. For simplicity, we did not focus on this part and just assumed the RCA being trustworthy, so it keeps the information secret.

To achieve privacy when the voting device is compromised requires of a coercion resistant strategy such as [18]. Our proposal provides privacy against external attackers. However, it could be adapted to cast the ballot in a way that prevents privacy disclosure when voting from a missbehaving voting machine using the above mentioned strategy.

4.3   Verifiability

The integrity of a voting scheme does not guarantee that its implementation also provides this security property. In order to provide tools to ensure the integrity of an implementation, our voting protocol generates a set of proofs which allow any verifier to check that an implementation performs all the steps properly.

Our solution is end to end verifiable because it provides recorded as cast, counted as recorded, and cast as intended verifiability.

Recorded as Cast: Being able to verify if a ballot is recorded as it was cast ensures the voter that her vote has not been modified after being cast. This kind of verification is usually performed by checking the digital signature. In our protocol, the voter digitally signs her ballot C_{v_i} and the ZKPs guaranteeing ballot correctness. Anyone can check the signatures in the bulletin board and be sure that the ballots where recorded as cast. This property is universally verifiable.

Counted as Recorded: This verifiability property guarantees that the results are a correct decryption of the received ballots. This was already addressed in the original proposal. As it was stated in [13], anyone can verify the aggregated ballots to come from the aggregation of the digitally signed ballots received by the polling station and published in the bulletin board. Moreover, the aggregated ballots are verifiably decrypted, hence, the tally can be universally verified.

Cast as Intended: The last verifiability property ensures that when a voter casts her ballot, the ballot generated by the voting client contains a vote for the voting option intended to vote.

We want to prove that a misbehaving voting client is not able to cast a valid vote containing a different voting option from the intended one, and nobody notices. We provide a game based [19] definition of the problem:

Game A: the Attacker tries to cast a valid vote different from the intended and nobody notices

Challenger ("Talliers" + "RCA" + "Voter"): generates
  $(Q, d) \leftarrow \mathsf{GenKeyPair}()$
  $(Q', d') \leftarrow \mathsf{GenKeyPair}()$
  $\ell_i \xleftarrow{\$} \{1, \ldots, m-1\}$
  for $j = 1, \ldots k$:
    $rc_j \leftarrow f(j \cdot d' \cdot \ell_i \cdot P)$
  Sends Q, Q', V, ℓ_i, and the voting option x to the Attacker. Assume these values as implicit inputs for the remaining algorithms.
Attacker: Computes
  $(C_{v_i}, T_i, X_i, \alpha_i, \beta_i, \delta_i) \leftarrow \mathsf{Alg1}(\ldots)$
  Sends $(C_{v_i}, T_i, X_i, \alpha_i, \beta_i, \delta_i)$ to the Challenger.
Challenger ("RCA" + "PS"): If $\mathsf{VerifyZKP}(C_{v_i}, T_i, X_i, \alpha_i, \beta_i, \delta_i) = 1$, then sends
  $rc' \leftarrow f(\mathsf{Dec}_{d'}(d' \cdot X_i))$.
  Else sets $\hat{rc} = \perp$ and finishes the game.

Attacker: Compute
$$\hat{rc} \leftarrow \mathsf{Alg2}(C_{v_i}, T_i, X_i, \alpha_i, \beta_i, \delta_i, rc', ...),$$
and sends $\hat{rc}$ to the voter.

Challenger ("Voter"): If $\hat{rc} = rc_x$ it sends z_i and finishes the game.

Attacker: If challenger does not send z_i then
$$\hat{z}_i \leftarrow \mathsf{Alg3}(C_{v_i}, T_i, X_i, \alpha_i, \beta_i, \delta_i, \hat{rc}, rc', ...)$$

Define S^A (attacker succeeds) as the event that $C_{ix} = \mathrm{Enc}_Q(\mathcal{O})$ and $\hat{rc} = rc_x$, or $\hat{z}_i = z_i$.

It is easy to see that Alg1 is highly limited to generate the values properly because of the ZKPs $\alpha_i, \beta_i, \delta_i$. The probability to cheat verifyZKP ϵ_{zkp} is negligible due to the soundness property of these proofs. Accordingly, the attacker depends on either Alg2 or Alg3 to succeed.

The attacker needs Alg2 to find $\hat{rc}$ such that $\hat{rc} = rc_x$. However, the algorithm does not receive d' or rc_x as input but receives $s\,\ell_i V$ and rc'. Since f function is one-way and random, Alg2 could try a brute force attack to find d' but with a message space of 2^{256} the success rate ϵ_{ow} is negligible. The remaining option is to randomly obtain rc_x with only one try which gives a success rate of 1 out of 10^6.

Apart from that, the attacker could also succeed if he directly obtains the confirmation code z_i and bypasses all voter interaction using Alg3. However, z_i is a random 16 characters alpha numeric value independent from the input of the algorithm Alg3. Therefore, the success rate of Alg3 is about 2^{-80}.

As a result, the success probability of the attacker is

$$\Pr[S^A] = \epsilon_{\mathrm{zkp}} + \epsilon_{\mathrm{ow}} + \frac{1}{10^6} + \frac{1}{2^{80}},$$

which is almost the same probability of randomly guessing rc_x or z_i.

5 Conclusions

We have proposed a secure voting scheme that provides end to end verifiability. Previous solutions required voters to have a second device because they used algebraic operations with long integers. Our scheme, in contrast, simplifies the verification by using short return codes that voters can use to validate that their ballots were cast as intended. Moreover, our proposal requires voters participation by means of a confirmation code. This way, an attacker can not bypass the voter and succeed casting a ballot for a different choice.

References

1. Fujioka, A., Okamoto, T., Ohta, K.: A practical secret voting scheme for large scale elections. In: Seberry, J., Zheng, Y. (eds.) AUSCRYPT 1992. LNCS, vol. 718, pp. 244–251. Springer, Heidelberg (1993). doi:10.1007/3-540-57220-1_66

2. Mateu, V., Sebé, F., Valls, M.: Constructing credential-based e-voting systems from offline e-coin protocols. J. Netw. Comput. Appl. **42**, 39–44 (2014)
3. Chaum, D.: Untraceable electronic mail, return addresses, and digital pseudonyms. Commun. ACM **24**(2), 84–90 (1981)
4. Mateu, V., Miret, J.M., Sebé, F.: Verifiable encrypted redundancy for mix-type remote electronic voting. In: Andersen, K.N., Francesconi, E., Grönlund, Å., Engers, T.M. (eds.) EGOVIS 2011. LNCS, vol. 6866, pp. 370–385. Springer, Heidelberg (2011). doi:10.1007/978-3-642-22961-9_29
5. Bayer, S., Groth, J.: Efficient zero-knowledge argument for correctness of a shuffle. In: Pointcheval, D., Johansson, T. (eds.) EUROCRYPT 2012. LNCS, vol. 7237, pp. 263–280. Springer, Heidelberg (2012). doi:10.1007/978-3-642-29011-4_17
6. Hirt, M., Sako, K.: Efficient receipt-free voting based on homomorphic encryption. In: Preneel, B. (ed.) EUROCRYPT 2000. LNCS, vol. 1807, pp. 539–556. Springer, Heidelberg (2000). doi:10.1007/3-540-45539-6_38
7. Adida, B., Marneffe, O.D., Pereira, O., Quisquater, J.J.: Electing a university president using open-audit voting: analysis of real-world use of helios. In: Electronic Voting Technology/Workshop on Trustworthy Elections (EVT/WOTE) (2009)
8. Joaquim, R.: How to prove the validity of a complex ballot encryption to the voter and the public. J. Inf. Secur. Appl. **19**(2), 130–142 (2014)
9. Sako, K., Kilian, J.: Receipt-free mix-type voting scheme. In: Guillou, L.C., Quisquater, J.-J. (eds.) EUROCRYPT 1995. LNCS, vol. 921, pp. 393–403. Springer, Heidelberg (1995). doi:10.1007/3-540-49264-X_32
10. Gjøsteen, K.: The norwegian internet voting protocol. In: Kiayias, A., Lipmaa, H. (eds.) Vote-ID 2011. LNCS, vol. 7187, pp. 1–18. Springer, Heidelberg (2012). doi:10.1007/978-3-642-32747-6_1
11. Allepuz, J.P., Castelló, S.G.: Internet voting system with cast as intended verification. In: Kiayias, A., Lipmaa, H. (eds.) Vote-ID 2011. LNCS, vol. 7187, pp. 36–52. Springer, Heidelberg (2012). doi:10.1007/978-3-642-32747-6_3
12. Galindo, D., Guasch, S., Puiggalí, J.: 2015 neuchãtel's cast-as-intended verification mechanism. In: Haenni, R., Koenig, R.E., Wikström, D. (eds.) VOTELID 2015. LNCS, vol. 9269, pp. 3–18. Springer, Cham (2015). doi:10.1007/978-3-319-22270-7_1
13. Mateu, V., Miret, J.M., Sebé, F.: A hybrid approach to vector-based homomorphic tallying remote voting. Int. J. Inf. Secur. **15**(2), 211–221 (2016)
14. ElGamal, T.: A public key cryptosystem and a signature scheme based on discrete logarithms. IEEE Trans. Inf. Theory **31**(4), 469–472 (1985)
15. Goldwasser, S., Micali, S., Rackoff, C.: The knowledge complexity of interactive proof systems. SIAM J. Comput. **18**(1), 186–208 (1989)
16. Wikström, D.: Simplified submission of inputs to protocols. In: Ostrovsky, R., Prisco, R., Visconti, I. (eds.) SCN 2008. LNCS, vol. 5229, pp. 293–308. Springer, Heidelberg (2008). doi:10.1007/978-3-540-85855-3_20
17. Chaum, D., Pedersen, T.P.: Wallet databases with observers. In: Brickell, E.F. (ed.) CRYPTO 1992. LNCS, vol. 740, pp. 89–105. Springer, Heidelberg (1993). doi:10.1007/3-540-48071-4_7
18. Yi, X., Okamoto, E.: Practical internet voting system. J. Netw. Comput. Appl. **36**(1), 378–387 (2013)
19. Shoup, V.: Sequences of games: a tool for taming complexity in security proofs. IACR Cryptol. ePrint Arch. **2004**, 332 (2004)

E-Government Cases - Data and Knowledge Management

Institutionalization of the Reengineering of Strategic Management Processes in the Brazilian Public Management: A Case Study in Federal Government Organizations

Marçal Chagas[✉], Ricardo Gomes, Paulo Henrique Bermejo, and José Martins

University of Brasília, Brasília, Brazil
marcalchagas@hotmail.com

Abstract. Strategic management processes have been increasingly seen as essential to the effectiveness of public organizations. In the context of the Brazilian public management, the administrative reforms that undertook efforts to transform strategic management processes, usually, show little institutional sedimentation. The objective of the research was to analyze which practices implemented by the public organizations studied contribute to the advancement in the stage of institutionalization of its strategic management processes and models. The work was based on an applied, descriptive research with a qualitative approach, in which a case study was done in two public organizations, which have models of strategic management for more than five years. The analyzes were carried out from three theoretical perspectives: historical-analytical, institutional and technical. The results show that the technical motivations overlapped the isomorphic pressures. It was observed that the greatest difficulty of organizations in the advance of institutionalization resided in the practices of governance, confirming the theoretical propositions presented. Confirming part of the institutional theory, the actor's perception regarding the benefits brought by Reengineerings have contributed to its maintenance. As for the adherence of the institutional theory, it was possible to observe theoretical gaps in the new institutionalism, with emphasis on the overestimation of the isomorphic mechanisms.

Keywords: Business process reengineering · Transformation and change management

1 Introduction

Strategic management processes have been increasingly seen as essential to the effectiveness of public organizations [1–3]. From the perspective of good public governance, the most recent literature offers a broad argument about the importance of this type of processes as one of the attributes of quality and institutional capacity of a public organization, functioning as a mechanism for building strategic agenda, legitimacy, convergence Of efforts, accountability and transparency [4–7].

In the public sector, strategic management processes can be framed within an area called public management policies [8], and essentially group activities and artifacts that deal with the formulation, unfolding and monitoring of organizational strategies.

© Springer International Publishing AG 2017
A. Kő and E. Francesconi (Eds.): EGOVIS 2017, LNCS 10441, pp. 221–235, 2017.
DOI: 10.1007/978-3-319-64248-2_16

Historically in Brazil, public administration reforms that dealt with public management policies, planning, management or any initiative analogous to strategic management processes, faced numerous problems and distortions [9–13], which are widely discussed in the literature and, although they may offer good explanatory power, they seem to resent an integrated approach that provides a practical overview of how historical, institutional, and technical issues relate, residing in this point one of the contributions of this work.

Another contribution of this article is to verify the stage of institutionalization of some recents initiatives in Brazilian public organizations, adopted here as defined by Tolbert and Zucker [14, 15], that is, in what measures such Reengineering initiatives are based in those organizations that were objects of the empirical investigation carried out by this work. According to Tolbert and Zucker [15], despite the considerable body of work, little attention has been paid to the conceptualization of the processes of institutionalization.

Bryson et al. [16] is another author who highlights the need for new research within the theme explored here. Referring more specifically to strategic management processes, Bryson et al. [16] states that:

"Given the increasing and widespread use of public sector strategic planning, new research on what exactly works best in which situations and why would be useful" [16].

Thus, the following research question was defined for this work: "How have brazilian federal public organizations been working to institutionalize the Reengineering in their strategic management processes?" From this questioning, this work aimed to investigate how public organizations institutionalize and transform their strategic management processes.

To achieve this objective, an investigation was carried out based on the theoretical frameworks on institutional theory and practices of process management and strategic management. Based on these theories and practices, a qualitative multicase study was conducted in Brazilian public organizations from August to December 2016, as it will be presented in the following sections.

Considering this first introductory section, this article is structured in a total of five sections: the second section presents and systematizes the theoretical bases that supported the research work; the third section discusses the elements that compose the research methodology used; the fourth section presents the initiatives of Reengineering of strategic management processes of the organizations that compose the case study and brings the main results achieved by this work and respective discussions; and the fifth and last section elaborates a set of conclusions of the work and proposes directions for new researches.

2   Theoretical Foundation

Considering the complexity of the topic, the paper addresses the issues that involve the Reengineering and institutionalization of strategic management processes in Brazilian public organizations from three specific perspectives. The historical-analytical perspective aims to generate a contextual reflection and therefore provides a panoramic view of the administrative reform attempts undertaken in the Brazilian government and the distortions and flaws that constituted them.

The institutional perspective is used to understand the motivations, the institutionalization process and the institutional capacity to promote the Reengineering of the strategic management processes of the organizations analyzed in here. The technical perspective provided theoretical support for the Reengineering initiatives to be appreciated prescriptively in the light of conceptual models of strategic management processes enshrined in the literature. The following topics will briefly present the theories that support each of these perspectives.

2.1 Historical-Analytical Perspective: Context of Administrative Reforms in Brazil

Motta's [10] statement that in the last 40 years, in the Brazilian public administration, new practices and expectations of modernization were developed, but many of its traditional characteristics were not removed, serves as a background for the analyzes reflected here.

It can be affirmed that there seems to be a pattern of discontinuity in the trajectory of reforms in the Brazilian public administration, a fact that is consequently harmful to the initiatives related to planning and management [17, 18]. For Martins [13], the Brazilian public administration persistently lives with a dichotomy between politics and bureaucracy.

Martins [13] demonstrates this dichotomous bureaucratic pattern by re-reading attempts to modernize the Brazilian administration, beginning with the Vargas era and the interventionist model undertaken at the time, mainly through the Administrative Department of the Public Service [DASP]. The author states that "the modernization of the natives was essentially dissociative: Implemented an administrative state off politics [...] constituting, in this period, forms of insulated autonomy and autocratic regulation" [pp. 11–12].

The period of redemocratization, between 1945 and 1964, as shown by Martins [13], was marked by institutional dismantling and the presence of clientelism. The sequence, post-1964, although marked by a strong modernizing character, notably by Decree Law no. 200, also practiced the dichotomy, insulating the state of politics, while at the same time not mitigating patrimonialist practices [13]. The new period of redemocratization, which began in 1985, had as its hallmark characteristics the physiology, the idea of corporatism and the excessive politicization of the public service, again resulting in the dissociation between politics and public administration, having a patronizing and standard political regulation insertion.

Even in a more current context, in which governance discussions gain strength and thus signal an increase in management's influence over politics [and vice versa], a functional integration between politics and administration does not seem to exist [13] For the author, the challenge is to establish a pattern where politics and bureaucracy interact with both the requirements of social insertion and political regulation.

Rezende [9] also examined the problem of permanent failure in administrative reform policies, exemplifying the process of conception and summary extinction of

MARE [Ministry of Federal Administration and State Reform] in the period 1995–1998. Cardoso [18], specifically discussing the relationship between planning and management processes, demonstrates that over the years these two components have been taking turns in terms of "primacy", sometimes in moments when management has been privileged over planning, sometimes in others where this situation is reversed.

2.2   Institutional Perspective: Transformation and Institutionalization

A reengineering initiative in any organization also needs to be analyzed from a "spatial" dimension, as Tolbert and Zucker [15] argue by stating that what each organization mobilizes for a given Reengineering initiative certainly influences its achievement and Institutionalization. Starting from this premise, the institutionalist theories gather high explanatory power. There is a consensus among the various currents of institutional theory about skepticism about full rationality, emphasizing that organizations, in an objective reality, reveal aspects that do not consist of a purely rationalist approach [20].

DiMaggio and Powell [20] bring the idea of isomorphism, basically arguing that organizations, in the quest for legitimacy, power and adequacy, aim at the homogenization of their practices and structures [20]. The authors understand that organizations are subject to continuous environmental pressures that force this homogenization, and the pressure mechanisms fall into three basic types of isomorphism: coercive, mimetic and normative. The coercive isomorphism is the result of pressures exerted by external organizations, whereas the mimetic is more propagated in institutional environments endowed with a high degree of instability and uncertainty, where organizations commonly become susceptible to imitation practices. The normative has links with the question of professionalization, when occupational groups seek to discipline a set of conditions and methods that must prevail in that particular area of activity, exerting, in this way, a cognitive pressure with the legitimacy and autonomy of the professionals located there.

Another contribution of institutional theory concerns the institutionalization process itself, which is essential for tracking how new constructions and social Reengineerings [organizational structures and practices] have [or do not have] a rule character in certain organizations. The concepts developed by Tolbert and Zucker [14, 15] offer propositions that allow an elucidation of how new structures and organizational initiatives are typically processalized and institutionalized in organizations.

The authors consider that a process of institutionalization and Reengineering is permeated by three sequential subprocesses: habitualization, objectification and sedimentation, according Fig. 1. Habitualization is found in what they consider as the stage of pre-institutionalization, where new structures are formulated to respond to organizational problems. Objectification represents a movement towards the stage of semi-institutionalization, when the structure launched advances in terms of diffusion and consensus on the results it promised. What authors classify as "total institutionalization" is in the stage of sedimentation, when a Reengineering demonstrates a historical continuity, with a wide spread of its results and is taken for granted by the actors.

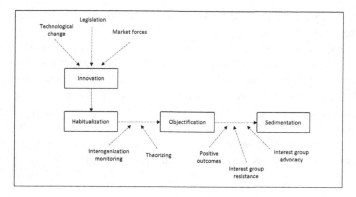

Fig. 1. Institutionalization processes (Source: adapted from Tolbert e Zucker [15])

2.3   Technical Perspective: Strategic Management Processes

It must be considered that the Reengineering of strategic management processes, as well as other organizational initiatives, will face problems in their institutionalization if they do not meet technical requirements [15]. In this logic, this section discusses models that form the knowledge field of strategic management processes in the public sector, aiming to list elements that are configured as technical requirements for the institutionalization of a Reengineering initiative.

Process management, more broadly, refers to practices, approaches and tools for managing business processes, in order to align them with strategic objectives and optimize them to achieve organizational efficiency [21]. In a context that governments must deal with financial pressures, demographic pressures and globalization, the management of processes becomes essential to enable the digitilization of activities and the efficiency of public organizations, especially in nations such as Brazil whose volumes of public expenses are increasing and are very expressive.

Typically, business processes are grouped into three main categories: end-to-end processes, support processes, and management processes. Strategic management processes fall into the latter category and typically respond to activities that provide technical support to organizations. Among these activities are those dealing with planning, strategic alignment and monitoring of organizational performance.

Given the relevance, strategic management processes have been widely discussed in the literature of private and public organizations [22], with some authors dedicated to the construction of specific concepts, approaches and models for strategic management processes.

Wheelen and Hunger [23] consider that the processes that make up the strategic management must include process of analysis of the environment, strategy formulation process, implementation process and results evaluation process, encompassing a larger scope than strategic planning only, worrying with how this plan will be implemented and monitored.

For Martins and Marini [24], strategic management processes should group activities into three blocks: building the strategic agenda; alignment of the implementing organizational architecture; and implementation of monitoring and evaluation mechanisms.

In a similar way, Joyce and Drumaux [25] proposes a model in which strategic management processes form a "decision flow diagram", starting with activities of definition of the organizational mission, passing a stage of strategic analysis [stakeholder analysis, situational analysis] And a formulation phase [definition of strategic objectives, definition of courses of action and feasibility analysis] and deployed to implementation plans. Kaplan and Norton [26] in their most recent publications, the authors present a system that has been termed a "closed loop of strategic management processes", adhering to private and public organizations. Figure 2 below represents this system.

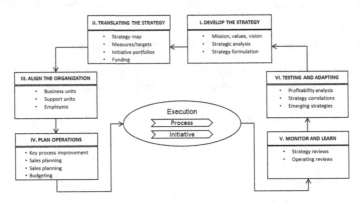

Fig. 2. System of strategic management processes (Source: adapted from Kaplan e Norton [19])

The system is composed of a sequence of six macroprocesses necessary to think strategic management. The first three steps are dedicated to the formulation, definition of results to be achieved and organizational alignment, all materialized in strategic components [strategic map, indicators, goals, strategic initiatives, budget]. The fourth step deals with organizational readiness to reach the strategic challenges and performs a diagnosis on the main elements of the operation. The last two steps are responsible for monitoring and adjusting the strategic definitions. The six steps generate as a product the strategic plan and the operational plan.

From this brief theoretical review of models and processes of strategic management and based on other authors of the field of knowledge, it was possible to construct a conceptual model of analysis that synthesizes the main processes that should be contained in an idealized model of applied strategic management processes. To the public sector, as shown in Fig. 3. The definition and implementation of such processes must be perceived with a set of requirements, without which an initiative of Reengineering in strategic management processes would suffer losses in the advance of its stages of institutionalization.

As it can be seen, the structure is organized in three main macroprocesses, supported by the respective processes, similar to the theoretical models presented here

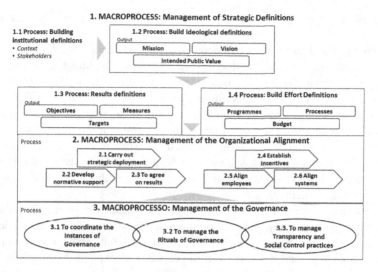

Fig. 3. Strategic management processes for public sector (Source: elaboration of the author).

previously in the previous section, but with some specificities and requirements, which were served as reference for an investigation of the strategic management processes of the organizations studied.

3   Research Methodology

The methodology chosen to develop the study was the qualitative research, with an explanatory objective, characterizing itself as descriptive, considering that, based on the analysis of the data obtained in the interviews and in the documentary research, the factors that may influence the institutionalization of the Strategic management processes in the analyzed organizations.

The case study structure chosen is that of multiple organizations, and the organizations were chosen considering the following criteria: federal public organizations that have initiated Reengineering initiatives in their strategic management processes for at least five years, adequate time to verify the internship stage. Institutionalization, which operate in different sectors, in order to observe possible differentiations or generalizations in different fields of action; And federal public organizations that demonstrated feasibility for the application of the study.

Based on these criteria, two organizations were defined, which at the request of these organizations, the confidentiality of the work was preserved and, therefore, we have agreed to denominate them as organization "A" and organization "B".

Organization "A" is a Federal Regulatory Agency, with the attribution of regulating the national services and basins and counts 355 servers. The "B" organization is a Public Company, whose corporate purpose is to plan, deploy and operate the postal service, to explore integrated logistics, financial and electronic postal services and to carry out other related activities, is present in all Brazilian municipalities and has 117,405 employees.

The research was developed based on primary and secondary data. The primary data were collected from semi-structured interviews, containing a script of main questions, built from the propositions previously presented and complemented by questions inherent to the momentary circumstances of the interview [27]. The definition of the interviewees took into account the role assumed by a particular actor in the process of institutionalizing strategic management. Among those interviewed, there are those who acted as champions [concept used by Tolbert and Zucker [15]] in the implementation project, who assumed a technical role, responsible for the operationalization and those who have some routine contact with components designed by the strategic management model.

The secondary data were accessed through documentary research. The data were treated through content analysis, based on inferences based on the characteristics of the analyzed content [28]. Thematic categories were created that served to encode the most frequent consensuses [and dissent], with the capacity to explain the problem.

In order to ensure the validity of the results, a double source of evidence, both documentary and field, was used through the interviews to perform the triangulation.

Concerning internal validity, because it is a study that is not exclusively explanatory, the concern with this nature of validity does not necessarily need to be sought, since it does not aim to offer causal propositions [29]. Regarding external validity, which specifically concerns the generalization of discoveries, it should be pointed out that from the present it would not be possible to have any kind of statistical generalization, given its limitation in terms of number of cases and of respondents.

4   Development of the Case Study, Results and Discussion

In order to facilitate the line of reasoning of the analysis in relation to the research objectives, the descriptions were carried out in a narrative form, divided into five categories, as shown in Fig. 4.

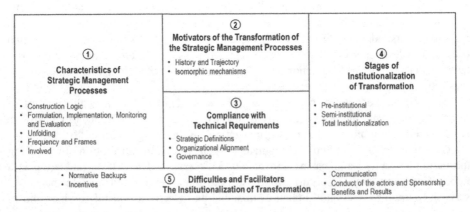

Fig. 4. Categories of analysis (Source: elaboration of the author).

The first category is used to describe what the processes of strategic management adopted by the analyzed organizations are and how they work. The motivators of adoption category was used to understand how decision makers became aware of the importance of implementing Reengineering in their strategic management processes and eventually whether practices adopted by similar organizations or coercive and normative aspects influenced the decision. The technical requirements category was based on the propositions made by the theoretical models described and the previously consolidated conceptual model of analysis, in an attempt to gauge the quality in which the formulation, implementation and monitoring and evaluation processes were conceived and are being conducted. By the stages of institutionalization category, it was inferred at what stage of the process of institutionalization of Reengineering the processes of strategic management would be framed, based on the stages and the sub-processes of institutionalization, proposed by Tolbert and Zucker [14], previously described. Finally, the last category had as its purpose to list the main elements that acted [and act] as factors that are difficult and facilitating the progress of Reengineering.

4.1   Results – Organization "A"

Organization "A" structures its strategic management processes in three main dimensions, each with its respective instruments: strategic dimension, with long-term management activities; tactical dimension, with processes that establish and manage definitions for four years; and operational dimension, with activities and instruments for the annual allocation of budgetary and operational resources.

In the perception of the interviewees in the area of strategic planning, the reasons that motivated the "A" organization to implement the Reengineering in its strategic management processes are more related to technical issues, appearing not to have the influence of mimetic or normative mechanisms. According to them, several environmental crises revealed the institutional ineptitude in predicting and responding to contextual changes, thus generating an urgent need to implant typical mechanisms of a strategic management model, leading to the need for process Reengineering.

From a structural point of view, the Organization "A" demonstrates that it meets the technical requirements. The existence of the various artifacts of the planning processes and of the management processes corroborate this assertion. There is formalization for the basic elements, institutional commitments [mission, vision and guidelines] are properly recorded. The connection and the various artifacts responsible for the link between strategic, tactical and operational are also formalized and organized. Other elements such as projects, indicators and goals are also defined and explained. There is also a computerized system that functions as a repository of all information and as a platform for monitoring and updating the results.

However, governance processes still have gaps. The rites of monitoring and evaluation follow an ad hoc agenda and the updating of the information of the results is still inefficient.

In a ten year period, it was only in the last six years that the strategic management processes began to gain some formalization, when at that time the organization contracted a consultancy to transform, formalize and communicate its great strategic declarations [mission, vision and values], moving on to a new stage of institutionalization, when efforts at objectification and diffusion began to gain momentum. These efforts gained momentum in planning 2008–2020, when it gained more materiality and consequently greater institutional strength. The fact that, since 2008, strategic management activities have been carried out, basically by the same team, has proved to be fundamental for maintaining the technical memory and the perenniality of the processes.

Figure 5 below illustrates the evolution curve of the Reengineering of the strategic management processes of Organization "A", as proposed by Tolbert and Zucker [15].

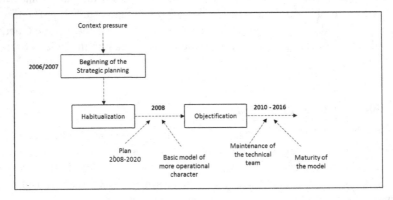

Fig. 5. Institutionalization process - Organization "A" (Source: elaboration of the author).

It is possible to perceive that the organization is in an advanced stage of the process of institutionalization. Obviously, it is necessary to consider the possible biases in the perception of those who analyze the stage of institutionalization of a particular practice. It is natural that the interviewees in the planning area have a greater sensitivity than those who are allocated in the finalist areas, a fact that was considered to establish the institutionalization stage described above.

The point of most attention really lies in the issue of governance. With respect to normative endorsements, their effects are considered neutral, that is, they were important but not preponderant. At present, the organization does not use the agreement of results, which causes a difficult effect in the process of institutionalization. With regard to incentives, the most eloquent practice was the variable compensation linked to the achievement of strategic planning goals, which is being reviewed, due to the distortions that had been causing the behavior of the servers. Communication is one of the factors that has been acting most in the sense of hindering the advance of institutionalization, especially to the more operational levels of the organization. As for the benefits brought by strategic management processes, managers in the planning area understand that the strategic management model currently underway brings innumerable benefits to the organization, since the interviewees of the finalistic areas do not attribute the same relevance. Finally, the behavior of the actors that work in the area of strategic planning demonstrates to function as a factor of greater positive impact in the institutionalization. On the other hand, the behavior of the actors in the finalist areas and the top management points to some kind of distancing and skepticism about the role of strategic management.

4.2   Results – Organization "B"

In organization "B" the strategic management model and processes are structured in the strategic, tactical and operational perspectives. The strategic formulation activities contemplate a stage of internal analysis, a stage of external analysis and the construction of scenarios, involving the participation of the directors.

The monitoring and evaluation are carried out monthly, having as object the indicators and the projects defined in the strategic planning. Regarding the governance and deliberative instances, the organization relies on the regimental involvement of the president, who ultimately responds through strategic management processes.

The interviewees reject the idea of some type of coercion or even normative imposition to implement the strategic management processes, this because of its legal-institutional autonomy. It is a consensus among all the interviewees and also for the evidences that could be evaluated, that the greatest deficiency would be in the strategic follow-up processes, which has an incipient involvement of the top management, with a clear gap in the directors' Strategic results.

The analysis of the process of institutionalization in the organization "B" and its respective stage, must take into account the constant changes in the management, highlighting a sudden rupture occurred in 2007, when the processes of strategic management were placed in the background and practically all the practices and rituals of strategic management were stationed. Since 2010 the process has been resumed and the model is again entering a kind of stability.

It was agreed among all the interviewees that the current strategic management model is consolidated. There is no longer any questioning about the fulfillment of its routines, being it possible to consider that the practice is no longer in an initial stage of institutionalization. However, in the engagements generated by the planning process, the organization seems to act erratically, with frequent changes throughout the execution of what was planned. Figure 6 below illustrates the evolution curve of the Reengineering of the strategic management processes of Organization "B", as proposed by Tolbert and Zucker [15].

Among the technical requirements, it is in the strategic definitions that the organization "B" demonstrates greater robustness. The most critical point is actually governance and the limited intensity with top management is involved in the process. Regarding the conduct of the actors involved in the process, the way of those who work in the planning area has an important positive effect on the process. On the part of the finalist managers, although the interviewed manager shows strong engagement with the process, there are gaps in the high leadership, therefore, a neutral effect was considered for this factor.

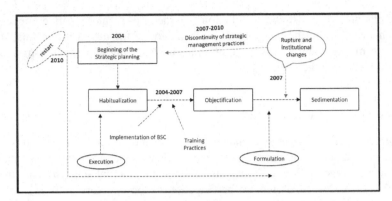

Fig. 6. Institutionalization process - Organization "B" (Source: elaboration of the author).

4.3 Compared Results - Organization "A" and Organization "B"

Figure 7 illustrates synthetically the results compared between Organizations:

Elements of Comparison	Organization	
	"A"	**"B"**
Model Features	• Very similar models and techniques	
Motivators of the Transformation	• Very similar motivators • Without isomorphic pressure	
Historical Milestones	• Start: 2006/2007 • Habitualization: 2006 - 2008 • Objectification: 2008 - 2020 • Without breaks	• Start: 2004 • Habitualization: 2004 - 2007 • Break: 2007 - 2010 • Objectification: : 2010
Stages of Institutionalization	• Close to Total Institutionalization	• Semi-Institutionalization
Facilitators of Institutionalization	• Technical requirements • Conduct of the actors	• Technical requirements • Perceived Benefits
Difficulties of institutionalization	• Governance • Communication	• Governance • Incentives

Fig. 7. Compared results: Organizations "A" and "B" (Source: elaboration of the author).

4.4 Discussion

The theoretical concepts presented in the second section of the paper offer references of factors that tend to influence the process of institutionalization. The analysis of the cases presented above, placed in a juxtaposed way with the theoretical propositions presented, serves to corroborate the importance of the technical requirements in the conception and attainment of the Reengineering of the strategic management processes. Both organizations have very specialized and experienced technical teams, which gives the majority of the activities a good quality and the fulfillment of the technical requirements, generating, in both organizations, legitimacy with the models and processes of strategic management.

However, the technical quality of the formulation is not sufficient to advance the process Reengineering. It is necessary, as the institutional theory itself suggests. an involvement of all relevant organizational actors. In this sense, the organizations analyzed show that they lack a more direct involvement of high-level managers, a fact that imposes a secondary role on governance activities, something that ultimately blocks progress in the stages of institutionalization.

Regarding the perception of the results brought by the strategic management processes, in the case of organization "B", in spite of the several historical ruptures, the practices and processes of the strategic management model have been sustained and seem to maintain a relative degree of institutionality, thanks to the instrumental relevance to the finalist actors.

It was also verified that besides these structuring factors, there are other accessory factors that can prompt progress in the institutionalization stage, among which three were highlighted in the study: communication, pacing of results and incentives.

5 Conclusions

The objective of this work was to analyze how the federal public organizations studied have been working to institutionalize the Reengineering in their strategic management processes. The study aimed to understand which factors favored or hindered progress in the institutionalization stage of these processes. The study indicated that even though there is a conceptual and instrumental convergence between the models adopted by the two organizations, the operationalization is idiosyncratic, meaning that each organization has its own specificities and, therefore, executes its models in a different way. In this sense, the theory of isomorphism in both organizations does not support itself, since the analyzes showed that technical motivations overlapped any other type of coercive, normative or mimetic pressure and, in this context, the understanding of historical trajectory and learning curve of each of the organizations was fundamental to explain the modus operandi and the institutionalization status of each organization.

It was observed that the greatest difficulty of organizations lies in governance. Whether due to design shortcomings, or due to low institutional capacity or even low management engagement, the organizations analyzed present gaps in the stability of their governance, governance rituals and especially in their practices of transparency and social control, aspects that limit and sometimes brake the process of institutionalization.

In terms of the research implications for theorists and practitioners, it is possible to affirm that the work can bring relevant contributions. For those who are more involved with the subject of strategic management processes, the work makes a contribution towards revealing strategic management practices that best adhere to the reality of the public sector and those that cannot be dispensed with, to create inertia in the Reengineering initiatives, for example in the case of governance processes. For those more connected to institutional theory, the implication of this work can be considered when it contributes to corroborate some of the shortcomings pointed out by Peci [30] regarding the new institutionalism. Among them, the argument of the presence of isomorphic mechanisms to explain the adherence of the studied organizations to Reengineering initiatives and strategic management models did not find empirical support, signaling a kind of overestimation of this type of mechanism [30].

As a suggestion for future studies, it is recommended to carry out new case studies in organizations of the different spheres of Brazilian public administration, aiming not only to enable the participation of a larger number of organizations, but also to understand how organizations positioned in different spaces behave in relation to the propositions presented. It is also suggested the use of quantitative methods, which would allow the establishment of statistical treatments, capable of signaling more precisely the causal relationships between the studied variables.

It is worth highlighting some delimitations of the research, noting that the theoretical perspectives used are not exhaustive, and it is inappropriate to disregard the fact that there are other factors that may influence the degree of institutional Reengineering of the strategic management processes.

References

1. Kaplan, R.S., Norton, D.P.: The Balanced Scorecard – Measures that Drive Performance, pp. 71–79. Harvard Business Review, January–February 1992
2. Bryson, J.M.: Strategic Planning for Public and Nonprofit Organizations: A Guide to Strengthening and Sustaining Organizational Achievement, 3rd edn. Jossey Bass Publishers, San Francisco (2004)
3. Andrews, R., Boyne, G., Law, J., Walker, R.: Strategic Management and Public Service Performance. Palgrave Macmillan, Basingstoke (2012)
4. Booz&Company: Center of Government: The Engine of Modern Public Institutions (2010)
5. Moore, M.: Recognizing Public Value. Harvard University Press, Cambridge (2013)
6. Gaetani, F.: O funcionamento do alto governo no Brasil. CLAD. Centro Latinoamericano de Administracion para el Desarrollo (2014)
7. Marini, C., Martins, H.F.: Governança pública contemporânea: uma tentativa de dissecação conceitual. Revista TCU (2014)
8. Barzelay, M.: The New Public Management: Improving Research and Policy Dialogue. University of California Press, Berkeley (2001)
9. Rezende, F.C.: Por que reformas administrativas falham? Revista Brasileira de Ciências Sociais 17(50), 123–142 (2002)
10. Motta, P.R.: A modernização da administração pública brasileira nos últimos 40 anos. Revista de Administração Pública – RAP/FGV 41, 87–96 (2007)
11. Martins, H.F.: A modernização da Administração Pública na Perspectiva do Estado. Dissertação [Mestrado em Administração]. Fundação Getúlio Vargas, Rio de Janeiro (1995)
12. Martins, H.: Uma teoria da fragmentação de políticas: desenvolvimento e aplicação na análise de três casos de políticas de gestão pública. Tese [Doutorado em Administração]. Fundação Getúlio Vargas, Rio de Janeiro (2003)
13. Martins, H.: Burocracia e revolução gerencial: a persistência da dicotomia entre política e administração. Revista Eletrônica sobre a Reforma do Estado, Salvador, no. 6, junho/julho/agosto (2006). Disponível em: http://www.direitodoestado.com.br. Acesso em 19 de outubro de 2006

14. Tolbert, P.S., Zucker, L.G.: Institutional sources of changes in the formal structure of organizations: the diffusion of civil service reform, 1880–1935. Adm. Sci. Q. **28**, 22–39 (1983)
15. Tolbert, P.S., Zucker, L.G.: The institutionalization of institutional theory. In: Clegg, S.R., et al. (eds.) Handbook of Organization Studies. Sage Publications, Thousand Oaks (1996)
16. Bryson, J.M., Ackermann, F., Eden, C.: Discovering collaborative advantage: the contributions of goal categories and visual strategy mapping. Public Adm. Rev. **76**(6), 912–925 (2016)
17. Gaetani, F.: As iniciativas de políticas de gestão pública do governo Lula. ResPvblica, Brasília, no. 3, pp. 104–138 (2003)
18. Cardoso Jr. J.C. (eds.): A reinvenção do planejamento governamental no Brasil. Projeto Diálogos para o Desenvolvimento, Brasília, livro 4. Ipea (2011)
19. Kaplan, R.: Mapas estratégicos – balanced scorecard: Convertendo ativos intangíveis em resultados tangíveis. Elsevier, Rio de Janeiro (2004)
20. DiMaggio, P.J., Powell, W.W.: The iron cage revisited: institutional isomorphism and collective rationality in organizational fields. Am. Sociol. Rev. **48**, 147–160 (1983)
21. Jeston, J., Nelis, J.: Business Process Management: Practical Guidelines to Successful Implementations. Routledge, Abingdon (2008)
22. Harmon, P.: Business Process Change: A Manager's Guide to Improving. Redesigning and Automating Processes. Morgan Kaufmann, Burlington (2003)
23. Wheelen, T., Hunger, J.: Strategic Management and Business Policy. Pearson Education International, New Jersey (2002)
24. Marini, C., Martins, H.F.: Um guia de governança para resultados na administração pública. Publix Conhecimento, Brasília (2010)
25. Joyce, P., Drumaux, A. (eds.): Strategic Management in Public Organizations: European Practices and Perspectives, 1st edn. Routledge, New York (2014). 348 p.
26. Kaplan, R.S., Norton, D.P.: A estratégia em ação: Balanced scorecard. Campus, Rio de Janeiro (1997)
27. Manzini, E.J.: A entrevista na pesquisa social. Didática **26/27**, 149–158 (1990/1991)
28. Vergara, S.C.: Métodos de Pesquisa em Administração. Ed. Atlas, São Paulo (2005)
29. Yin, R.K.: Estudo de Caso: Planejamento e métodos, 2nd edn. Bookman, Porto Alegre (2001)
30. Peci, A.: A nova teoria institucional em estudos organizacionais: uma abordagem crítica. In: Encontro anual da associação nacional de programa de pós-graduação em administração, Brasília, vol. 19 (2005)

The Potential of the Estonian e-Governance Infrastructure in Supporting Displaced Estonian Residents

Lőrinc Thurnay[1(✉)], Benjamin Klasche[2], Katrin Nyman-Metcalf[1], Ingrid Pappel[1], and Dirk Draheim[1]

[1] Tallinn University of Technology, Akadeemia tee 15a, 12618 Tallinn, Estonia
thlorinc@gmail.com,
{katrin.nyman-metcalf,ingrid.pappel,dirk.draheim}@ttu.ee
[2] Tallinn University, Narva mnt 25, 10120 Tallinn, Estonia
benjamin.klasche@tlu.ee

Abstract. This paper examines the possibilities of using the Estonian e-Governance infrastructure in an innovate manner to help displaced Estonian residents in a hypothetical national emergency. We begin by exploring the challenges that displaced persons and aid organizations face throughout three key stages of displacement – flight from conflict zones, temporary displacement, and long term integration. On this basis we analyze how the Estonian e-Governance infrastructure can be used in a refugee emergency. We provide a definition of intangible e-Governance infrastructure. We identify the key component of the existing Estonian e-Governance infrastructure as well as the proposed Governmental Cloud and Data Embassy initiatives. We analyze linkages where the utilization of the infrastructure could potentially counter the challenges of displaced persons and aid organizations. To realize these linkages, we propose a policy to make certain refugee-related, otherwise restricted governmental datasets accessible to international aid organizations. Additionally, we introduce a legal framework for the policy, analyze the technological requirements of its implementation, and discuss its communicational and technology export-related implications.

Keywords: Data embassy · Displacement · e-Governance infrastructure · National emergency · Policy recommendation · Refugee · UNHCR

1 Introduction

Estonia can be considered a pioneering country in ICT and e-Governance solutions [17,18]. In the last 25 years, Estonia introduced a number of unprecedented new technology-driven solutions in the public sector, such as Internet voting [7], nation-wide digital signatures [20] and the e-Residency program [12]. One of the most recent e-Governmental projects is the Data Embassy initiative, which – when finished – will guarantee that Estonia's heavily relied upon e-Governance

© Springer International Publishing AG 2017
A. Kő and E. Francesconi (Eds.): EGOVIS 2017, LNCS 10441, pp. 236–250, 2017.
DOI: 10.1007/978-3-319-64248-2_17

services would remain functional even if the country's territorial integrity was breached [15]. The idea of the Data Embassy initiative is intriguing. The unconditional continuous operation of e-Governance that it provides, implies that a state does not necessarily cease to exist if it loses its powers and controls in the conventional sense of the words – it can continue to live on in an extended, digital form. This is a new element of the idea of exile governments. It is not the aim of this work to assess the likelihood of such a scenario. However as the Estonian Government has made this topic a relevant matter of national security it does not need further explanations from our side.

The main questions that we will discuss in this paper are if and how displaced persons with Estonian digital identities can be supported by the Estonian e-Government infrastructure and what the challenges are that displaced persons and organizations aiding them face. In this discussion, we will identify what are the components of the Estonian e-infrastructure that are relevant to the challenges of displaced persons and aid organizations and what steps could be taken to enable the relevant components to be used to counter the challenges. This discussion will be of wider interest than just for Estonia, as many countries are inclined to build an e-Governance structure based on the Estonian e-Governance model. To answer these questions, we use qualitative data analysis methods and data sets. This is mostly, due to the lack of large quantitative datasets available on several of the subject matters, and most notably on the topic of Data Embassies [15], which is a project in its early pilot phases. All results in this paper are outcome of the research conducted for a Master Thesis by Thurnay [23].

In Sect. 2, we look at the challenges that displaced persons and aid organizations face throughout different stages of displacement. Following that, Sect. 3 discusses components and features of the Estonian e-Governance infrastructure. In Sect. 4, we attempt to define linkages between the infrastructural features and the challenges of displaced persons and aid organizations discussed in the previous sections. Based on this, we make a policy recommendation to realize the potential benefits identified in Sect. 5. Finally, we make some concluding remarks in Sect. 6.

2   Challenges of Displaced Persons and Aid Organizations

There are no universally applicable stages of displacement that every displaced persons would go through. Each journey is different due to the differences in crises refugees are fleeing from, the world's political climate, the individual's life situation, and other non-traditional security threats, such as the weather. We identify the challenges that refugees face during three stages of a – relatively positive – scenario. In this scenario refugees first flee an armed conflict wreaking havoc in their native land, then arrive somewhere where aid organizations manage their displacement temporarily, and lastly, as their homeland's conflict does not get resolved and as their displacement becomes permanent, they face the challenges of integration into the host community.

2.1   In Transit – Flight from an Armed Conflict

The main aim of people fleeing war, armed conflicts and destruction is to survive, to be in a place of safety and stability, at least until the conflict is resolved. The first set of challenges they face is during the flight away from their homes to safety. The most prominent challenges that displaced persons might face are:

– Survival. Leaving a zone of active conflict might relieve people of the primary dangers they are running away from but will introduce new challenges that might be equally threatening to their survival. The route to safety might lead through the conflict zone itself. Armed forces might actively seek to arrest or kill those who try to escape. Even when conflict zones are already behind them, refugees are often left to their own devices, where natural obstacles, weather, hard terrain, and lack of shelter can pose intermediate danger to their lives. Essential resources are scarce, if at all available – and are often expensive.
– Coordination. Once someone comes to a decision that they will attempt flee-ing the armed conflict in their home-land, they must come to a decision con-cerning their desired destination. Information on optimal destinations and routes from different media, as well as social networks, are often contradict-ing, volatile, and hard to come by [9]. Up-to-date and reliable information is vital for refugees in planning their journeys, which are often dangerous [9].
– Transportation. As transportation services are typically discontinued in active conflict zones, due to embargoes, the risks that transportation personnel would face, or the destruction of infrastructure [8], large numbers of peo-ple who are fleeing a conflict zone will not be able to use conventional forms of transportation to get to safety. Often, refugees will have to travel on foot, or if that is not possible, revert to the services of human traffickers.
– Communication. During their time in transit, refugees have the need to com-municate: with authorities; with locals or aid organizations that they ask information or resources from; with their friends and families back home, in the countries of their destination or also on the road, to know if they are safe; and with each other, to exchange information, resources, and to estab-lish some comfort of human contact. The changing locations, distances, and the multitude of languages can make the aid of ICT, most typically phones, ideally smartphones with internet connection, useful in many though not all situations [9].

The challenges that refugees face during flight are many. Physical resources, such as food, shelter, medicine and clothing are essential to survival. Information is of key importance throughout the journey – the quality of information available to refugees can be in direct correlation with the chance of survival. This is likely to be an issue that the e-Government infrastructure could deal with. We use these categories as the basis of further analysis of challenges that refugees face while fleeing a dangerous zone of conflict. The next stage in a refugee's journey towards safety might be arriving at a place that is safe and stable enough for aid organizations to be able to offer help in people's displacement.

2.2   Emergency Response of Aid Organizations

Just as every region, refugee crisis and every individual refugee faces different challenges during flight, also organizations aiding refugees have to address different challenges in every situation they work in. To be able to quickly and efficiently react to the diverse challenges that may arise during different refugee crises, the UNHCR developed a Needs Assessment for Refugee Emergencies (NARE) Checklist [24]. The NARE checklist is a tool, designed to be used by UNHCR and other aid organizations to help them assess and manage their reaction to refugee crises – to understand the nature of the refugee crises, to identify the main challenges that coordinating the refugees pose, and to suggest actions based on these assessments. The checklist is designed to be general enough, and customizable so it could be applied effectively in any refugee scenario. The NARE checklist suggests using several methodologies to assess the nature and severity of refugee crises. Based on the content of and the methodologies suggested by the NARE checklist, we identify the following, high-level challenges that refugee aid organizations, specifically UNHCR, face during a general refugee emergency:

– Resources – each issue outlined in the checklist's sections (water, sanitation, hygiene, food, education, etc.) require resources, both physical goods (food, medicine, infrastructure, etc.) and human resources (security personnel, social workers, medics, etc.). In a refugee emergency, adequate resources have to be identified, acquired and distributed urgently.
– Coordination – the acquisition, storage and distribution of resources, the performance and efficiency of services, the safe and secure registration and housing of refugees requires systematic coordination.
– Stakeholders – key persons in the refugee community, officials and authorities of the host, transit and home countries, other organizations and NGOs have to be informed, consulted or observed, to provide aid, to help the aid process and to mitigate issues and threats.
– Information is a key tool that supports all the above challenges and is gathered using the methodologies recommended by the checklist and summarized above.

We will consider these general categories as the basis of further analysis of challenges that aid organizations face in a refugee emergency situation, e.g., when managing a refugee camp.

2.3   Legal Integration into Host Societies

In the case of a long-term displacement, the displaced persons' integration into the host societies is in the interest of both the displaced person and the host society. The more a displaced person is integrated into the host society in cultural, legal and economic terms, the more they benefit by accessing larger social networks, education and health services, legal protection, career opportunities, etc. The host society benefits from the displaced persons' integration by gaining economically active residents, as opposed to passive residents who do not contribute to the country's economy but only use up resources. If we consider the goal of integration as being included in the host society, the purpose of the legal process leading to integration is to have similar legal status or rights that the members of the host community have.

Integration presupposes certain legal steps, primarily in order to determine the identity of persons based on which a clear legal status for the displaced person can be established. This can best be achieved with the help of documents, proofs and certificates that verify the identity and provide a basis for any claims made. Re-establishing and preserving identities is key to ensuring protection and solutions for refugees [25]. The lack of documents due to losing them during transit or the inability to carry them around is a critical issue in establishing a clarified legal status [27]. Host states enforce the identification of incoming refugees and displaced persons because taking in people with unclear identities carries risks. Missing legal documents, proofs, and certificates make legal proceedings in the host country challenging, since supplementing them is often impossible due to the disruption of the home state and lost identities of the displaced persons. These people fleeing persecution are often unable to contact home state authorities. These challenges are further aggravated by the fact that the legal requirements might differ significantly between the home country and the host country. Apart from having to prove their identity, legal issues displaced persons face can typically be, but are not limited to, family-related issues (marriage, children), issues related to ownership, labor-related issues and certifications, health problems, or criminal cases. Legal proceedings in such situations can be problematic if the legal history of the involved parties is missing [27].

3   Estonian e-Governance Infrastructure Components

When discussing electronic government, the concept of infrastructure can be interpreted in different ways. We can talk about the physical infrastructure that e-Governance services utilize – the servers and network devices, the networks connecting servers with users, the electric grid that powers the servers and network devices, etc. We can also discuss the intangible e-Governance infrastructure – architectural and design concepts, standards, software, and key services upon which e-Governance services that face end users are based. In this work, we chose to study infrastructure in the non-tangible sense. This decision was made based on the fact that the physical infrastructure under the Estonian e-Governance is not the differentiating factor between e-Governance in Estonia and other countries; the striking distinction of the Estonian e-Governance are found in the intangible components. The key components are:

- X-Road is a distributed, secure, unified web-services based inter-organizational data exchange framework [1], and as such it is the backbone of the Estonian e-Government infrastructure. X-Road has a standardized Application Programming Interface (API) that Estonian e-Government services

and datasets implement, to form a linked, interconnected, decentralized portfolio of services and datasets [1].
- Public Key Infrastructure. In the Estonian national PKI, every e-Citizen[1] is
  issued with a public key – everyone can benefit from the features of PKI.
  Citizens are issued an identity card, which – in addition to a portrait photo
  of the citizen, enabling face-to-face visual identification – has a built-in chip,
  with the basic data and the citizen's public key in digital format.
- eID. Every e-Citizen has a personal identification code. This code is used
  as a basis of the citizen's identity by the state, throughout their lives. Most
  of the Estonian public registers and documents containing citizens' personal
  information is managed digitally, and these documents are attributed to the
  citizen by the citizen's personal code, therefore the personal code is also a
  basis of the citizens' digital identities, or electronic identities (eID).

In addition to the key components, we also identified the Government Cloud
and Data Embassies project [15] that – once implemented – will be a key component of the Estonian e-Government infrastructure, but is missing from the
literature cited above, since the project is still in its early stages; it does not yet
play a considerable role in the infrastructure. Many European countries, including Estonia, have concluded that features of cloud computing such as rapid
elasticity, continuous operation, location independence could be used as the
infrastructural basis of their e-Government services [15]. However, the assessment of the possibility of implementing governmental cloud in Estonia shows
that the ubiquitous service portfolio, the advanced Estonian information society
and the e-Residency project – issuing Estonian digital identities for and granting
access to the e-Service portfolio to citizens of any country – warrant additional
components complementing the solutions used commonly by other states [15].
These peculiarities of the Estonian e-Government system were the basis of the
Concept of the Estonian Government Cloud and Data Embassies [15], which
considers three main technological components, i.e., cloud infrastructure located
in Estonia proper, public clouds offered by big international service providers,
and data embassies:

- Cloud infrastructure in the country's territory – creating a governmental
  cloud infrastructure in the country's territory is the most common strategy; it is the first and most relied upon component of the three. In essence,
  it refers to the creation of a standardized and distributed network of data
  centers complying with the above cited definition of cloud computing, where
  the data centers are located in the territory of Estonia [6].
- Public clouds – as a government cloud pilot project, Estonia already migrated
  some of its services to Microsoft public cloud Azure – services that contain
  no sensitive data, but may be subject to significant growth of demand temporarily and whose availability carry national symbolic significance – so as

---

[1] Throughout this work the term e-Citizen is used to refer to people who hold Estonian
digital identification and profile: Estonian citizens, residents of Estonia, and Estonian
e-residents.

to better guarantee their availability, e.g., the website of the President or the Government [13,16]. The possibility of migrating sensitive data to public cloud services – despite the inherent security risks – which would allow to guarantee digital continuity in case the territorial integrity of the country is breached, is also discussed [15].

– Data embassies – to combine the benefits of a territorial cloud infrastructure, i.e., exclusive control over the cloud infrastructure, with the benefits of using multinational private cloud providers – i.e., global distribution, infrastructure integrity not dependent on the country's territorial integrity – there is a proposed solution to establish data centers on the premises of Estonian diplomatic missions in friendly foreign countries [15].

4   Estonian e-Government Infrastructure Components Relevant to Issues of Refugees and Aid Organizations

4.1   (Re-)Establishment of Identities of Displaced Persons

In Sect. 3 we concluded that identity-related issues can cause significant challenges to both displaced persons and organizations aiding them. If a displaced person's identification documents are lost, verifying their identity is going to be difficult. If a displaced person's identity is not verified, authorities of host and transit countries might not grant them entry, since their claims of fleeing dangerous regions, which would be their legal basis of entry, cannot be verified. The same issue arises when a displaced person applies for asylum.

The Estonian e-Governance stores e-Citizens' names, personal codes and biometric data in digitized, linkable databases. In theory, if displaced persons who lost their identity document provide their name or personal code, and have their fingerprints scanned, their names or IDs could be matched up by querying the relevant datasets, and their identity could be re-established. The digital profiles[2] of e-Citizens have the potential to be used to re-establish the identities of displaced e-Citizens who have lost their identification documents.

Even if the identification document of the displaced person in question is available, the possibility of performing biometric identification provides an additional guarantee of the genuineness of the identity. Biometric identification could be used to filter out counterfeit identity documents. Also, while authentication using PKI, i.e., with national ID card or mobile ID, is primarily intended to be used for authentication in digital environments, it could also be used to provide additional guarantee of authenticity in an interpersonal situation, e.g., an officer verifies the identity visually, and also prompts the citizen to authenticate themselves digitally. In fact, biometric identification is already being used by UNHCR to register and identify refugees [25]. Being able to use the already established

---

[2] Digital profiles of e-Citizens maintained by the state differs from digital profiling carried out by social media providers such as Facebook, the latter not having the potential to be used to re-establish identities of displaced persons, since they are not verified by the state and carry no legal authenticity.

biometric identity of an e-Citizen would have the benefit of the continuation of their identity, as opposed to losing their old identities and then gaining a new one from UNHCR. It would make processing their cases and requests more efficient, and with a clear, credible and rich – in terms of data and history – digital profile, it would likely make the life and integration of the displaced person into the host country's society easier.

4.2   Information About Displaced Persons

Each refugee crisis has its own complex set of challenges. In Sect. 2 we found that in order to be able to identify and assess these challenges, and to provide survival, safety and acceptable conditions to displaced persons during their temporary displacements, aid organizations need several diverse sources of information. Large, quantitative datasets about the displaced persons, the home and host country's population, geography, economy, as well as qualitative data from interviews and focus groups and field reports are needed. The Estonian e-Governance has a high degree of maturity, and most state and public registers and databases as well as documents are managed in digitized, standardized formats, linkable by X-Road. In theory, these databases could be sources for rich, quantitative data of demographics with information on the population health and education that could support aid organizations in their efforts to understand the complex challenges they are facing.

Given that the identities of displaced persons' normally have been re-established, verified and registered upon their arrival, the a list on the members of the refugee community can provide an additional valuable dimension to the datasets above. Data analysis of state and public databases, cross referenced with the list of citizens in the refugee community could be used to create detailed profiles to help in identifying not only community key informants and ideal focus group discussion participants, but also to identify potential community liaisons, persons or groups that are likely to be in vulnerable situations, or who are likely to cause security concerns. With conventional methods, these benefits could only be achieved if each displaced person would be interviewed in depth, which – depending on the refugee emergency – would be either very difficult, or completely unfeasible. The availability of rich, linkable, computer-analyzable datasets about the refugee community would enable aid organizations to make data-driven decisions.

4.3   Supplementing Missing Documents

Above, we identified the legal dimension of local integration as a challenge that displaced persons are likely to face during their long term displacement. The prerequisite of legal integration into the host society is a clear legal status. Displaced persons are often unable to carry certificates and proofs – documents that should be the basis of their cleared legal status in the host country – or lose them during the displacement. The Estonian State manages many of its citizens' legal statuses electronically. Records of documents and certificates are stored digitally, in machine readable formats. So long as the e-Government infrastructure and related servers are operational, citizens' documents are going to be available online.

Their genuineness is guaranteed by digital signatures, and as such, the creation of fake electronic documents in implausible. In theory, the electronic availability of documents could enable e-Citizens to establish their clarified legal status and prove their further legal claims, thus facilitating their legal integration into the host society. For instance, citizens can view their education records and diplomas online [4], which might help them to have their education and skills recognized by the host state, helping them to better career possibilities. They can access several of their health-related records [5] and records related to benefits, which might not only render repeated medical examinations unnecessary and make receiving treatment quicker, it might help in re-establishing statuses of disability or reduced capacity to work. Legal cases concerning family reunification, marital issues, and heritage and alimony rights could be supported by a multitude of family-related datasets and services.

4.4 Continuous Operation

In time of an armed conflict, conventional government services are often severely disrupted, or even seize to be offered completely [11]. Assuming that the Data Embassy initiative would be fully implemented and operational, e-Government services migrated to the government cloud could remain operational even during a severe impairment of other governmental functions [15]. Services that require the active, manual involvement of a public servant, e.g., approving requests, could be provided with the condition that the public servant also has access to the online service environment, wherever they might be. Fully automated, autonomous or pro-active services, e.g., making queries to the e-Recipes environment, authentication using national ID cards, and the issuing of digital signatures, on the other hand could remain operational and fully functional – at least temporarily – even in a case of a severe disruption when no public servants are able to carry out their functions.

The Estonian e-Governance infrastructure has the technical potential of helping e-Citizens in re-establishing their identities, clarifying their legal status, and the potential of supporting the work of aid organizations by providing rich data sources to analyze. However, in practice, the technical realization of such potential would require the continuous operation of the underlying infrastructural components. The Data Embassy concept is proposed specifically to guarantee continuous operation in scenarios that are likely to trigger the displacement of people, i.e., the Government's loss of control over the territory of Estonia [15]. Therefore, we consider the full implementation of data embassies to be a prerequisite of the realization of the potential identified above and classify data embassies as a key component of the Estonian e-Governance infrastructure in a refugee emergency scenario.

5   Policy Recommendations

As concluded above, aid organizations could use rich, digital databases and documents that concern displaced persons to better assess the challenges of the emergency and provide aid to the displaced persons more efficiently and effectively. Such databases and documents are currently not available to third parties, but the technological infrastructure of granting aid organizations access to these dataset, even if the country's integrity is severely disrupted, is available. Therefore, our policy recommendations are the following:

> In case of a national emergency that triggers the mass displacement of Estonian residents, certain refugee-related, otherwise restricted governmental datasets should be made accessible to international aid organizations.

This policy would have benefits similar to open data initiatives. Open data has the widely accepted benefit of enabling well informed, data-driven management and decision-making in organizations [2]. The United Nations specifically encourages the increased publishing and use of open data for helping people in vulnerable situations [28]. However, unlike usual open data policies, the implementation of our recommendation would provide an even wider breadth of data for the targeted support of the work of aid organizations in critical times; data that could not be made open to the general public, due to its sensitive nature.

5.1   Legal Framework

This policy recommendation has several legal implications. To implement this policy, the definitions and conditions of its subjects must be clarified. The conditions in which aid organizations could be granted access to restricted databases should be codified in law. The possibility of codifying these conditions as an amendment to the State of Emergency Act should be examined, since this Act is relevant to the policy recommendation: the purpose of the State of Emergency Act is to provide the basis, conditions and procedure for declaration of a state of emergency, and the competence of authorities managing a state of emergency [and] the measures to be implemented during a state of emergency, and the rights, duties and liability of persons during a state of emergency, compare with [22], Sect. 1. In other words, this Act already addresses the question of what a national emergency is, which institutions are responsible for decisions related to national emergencies, and provides a list of exceptional measures that are only valid in case of national emergencies. Similar legislation exists in most countries, which is why our recommendations can be relevant in the future also elsewhere, in countries that may develop similar e-governance to Estonia.

An alternative approach of determining the conditions in which access could be granted to restricted databases could be using the national security model proposed by Kotka et al. [14] to determine the operation modes of Data Embassies, i.e., the infrastructural components that are a prerequisite of this policy recommendation. This model makes a distinction between full control, fragile control and no control operation modes of the Government Cloud; modes that are functions of the Estonian government's level of control over the country's territory, and the constraints that core technical and policy staff may have in accessing computer services.

The possibility of granting international aid organizations access to personal data without the explicit agreement of the citizens in question should be examined in the context of section 14 of the Personal Data Protection Act. This Act is relevant to the policy recommendation since it states that the communication of personal data or granting access to personal data to third persons for the purposes of processing is permitted without the consent of the data subject: (1) if the third person to whom such data are communicated processes the personal data for the purposes of performing a task prescribed by law, an international agreement or directly applicable legislation of the Council of the European Union or the European Commission, compare with [21] section 14. Estonia, as a member state of its Executive Committee, has international agreements with UNHCR [26], which could be the legal basis of this policy. As a sub-organization of the United Nations, with over 60 years of operation, presence in 123 countries and an active cooperation with Estonia, UNHCR could be an ideal aid organization to whom access could be granted to restricted refugee-related datasets in case of emergencies. The possibility of granting UNHCR the right to further share these datasets with other organizations could also be discussed – based on their involvement and the relevance of their work assessed by the NARE checklist in the context of a concrete refugee emergency. It is not unusual that explicit consent is not needed for data use provided it is for the purpose of carrying out a task of public interest or in the interest of the individual, which is set out in law or in other form – such as an international agreement.

As explained in Sect. 4, aid organizations might also benefit from the use of data such as biometric data, data on the state of health or disability, data revealing ethnic or racial origin, or certain crime-related information. These data are classified as sensitive personal data, compare with [21], section 4, and as such cannot be granted access to based on section 14 of the Personal Data Protection Act, compare with [21], section 14. Instead, sensitive personal data of individual displaced persons could be collected on the condition of their explicit consent, compare with [21], section 12, supporting the efforts of aid organization in providing better individualized services to displaced persons. In exceptional circumstances there may be a possibility to collect data also without explicit consent, but this issue will not be further discussed here as it is a major topic in its own right and not necessary for the main argument of this article.

5.2 Technological Considerations

The Estonian e-Governance infrastructure provides connectivity to and between datasets with the help of X-Road. X-Road has been one of the bases of the Estonian e-Governance infrastructure for over 15 years, and as a highly mature, reliable piece of technology, it could also serve as the facilitator for aid organizations, enabling them to connect and query databases that they are granted access to. To maximize effectiveness of our policy recommendation, the aid organizations' efforts in developing solutions that query and analyze data from Estonian e-Governmental databases should be supported by making documentation, know-how and best practices produced and gathered by Estonian e-Governance professionals available to them. X-Road is a preferable choice from this perspective as well. The technical specification needed to implement X-Road for data exchange is publicly available, written in English [19], making it ideal for developers of international organizations. An open source API solution has also been published as part of the effort of making the Estonian and Finnish implementation of X-Road connected and interoperable [3]. The Java codebase is accessible to anyone under the European Union Public Licence, and offers documentation. As such, this code base can be a valuable example resource for developers of aid organizations working on accessing and analyzing data granted to the organization via X-Road.

5.3 Communication and Export Implications

As argued earlier, the relevance of this work lies not in the likelihood of a national emergency, but in the fact that the Estonian state is implementing measures to mitigate a hypothetic future national emergency, i.e., the Data Embassy project is meant to provide continuous operation in case of loss of control over the country's territory [15]. If this policy recommendation was implemented as law, the question of its relevance might also arise in the public discourse. Preparatory measures taken by the state to mitigate a future risk can bring the risk in the field of view of the public [10], and might be interpreted as a sign of increased risk, potentially causing unwarranted public unease or panic. Therefore, we think it is worth taking this into account when preparing the public communication regarding the policy's implementation.

As yet another novel, technology-driven public policy from Estonia, implementing this recommendation has the potential of further strengthening the country's international recognition for being a technological pioneer, which could also strengthen the country's position in international organizations such as the UNHCR – just as the precedent setting national cyber defense achievements cemented the country's position in NATO. One of the infrastructural components enabling the benefits of this policy recommendation is X-Road. The technology of, and the know-how on, X-Road are some of the e-Governance-related products that Estonia exports abroad. X-Road is being implemented in a number of states and territories. Enabled by the implementation of X-Road, this policy recommendation could be considered by all of these countries and territories, especially if it was in the future combined with an initiative similar in nature to the Estonian Data Embassy initiative, guaranteeing continuous operation. The recommendation could especially be relevant to countries who have historical or present struggles with displaced persons, as do Namibia and Palestine – countries that have implemented or are in the process of implementing features of the X-Road, with Estonian help. Consequently, the benefits of this policy recommendation could be used as an additional argument in the marketing and sales process of technologies and know-how related to X-Road, potentially positively stimulating the Estonian ICT export sector.

6   Conclusion

The idea behind the Data Embassy initiative is to achieve the continuous operation of the Estonian e-Governance, so even if the government lost power, even if the country's border were breached, even if its sovereignty diminished, the core operation of the government could continue, and Estonia's symbolic and constitutional integrity could live on in an extended, intangible digital form. The goal of continuous operation is clearly pronounced in the literature and in governmental communication. However, we think that it is also worth taking a look at whether there are some other, more practical implications of these key governmental functions that could be taken advantage of during a worst case scenario.

This paper shows that the Estonian e-Governance could provide real life, practical help to those who are perhaps in the most vulnerable positions in a national crisis – those who leave everything behind to seek refuge. It could help people who lost their identification while fleeing from danger by proving their identities to foreign states, granting them entry to safety. It could save their medical records thus helping them get better medical care. It would keep their legal documents, certifications, and licenses, so they could go back to school quicker, enter the work force easier – it would help them find solid ground under their feet in their new host countries.

Estonian e-Governance could also help international aid organizations who give essential support to these refugees by providing them with plenty of valuable detailed information on the refugees' backgrounds. Aid organizations could use this information to understand the complex situation they are working in, and make data-driven decisions on how to help refugees in the best possible way. These potential benefits are inherent of the Estonian e-Governance infrastructure. Once the Data Embassies initiative is realized, all the necessary technological components will exist, and no expensive additional development would be needed to take advantage of e-Governance to the benefit of the citizenry. The legal basis of using e-Governance to help those who had to flee the country also exists. The concept of providing aid organizations with restricted data to be used to help Estonian residents in displacement could be turned into a policy, just like the concept of Data Embassies – the very concept enabling this suggestion – was turned into a policy, and is being implemented.

References

1. Cybernetica: X-Road eGovernment Interoperability Framework (2013). https://cyber.ee/uploads/2013/03/cyber_xroad_NEW2_A4_web.pdf
2. Davies, T.G., Bawa, Z.A.: The Promises and Perils of Open Government Data (OGD). J. Commun. Inform. **8**

3. EduCloud Alliance: Joint X-Road REST Gateway Development (2016). https://github.com/educloudalliance/xroad-rest-gateway
4. https://www.eesti.ee/eng/services/citizen/haridus_ja_teadus/isikukaart_eesti_ee_portaali
5. https://www.eesti.ee/eng/services/citizen
6. ENISA: Good Practice Guide for Securely Deploying Governmental Clouds. European Union Agency for Network and Information Security (2013)
7. Estonian National Electoral Committee: E-Voting System - General Overview (2010). http://vvk.ee/public/dok/General_Description_E-Voting_2010.pdf
8. Gates, S., Hegre, H., Nygrd, H.M., Strand, H.: Development consequences of armed conflict. In: World Development, vol. 40 (2012)
9. Gillespie, M., et al.: Mapping Refugee Media Journeys - Smartphones and Social Media Networks. The Open University and France Medias Monde (2016)
10. Hansen, L., Nissenbaum, H.: Digital disaster, cyber security, and the Copenhagen School. Int. Stud. Q. **53**, 1155–1175 (2009)
11. ICRC: Urban services during protracted armed conflict - a call for a better approach to assisting affected people. International Committee of the Red Cross (2015)
12. Kotka, T., del Castillo, C., Korjus, K.: Estonian e-residency: benefits, risk and lessons learned. In: Kő, A., Francesconi, E. (eds.) EGOVIS 2016. LNCS, vol. 9831, pp. 3–15. Springer, Cham (2016)
13. Kotka, T., Johnson, B., Cebul, T., Lovosevic, L., Liiv, I.: E-Government services migration to the public cloud: experiments and technical findings. In: Kő, A., Francesconi, E. (eds.) EGOVIS 2016. LNCS, vol. 9831, pp. 62–76. Springer, Cham (2016). doi:10.1007/978-3-319-44159-7_5
14. Kotka, T., et al.: Policy and legal environment analysis for e-Government services migration to the public cloud. In: Proceedings of ICEGOV 2015–2016 - 9th International Conference on Theory and Practice of Electronic Governance. ACM (2016)
15. Kotka, T., Liiv, I.: Concept of Estonian Government cloud and data embassies. In: Kő, A., Francesconi, E. (eds.) EGOVIS 2015. LNCS, vol. 9265, pp. 149–162. Springer, Cham (2015). doi:10.1007/978-3-319-22389-6_11
16. Microsoft, MKM: Implementation of the Virtual Data Embassy Solution - Summary Report of the Research Project on Public Cloud Usage for Government. Microsoft Corporation, Estonian Ministry of Economic Affairs and Communications (2015)
17. MKM: Cyber Security Strategy 2014–2017. Estonian Ministry of Economic Affairs and Communications (2014)
18. MKM: Digital Agenda 2020 for Estonia. Estonian Ministry of Economic Affairs and Communications (2013)
19. RIA: Protocol for Data Exchange Between Databases and Information Systems - Requirements for Information Systems and Adapter Servers. Republic of Estonia Information System Authority (2014)
20. Sertifitseerimiskeskus: The Estonian ID Card and Digital Signature Concept - Principles and Solutions (2003). http://www.id.ee/public/The_Estonian_ID_Card_and_Digital_Signature_Concept.pdf
21. Riigi Teataja: Personal Data Protection Act, RT I 2007, 24, 127 (2008)
22. Riigi Teataja: State of Emergency Act, RT I 1996, 8, 165 (1996)
23. Thurnay, L.: The potential of the Estonian e-Governance infrastructure in supporting displaced estonian residents in national emergencies. Master thesis, School of Information Technologies, Tallinn University of Technologies, December 2016

24. UNHCR: Needs Assessment for Refugee Emergencies (NARE) Checklist. United Nations High Commissioner for Refugees (2016)
25. UNHCR: Biometric Identity Management System - Enhancing Registration and Data Management. United Nations High Commissioner for Refugees (2015)
26. UNHCR: Global Report 2014. United Nations High Commissioner for Refugees (2014)
27. UNHCR: Refugee Integration in Europe. United Nations High Commissioner for Refugees (2013)
28. United Nations: E-Government Survey 2016 – e-Government in Support of Sustainable Development (2016)

The Challenge of Accelerating Greek Judicial Procedure

Demetrios Sarantis(✉)

United Nations University – Operating Unit on Policy-Driven Electronic
Governance, Campus de Couros, Rua Vila Flor 166,
4810-445 Guimarães, Portugal
sarantis@unu.edu

Abstract. Ten years ago, the digitalization of public administration was put on
the agenda in Greece by the Digital Strategy policy. Only now, though, does
e-Justice appear to be gaining ground. The article explains the current situation
in Greek judicial operation and highlights the problems, such as judicial delays.
It then outlines the new Civil and Criminal Court Case Management System.
Against this background, the potential of Greek e-Justice reform is discussed,
along with the future challenges it faces. The aim of this paper is twofold. On the
one hand, it provides a contribution to the debate on judicial efficiency by
conducting an analysis on the existing data. On the other hand, it presents the
attempt to resolve these problems through the introduction of a new system.

Keywords: Court case management system · e-Justice · Judicial efficiency

1 Introduction

The judicial system is vital to society for several reasons. It is pivotal in protecting
human rights and in supplying citizens with what they perceive as justice. It is fundamental in the interplay with the legislature and the executive to jointly contribute in
providing socially and economically valuable outcomes. Moreover, it performs a role
in fostering sustainable development and in making the economy sound by effectively
enforcing private property rights and by having a very significant impact on economic
behavior, investment choices and economic development [1].

Citizens and businesses might deliberately exploit delays in justice delivery to
craftily postpone their financial obligations to other parties [2]. For example, debtors
might choose purposely to be sued by their creditors hoping to obtain a substantial
delay of the repayment deadline [3].

The recent financial crisis has produced an increasing interest of the need for
structural reforms in order to increase the public service efficiency and achieve higher
economic prosperity [2]. One of these reforms concerns the acceleration of the judicial
system operation. International organizations like the World Bank and the European
Community pay attention on the connection between the judiciary and sustainable
development encouraging the reform of national judiciaries in order to make them
effective [4].

One of the essential elements for a smooth functioning of courts is the safeguarding
of the fundamental right to a fair trial within a reasonable time (ECHR Article 6) [5].

© Springer International Publishing AG 2017
A. Kő and E. Francesconi (Eds.): EGOVIS 2017, LNCS 10441, pp. 251–260, 2017.
DOI: 10.1007/978-3-319-64248-2_18

This principle must be fully considered when managing the workload of a court, the duration of proceedings and specific measures to reduce their length and improve their efficiency and effectiveness. The Council of Europe and its European Court of Human Rights (The Court) pay specific attention to the "reasonable time" of judicial proceedings and the effective execution of judicial decisions. On several occasions the European Court of Human Rights considered that one of the ways of guaranteeing the effectiveness and credibility of judicial systems is to ensure that a case is dealt with in a reasonable time (H. v. France, No. 10073/82, of 24 October 1989). The Court highlights that "significant and recurring delays in the administration of justice were a matter of particular concern and likely to undermine public confidence in the effectiveness of the judicial system", and that in exceptional cases, "the unjustified absence of a decision by the courts for a particularly prolonged period could in practice be regarded as a denial of justice" (Glykantzi v. Greece, No. 40150/09, of 30 October 2012).

Studies and related projects focused on judicial systems performance improvement, on the optimal organization of courts, and on incentives governing the judges' activities have become a flourishing portion of eGovernment initiatives [6].

Therefore, implementation of effective policies, procedures and systems aimed at improving the overall efficiency of judicial operation is of outmost importance. In this paper, we investigate the efficiency of Greek courts of justice and illustrate an integrated system which aims to optimize their performance.

The paper is organized as follows. In Sect. 2, we sketch out Greek courts' performance regarding cases completion. The new court case management system is presented in Sect. 3. The main policy implications and possible extensions of this e-Justice system are discussed in Sect. 4. Finally, conclusions are illustrated in Sect. 5.

2   Motivation

The Council of Europe and its European Court of Human Rights (The Court) has established criteria for assessing the reasonableness of the length of proceedings and rules for calculating the length of proceedings [6]. These elements offer a useful benchmark, against which, state performance in relation to court efficiency can be assessed. In addition to and as a specification of these, the CEPEJ (The European Commission for the Efficiency of Justice) has developed two performance indicators to assess court efficiency at the European level. The first indicator is the Clearance Rate[1], which measures how effectively courts within a country or entity are keeping up with the incoming caseload. The second indicator is the calculated Disposition Time[2], which measures the estimated number of days that are needed to bring a case to an end. The

---

[1] The Clearance Rate is a simple ratio, obtained by dividing the number of resolved cases with the number of incoming cases, expressed as a percentage: *Clearance Rate (%) = Resolved cases in a period × 100/Incoming cases in a period.*

[2] Disposition Time is obtained by dividing the number of pending cases at the end of the observed period by the number of resolved cases within the same period multiplied by 365 (days in a year): *Disposition Time = Number of pending cases at the end of a period × 365/Number of resolved cases in a period.*

two indicators can be studied together to achieve an initial general picture of the efficiency of courts in a certain country; analysis of their evolution over time allows a better understanding of the efforts of the judiciary to maintain or improve efficiency.

A well-functioning judiciary with an efficient court system is central to effective access to justice. This is not the case with the Greek judiciary, where cases usually proceed with substantial delay, multiple adjournments, and suboptimal guarantees of due process for victims and witnesses. Few will deny that the Greek judiciary is slow, and therefore not suitable for an EU member state. In Greece, judicial reforms are moving rather slowly. Distinguished jurists are being critical, pointing out the immediate need of reforms, underlining current underperformance of judicial system. Despite not being the general rule, there are cases which are not being resolved early or resulting in mistrial.

Greece is in first place in the number of pending administrative cases among the 26 European Union member states, according to president of the Association of Administrative Judges (EDD) [7]. She addressed the annual EDD meeting (2017) held by the Athens Bar, saying that lawsuits filed today in Administrative Courts take seven years to be resolved, as tax affairs are the top priority. Indicatively, in Greek courts 995.399 cases were pending on June of 2014 [8]. Specifically, in Greek Administrative Courts there are currently 288,229 cases pending, of which 245,795 cases are pending in first instance courts and 42,434 in appeal courts. Of the pending cases, 58,082 are tax related, while the remaining 230,147 cases are related to other issues. In recent years, the EDD president said, 38 bills for speeding the administration of justice passed in Greek Parliament, but the problem is not solved, since the new legislation "did not touch the root of the problem". Data show low clearance rates for Greece 79% (2010) 58% (2012) compared to respective average European values 98% (2010) 104% (2012) [9].

By international standards, the Greek judicial system is quite inefficient. According to the World Bank's Doing Business 2017 [10], in terms of enforcing contracts, Greece ranks 108th out of the 183 countries covered in the survey (compare this, for example, to Germany (17th), Portugal (19th), Croatia (7th), and Bulgaria (49th)). In addition, while in most European countries the maximum time needed to resolve civil, commercial, administrative and other cases was 200 days, in Greece the respective time was 510 (2010 data) days and 677 (2012 data) days. In fact, of the 24 European countries considered in the survey, only Malta and Portugal were less efficient than Greece [11]. Greece had the lowest rate, 79% in 2010 and 65% in 2012, of resolving civil, commercial, administrative and other cases in Europe [11]. In 2013, only Cyprus had bigger number (6.1) of litigious civil and commercial pending cases (first instance/per 100 inhabitants) than Greece (5.6).

A strong increase has been recorded in Greece, in the Disposition Time of civil and commercial litigious cases of first instance between 2010 and 2012 and a reduction thereof between 2012 and 2014, but it remains high compared to the rest of European countries (Fig. 1).

The global World Justice Project's Rule of Law Index ranks Greece forty first in the overall assessment, and better only to Hungary and Bulgaria in Europe, 44th when it comes to civil justice and 50th in Criminal justice in particular. Specifically, regarding the indexes 'Civil justice is not subject to unreasonable delay' and 'Criminal

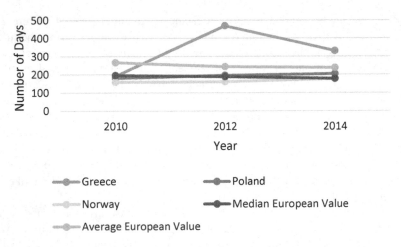

Fig. 1. Evolution of the disposition time of civil and commercial litigious cases between 2010 and 2014

adjudication system is timely and effective' the performance is significantly low 0.22 the first and 0.46 the latter one.

The above numbers explain why e-Justice has climbed high on the e-agenda in Greece. Looking ahead, we present the Integrated Judicial Case Management System, an e-Justice reform of Greek civil and criminal court procedure and the relative challenges that such reform faces.

3   The Integrated Judicial Case Management System

One activity emerging as being common to more Member States, which identifies justice systems as a priority area, is the introduction of case management systems in courts. The administration of the courts has been defined as "the way in which a court is organized so that judicial decisions can be delivered" [12]. Case management refers to the court's role in management of proceedings. This raises issues relating to the course of proceedings and the functioning and efficiency of the judicial system.

The Greek Integrated Judicial Case Management System for Civil and Criminal Procedure (OSDDY) has been partly completed and its full completion (roll-out) is envisaged, under the National Strategic Reference Framework (NSRF), until 2020. Initially it supports the processes of courts in four cities, Athens, Thessaloniki, Piraeus and Chalkida. Participant courts include, county court, police court, court of the first instance, court of appeal and supreme court.

The initiative refers to the development, installation and commissioning of an Integrated Judicial Case Management System (OSDDY), for managing the flow of criminal and civil procedures, the enrichment of services to the public and provision of assistance to the back office operations of the respective courts. An integrated information system has been designed and implemented, which includes separate applications (subsystems) to support the operation of the units at all levels of the courts that are involved in the court case flow. Once the court process has started, the system also allows the user to track the various stages online.

The introduction of such a homogenized IT environment for the Greek courts charged with criminal and civil cases, improves the quality and speed of justice administration. All involved stakeholders, judges, prosecutors, advocates, court-appointed experts, lawyers and translators, upon registration on the web portal, submit the case related documents electronically to the portal, including written pleadings, writs of summons, replies, applications, notices of appeal, written closing submissions, expert declarations, related reports and attachments, as well as fee claims from lawyers involved in cases where their fees are to be paid from the public purse.

The system supports several processes requesting the essential input and providing the relative output (Fig. 2). It has been implemented complying with international standards and e-Justice processes such as the European Case Law Identifier (ECLI), the European Law Institute (ELI), the e-CODEX project results and the European Commission decisions (315/2009 and 316/2009) regarding criminal record data exchange. It has been designed foreseeing the provision of open data such as public information and communication with other organizations and assuring the interoperability with other organizations and systems (e.g. National Criminal Record Registry, Integrated System of Courts Proceedings, Detention Facilities, Bar Association Systems, National Portal ERMIS, Police, TAXISnet, eKEP, eProcurement).

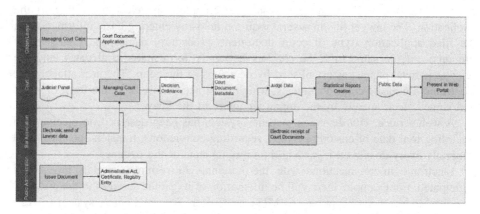

Fig. 2. Cross-functional process flow support of criminal/civil procedure in integrated judicial case management system

Regarding the civil court procedure, the system supports the court document deposition workflow, the court composition definition, the judicial panel's publication, the case update with current discourse results and the publication of possible remedies. Simultaneously it supports the procedure of certificates issuance regarding the specific civil court case.

Regarding the criminal court procedure, the system initially supports the creation of judicial panel using the incoming digital data from prosecutor's office. Then, it supports the liquidation process by relative decisions publishing, payments data update, filing the possible appeal, writing of criminal record data, editing of monthly payments statements, updating statistical bulletins of accused people and settling payment penalties (facilitating instalments). It also, follows all the decision workflow regarding criminal record data update, it monitors pending decisions and it keeps record of attestations and remedies.

Specific supported services include disclaimer heritage, registration of the establishment of a company, companies' bankruptcies, monitoring the progress of a union legal entity and leasing information. Criminal Record information update, after judicial decisions, is sent through appropriate implemented web services to the National Criminal Record Registry. Conversely, after judge's request, criminal record information is retrieved from the National Criminal Record Registry through web service use [13]. There is an interface with the central proceedings judicial system. In this way, the judge has access to trial minutes whenever he needs it. There is also an interface with the Bar Association system to facilitate the electronic submission of court documents. Greek lawyer, using a fully automated, fast and easy procedure, can submit electronically documents directly to competent court. After authentication, the lawyer enters his personal working environment in Bar Association system and he initiates the court document filing process. The user fills in the required fields (customer name, procedure, number of copies requested), while the system automatically calculates the payment amount and the relative tax. The user completes the payment through a secure window of the affiliated bank. Then the user is automatically transferred to the Integrated Judicial Case Management System to complete the electronic filing of the application. The lawyer fills in several required fields by entering basic information on the filed application (type of court document, procedure, names and addresses of litigants). At the same time, he chooses between the available trial dates, and the relative judicial panels, as established by decisions of the court. The user attaches the electronic file of the court documents, which must necessarily be in the form of .docx and signed electronically by the digital signature of the lawyer.

A web service with detention facilities system has been designed, to receive data regarding trial date of custody persons, regarding convictions, transfers, penalties and generally every document regarding the criminal state of the detainee.

Electronic interconnections with the national eGovernment portals have been anticipated. For example, there will be integration of its public services to the National Portal of Public Administration (ERMIS), to Citizen Service Centers system (eKEP) and with Ministry of Finance systems (TAXISnet). The latter interface will allow to monitor fines payment imposed by courts. Interface exists with the eProcurement system to provide information regarding the candidate suppliers of public sector and there will be integration with police information systems (lawsuits, fugitive data etc.), port authority, fire authority, customs authority and electronic interconnection with chambers registries to retrieve relative data. The system is implemented satisfying the standards set from eGovernment Interoperability Framework (Greek e-GIF) [14].

The knowledge management system aims to collect all the structured and unstructured information from the court integrated system and transform it on accessible knowledge resource for the stakeholders.

4 Policy Implications – Future Extensions

Greek government implements the specific reform in order to meet the EU country-specific policy recommendations aimed at increasing the efficiency of the judicial system [15]. The problems associated with the Greek judicial system have quite a long history, and there has thus been a long on-going policy debate on the reforms needed to bring the system towards more efficiency. This Integrated Judicial Case Management System (OSDDY) aims to justice modernization, acceleration of justice processes, stakeholders' service improvement and fully informing citizens regarding the progress of their court cases. The court case will be followed from certified users (judges, lawyers etc.) following the court panel. According to ELTRUN study the expected Clearance Rate of Greek courts (2015 data) will be near 100% and the cost and time savings will be improved at approximately 70% after new system's application [8]. Provided that the necessary funding will be made available, the ambition of the Greek Courts Administration is to have the courts 'fully digitalized' by 2020.

Decrease of pending cases and qualitative improvement of provided services to citizens are anticipated after system's full application. The administrative burden of judicial system bodies will be reduced and the justice award process will be upgraded by supporting judicial officers' duties. Communication among justice officers and other government sector bodies will become more effective by use of appropriate electronic interfaces. The need for physical presence regarding public administration services provision such as submitting and receiving documents will be drastically reduced.

Management of justice system is expected to be improved. Statistical and administrative data will be produced systematically, leading to objective information about justice operation and supporting the justice control mechanisms. Publication of statistics regarding justice's operation will also increase transparency in justice operation. Quality control will be enhanced through electronic archiving and monitoring of cases.

Lost revenue because of delays and final deletion of fine will be avoided by using interoperability with ministry of finance systems. Cost savings will be achieved by decreasing operational costs (storage areas, search time, printing documents, consumables) and by decreasing infrastructure costs and reducing administrative burden.

The Integrated Judicial Case Management System (OSDDY) could possible address some additional challenges. Such a court case management system may also have early warning devices, allowing proactive case management. Such warnings may relate to deadlines to prevent an accumulation of cases or the overrunning of predefined limits. Budgetary and financial monitoring could be also facilitated with related tools. For example, budgetary and financial court management could be assisted, providing court heads with information on the budget and on the monitoring of expenditure (operating, payroll, building management, etc.). Furthermore, it could be used to provide court heads with information on court costs alone, that is, the full costs of court proceedings, together with other case-related services, paid by the parties in the course of those proceedings (taxes, legal assistance, legal representation, travel costs, etc.). Such a budgetary and financial monitoring could be possibly improved by establishing communication with systems in the ministry of finance and ministry of justice. It could also be exploited for regular courts and case management, measuring not only court activity but also the workload of judges, prosecutors and court clerks, the number of incoming cases, the handled cases and the pending cases.

In the light of the quantitative assessments, such a system, has a more forward-looking role in improving the efficiency of the judicial system. Business intelligence tools can be developed to collect, consolidate, model and report court's data to give the head of the court an overview of activity as a decision making aid. The court activity data collected, could be used to prepare human and budgetary resource allocation plans.

General-interest information can be easily provided to public users. Such information may describe courts' work or provide a judicial map showing the distribution of courts across the country.

The system can be also used to notify summons for hearings and pre-hearing appointments electronically. This method of notification can take several forms: a text message (SMS) or email to the court user, or else a special computer application for dedicated websites, which court users can access with a pre-notified user name and password and on which notices and summonses can be filed securely.

In addition to lawyers, other professionals may also make use of electronic communication. These include enforcement agents (e.g. police officers), or experts who are invited from the court ad hoc.

Lastly, to facilitate and support various forms of communication, other types of technology could be used between the courts, professionals and users for judicial proceedings. Videoconferencing (e.g. 'distance meetings' or 'distance examinations'), as an alternative to ordinary court hearings and electronic recording of testimony of parties and witnesses during the investigation or trial stages could be also considered. The purpose is two-fold. Firstly, recordings limit the need for examination of parties and witnesses before the courts of appeal, thereby saving both time and money. Secondly, in cases where parties or witnesses are still to be examined anew before the court of appeal, the recordings from the court of first instance can counter any inconsistencies or 'adjustments' in their testimonies.

Interoperability mechanisms can be used to exchange information with National and European Union systems. A first application of e-Justice interconnection could be with e-Codex (e-Justice Communication via Online Data Exchange) which has been designated to provide European citizens, companies and legal professionals with easier access to cross-border proceedings, improve cross-border collaboration between the courts and agencies and improve efficiency through interoperability between the existing national ICT solutions.

The array of policies needed to increase the efficiency of the judicial system is wider than one system. Major contributors to increase the inefficiency of the Greek judicial system would be best practice adoption of successful European countries' cases. In the long term, the Greek justice system would converge on a trial duration comparable with other European countries, promoting a fairer justice system and higher economic growth. The only real obstacle to further such development appears to be of a financial nature. As far as funding is concerned, one may assume the necessary funds will be made available by the government sooner or later.

5 Conclusions

The judicial system plays a pivotal role in the enforcement of law, the safeguarding of human rights, the definition of civil rights and, thus, for the smooth functioning of society. In this paper, we highlighted the performance problem of Greek courts of justice, regarding the large amount of pending cases that affects the lives of citizens, discourages foreign investments, and ultimately hinders economic growth.

By adopting the new Integrated Judicial Case Management System (OSDDY), Greek courts could increase drastically the Clearance Rate approaching a value of 100% and simultaneously saving time and reducing relative costs. Following the introduction of the new e-Justice system, we thus propose a complementary set of actions adopting best practices in technically inefficient courts.

Jurists have stressed on multiple occasions that Greece's judiciary is in critical need of reform, it should become a modern, effective judiciary in line with international best practice and EU standards [16]. Strategic governance in central level of e-Justice initiatives is needed in order to identify the modernization issues of the judicial system, to set priorities with defined objectives and to initiate reforms attached to these objectives.

Efficient justice process is essential to economic development and sustainable growth [17]. Economies with an efficient judiciary in which courts can effectively enforce law obligations have more developed economies and a higher level of overall development [18]. A stronger judiciary is also associated with more rapid growth of entrepreneurship [19] and enhanced judicial system efficiency can improve the business climate, foster innovation, attract foreign direct investment and secure tax revenues [20].

Contemporary judicial reform efforts focus on attaining a higher level of court automation. Some countries have started to introduce sophisticated and comprehensive electronic case management systems. Reducing in-person interactions with court officers minimizes potential opportunities for corruption and results in speedier trials, better access to courts and more reliable service of process. These features also reduce the cost to enforce a contract—court users save in reproduction costs and courthouse visits while courts save in storage, archiving and court officers' costs. Public authorities expect the system to result in considerable cost and time savings along with increased transparency and more reliable statistical data on court operations.

Acknowledgements. This paper is a result of the project "SmartEGOV: Harnessing EGOV for Smart Governance (Foundations, methods, Tools)/NORTE-01-0145-FEDER-000037", supported by Norte Portugal Regional Operational Programme (NORTE 2020), under the PORTUGAL 2020 Partnership Agreement, through the European Regional Development Fund (EFDR).

References

1. Aldashev, G.: Legal institutions, political economy, and development. Oxf. Rev. Econ. Policy **25**(2), 257–270 (2009)
2. Peyrache, A., Zago, A.: Large courts, small justice!: the inefficiency and the optimal structure of the Italian justice sector. Omega **64**, 42–56 (2016)

3. Jappelli, T., Pagano, M., Bianco, M.: Courts and banks: effects of judicial enforcement on credit markets. J. Money Credit Bank. **37**(2), 401–411 (2005)
4. Falavigna, G., Ippoliti, R., Manello, A., Ramello, G.B.: Judicial productivity, delay and efficiency: a directional distance function (DDF) approach. Eur. J. Oper. Res. **240**(2), 592–601 (2015)
5. European Court of Human Rights: Guide on Article 6 of the European Convention on Human Rights (2013)
6. European Commission: Quality of Public Administration a Toolbox for Practitioners, Theme 6: Strengthening the quality of judicial systems (2015)
7. Chrysopoulos, P.: Greece First in Europe in Number of Pending Administrative Cases. Greek Reporter (2017)
8. Hellenic Federation of Enterprises, ELTRUN: Benefits of applying e-Justice in the Greek judicial system, Enterprises and Digital Economy 3rd chapter (2015)
9. The European Commission for the Efficiency of Justice: European judicial systems Efficiency and quality of justice. CEPEJ STUDIES No. 23 (2016)
10. World Bank Group: Doing Business 2017, Equal Opportunity for All (2017)
11. European Commission: EU Justice Scoreboard (2016)
12. CEPEJ Studies No. 4, "L'administration de la justice et la qualité des décisions de justice" ("Administration of justice and quality of court decisions"), in CEPEJ, "La qualité des décisions de justice" ("The quality of court decisions"), (Hélène PAULIAT, edited by Pascal MBONGO - French only)
13. Sarantis, D., Askounis, D.: Electronic criminal record in Greece: project management approach and lessons learned in public administration. Transylv. Rev. Adm. Sci. **5**(25), 132–146 (2009)
14. Sarantis, D., Askounis, D.: Electronic government interoperability framework in Greece: project management approach and lessons learned in public administration. J. US-Chin. Public Adm. **7**(3), 39–49 (2010)
15. European Commission: Task Force for Greece: Progress on technical assistance, Memo, Brussels (2013)
16. Sitaropoulos, N.: Delayed Justice in Greek Administrative Courts and Lack of an Effective Domestic Remedy-Comment on Interim Resolution CM/ResDh (2007) 74 (2011)
17. Ball, G.G., Kesan, J.P.: Judges, courts and economic development: the impact of judicial human capital on the efficiency and accuracy of the court system. In: 15th Annual Conference of the International Society for New Institutional Economics, Stanford University, Stanford (2010)
18. Kenneth, K.: The judiciary and economic development. University of Chicago Law & Economics, Olin Working Paper 287 (2006)
19. Islam, R.: Do more transparent governments govern better? Policy Research Working Paper 3077, World Bank, Washington, DC (2003)
20. Esposito, G., Sergi, L., Pompe, S.: Judicial system reform in italy: a key to growth. IMF Working Paper. 14/32, International Monetary Fund, Washington, DC (2014)

Knowledge Management in the Context of e-Government

Social Network for Education: What Are the Resources Desired by Students?

Guilherme Henrique Alves Borges[1]([⊠]) [iD],
Paulo Henrique de Souza Bermejo[2] [iD],
Everton Leonardo de Almeida[1] [iD],
and Thiago Almeida Martins Marques[1] [iD]

[1] Universidade Federal de Lavras, Lavras, Minas Gerais, Brazil
ghaborges@gmail.com, evtufla@gmail.com,
thiagomartins.marques@gmail.com
[2] Universidade de Brasília, Brasília, Distrito Federal, Brazil
paulobermejounb@gmail.com

Abstract. In the educational field, new technology appears all the time, making the teaching and learning process more interesting and effective. In this scenario, one of the tools that has gained prominence is educational social networks. Despite the progress made, there is still no consolidated field of study for educational social networks. Therefore, the objective of this research was to identify the resources desired by students in this type of network. For this, 369 questionnaires were given, and to analyze the results, cluster analysis and discriminant analysis were used. The results reveal that the most relevant resources in an educational social network are the note consultation service, the evaluation of various aspects of the institution, and the sending of suggestions and improvements. Among the less important resources were the consultation of menus of canteens at the university restaurant and the sharing and evaluation of newsrooms. These results highlight the idea that an educational social network can contribute to collaborative learning and closer relationships between students and teachers.

Keywords: Education · Educational social networks · Educational technologies

1 Introduction

The various improvements in teaching methodologies that have traditionally been adopted are only possible because of the emergence of the Internet and other digital tools [39], one of them being social networks [7]. The tools present in social networks provide several opportunities for the accomplishment of educational activities [23]. Many educational institutions have gained significant benefits by adopting social networks as a way of maintaining the educational process [45].

[37] argue that the use of Internet technologies for educational purposes can be considered one of the major changes that have occurred in the academic world over the past few years. It had provided new platforms, tools, and applications, allowing people to develop socially [32].

© Springer International Publishing AG 2017
A. Kő and E. Francesconi (Eds.): EGOVIS 2017, LNCS 10441, pp. 263–277, 2017.
DOI: 10.1007/978-3-319-64248-2_19

Recent studies have demonstrated that social education networks are useful in teaching and learning, as well as in the student's career management [4]. These networks allow for enriching activities related to education through the construction of environments where students can interact with each other and share experiences, difficulties, results, materials, comments and other actions that enhance learning. According to [34], for educational institutions to remain relevant, they must promote literacy in a social network.

[15] argue that the ability to contact groups of people should be the main quality educational institutions should explore. The use of technology in teaching significantly increases effectiveness, making it perfect for students and teachers to become more involved with the information needed to build learning. A similar conclusion was made by [31], holding that online social networks facilitate the interactions among individuals and learning.

Despite all the advances in educational social networks, there are still important gaps in the literature that need to be filled; there is still not enough experience regarding the scope and consequences of the development of new technologies in education [32], especially regarding their role in the teaching and learning process [14]. It is also necessary to discover if social networks can be another evolution in the use of technologies for the educational process [43].

[46] points out that the main studies on educational technologies have focused on open resources, such as e-mail and blogs, but emphasize the need to develop studies focused on the use of social networks as a learning tool. This aligns with [48], who defend the need to create new tools for students and teachers.

[1] points out that there is an opportunity to structure a new area of study when analyzing educational social networks and that these debates are important for the development of young people. [50] indicates that one must also investigate what the motivating factors are for participation in social educational networks.

This research aims to answer the following question: What are the relevant resources in an educational social network from the view of its users? In this sense, the general objective of this research was to identify the resources desired by students in a thematic social network for education by using multivariate data analysis (cluster analysis and discriminant analysis). At the same time, the important resources from the point of view of non-students were sought as well because the opinion of this group is important in the study of educational social networks, and they represented almost 26% of the study's sample.

2 Theoretical Reference

2.1 Defining Social Networks and Its Main Attributes

Several researchers consider the starting point of social networks to be the system devised by Murray Turoff, an American researcher who in 1976 proposed the electronic information exchange system (EIES) [9]. Since then, the use of electronic equipment as mediator of relations between individuals and communities has only grown, especially since the 2000s with the expansion of the Internet [12].

A social network can be defined as a service offered on the Web that meets the following characteristics: (i) limited system where people can build a public or semi-public profile; (ii) users can create a list with other users with whom they share connections; (iii) it is possible to view and interact with the list of user and third-party connections [14]. Other authors define social networks as sites where a user can create a profile and build a personal network and where it is possible to connect to other users with different goals, whether professional or personal [24].

Based on these definitions, [14] points out that the first social networking site, Six Degrees, came into being in 1997. In this network, it was possible to create a profile, have a list of friends, and see a friend's list of other friends. These features already existed on other systems, but it was the first time they were combined into one. [42] suggests that social networking tools have five effective functions: building a community; access to the most diverse perspectives; the construction and sharing of knowledge; mobilization of people; and the coordination of resources and actions.

2.2   The Social Educational Networks and the Fundamental Factors in Their Composition

With the evolution of social networks, diverse and specific applications have emerged and are being used as, for example, health [21], social inclusion [28], and society of development [18]. In the educational area, it was not different; applications aimed at helping the teaching and learning process were created and were being used by students in the most diverse places and in the most different forms [8, 38, 44]. Social networks are important in education because they facilitate interaction with a larger group of people, help the student explore his or her professional identity, and assist in the enhancement of the student's social and cognitive abilities [20]. In addition, social networks allow for deeper approaches, increase learning time, and support development and social learning [47]. Social networks can still be used in research groups or as teaching tools, bringing changes to the dynamics of the learning process [27].

[49] discuss and present five principles for the use of social networking technologies in education: their use to improve student learning; their use as an integral aspect of teaching; professional support for their use; planning, budgeting, and evaluation as key activities; and the infusion of users into the network being supported by collaborative efforts. [41] affirm that there are four widely accepted principles of social networks in support of the educational process: knowledge content; dialogue; agency; and collaboration.

Several authors sought to identify the main factors that influence the use of technologies such as social networks in education. For [13], utility and ease of use are fundamental dimensions of students' attitudes toward technology. Other authors, such as [29], went deeper and identified behavioral intention, direct experience with technology, individual beliefs, communication and information, change management, support for use, easy access and use support, ease of use, increased efficacy with technology, learning time, utility, and relative value as important factors.

[52] identified some benefits of social networking technologies for education, such as greater student engagement, greater efficiency for both teachers and students through the creation of workgroups that help students understand complex concepts, and the ability to learn through technology.

Especially in the Brazilian case, there are also obstacles related to Internet coverage and its quality, mainly within educational institutions, as well as issues involving privacy because in many places, access to social networks is blocked [25]. In addition, despite their widespread use, social networks, including those geared toward education, have garnered some negative reactions [23]. One of the main criticisms relates to the quality of information that is made available in malware by malicious users [10].

Another point that receives criticism is the division (nationality, age, sex, etc.) that occurs in some social networks; although in their conception, they are all widely accessible [14]. It is necessary to consider the resistance to change on the part of education professionals who treat the use of social tools as one more task that they must carry out [11].

2.3   The Evolution of the Process of Teaching and Learning Through Technologies, Online Tools, and the Use of Social Networks

The term education has undergone modifications over time, and often, some adjectives are included as complements or synonyms of educational activities, such as environmental education, health education, traffic education, social education, and many others [33].

In this scenario, information and communication technologies (ICTs) have been important and have facilitated the activities of the most diverse sectors of society, not only in education, but also in the banking, commercial, and transportation sectors, among others [40].

The growth of new technologies has transformed teaching and learning. New doors were opened, allowing for more innovative and stimulating ways of working with ICTs to make teaching and learning dynamic, varied, and attractive to young students [40].

[3] addresses the use of informal writing through a series of text messages. For [51], teachers can discuss the use of informal writing through text messages among students of higher education because they are familiar with instant communication. Communication does not only need to occur through text messages, but also through instant messages or messages between friends on Facebook [51].

Facebook is the social network that has the largest number of users in the world, exceeding one billion people [25]. Often, it has supported educational activities; although, this is not the main focus of the network [25, 35, 36, 40].

Virtual learning environments (AVAs) are other types of non-face-to-face mediation software that are often used by teachers and students to conduct educational activities.

3   Methodology

This work can be classified as applied and descriptive research because it seeks to solve problems related to concrete applications and to describe the characteristics of a population and because the subject is already known [19]. It is still characterized as a quantitative study because it is based on the principle of objectivity, where its results are quantified and analyzed on the basis of numbers [16]. Quantitative studies generally seek to follow, with methodological rigor, a previously established plan based on variables that are the object of operational definition [7]. The survey was used as a research method because according to [17], it is commonly used in obtaining information about a certain group of people to produce descriptions about it, which is done by making use of a predefined instrument [6].

To analyze the data obtained through the survey, multivariate analysis techniques were used [22]. The Cronbach's alpha coefficient was also used to measure the reliability of the studied variables. Thus, the Cronbach's alpha coefficient was obtained with the general value of 0.888. According to [30], Cronbach's alpha coefficient varies between 0 and 1, and above 0.6, the reliability of the scale can be considered satisfactory [22].

These analyzes were performed using the Statistical Package for Social Sciences (SPSS) software version 21.0. SPSS was considered more appropriate to the nature of the data collected and helped enable the application of multivariate analysis techniques commonly used in social science studies.

Because the researchers had access to a list of 4,000 people who had already taken part in similar research related to a federal higher education institution, several rounds of e-mailing were conducted until 369 questionnaires were answered. To do so, simple random sampling was used without replacement, which occurs when each sampling unit is sequentially selected so that each one has the same chance of being chosen with the previous element being removed from the population [5]. The 369 respondents represented 14% of the initial population.

The online questionnaires were applied between the months of November 2015 and January 2016 and were structured with a series of initial questions to identify the profile of the respondent; this was followed by the perception of the users regarding certain resources commonly used in educational social networks.

For each proposed resource, the person indicated the degree of importance of that resource and the frequency of its use. If the respondent was not a student, he or she would only answer the question about the importance of the appeal. The scales of frequency of use and importance were 5 points, ranging from "never" and "always" to frequency and "unimportant" to "very important" to importance.

The resources were identified in the literature, and some were proposed by the authors to cover aspects relevant to students. The identification of resources is described in Table 1.

Table 1. Resources for educational social networks proposed in the reports.

Resource	Reference
Evaluation of the educational institution and related aspects	[25, 26, 32]
Monitoring statistics of educational institutions	Authors' suggestion
Space to suggest improvements in educational institutions	Authors' suggestion
Viewing and sharing photos and videos	[11, 15, 25]
Writing and writing essays	[25]
Video classes	[2, 25]
Chat	[15, 25, 26]
News and events	[15, 25, 32]
Discussion forums	[11, 15, 25, 32]
Services—consultation of canteen and restaurant menus	Authors' suggestion
School calendar	[2, 11, 15]
Security alerts	Authors' suggestion

Source: Prepared by the authors.

4   Results and Discussion

4.1   Characterization of the Sample

Of the 369 respondents to the questionnaire, 274 (74.25%) are students and 95 (25.75%) are non-students. Of the respondents, 48.24% are attending higher education while 42.28% have completed higher education. Also, 189 are men and 180 are women, and as far as the age group is concerned, only 1% are under 18 years of age, 52% are between 18 and 24 years old, and 47% are over 24 years old.

As far as technology is concerned, 95% have a smartphone with Internet access, and the most common means of access is Wi-Fi (46.90%), followed by 3G and 4G (4.90%). The most used operating system is Android, which is present in 71% of the handsets, followed by iOS with 16%. The other information collected is described in Table 4.

4.2   Degree of Importance of the Resources of a Thematic Social Network for Education

Regarding the degree of importance observed by the respondents for each resource, both for students and those who are not studying, the most important feature in their perceptions is the note consultation service, obtained at more than 68.56% as "very important." As a result, the video-teaching and assessment resources of the educational institution were evaluated as the most important while for non-students, the most important resources were the monitoring of statistics on teaching and video institutions classes.

Among the less important resources for students were the consultation of canteen menus and restaurants, the sharing and evaluation of essays, and the recording and control of activities. For the non-students, the resources classified as less important were the space for proposing improvements and the resource to consult notes. Table 2 shows the degree of importance attributed to all the proposed resources.

Table 2. Degree of importance attributed to resources by students and non-students.

Variables		Unimportant	Little important	Medium important	Important	Very important
Evaluation of several aspects of the educational institution	Student	2.9%	0.7%	10.2%	35.8%	50.4%
	Non-students	2.1%	1.1%	6.3%	28.4%	62.1%
Follow-up of statistics on the institution	Student	4.0%	4.8%	19.4%	41.0%	30.8%
	Non-students	2.1%	1.1%	7.4%	36.8%	52.6%
Sending of suggestions and improvements	Student	5.1%	1.1%	8.4%	38.3%	47.1%
	Non-students	40.0%	–	4.2%	14.7%	41.1%
Sharing of photos and videos	Student	6.6%	12.0%	28.8%	33.2%	19.3%
	Non-students	4.2%	8.4%	16.8%	40.0%	30.5%
Sharing of essays	Student	9.5%	11.7%	22.6%	33.9%	22.3%
	Non-students	4.2%	6.3%	14.7%	38.9%	35.8%
Video classes	Student	7.3%	1.8%	10.2%	28.8%	51.8%
	Non-students	5.3%	3.2%	2.1%	24.2%	65.3%
Educational chats	Student	8.0%	7.3%	23.7%	37.2%	23.7%
	Non-students	5.3%	3.2%	15.8%	35.8%	40.0%
Event calendar and notifications	Student	6.6%	3.6%	18.2%	40.5%	31.0%
	Non-students	5.3%	3.2%	22.1%	36.8%	32.6%
Creation and participation of discussion forums	Student	8.4%	5.5%	19.7%	38.7%	27.7%
	Non-students	6.3%	3.2%	9.5%	43.2%	37.9%
Consult of grade	Student	6.9%	0.7%	2.9%	20.4%	69.0%
	Non-students	7.4%	–	3.2%	22.1%	67.4%
Restaurant/canteen menu consult	Student	10.6%	9.5%	17.2%	33.6%	29.2%
	Non-students	7.4%	18.9%	28.4%	27.4%	17.9%
Registration and activities control	Student	9.5%	3.6%	20.4%	33.9%	32.5%
	Non-students	7.4%	2.1%	12.6%	38.9%	38.9%
Alert of authorities about occurrences in the educational institution	Student	9.1%	6.6%	10.6%	31.4%	42.3%
	Non-students	6.3%	4.2%	12.6%	36.8%	40.0%

Source: Prepared by the authors.

As for frequency of use, the resources students would most use were the examination of grades and video-lessons, which obtained 67.5% and 49%, respectively, of classifications as "always." Among the less-used resources, the sharing and evaluation of essays and the sending of suggestions and improvements to the managers of educational institutions were selected. Table 3 shows the frequency of use indicated by the respondents who declared themselves as students.

Table 3. Frequency of use indicated by respondents who declared themselves students.

Variables	Never	Few times	Sometimes	Many times	Always
Assessment of several aspects of the educational institution	0.8%	9.0%	48.9%	29.3%	12.0%
Follow-up of statistics on the institution	0.8%	15.5%	50.8%	26.5%	6.4%
Sharing of suggestions and improvements	–	4.6%	44.1%	35.2%	16.1%
Sharing of photos and videos	2.3%	25.1%	35.9%	27.8%	8.9%
Sharing of essays	6.2%	22.6%	30.4%	27.2%	13.6%
Video classes	1.9%	4.7%	13.2%	31.1%	49.0%
Educational chats	3.1%	12.1%	37.1%	29.7%	18.0%
Event calendar and notifications	0.8%	6.3%	30.9%	34.8%	27.3%
Creation and participation of discussion forums	2.7%	10.6%	36.1%	33.3%	17.3%
Consult of grade	–	2.0%	9.4%	21.2%	67.5%
Restaurant/canteen menu consult	2.4%	12.5%	18.8%	24.7%	41.6%
Registration and activities control	1.6%	6.3%	24.2%	31.3%	36.5%
Alert of authorities about occurrences in the educational institution	1.2%	16.3%	31.0%	19.8%	31.7%

Source: Prepared by the authors.

Among respondents who are students, 95 (25.74%) consider that teaching quality, physical structure, support equipment and materials, library and didactic material, food, space for physical activities, teacher qualification, and research laboratories are relevant items in the evaluation of educational institutions.

Regarding services related to the subjects, 80 students and non-students, which represents 21.70% of the sample, would like all the items (time and place, subjects' syllabus, lesson plan, telephone list and e-mails, school schedule, bus timetables, and hitchhiking) to be available for consultation on a virtual teaching platform.

4.3   Cluster Analysis

To deepen the characteristics of the respondents, a cluster analysis was applied to the research data. As previously mentioned, the hierarchical agglomeration method (Ward) was used in the cluster analysis with two groups: Group 1 is composed of 346 respondents, and Group 2 is composed of 22 respondents, whose profiles are presented in Table 4.

Table 4. Profile of groups composed of cluster analysis.

Specification	Groups				
	1			2	
Total people	346			22	
	Count	% (of total)		Count	% (of total)
Sex	Male	177	48.1%	Male 11	3.0%
	Female	169	45.9%	Female 11	3.0%
Age group	Between 15 and 17 years	3	0.8%	Between 15 and 17 years –	–
	Between 18 and 24 years	180	49.0%	Between 18 and 24 years 11	3.0%
	Above 24 years	162	44,1%	Above 24 years 11	3.0%
Scholarity	Complete primary education	1	0.3%	Complete primary education –	–
	Incomplete high school	1	0.3%	Incomplete high school –	–
	Complete high school	21	5.7%	Complete high school 1	0.3%
	Complete technical education	11	3.0%	Complete technical education –	–
	Incomplete higher education	167	45.4%	Incomplete higher education 10	2.7%
	Complete higher education	145	39.4%	Complete higher education 11	3.0%
Smartphone with Internet access	Yes	329	89.4%	Yes 20	4.6%
	No	17	5.4%	No 2	0.5%
Smartphone internet access mode	Wi-Fi	159	43.2%	Wi-Fi 14	3.8%
	3G and 4G	17	4.6%	3G and 4G 1	0.3%
	Both	153	41.6%	Both 6	1.6%
	Not applicable	17	4.6%	Not applicable 1	0.3%
Operational system of the smartphone	Android	246	66.8%	Android 15	4.1%
	IOS	55	14.9%	IOS 4	1.1%
	Windows phone	24	6.5%	Windows phone 1	0.3%
	Not applicable	19	5.2%	Not applicable 2	0.5%
	Others	2	0.5%	Others –	–
Is studying at the moment	Yes	256	69.6%	Yes 90	24.5%
	No	17	4.6%	No 5	1.4%

Source: Prepared by the authors.

The analysis is based on the identification of the opinions of the interviewees according to each group formed. The results obtained for Group 1 respondents showed that the three of the most important resources are consultation of grades, evaluation of various aspects of educational institutions, and sending of suggestions and improvements. On the other hand, the three resources considered less important for this group are menu consultation, registration, and control of activities and sharing of essays.

As for Group 2 respondents, the three most important resources are evaluation of various aspects of the institution, monitoring statistics on institutions, and sending suggestions and improvements. The three resources considered less important for this group are menu query, event calendar query, and newsroom sharing. These results can be seen in Table 5.

Knowing that the evaluation of the educational institution in several aspects was considered one of the most important resources in an educational social network, [25] reinforce that in addition to the benefits linked to the teaching–learning process, it is expected to generate a self-promotion of the educational institution because the activities are published and the content is shared. In this sense, another result achieved by using social networks in relation to virtual learning environments is that it is possible to involve other actors, such as companies, parents, and the community in which the institution is inserted [25].

Table 5. Opinion of respondents according to each cluster formed.

Groups					
1			2		
346 people			22 people		
More important	Count	% (of total)	Less important	Count	% (of total)
Grade consult	253	68.8%	Evaluation of several aspects of the educational institution	6	1.6%
Evaluation of several aspects of the educational institution	191	51.9%	Monitoring statistics on institutions	4	1.1%
Sending suggestions and improvements to institutional managers	165	44.8%	Sending suggestions and improvements to institutional managers	3	0.8%
Groups					
1			2		
346 people			22 people		
Less important	Count	% (of total)	Less important	Count	% (of total)
Conult of menu	13	3.5%	Conult of grades	22	6.0%
Registration and control of activities	10	2.7%	Notifications and consultation of events calendar and news related to the institution	22	6.0%
Sharing of essays	9	2.4%	Alert authorities about incidents in institutions	22	6.0%

Source: Prepared by the authors.

The space for suggesting improvements in educational institutions is also pointed out as desired in both groups because the interaction between students or users and managers contributes to the common welfare of the actors involved. From this perspective, [15] have identified, for example, that voting proposals in an educational social network may produce positive results.

Regarding all the important variables, it should be noted that most respondents in Group 2 considered these resources as "unimportant" compared to the number of people who assigned some degree of importance to these variables. For this reason, Group 1 was composed of respondents considered "more interested". On the other hand, Group 2 was composed of respondents considered as "less interested".

4.4 Discriminant Analysis

The discriminant analysis evaluates which variables best discriminate the groups in question ("more interested" and "less interested"). The canonical correlation is used to verify the adjustment of the variables extracted by the method, and raising its value squared is a similar method to obtain the coefficient of determination. In the case analyzed, the canonical correlation presented a value of 0.859, which means that 73.8% of the variances of the variables are explained by the discriminant model.

To know the degree of importance that each variable has within the discriminant function, the most indicated method is the analysis of the standardized coefficients of the canonical function. Thus, the most relevant variables for the study in order of importance were the following: "alerting authorities about incidents" (0,188) "sending suggestions and improvements to managers of institutions" (0.123), "video-lessons" (0.378), "Receive notifications and query the event calendar" (0.259), and "note query" (0.638).

The degree of correctness of the discriminant function was also verified when trying to classify the groups formed. As can be seen in Table 6, the percentage of correctness is 99.2% of the original cases, which represents a good percentage.

The results of Table 6 show that three respondents showed a certain interest in the functional resources of a social network and were indifferent to such resources whereas no respondents who showed lack of interest were misclassified as being interested in using them.

Table 6. Results of classification[a] by discriminant analysis.

		Group	Association to the group planned		Total
			1	2	
Original	Count	1	343	3	346
		2	0	22	22
	%	1	99.1%	0.9%	100%
		2	0.0%	100%	100%

[a]99.2% of original cases grouped correctly classified.
Source: Prepared by the authors.

Through a multivariate analysis of all the resources proposed in the questionnaire, it was verified that the most relevant social network aspects for the users of a higher education institution are evaluation of various aspects of the institution, the consultation of grades, access to video lessons, the possibility of receiving notifications and consultations to the agenda of academic events, an area for sending suggestions and improvements to managers, and alerting the authorities about occurrences at the university. On the other hand, the resources considered irrelevant were the consultation of menus of canteens and the university restaurant, the recording and control of activities, and the sharing and evaluation of essays.

In general, the results of this research were positive, showing the importance of the use of an educational social network as a favorable space for school learning. These results demonstrate at the same time the interest and desire of people to use in their day-to-day networks with these characteristics and also the latent need to develop initiatives that overcome the difficulties and demands of a new generation of teachers and students.

5 Conclusion

In the educational field, new technologies have emerged, making the teaching and learning process more interesting and effective. In this scenario, one of the tools that has gained prominence over traditional teaching methods is educational social networks. Therefore, the objective of this research was to identify the resources desired by students in a thematic social network for education; this was carried out through the application of 369 questionnaires and multivariate analysis techniques, such as cluster analysis (for knowledge of respondents' characteristics), and discriminant analysis (to identify the resources that were discriminated the most). Also, there was a search for the important resources from the point of view of non-student respondents, considering that this group corresponded to almost 26% of the sample.

Based on the characteristics identified, the two groups were called "more interested" and "less interested" respondents, bringing together a total of 346 and 22 people, respectively. The group of less-interested respondents received this definition because most of these respondents considered these variables as "unimportant" compared to the number of people who assigned some degree of importance to these variables. Next, which of the variables discriminate the two groups was carried out.

The degree of dissimilarity between the groups was also analyzed with a statistical test of mean difference, which showed that the variables indicated a difference between the groups (more and less interested). Thus, based on these results, the desired resources for those who showed a greater interest in social networks in education are the following: allow the evaluation of various aspects of the institution, the consultation of notes, access to video lessons, the possibility of receiving notifications and consultations to the agenda of academic events, an area for sending suggestions and improvements to managers, and alerting authorities to occurrences at the university. On the other hand, the resources considered irrelevant were the consultation of menus of canteens and the university restaurant, registration and control of activities and the sharing and evaluation of essays.

The desire for the resources cited and the degree of importance attributed to each of them reinforces the idea that an educational social network can contribute to collaborative learning and closer relations between the actors. In addition, the research results provide support not only for researchers, but also for entrepreneurs as it provides relevant and prioritized information for the construction and diffusion of such platforms. The limitation of this research includes a lack of practical examples for the evaluation of resources. In addition, as indications for future work, the expansion of the sample of respondents and the development of technological solutions with these resources, along with the application of high school, technical, and graduation students, to evaluate the contributions that these resources could provide to improve students' socialization and learning can be carried out.

Acknowledgments. A special thanks goes out to the National Council for Scientific and Technological Development (CNPq, Brazil) – Process 402789/2015-6 for their support of this research.

References

1. Ahn, J.: The effect of social network sites on adolescents' social and academic development: current theories and controversies. J. Am. Soc. Inform. Sci. Technol. **62**(8), 1435–1445 (2011)
2. Álvarez, E.C.M.: Redes sociales educativas: caso edmodo en educación secundaria. Campus Virtuales **4**(2), 10–15 (2015)
3. Aronson, E.: Not by Chance Alone: My Life as a Social Psychologist. Basic Books, New York (2010)
4. Benson, V., Morgan, S.: Student experience and ubiquitous learning in higher education: impact of wireless and cloud applications. Creat. Educ. **4**(08), 1 (2013)
5. Bolfarine, H., Bussab, W.O.: Elementos de Amostragem. USP, São Paulo (1994)
6. Bryman, A., Becker, S., Sempik, J.: Quality criteria for quantitative, qualitative and mixed methods research: a view from social policy. Int. J. Soc. Res. Methodol. **11**(4), 261–276 (2008)
7. Cabero-Almenara, J., Marín-Díaz, V.: Educational possibilities of social networks and group work. University students' perceptions. Comunicar **21**(42), 165–172 (2014)
8. Cheston, C.C., Flickinger, T.E., Chisolm, M.S.: Social media use in medical education: a systematic review. Acad. Med. **88**(6), 893–901 (2013)
9. Da Costa, R.: Por um nov or um nov or um novo conceito de comunidade: o conceito de comunidade: Redes sociais, comunidades pessoais, inteligência coletiva. Interface-Comunic. Saúde Educ. **9**(17), 235–248 (2005)
10. Dascalu, M.I., Bodea, C.N., Lytras, M., De Pablos, P.O., Burlacu, A.: Improving e-learning communities through optimal composition of multidisciplinary learning groups. Comput. Hum. Behav. **30**, 362–371 (2014)
11. dos Santos, M.D.S., dos Santos, J.D.M.M.: Primeira avaliação do projeto piloto para uma Rede Social Educacional do Município de Novo Hamburgo. UFSM, Santa Maria (2013)
12. Drigas, A., Leliopoulos, P.: Business to consumer (B2C) e-commerce decade evolution. Int. J. Knowl. Soc. Res. (IJKSR) **4**(4), 1–10 (2013)

13. Edmunds, R., Thorpe, M., Conole, G.: Student attitudes towards and use of ICT in course study, work and social activity: a technology acceptance model approach. Br. J. Edu. Technol. **43**(1), 71–84 (2012)
14. Ellison, N.B.: Social network sites: definition, history, and scholarship. J. Comput.-Med. Commun. **13**(1), 210–230 (2007)
15. Fardoun, H.M., López, S.R., Alghazzawi, D.M., Castillo, J.R.: Looking for leaders: reaching the future leaders in education through online social networks. Procedia-Soc. Behav. Sci. **47**, 2036–2043 (2012)
16. Fonseca, J.J.S.: Metodologia da Pesquisa Científica. UECE, Fortaleza (2002)
17. Freitas, H., Oliveira, M., Saccol, A.Z., Moscarola, J.: O método de pesquisa survey. Revista de Administração. **35**(3), 105–112 (2000)
18. Furini, L.A.: Redes sociais temáticas: o caso das redes sociais de assistência à criança e ao adolescente em Presidente Prudente (SP) e suas representações sociais. UNESP, Presidente Prudente (2008)
19. Gil, A.C.: Como elaborar projetos de pesquisa. São Paulo **5**, 61 (2002)
20. Green, J., Wyllie, A., Jackson, D.: Social networking for nurse education: possibilities, perils and pitfalls. Contemp. Nurse. **47**(1–2), 180–189 (2014)
21. Greene, J.A., Choudhry, N.K., Kilabuk, E., Shrank, W.H.: Online social networking by patients with diabetes: a qualitative evaluation of communication with Facebook. J. Gen. Intern. Med. **26**(3), 287–292 (2011)
22. Hair, J.F., Black, W.C., Babin, B.J., Anderson, R.E., Tatham, R.L.: Análise multivariada de dados. Bookman Editora, Porto Alegre (2009)
23. Işık, F.: Comparison of the use of social network in education between North and South Cyprus. Procedia-Soc. Behav. Sci. **103**, 210–219 (2013)
24. Jucevičienė, P., Valinevičienė, G.: A conceptual model of social networking in higher education. Elektronika ir Elektrotechnika **102**(6), 55–58 (2015)
25. Juliani, D.P., Juliani, J.P., de Souza, J.A., de Bettio, R.W.: Utilização das redes sociais na educação: guia para o uso do Facebook em uma instituição de ensino superior. RENOTE **10** (3), 1–11 (2012)
26. Junior, E.V.B., Gomes, A.S., Souza, F.V.: Plataforma social educacional redu. In: Anais dos Workshops do Congresso Brasileiro de Informática na Educação, vol. 1, no. 1 (2012)
27. Kakushi, L.E., Évora, Y.D.M.: As redes sociais na educação em enfermagem: revisão integrativa da literatura. Rev. Latino-Am. de Enferm. **24**, 2709 (2016)
28. Kaminski, D.: Redes sociais temáticas inclusivas. Doctoral dissertation, Universidade Federal de Santa Catarina (2014)
29. Kent, J.: Enhancing the adoption of educational technologies in a postsecondary environment. Doctoral dissertation, Royal Roads University (2015)
30. Malhotra, N.K.: Pesquisa de marketing: uma orientação aplicada. Bookman Editora, Porto Alegre (2012)
31. Mayer, A.: Online social networks in economics. Decis. Support Syst. **47**(3), 169–184 (2009)
32. Mora, H.M., Pont, M.T.S., Casado, G.D.M., Iglesias, V.G.: Management of social networks in the educational process. Comput. Hum. Behav. **51**, 890–895 (2015)
33. Munhoz, A.V.: Práticas investigativas: experiências não escolarizadas. Diálogos na Pedagogia Coletâneas **1**(11), 11–26 (2012)
34. Pegrum, M.: Mobile Learning: Languages. Literacies and Cultures. Springer, New York (2014)
35. Pretto, N.D.L.: Redes sociais e educação: o que quer a geração alt + tab nas ruas? | Social Networks and education: what does the alt + tab generation protesting on the streets want? Liinc em Rev. **10**(1), 344–350 (2014)

36. Pretto, N.D.L.: Reflexões: Ativismo, redes sociais e educação. EDUFBA, Salvador (2013)
37. Sánchez, R.A., Cortijo, V., Javed, U.: Students' perceptions of Facebook for academic purposes. Comput. Educ. **70**, 138–149 (2014)
38. Ruibal, A.R., Vegas, M.I.: Uso de la red social Edmodo en asignaturas de secundaria: Biología y Geología. Rev. Tecnología Ciencia y Educ. **1**(3), 97–103 (2016)
39. Sangrà, A., Wheeler, S.: New Informal ways of learning: or are we formalising the informal? Int. J. Educ. Technol. High. Educ. **10**(1), 286–293 (2013)
40. Santos, R.A., Campos, T.C.: Redes sociais na educação: uso do Facebook no estudo de trigonometria no triângulo retângulo. IFF, Rio de Janeiro (2013)
41. Scardamalia, M., Bereiter, C.: Pedagogical biases in educational technologies. Educ. Technol. **48**(3), 3–11 (2008)
42. Scearce, D., Kasper, G., Grant, H.M.: Working Wikily 2.0: Social Change with a Network Mindset. The Monitor Institute (2009)
43. Tadeu, P., Lucas, J.: Social network in education: a mathematical pilot test. Procedia-Soc. Behav. Sci. **106**, 2409–2418 (2013)
44. Tess, P.A.: The role of social media in higher education classes (real and virtual)–a literature review. Comput. Hum. Behav. **29**(5), A60–A68 (2013)
45. Tinmaz, H.: Social networking websites as an innovative framework for connectivism. Contemp. Educ. Technol. **3**(3), 234–245 (2012)
46. Toetenel, L.: Social networking: a collaborative open educational resource. Comput. Assist. Lang. Learn. **27**(2), 149–162 (2014)
47. Tower, M., Latimer, S., Hewitt, J.: Social networking as a learning tool: nursing students' perception of efficacy. Nurse Educ. Today **34**(6), 1012–1017 (2014)
48. Usluel, Y.K., Mazman, S.G.: Adoption of Web 2.0 tools in distance education. Procedia-Soc. Behav. Sci. **1**(1), 818–823 (2009)
49. Van Melle, E., Cimellaro, L., Shulha, L.: A dynamic framework to guide the implementation and evaluation of educational technologies. Educ. Inf. Technol. **8**(3), 267–285 (2003)
50. Veletsianos, G., Navarrete, C.: Online social networks as formal learning environments: learner experiences and activities. Int. Rev. Res. Open Distrib. Learn. **13**(1), 144–166 (2012)
51. Viju, M.J.: The role of web technologies and social media at higher education level in India. Int. J. Engl. Lang. Lit. Humanit. **3**(1), 361–367 (2015)
52. Watty, K., McKay, J., Ngo, L.: Innovative teaching, learning and assessment in accounting education: engaging with digital technologies that enhance student learning. CPA Australia/Deakin University (2014)

Driving Forces and Design of the TTÜ e-Governance Technologies and Services Master's Program

Ingrid Pappel[1]([✉]), Karin Oolu[1], Ingmar Pappel[2], and Dirk Draheim[1]

[1] Large-Scale Systems Group, Tallinn University of Technology,
Tallinn, Estonia
{ingrid.pappel,karin.oolu,dirk.draheim}@ttu.ee
[2] Interinx Ltd., Tallinn, Estonia
ingmar.pappel@interinx.com

Abstract. The development of e-governance is impossible without appropriately training qualified professionals in this field. The lack of untrained personnel in government offices provided the need to create an interdisciplinary program linking different domains such as IT, law and public sector. This paper discusses the creation and development of a Master's study program in e-Governance Technologies and Services, highlighting the most common obstacles and providing solutions. The curriculum prepares managers and specialists to be responsible for the development of e-Governance in organizations and e-Government initiatives. It enables them to master the management and business processes related to e-Governance. Students gain broad knowledge about the makings of a modern state and the transition process into e-Governance.

Keywords: e-Governance training · e-Governance awareness · Curriculum development · Higher education · Knowledge management · e-Government policies and strategies

1 Introduction

Undoubtedly, e-Governance can help improve overall governance both in the public and the private sectors. The required reforms of underlying working processes provide state and local governments with new opportunities to engage in governance.

Moreover, civil society and the private sector are both engaged in the design of effective public services. E-governance is also instrumental to raising public awareness about environmental conditions and ecological problems as well as gender equality. It has the potential to supply a reinforced context to advance equal opportunities for women in the management of democratic institutions, through gender-blind education in e-governance, e-access and e-services provision, and to promote political correctness in institutional governance discourse. The Digital Agenda for Estonia 2020 aims for a "simpler state 2020" [1], which also entails highly trained public officials.

In order to make the public sector more efficient, several solutions have been developed in Estonia [2], e.g. the document exchange center (DEC) and e-services at the citizen portal eesti.ee environment. However, whether these solutions are utilised in

© Springer International Publishing AG 2017
A. Kő and E. Francesconi (Eds.): EGOVIS 2017, LNCS 10441, pp. 278–293, 2017.
DOI: 10.1007/978-3-319-64248-2_20

full depends on the awareness and willingness of people. For instance, over the years, the volume of paper documents exchanged between authorities has decreased significantly [3], which in turn shows a rather high level of competence in the public sector. Nevertheless, recourse to training and constant teaching has not decreased sufficiently, and the need to have trained officials from the high level education has persisted. In addition, in the framework of globalization, information society development and social strife against corruption and inefficiency in government, traditional methods have become less satisfactory. In order to avoid the emergence of corruption components and to create new and more convenient methods for service provision, new routines and skills are required.

This is where e-governance steps in as a form of government providing a new level of open cooperation between the state and society with the widespread use of modern ICT, supplying a full range of public services for all categories of citizens and enterprises. However, with the use of new ICT in public government there is a need for training highly qualified specialists in the field of public administration and management.

Therefore, the Master's Program in e-governance should promote the state policy in the field of information, e-governance, development and use of national electronic information resources. The curriculum must include a wider overview of the administrative and legal aspects of e-governance. Furthermore, future public sector employees should have the capacity to create and apply the solutions that respond to that [4]. In 2011, the first steps were taken to create a field of study that would merge the science and practice of e-governance [4]. This curriculum (accreditation by Estonian Ministry of Education and Research in March 2013) enables public sector institutions in Estonia as well as abroad to send their officials to acquire further education and field-specific knowledge. The program gives students insight into the makings of a modern state: the transition into e-governance, its management and development, including an overview of the administrative and legal aspects of e-governance. In that context, the focus is on designing, developing and improving governmental systems and implementing e-government components on every level of the state. There is an option to specialise in IT technologies, innovation/services in the public and private sector or the adoption and marketing of e-governance. Moreover, the course covers ICT-based user-oriented services offered by the government alongside providing experience in the industry, practical research and project work during the studies.

This paper elaborates on the necessity and utility of our study program and how it was designed, also including the feedback already received for the teaching process. Section 2 provides an overview of the theories and practices for curriculum development, the current state of the study programme and the method for its design. The background of the students is also considered. Section 3 contains the results of the curriculum design process, including feedback from the students. In Sect. 4, experience and results are considered to derive factors and recommendations for improvement. This is followed by a discussion of related work in Sect. 5, future work in Sect. 6 and conclusion in Sect. 7.

2   Theory and Practice of the Curriculum Development

This paper presents the curriculum development for e-Governance Technologies and Services at Tallinn University of Technology. The first admissions to the program were in 2013 and the first cohort graduated in 2014. We were faced with the question of how to develop a curriculum which integrates theories, methods and practice in the e-governance field, and simultaneously enhances the skills and competencies of the students, includes field experts and meets the requirements of employers.

However, all university study programs should strive to combine theories, best practices and entail research to the greatest extent possible. For instance, the accumulation of educational materials and research personnel will provide a common ground for knowledge transfer. ICT tools and media resources, research data and research resources should create the portfolio for the practices. These practices can be used in different competence centers such as e-Governance Academy and other similar institutions world-wide. In addition, the creation of a theoretical and empirical framework to analyze the e-governance of the subject in the education system of Estonia and the European Union helps to involve practical side by participation in different e-Governance related projects. Finally, the accumulation of research materials gained from the different projects should be the basis for the preparation of publications, designed to identify the phenomenon of e-governance and analyze the features of its manifestation in the competitive environment of a multicultural Europe. It can be also achieved through international mobility by exchanging experiences and sharing best practices at the university network level.

2.1   Theoretical Approaches of the Curriculum Development

The idea of a curriculum is not new. It is commonly understood as the foundation of the teaching-learning process in higher education institutions. The term has its origins in the running/chariot tracks of Greece. It was, literally, "a course." In Latin, curriculum was a racing chariot; the word *currere* meant "to run".

Curriculum development as a research field has its origins in the beginning of 20th century. A number of paradigms, models, and approaches have been discussed over the decades, resulting in a vast amount of academic literature. "Designing an appropriate curriculum is considered the foundation stone for high quality programs and services, regardless of the type of educational program and institution" state Khan and Law [5]. They argue that curriculum development should be the central focus of the strategic planning activity. "A curriculum development approach should encompass its design, implementation and assessment" [5]. Figure 1, according to Khan and Law, shows that "curriculum development requires a systematic approach and therefore, should be undertaken in stages:

- In stage 1, both the internal and external environment should be studied in order to have a comprehensive understanding of the circumstances in and around the educational institutions.

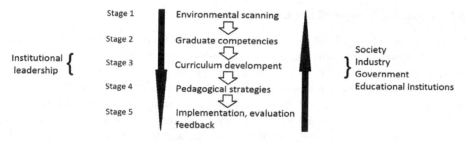

Fig. 1. Curriculum development process and system [5]

- In stage 2, which is more closely related to and based on the knowledge of stage 1, specific competencies to be developed in students are identified and analyzed. These competencies are then classified into personal, professional and institutional competencies.
- In stage 3, the actual curriculum is designed and developed keeping in mind the knowledge from previous two stages.
- In stage 4, specific pedagogical strategies most relevant and effective in imparting the intended knowledge in the curriculum are identified and proposed. In stage 5, it is critical for educational institutions to establish the necessary mechanisms to follow-up on the planned implementation of the curriculum; perform regular evaluations of the learning outcomes; provide necessary and timely feedback to interested parties, including policymakers, academic directors, parents, teachers and students to name a few" [5].

Figure 1 also suggests that while developing a curriculum, other factors such as society, industry, and the role of government have to be fully taken into account. This requires dynamic, participative and pro-active institutional leadership.

According to different sources available in the existing literature, curriculum development can be considered from different perspectives, for example (according to Mednick):

- "Curriculum as a Body of Knowledge/Product
- Curriculum as Process
- Curriculum as Praxis (practice)
- Curriculum as Context" [6].

In the curriculum as process model the learners are not objects to be acted upon, and the focus is instead on interactions - attention shifts from teaching to learning. "It need to be emphasized that "Curriculum as Process" is not a physical thing, but rather the interaction of teachers, students, and knowledge" [6]. Moreover, there is a growing need for higher education institutions to respond to the changing conditions and environment. According to Nygaard et al. "the development of a learning-centred education has become increasingly important as the tasks, roles and identities of the modern worker have changed with the introduction of new technologies and the establishment of the knowledge economy" [7]. Hence, the "e-Governance Technologies and Services" curriculum elaborated on below is guided by the newer approaches where the focus is shifted to learners.

2.2 Designing Process of the Curriculum

Many factors supported the development of the "e-Governance Technologies and Services" Master's program. For instance, the e-State Charter was prepared in 2008 to provide the principles and criteria for assessing the relevance of the work done by the institutions when utilising the possibilities of information technology for the interests and needs of the people. In addition, the practical necessity arose from the personal experience of the author [1]. Long-time experience leading the Estonian e-government related projects revealed a vast gap between public sector officials and IT personnel. The latter do not understand public administration procedures and the relevant legal framework, and public sector could not explain the requirements for the e-governance related systems in the development process. Based on the interdisciplinary experiences, the program considers the transition to e-governance in various disciplines and combines administration, IT, legal and economic perspectives [4]. The combination of an undergraduate degree in law with a PhD in the field of informatics gave the author a notable advantage regarding the state-related e-governance development process due to insight into state functions and legal requirements. In that context, the practical need for this Master's programme was recognised.

Along with the e-Governance Academy (eGA), the e-Governance and Technologies study program was launched in 2013. The curriculum gives an opportunity to study natural sciences, social sciences, and humanities from a broad perspective. This well-rounded program enables students to combine subjects from the different domains including IT, legal environment and public administration. Allowing to tailor courses by individual design in turn helps to meet the public sector career goals of the students.

The program has a far-reaching impact. Firstly, in higher education, it enables to transfer knowledge abroad and introduce Estonian e-Governance implementations, alongside the development of a generic study program about e-governance using the example of Estonia's experience. Secondly, as a comprehensive e-democracy educational standard is developed, civil society institutions and the public sector are impacted. Lastly, awareness is raised in democratic institutions by providing comprehensive training for institutional decision-makers about the principles and vehicles of e-governance.

The design process itself mirrors the action research approach (AR) where every cycle of investigation irritates the new one. The use of the AR approach is at once a dynamic force of change within the social setting as well as a highly effective method of studying and evaluating this change. The elements of the action design research (ADR) are identified in Fig. 2. ADR is a research method for gaining prescriptive design knowledge through building and evaluating an ensemble of IT artefacts in an organisational setting [8], and the same principle has been applied in the curriculum design as well.

As action research can in particular be used by professionals who want to investigate and improve their own working practices, this participative approach suited the research activities. Considering the fact that this field of research has developed mostly through practice, AR methods have proven to be useful in the process for understanding the e-governance needs and competence in the public sector. As mentioned above, the author possessed knowledge about the subject matter which facilitated the

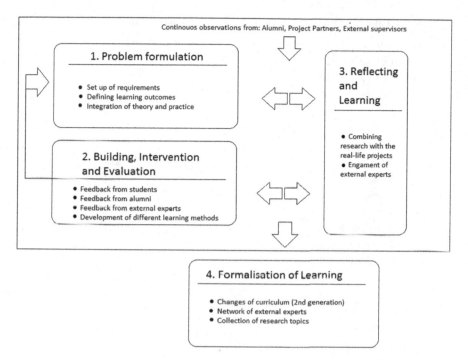

Fig. 2. Different cycles of Investigations based on the ADR approach [8]

curriculum development project, specifically combining the theoretical input with the process. Moreover, being a student at the same university for years gave valuable input for avoiding mistakes which had occurred in other study programmes. Finally, as professionalism is a complex interplay between theories, research methods and practice, the most highly valued experts in the field were also involved into development process.

Our curriculum development process can be also seen as a combination of contextual learning theories [9–12] in a diverse and constantly changing environment. As regards teaching e-Governance, the learning context changes over time, rather than being static or clearly mixed. Learning can be seen as a social process which takes place between embedded learners (Table 1).

2.3 Curriculum Status

The first admission cycle was in 2013 and there were 18 students from 5 different countries. By spring 2017, three cycles of graduation have taken place. At the moment, there are 63 active students and there have been 34 graduates between 2014 and 2016. As shown in Table 2, the largest number of students are from Estonia, followed by Ukraine and Georgia which are also very actively supported by EGA activities. Furthermore, there are 7 target countries (Afghanistan, Georgia, Ukraine, Belarus, Moldova, Palestine and other OECD-suggested countries) for the scholarship offered by the

Table 1. Origin of active students and graduates (April 2017)

Citizenship	Amount of students	Amount of graduates	Total
Estonia	28	12	40
Ukraine	10	4	14
Georgia	5	8	13
Niger	4	2	6
Turkey	1	2	3
Palestine		3	3
USA	2	1	3
Nepal	2		2
Russia	2		2
Pakistan	2		2
Bangladesh	1		1
Indonesia	1		1
Moldova	1		1
Namibia	1		1
Norway	1		1
Portugal	1		1
Germany	1		1
Sri Lanka		1	1
Hungary		1	1
	63	34	97

Table 2. Results of successfully defended Master's theses (April 2017)

Year	Defended theses	Cum laude (incl)	Countries
2014	1	1	Estonia
2015	7	1	Estonia (5), Palestine, Turkey
2016	26	6	Estonia (6), Ukraine (4), Georgia (8), USA (1), Palestine (2), Turkey (1), Niger (2), Sri Lanka (1), Hungary (1)
TOTAL	34	8	

Estonian Ministry of Foreign Affairs which explains the high number of students from specific countries.

3 Competences and Practical Values for Students

Nygaard et al. [7] have researched the learning-based paradigm for higher education and demonstrate the close relationship between curriculum development and the learning processes of the students. In their view, "the mastery of an academic profession requires students to acquire at least three important competencies:

– Competent use of **models and theories**
– Competent use of **research methods**
– Competent analysis of **empirical practice**" [7].

3.1   Content Delivery

Our curriculum gives a systematic overview of the relationship between ICT and public administration along with the basic concepts, theoretical principles and research methods for the different fields. A graduate can analyze, model, plan and apply the IT solutions needed for reorganizing public administration processes as well as identify the requirements for new developments. The learning capacity of the curriculum is 120 ECP-s, i.e. two years of full-time studies. The organization of the study process and the academic workload of the students are determined by the Tallinn University of Technology Study Regulations. The significant dates in the cycle of the academic year and deadlines related to the organization of the course are fixed in the academic calendar.

The structure of the E-Governance Technologies and Services study program is divided into basic modules, core modules and the main specialty. Most compulsory courses are focused on IT, business process design, including service design, and the legal framework together with intellectual property. Elective courses can vary from project management to economics. The fourth semester is typically allocated for thesis writing and an internship.

At first, most of the lecturers for this programme came from outside of the university, and eGA experts in particular were significantly involved. Engaging field experts is a positive trend and provides students with real-life practical knowledge. However, from a didactic point of view, the academic integrity is somewhat broken. Many combinations of learning are involved in the curriculum learning process, including online learning and some formulation of the flipped classroom. Within various learning approaches, reflective learning can be facilitated through group debates, panel discussions, group assignments and individual assignments which give students the opportunity to actively participate in the entire learning process. Over the three-year development process, a number of courses are either partly or almost fully taught using e-environments. The most basic and introductory course "Information Society Concepts and Principles" and "Information Management and Digital Archiving" are MOOC (Massive Online Open Course) courses. Thus, most of the learning process is designed and carried out on the Eliademy platform. In addition, the majority of other courses include support from the closed e-learning environment Moodle.

However, as we took the approach of constantly improving the program and validating the real needs of our consumers (students), various questionnaires and surveys were conducted. Ornstein [13] suggest that "Curriculum development encompasses how a curriculum is planned, implemented and evaluated, as well as what people, processes and procedures are involved". Therefore, the feedback has been obtained from stakeholders and students on a regular basis. Our goal has been to get students to objectify and negotiate their subjective meanings. It is always difficult to obtain

feedback from all the relevant parties. However, at the very least, we received information from the more active ones. The feedback from students has been an important
input for the curriculum development process. Constant interaction with students and
semester-based surveys have provided honest feedback and highlighted the requirements for changes. For instance, the figures below (Figs. 3 and 4) show the survey
results from spring 2015.

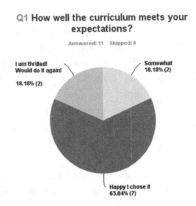

Fig. 3. Satisfaction rate of students

As seen on Fig. 4, the most valued course according to the feedback from students
is "Legal Framework of e-Governance", which has actually gained maximum points
every single year. In that course, the content as well as the teaching-learning process
are balanced and updated. E-Learning is mixed with classical classroom lectures given
by a university professor with a very high level expertise, including from practical
e-governance activities worldwide. The professor for this course is also involved in
different eGA projects and activities abroad. Therefore, there is a clear combination of a
theoretical background coupled with real-life experiences.

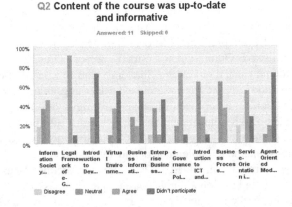

Fig. 4. Course content

3.2   Research and Project Work of Theses

Competent use of research methods will be taught to students through the Master's seminar and Master's thesis. By writing the Master's thesis and conducting research on the chosen scientific problem related to their specialty, students acquire the skills for establishing a research problem, selecting suitable methodologies for solving it, and logically structuring their work.

The workload of the students for writing their thesis compared to the whole curriculum is relatively high (30 ECTS[1]). Tallinn University of Technology has settled that 26 academic hours of work equals 1 ECTS. Thus, a thesis amounts to 780 h of work by the student, recommended to be carried out during the last semester. Completing the required volume of studies and successfully defending one's thesis are the essential requirements for graduation. After three admission cycles, 34 Master's theses have been defended, as shown in Tables 2 and 3 (Table 3 in Appendix A).

The research methods most used in theses are qualitative (case-studies and action-design science), but the amount of design-science methodology and engineering works is progressively growing. The problems analysed in theses are concerned with different fields of e-governance research. Most of the theses are focussed on describing service design and the creation of a better service provision environment. Three alumni are continuing their studies at the PhD level. A more detailed overview about the theses can be found in Table 3 in Appendix A.

3.3   Practice and Hand-on Teaching with e-State Laboratory

Nevertheless, due to a lack of resources, many good ideas and thoughts could not be put into action. Thus, it became clear that partnerships and networks with many different stakeholders were required for more comprehensive research and knowledge transfer. Consequently, the need arose for the formalization of the laboratory [4], as it was understood that only technological development work would not achieve the best results for local governments. In autumn 2011, the e-State Technologies Laboratory was formalized under the Institute of Informatics. For further system development, it is necessary to import the methodologies of other countries. The e-State Technologies Laboratory shall facilitate training and workshops, and enable students to participate in practical experiments related to e-governance and the improvement of the local government processes. The aim is to export models, prototypes and know-how produced by the students and the laboratory to foreign countries through public sector institutions and academic research. Furthermore, practitioners and lecturers are engaged in the laboratory which further has a practical implementation platform and allows for the involvement of students from other countries. The biggest achievement thus far has been the project "E-government 2.0 in practice", carried out as part of the ERASMUS + Program under the Cooperation for Innovation and the Exchange of

---

[1] European Credit Transfer and Accumulation System (ECTS) is a standard for comparing the study attainment and performance of students in higher education across the European Union and other collaborating European countries.

Table 3. Overview of defended theses and used research methods (2014–2016)

	Title of the thesis	Used research method (s)
IG and governmental procedure	Concept of Estonian government cloud and data embassies	Case study
	Attracting foreign entrepreneurs to open businesses in estonia	Case study, action-design research
	Analyses of return on investments in Estonian eGovernment development projects	Case study
	Modern governments need no legacy policy to keep ICT cost under control	Semi-focused interviews, quantitative study
	Georgian ID card and its relation to the e-Governance and citizen awareness	Case study, action-design research
	Development of e-Service environment in public sector at the local government (case of georgia)	Case study, action-design research
	Perspectives of local e-Governance development in ukraine	Qualitative methods, legal analysis
	Digitalization of the national diplomatic systems: Small powers dimension	Case-study, descriptive methods
	Improving knowledge transfer processes of e-Governance competence example of estonia	Design-science, reactive research
	The potential of the Estonian e-Governance infrastructure in supporting displaced Estonian residents in national emergencies	–
	ICT in water governance and stakeholders enhancement in palestine	Qualitative methods
Service design	How new e-Services for e-Residency project can be designed: the case of virtual incubation service	Online survey
	Designing a proactive service to disabled child's parents	Qualitative methods, case-study, agent-oriented modelling
	Decreasing public sector spending through the increment of E-Service usage by implementing marketing in E-Governance. Example of the road administration	Case-study
	The improvement of a self-service process of employment mediation in estonian unemployment insurance fund	Action-design research
	Trust towards services of e-Government	Mixed methods
	Impact of service process improvement in a public-private organisational environment: case of purchasing process of petroleum products in Lagos seaport, Nigeria	Action-design research
	Contribution of living labs for territorial development and innovation	Case-study

(continued)

Table 3. (*continued*)

	Title of the thesis	Used research method (s)
IT and engineering cyber and information security e-Democracy and legal framework	Service brokering environment for an airline	Design-science, business process modelling
	Analysis of integrity: cloud service provider case	–
	Citizen centric e-Health information system model for Turkey	Design-science
	Analysis of digital security threats in aviation sector	Design-science
	Creating ontology prototype based on x-road system	Design-science
	Increasing a digital invoice handling maturity model	Design-science
	Suggesting the best information security management system for palestinian e-Government	Qualitative methods
	Cyber security capability assessment	Case-study
	Georgian cyber defence unit cyber reserve	Case-study, descriptive methods
	The effects of the digital divide in the society and analysis of digital divide in Turkey	–
	Engaging youth voter participation with internet voting in Estonia	Case-study
	The introduction of RFID Microchipping, lessons from e-Voting	Case-study
	Building trust in digital age	Action research
Knowledge transfer	The introduction to E-Learning design to school teachers in Georgia	Case-study
	Factors influencing the use of e-Learning in schools in crisis areas: syrian teachers' perspectives	Quantitative survey
	A MOOC for teaching a MSc-level Blockchain-tech course	Design-science

Good Practices. The project included the creation of a knowledge base and the analysis of key strategic documents and case-studies illustrating how highly effective e-government 2.0 policies are being implemented in individual countries. The main outcome of the second phase was the design of curricula and educational materials in the area of e-administration for Polish universities.

4   Discussion and Recommendations

Over the years, a combination of good practices and theory has been developed. Firstly, students must be explained the theory behind e-governance as well as the scope of governance in general. Secondly, real life experiments must be introduced, for instance those based on Estonian success nor non-success stories. This provides an understanding of how to re-engineer processes in the home countries of the students. The underlying idea behind the study program is that after graduation students are able to create an e-governance concept for their countries. Finally, students must apply the string of theories and research methods in order to investigate practices in the real world, outside of the university environment. In order to do that, constant collaboration with different authorities is needed. For instance, most of the theses topics have been provided from the different ministries from Estonia and abroad. In addition, there are immediate learning requirements which need to be taken into account when engaging in curriculum development.

5   Related Works

It can be said that designing a curriculum is creating an intellectual path for one's students, and it results in a series of experiences that the students will gain. Curriculum design includes the consideration of aims, intended learning outcomes, syllabus, learning and teaching methods, and assessment. In that sense, the process is similar world-wide. However, the design process itself can vary as well as the learning and teaching methodologies and approaches. Nygaard [7, 14] provides a good overview of different designing approaches and learning methods. According to him, several theories can be considered while developing a curriculum. The biggest similarity to our curriculum development is the involvement of students. As mentioned before in Sect. 3, Nygaard discusses a learning-based paradigm for higher education and demonstrates the close relationship between curriculum development and the learning processes of students [7]. Besides, a lot of attention has been drawn to the learning process, which appears to be a social process. In the curriculum development process, the working group (students, teachers and other key actors) constitutes a unique ongoing system of social relations [14]. In addition, contextual learning is a useful foundation for curriculum development in today's changing society. A curriculum must respond and adapt to the changes in society.

The necessity to respond to the changes in society is also highlighted in other papers. For instance, Yastrebova [15] seeks to reveal how modern university education could respond to changes that take place in contemporary society development. He tries to follow the task of bridging the Academy and Society needs. Although this paper analyzes needs from the law perspective, the same applies to the field of e-governance as well. The curriculum must constantly adapt, as changing technologies and public service provision are in continuous development. Although the transformation is ongoing, nevertheless, the relevant academic disciplines remain yet comprehensive in order to guarantee academic integrity. However, the optimal sequence of training and the different learning possibilities must be considered and included. According to

Yastrebova [15], structuring cognitive elements of the training system should be considered as well.

To conclude, according to Khan and Law [5] the importance of a curriculum depends on providing high quality educational programs and services. However, he also highlights the gaps between how a curriculum is supposed to be developed in theory and how this is done in practice. Although the development of our curriculum did not strictly follow all of the most common theories, still observing and learning from others approaches has provided valuable input for building academic integrity.

6 Future Work

The 8th Framework project of European Commission Horizon 2020 academic collaboration incorporates a specific creed of Europe in the Changing World studies, which unfolds into a range of problematic issues open for project studies and development, including *Understanding Europe - promoting the European public and cultural space, including civil society development as an operative foundation for e-democracy elaboration.* Further development should aim to elaborate extensively on the findings and expertise of the 7th Framework Project of EC IRNet - International Research Network for the study and development of new tools and methods for advanced pedagogical science in the field of ICT instruments, e-learning and intercultural competences in terms of relevant blended learning tools and techniques for the e-governance program development. To conclude, the sustainability of the study program is planned to achieve through many contingency means. Firstly, a functional educational system is implemented in governance, sustained by the national and regional level institutions involved in the project consortium. Secondly, there will be advanced continuous training of staff and faculty to sustain the implemented master's program. Thirdly, close collaboration is undertaken with eGA and similar institutions abroad in order to fulfil their needs by teaching the staff for their projects. Finally, sustainable LMS and other e-learning (b-learning and u-learning) platforms are elaborated on, namely a MOOC of comprehensive parameters of e-government. The necessity of such a program is justified of itself as the applications for admission in 2016 were 7 students per seat. This clearly shows the societal demand to gain the knowledge for how to re-engineer the state and move towards e-governance.

7 Conclusion

By today, the academic integrity of the study program has been established. Most of the lecturers are from the university staff and related to different research groups. Almost 30% of the lecturers are members of the Large Scale Systems group (LSS), which is beneficial for the scientific foundation of the study program. Nevertheless, more attention should be paid to real-life practical research by involving students in projects outside university. The implementation and development of e-governance related projects is one of the important activities of the e-Governance laboratory. Here, different parties from the state, local governments, the private sector and scientific research organization are working together. Currently, we are discussing with local governments the conditions under which they would provide their data for statistical and scientific purposes. Such agreements must certainly be regulated in accordance with copyrights and other principles. Many local governments have already agreed to be involved in research projects. Once the curriculum has been developed, its implementation and evaluation is a long-term process. Therefore, an approach to developing a curriculum should encompass its design, implementation and assessment. Feedback from stakeholders and students has been obtained on a regular basis. The results of roundtables with employers have shown the need for continuous development of the curriculum. Today the majority of the teaching requirements originate in the needs of employers from the public sector. In our opinion, it is equally important to consider and maintain the academic perspective as well.

A Appendix

See Table 3.

References

1. Ministry of Economic Affairs and Communications, Digital Agenda 2020 for Estonia (2013)
2. Pappel, I., Pappel, I.: Implementation of service-based e-government and establishment of state IT components interoperability at local authorities. In: The 3rd IEEE International Conference on Advanced Computer Control (ICACC 2011), Harbin (2011)
3. Draheim, D., Koosapoeg, K., Lauk, M., Pappel, I., Pappel, I., Tepandi, J.: The design of the estonian governmental document exchange classification framework. In: Kő, A., Francesconi, E. (eds.) EGOVIS 2016. LNCS, vol. 9831, pp. 33–47. Springer, Cham (2016). doi:10.1007/978-3-319-44159-7_3
4. Pappel, I., Pappel, I., Saarmann, M.: Conception and activity directions for training and science centre supporting development of Estonian e-state technologies. In: 5th International Conference on Theory and Practice of Electronic Governance ICEGOV, Tallinn (2011)
5. Khan, M.A., Law, L.S.: An integrative approach to curriculum development in higher education in the USA: a theoretical framework. Int. Educ. Stud. 8(3), 66 (2015)
6. Mednick, F.: Curriculum theories. http://cnx.org/contents/VMr1OpSY@9/Curriculum-Theories
7. Nygaard, C., Højlt, T., Hermansen, M.: Learning-based curriculum development. High. Educ. 55, 33–50 (2008)
8. Sein, M., Henfridsson, O., Purao, S., Rossi, M., Lindgren, R.: Action research design. MIS Q. 35(1), 37–56 (2011)
9. Bruner, J.: The Culture of Education. Harvard University Press, Cambridge (1996)
10. Hermansen, M.: Relearning. Copenhagen Business School Press/DPU Press, Copenhagen (2005)
11. Lave, J., Wenger, E.: Situated Learning: Legitimate Peripheral Participation. Cambridge University Press, Cambridge (1991)

12. Vygotsky, L.S.: The Collected Works of L.S. Vygotsky, Volume 1: Problems of General Psychology. Plenum Press, London (1987)
13. Ornstein, A.C.: Curriculum Foundations, Principles, and Issues (2001)
14. Nygaard, C., Andersen, I.: Contextual learning in higher education. In: Milter, R.G., Perotti, V.S., Segers, M.S. (eds.) Educational Innovation in Economics and Business IX. Breaking Boundaries for Global Learning, pp. 277–294. Springer, Dordrecht (2004)
15. Yastrebova, O.A.: Renewing university-based curriculum in line with societal needs: a case of legal education in Russia. Int. J. Environ. Sci. Educ. 11(16), 9010–9016 (2016)

Strategic Planning in the Public Sector: How Can Brazilian Public Universities Transform Their Management, Computerise Processes and Improve Monitoring?

Lucas Cezar Mendonça[1]([⊠]) [iD], Fábio Henrique dos Anjos[1] [iD],
Paulo Henrique de Souza Bermejo[2] [iD], Tomás Dias Sant'Ana[1] [iD],
and Guilherme Henrique Alves Borges[3] [iD]

[1] Universidade Federal de Alfenas, Alfenas, Minas Gerais, Brazil
{lucas.mendonca,fabio.anjos,
tomas.santana}@unifal-mg.edu.br
[2] Universidade de Brasília, Brasília, Distrito Federal, Brazil
paulobermejounb@gmail.com
[3] Universidade Federal de Lavras, Lavras, Minas Gerais, Brazil
guilherme.borges@progolden.com.br

Abstract. The need for efficiency and quality in high-level educational institutions (HLEIs) has been increasing. When determining the future direction of these institutions, planning is playing an increasingly important role, as it involves rethinking the application of resources and developing processes to achieve the goals and mission of the organisation. Planning requires analysing the environment, establishing organisational guidelines and formulating a strategy and strategic control measures. Thus, it is no easy task. The objective of this study is to evaluate the management of institutional development plans (IDPs) in Brazilian public universities and, based on the results, propose software and a reference document (guidelines) to aid the elaboration, implementation and management of IDPs in these organisations. This applied social research used a qualitative approach. After analysis, it was revealed that public managers demand support in HLEIs. Based on this finding, we propose a reference document and software to support managers in the elaboration, implementation, management and monitoring of IDPs.

Keywords: Strategic planning · Institutional development plan · High-level educational institutions · Software · Reference document

1 Introduction

One of the greatest challenges governments face in democratic societies is achieving public management that rewards society for paying taxes and making it worthwhile with well-provided services and transparent use of public resources. To that end, studies on public administration are increasingly focusing on ways to improve citizens' living conditions and well-being through well-developed public policies.

© Springer International Publishing AG 2017
A. Kő and E. Francesconi (Eds.): EGOVIS 2017, LNCS 10441, pp. 294–306, 2017.
DOI: 10.1007/978-3-319-64248-2_21

In Brazil, despite many remnants of its patriarchal history, there has been progress towards improvements and transparency in public administration after the 1995 state management reform inspired by so-called *new public management* (NPM). According to this perspective, *managerialism* is based on the political project of its own structural adjustment to propose recommendations and reorganise the state apparatus [17].

According to Newman and Clarke [15], in past decades—especially the 1980s—the process of building welfare institutions in Brazil was constrained by economic and political obligations. Its strong foundation in the demands and complaints of social movements, however, has resulted in adjustments in administrative processes and democratic participatory politics. However, this process has not yet been completed, and the expectation that this new approach to public management will become the government standard has not been met [16].

The most recent goal in Brazil is to achieve an efficient administration with controlled results and flexible forms of management that grant managers autonomy in executing their tasks, whether they are related to material, financial or human issues [4]. This work intends to focus on managerial practices associated with the search for efficiency in the public sector. As an integral part of public administration, high-level educational institutions (HLEIs) are not taken for granted in the process of improvement of public management. In fact, these organisations are expected to produce ideas and innovative projects that can benefit society. In order to improve management and public policies, HLEIs' academic and administrative organisation must become a reference for other public organisations in terms of planning, monitoring and controlling activities.

One of the main tools for improving the management of these organisations is strategic planning (SP) as it allows the organisation to diagnose its situation in order to design future situations as well as establish its mission, vision and values to show society its raison d'être. Educational institutions' medium- and long-term strategic plans are called institutional development plans (IDP), and they have become mandatory in HLEIs due to Decree No. 5.773 May 9, 2006, which links these plans to the institutions' accreditation. This decree stipulates the minimum elements that must be addressed in educational institutions' organisational planning. It is important to highlight that, despite the fact that planning is mandatory, the effectiveness of the plan is not guaranteed within organisations and training systems.

This raises a few questions: How much effort are Brazilian HLEIs putting into their IDPs? What is the current scenario regarding IDPs' design, implementation and management? Have mechanisms been developed to serve these functions? To answer these questions, the present work aims to investigate the development, implementation and management of IDPs in 63 Brazilian public universities. Based on this investigation, the present study proposes a reference document (guidelines) and software to support the implementation of IPDs in public universities throughout the country. The software will be used by HLEIs to monitor and manage IDPs, while the guidelines will serve as a reference upon which HLEIs might base elaboration, implementation and management of their IDPs. The document is intended to guide the construction of IDPs in line with the current legislation. The software initiative is aligned with the National Education Plan, which emphasises that innovation should be a priority in universities.

This study uses a qualitative descriptive approach, which, through an applied social research model, seeks to generate knowledge for practical application to specific problems—in this case, to the elaboration, implementation and management of IDPs in government-run HLEIs.

The introduction of this study seeks to contextualise and problematise its subject to fuel debate and initiate investigation. Next, a brief theoretical framework is presented to contextualise IDPs and universities as strategic resources. The methods and results of the study are discussed next. Finally, conclusions are made, the theoretical and practical contributions as well as the limitations of the study are mentioned and recommendations for future work are presented.

2 Theoretical Background

2.1 Institutional Development Plan

Law No. 9,394 December 20, 1996 is the Law of Directives and Bases of National Education (DBL). It was the result of discussion and reflection between the executive, legislative and judicial branches of the Brazilian government as well as Brazilian citizens [18]. After the DBL was introduced, there was a need to introduce evaluative processes in HLEIs. Thus, the Governmental Assessment System for High-Level Education was instituted in 2004 in order to regulate and evaluate HLEIs [8].

An IDP is a document that identifies an HLEI's philosophy, mission statement, pedagogical guidelines, organisational structure and academic activities and ensures these elements' adequacy [2]. The guidelines on which the IDP is based include the institution's profile, mission, objectives and goals, field of academic performance, social responsibility, teaching policies and extension and research policies [13]. According to Souza [23], the IDP is a starting point for HLEIs that guides their development and helps them fulfil legal requirements. For Picawy [18], the IDP describes the HLEI part by part, including everything and everyone that participate in the administration, pedagogy and labour at the institution, thus determining its profile. In other words, the IDP is a guiding directive for the institution's measures and principles [18]. Mello et al. [13] point out that IDPs must be closely linked to the practice and results of institutional evaluations. In addition, it is essential to consider the principles, clarity, objectivity, coherence and feasibility of the document during its development in order to demonstrate its legal viability and integrity. According to Silva [21], IDPs have a positive impact on HLEIs; the greater the planning culture at the institution and the better managers understand how to use this tool, the better the institution can be.

Guidelines were created for developing IDPs in order to gain institutional support for them [2]. However, according to Picchiai [19], despite these guidelines, public servants' attitudes toward the document, including concerns regarding job security, the excessive formality of the document and limitations regarding interactions between the organisation and beneficiary, are the main challenges that must be overcome to achieve efficient planning in public organisations. This topic is discussed in more detail below.

2.2   Strategic Debate in Universities

The behavioural and cultural contexts of public administration, including in universities, are influenced by Brazil's Portuguese cultural roots. For instance, there are remnants of the country's patriarchal history and bureaucratic juridical–formal state, which require run-ins and improvisation to overcome the lack of organisational structure [19]. The Governmental University Restructuring and Expansion (REUNI) program, which was intended to eliminate these difficulties impeding planning, was implemented by the federal government in 2007. Despite the great benefits of this program in terms of expanding higher education, there was no initial planning or sufficient time for HLEIs to discuss expansion, since the announcement was published six months before proposals had to be submitted.

Currently, the desire for efficiency and quality in HLEIs is increasing. In particular, public universities have been questioned by society and the government regarding their real objectives, the rigidity of their bureaucratic structure, their inefficient use of government funds and the limited social relevance of the services they provide. Strategic planning plays a very important role in determining the course of an institution, since it allows for rethinking of the activities that will be developed in the period and takes into account the goals and objectives that will lead to the practical achievement of HLEIs' missions [23].

When creating a strategic plan, it is necessary to first analyse the environment in order to establish organisational guidelines and formulate an organisational strategy, and then to implement the strategy and strategic control. Information management is also relevant to strategic planning. The information should be used as a strategic resource to ensure that the legal and political requirements of the organisation are met, which is the most important step to spreading the institution's mission and objectives [14]. For Souza [23], planning in the field of education evolves over time from a practical to participatory principle, with knowledge ceasing to be considered the property of specialists and construction, participation, dialogue, collective local power, awareness and critical thinking increasing in value due to reflection on the practice of change.

As a flexible management tool, the IDP is guided by institutional objectives and goals, and its elaboration must be collective. Through the adoption of a participatory methodology, the IDP allows an organisation to take the opinions of the academic community and society into consideration when determining how to allocate its resources [23]. Thus, universities need to be organised and efficient to align with a contemporary managerialist model.

3   Methods

Using a qualitative descriptive approach, this research aims to propose guidelines and software to support the elaboration, implementation and management of strategic plans in Brazilian universities. In line with the nature, objectives and procedures of social research, the study is based on Gil's [7] method, which involves planning, data collection, analysis and interpretation and final writing of the report.

First, it was necessary to understand the management of IDPs within HLEIs by means of a questionnaire distributed to the planning and management departments of each Brazilian university. Based on the results of this questionnaire, guidelines and software are proposed to support IDP management. This research topic was chosen because HLEIs face difficulties when designing, implementing and managing IDPs. Applied research such as this study aims to produce knowledge for practical application to specific problems involving local interests [6]. Gil [7] argues that applied research is enriched in the course of its development, and its fundamental characteristics are interest in practical application and consequences of knowledge.

A comparative study of FORPDI software and similar systems was performed using a descriptive methodology based on experimentation with free trial software. The topics covered in this study, including the use and management of IDPs in Brazilian federal universities, reference document, IDP development process, implementation and management of IDPs and FORPDI, and the methods by which they were investigated are presented below.

3.1 Research Outline

Here, outlining refers to broad research planning, including graphical representation of the goals of the research, predicted results of analysis and anticipated interpretation of the data. This step was taken based on literature about strategic planning in the public sector, legislation regarding IDPs and the 63 HLEIs' approaches to analysing strategic plans. The research sought support from the National Forum of Planning and Administration Pro-Rectors (FORPLAD) to achieve a 100% response rate on the questionnaires. The methods used to answer the research questions, a literature search and survey, were defined in the research outline.

Literature Search. Through a search of related books and legislation, we sought to understand how strategic planning works in public organisations, how it is elaborated and which methodologies (Balanced Scorecard, SWOT analysis, etc.) are used to create strategic plans. The main objective of the search was to obtain information to serve as a basis for proposed guidelines regarding the management of IDPs in public HLEIs. The flexibility literature search allowed us to take the context of each university into account.

Survey. To understand the processes of elaboration, implementation and management of IDPs in HLEIs, a questionnaire was developed for distribution to 63 Brazilian universities (100%). A questionnaire is an instrument of data collection that consists of an ordered series of questions that are answered in one's own language, without an interviewer [11]. The procedure for this type of research is the same as that of a survey [1], and it allows data to be collected from a sample or group about the problem under study [7]. Surveys' main objective is to contribute the collected information to the area of interest [6]. The questionnaire in this study enabled accurate evaluation of the implementation, monitoring and control of IDPs in public universities since the questionnaire was completed by the primary users of IDPs (the planning and management departments). The questionnaire was hosted on an online platform, SurveyMonkey, to allow respondents to easily access it.

3.2   Reference Document Methodology

There are methodologies used in both the private and public sectors for strategic planning that can contribute to the implementation of the IDP. These methodologies are well tested. However, it is necessary to observe their application in the context of a public organisation. Therefore, some of the main methods used for strategic planning in the public sector will be discussed, namely, the Balanced Scorecard (BSC), Strategic Map of Higher Education (SMHE), Strategic Situational Planning (SSP) and SWOT (Strenghts, Weaknesses, Opportunities and Threats) analysis.

BSC. Kaplan and Norton [10] define the BSC as a new strategic instrument that allows new vectors without neglecting the financial measures of performance. These measures cover four perspectives: external clients, internal processes, learning and growth and financial needs. They are born from conscious and rigorous effort to translate organisational strategy into tangible objectives and measures. Thus, BSC is a management system, not just a measurement system, in line with Martins [12].

SMHE. The SMHE is the result of adaptation of the BSC's organisational performance measurements and control tools to IDPs in Brazilian HLEIs. The SMHE is a tool for visual representation of the IDP's strategy based on the BSC's quantum approach as an adaptive complex system [5].

SSP. The SSP aims to break from the deterministic, superficial view of traditional planning approaches in order to build a holistic approach that does not neglect important aspects of reality [9]. According to Rieg and Filho [20], the three main characteristics of the model are (i) gathering information (subjectivity), (ii) predicting future changes (uncertainty) and (iii) the conception of an unwanted result (plan-proposal).

SWOT. SWOT is a strategic management tool used to analyse an environment [24] in order to enable expansion of the positive aspects and elimination of the negative aspects of an organisation [3]. Widely recognised and used in both corporate and academic settings, SWOT analysis allows one to learn from and reflect on the present to create future plans [22].

4   Results

4.1   Survey of the Application and Management of IDPs in Brazilian Governmental Universities

The need for evaluation of the management of IDPs in HLEIs motivated the present work, becoming one of its research problems and objectives. Without a formal overview of how IDPs are managed in HLEIs, there is no way to propose interventions such as software and guidelines for managing IDPs.

To perform this evaluation, 63 questionnaires were sent to Brazilian universities to determine the stage of development of IDPs at HLEIs throughout the country. The questionnaire had a 100% response rate, which made it possible to perform a complete analysis of the management of IDP in HLEIs.

The main goal of this survey was to determine how IDP is managed. It is noteworthy that this work highlights the relationship between IDP and its complementary documents as well as the methods for elaboration and follow-up.

Only 1 of the 63 federal universities did not have a definite term. Nine universities were completed in 2015, while 53 (84.1%) are still developing their IDPs. There does not seem to be a standard time for developing an IDP. However, a five-year period was most common, with 42 HLEIs (66.67%) responding in this way.

Despite the wealth of research on strategic planning, 18 universities did not use a specific planning strategy for elaboration/management of their IDPs. The other 45 institutions used at least one method. SWOT analysis and BSC were the most frequent, used by 19 and 17 universities, respectively.

According to the questionnaires, IDP monitoring was considered one of the greatest challenges regarding strategic planning. Of the 53 HLEIs, 6 did not follow the IPD at all, 7 monitored their progress using specific software and 16 used a spreadsheet. It is worth noting that 34 institutions used other forms of follow-up, including an annual management report (14%), special committee (13%), periodic meetings (13%), development of personalised software (8%), occasional meetings (5%) and technical advice from a contracted company (2%).

Finally, in 28 universities (45%), the administrative and planning pro-rector departments were responsible for development of the IDP. A significant number of universities (19; 31%) created specific committees for IDP development. One can spot the differences in IDP management among various universities throughout Brazil, demonstrating the importance of a reference document and software, which are discussed in the following sections.

4.2   Reference Document

Development of a reference document to serve as guidelines for elaboration and management of the IDP is one of the main goals of this work. The idea for this document originated from federal universities' demands of FORPLAD, and the document is being managed by the Federal University of Alfenas (UNIFAL) in partnership with the Federal University of Lavras (UFLA) and the University of Brasília (UNB).

The reference document is divided into two parts: how to develop an IDP and how to execute and manage an IDP. The first part is based on observation of pertinent legislation and their requirements for IPDs as well as recurring issues mentioned in the literature. The second part involves putting IPD into effect and managing it using the Project Management Guide (PMBOK).

IDP Development Process. Based on the pertinent legislation (Decree No. 5.773 May 9, 2006) and a survey involving different IDPs at various federal universities, a process for elaborating the IDP is proposed. This process consists of three broad stages: preparation, diagnosis and planning.

In the preparation stage, all the activities and resources necessary for the development of the IDP are taken into account. Prior to planning activities, the scope and duration of the IDP are defined and the team responsible for its preparation is chosen. It is useful to determine which people will take on the project as the composition of the execution and support teams as well as the engagement activities they will perform may influence the development of the IDP. Communication among the teams managing the IDP should take place through channels that ensure efficient exchange of information.

After these initial definitions, activities are performed to elaborate the IDP, consolidate the documents that will be referenced (laws, regulations, other IDPs, etc.) and identify the mission, vision and values of the HLEI. All of these elements should be mentioned in the teams' initial work proposals. It is important to record all the information and documents that arise in each of the stages so a document that contains lessons learned and areas for improvement during the development of the IDP can be composed.

Once the IDP is prepared, the diagnosis phase begins. During this phase, the current situation of the HLEI is examined to identify external opportunities and threats as well as internal strengths and weaknesses in order to inform future actions. Some of the activities carried out during this phase are analysis of the previous IDP and its results, HLEI SWOT analysis and identification, consolidation and evaluation of needs and areas for improvement. When identifying needs, it is not necessary to create an exhaustive list, but those that are most relevant to each context should be included.

Based on the results of the diagnostic phase, an effective strategic plan is created. This plan includes ways in which needs will be met and the plans and actions necessary to reach the objectives will be defined. At this point, certain needs are prioritised and paired with goals and actions related to, for example, human resources, budgetary resources, physical infrastructure, the specific context of HLEIs and legislative demands. After this phase is complete, a consolidated document with all the relevant results can be created.

IDP Execution and Management. After the IDP is created, it must be implemented. The IDP can be managed by HLEIs, and to do so, many universities use the concepts and methods in the PMBOK as a reference.

For IPD implementation to occur properly, it is necessary to define a plan for managing the project, which will be the primary reference for information on how it will be planned, executed, monitored, controlled and closed. It also includes documentation of the actions required to define, prepare, integrate and coordinate all ancillary plans.

Next, preparation begins for the IDP's project analytical framework (EAP), which is a document containing the project's deliverables, subdivided into smaller components that can be managed more easily (Ex: Goal Plan). Based on the goals and objectives outlined for each strategic axis of the IDP and the available resources, the specific activities that must be executed are defined and scheduled.

When this information is compiled, the project managers estimate the duration of the activities and produce a schedule. At this point, it is important to establish a communication policy among the various actors involved in implementing the IDP in order to ensure that all information and stages of project development are up to date.

The project implementation phase involves coordinating people and resources as well as integrating and executing project activities in accordance with the schedule. It is possible that, by the time the project is executed and the results are obtained, there will be a need to update the plan, so this is considered.

Monitoring and control processes are required to oversee, review and regulate the project's progress and performance, detect areas in which the plan must be changed and make appropriate changes. The changes must be approved by the team in charge, communicated to interested parties and then performed.

When executing monitoring and control processes, reports are produced that provide information on the project's performance in terms of its scope, schedule, cost, resources, quality and risk. After required changes are noted, the integrated change control is used to evaluate the requested changes, approve changes and manage them. The project team must always document these changes.

At this point, controlling the schedule is very important. The progress of the project is monitored to identify any required changes to the schedule. It is also necessary to control costs by updating the budget and managing any changes. Finally, it is necessary to determine the performance of the schedule using information from progress reports, progress measurements and predictions.

Due to page restrictions, only a few points that are considered indispensable in the development/implementation of the IPD are listed here. Other activities can also be carried out by the HLEI, and other strategies can be employed. However, it is possible to effectively implement an IPD following only what is included in this paper. Regardless of the strategy used, it takes a significant amount of attention and dedication on the part of those involved in the project to achieve favourable results.

The following section compares FORPDI and similar systems in the context of this research project and identifies some of the advantages of this software.

4.3   FORPDI

FORPDI is an open platform for IDP management and monitoring in Brazilian federal universities that is still under construction. The software was developed by FORPLAD, UNIFAL, UFLA and UNB.

The project involves the development and implementation of a system available to public universities through Brazilian Public Software. The economical attitude of public administration must be kept in mind when developing this system. It is important to mention that there is no interest in entering the field of software programming and actually developing the software, but rather in proposing a concept for software that reflects the study and the empirical view of the work.

In 2015, the Ministry of Education (MEC) provided the project with a budget of one million reais to computerise the IDP and integrate the plan and budget. The project already has access to a platform for experimental data insertion, and some of its features are worth mentioning.

Currently, FORPDI has a structured format that is conducive to the creation of a reference document, which serves as an initial parameter for developing IDPs in HLEIs in compliance with the minimum elements required by law. Currently, it is already possible to input goals, targets and indicators in the program, with improvements planned for the future.

Another important topic is the relationship between the budget and the IDP's goals—in other words, how much has been invested in each identified goal. Through the system's flexible, personalised interface, the on-board panels guarantee that the resources (objectives, goals, indicators, graphs, budgets, thematic axes, etc.) meet the needs of each institution.

FORPDI is still in the testing phase, which is currently being carried out by thirteen federal universities, including the Federal University of Espírito Santo, Federal University of Santa Maria, Federal University of Paraná and Federal University of Tocantins, and the software developers, UNIFAL, UFLA and UNB. Sixteen additional universities have requested access to the software. The deadline for completion of the software is November 2017.

4.4   FORPDI and Similar Systems - A Comparative Study

FORPDI is an open platform for elaboration, management and monitoring of IDPs. This section will identify tools, software and systems available in the market that have similar functionalities.

Competitors to FORPDI were identified in two ways: (a) online experimentation with tools that are available through free trials, including Quickscore, Flag, EPM Suite and BSC Designer; and (b) questionnaire responses that mentioned software that is available through a free trial, including Redmine, SPSS, GP-Web and Stata.

In general, the comparable software is designed for statistical analysis, project management, quality management, management of indicators and/or strategic management, and it usually used for planning organisational goals and actions. The main features of each strategic management program are briefly presented below, as is a brief comparison of those programs and FORPDI.

Online Testing of Tools with Free Trials. QuickScore is a software for BSC, metrics tracking and strategic management. One of its main advantages is that it is available on iPhone, iPad and Android. Flag is an indicator management module that presents the accumulated results, generates customised charts that compare results and analyses the collected data to identify opportunities for improvement. EPM Suite is a program for managing enterprises' performance using the BSC methodology. This software creates strategic maps and customised visualisations of performance indicators. Finally, BSC Designer is performance management software. It can create and share projects, add actions/initiatives to the overall goal, produce performance reports, export HTML and Excel reports and provide automatic alerts.

Software with Free Trials Reported on the Questionnaire. Redmine is a free project manager used by Fluminense Federal University and the Federal University of Amazonas to access, register and monitor IPD. IMB SPSS is a statistical analysis software that provides resources for each stage of the analytical process. The Federal University of Pernambuco and the Federal University of Sergipe use SPSS to assist in IPD monitoring. GP-Web is intended for strategy and project management, and it was adopted by the Federal University of Santa Catarina. It is able to manage project portfolios and the budget for resources. Stata is statistical software capable of computing everything from simple tasks to complex statistics. The Federal University of Sergipe also uses Stata to assist in IPD monitoring.

Comparison to FORPDI. Strategic management programs other than FORPDI have been on the market long, and some of them are already consolidated. However, no current software except FORPDI is able to create custom levels and attributes or link budget issues with governance systems.

One of the strengths of FORPDI is that it allows free definition of strategic planning levels. In other words, institutions are not limited to a structure of levels imposed by the tool; the tool will create the levels that the institution needs. The FORPDI interface follows most modern design and usability standards in order to serve as an intuitive and easy-to-use tool.

FORPDI is undoubtedly comparable to the best technologies and software analysed here since it offers the same functionalities as well as customisability. In addition, FORPDI has an 'open source' proposal, which allows the creation of dynamic levels based on the structure of other strategic planning levels.

FORPDI is a free tool specifically designed to provide universities with a way to develop and monitor IDPs. Compared to other software, the universities have more freedom in terms of their strategic levels, and thus FORPDI is the most appropriate tool for IDP preparation and monitoring at Brazilian HLEIs.

5 Final Considerations

This paper seeks to provide information on the strategic planning process in Brazilian HLEIs by investigating the development, implementation and management of IDPs in 63 Brazilian federal universities. This subject was analysed to improve the effectiveness of IDP management in universities.

Questionnaires distributed to 63 HLEIs revealed different aspects of IDP management. For example, five years was determined to be the most common period for which an IPD was valid. In addition, it was found that 18 of the universities do not use any method of strategic planning. Among the universities that do use strategic planning methods, BSC and SWOT analysis were the most common.

Analysis of the questionnaire revealed that follow-through was the greatest difficulty faced by the universities. In fact, six universities did not follow through at all. Those universities that did follow through used a variety of means to do so, including specific software, spreadsheets, annual management reports, committees, regular meetings, proprietary software and technical advice from a contracted company.

Some methodologies played an important role in the development of the reference document or strategic planning in public organisations. These methodologies include the SWOT analysis, which has become an indispensable tool for self-assessment and environmental analysis in organisations, and the BSC, which is the most objective tool for achieving more effective public administration because it values the means to achieve the objectives. Its outlook structure contributes to the design and management of strategic plans and, more specifically, IDPs. Through financial analysis, external clients, internal processes, growth and learning, HLEIs can see that they exist for reasons other than the number of graduates and published research.

In terms of practical contributions, the present work proposed software to support the survey of legislation related to IDPs and a reference document for elaboration, implementation, and management of IDPs. Software for IDP management is needed to facilitate planning and monitoring in public organisations. It is also believed that software for supporting the management of IDPs can increase community participation in organisational politics as it becomes a vehicle that didactically conveys and monitors the objectives, goals and indicators of universities.

FORPDI is aligned with most modern strategic planning systems used within universities. However, the research is limited since the IDP management software is still in the testing phase and will not be released until November 2017. Thus, the comparisons to existing software provide only partial results.

It is suggested that future research on IDPs determine whether HLEIs actually use FORPDI or the reference document to support the elaboration, monitoring and strategic management of IDPs. Additionally, if HLEIs show improvements in IPD management, it is advisable to replicate the questionnaire to verify the results and determine whether the software and reference document had any impact on HLEIs.

References

1. Berto, R.M.V.S., Nakano, D.N.: A produção científica nos anais do encontro nacional de engenharia de produção: um levantamento de métodos e tipos de pesquisa, Rio de Janeiro, pp. 65–75 (2000). doi:10.1590/S0103-65131999000200005
2. Brasil. Presidência da República. Decreto No. 5.773, de 9 de maio de 2006. http://portal. mec.gov.br/seed/arquivos/pdf/legislacao/decreton57731.pdf
3. Capuano, E.A.: Construtos para modelagem de organizações fundamentadas na informação e no conhecimento no serviço público brasileiro. Ciência da Informação 37(3), 18–37 (2008)
4. Coelho, D.M.: Elementos essenciais ao conceito de administração gerencial, Brasília, vol. 37, no. 147 (2000)
5. Corrêa, A.C., et al.: Resistência à mudança na educação superior: design e operacionalização de um instrumento de medida para o MEES. GUAL, pp. 55–78 (2013). doi:10.5007/1983-4535.2013v6n2p55
6. Gerhardt, T.E., Silveira, D.T. (Org.): Métodos de pesquisa. Editora da UFRGS, Porto Alegre (2009)
7. Gil, A.C.: Como elaborar projetos de pesquisa. São Paulo (2008)
8. Guedes, E.P., Scherer, F.L.: O Processo de Elaboração do Plano de Desenvolvimento Institucional (PDI): um Estudo de Caso na Universidade Federal do Paraná. Gestão e Conhecimento, João Pessoa, pp. 240–253 (2015)
9. Huertas, C.: Entrevista com Carlos Matus: o método PES. Edições Fundap, São Paulo (1995)
10. Kaplan, R.S., Norton, D.P.: A estratégia em ação: balanced scorecard. Gulf Professional Publishing, Houston (1997)
11. Marconi, M.A., Lakatos, E.M.: Fundamentos de metodologia científica. São Paulo (2003)
12. Martins, V.A.: Proposta de um Mapa Estratégico para uma Universidade Pública. Revista Evidenciação Contábil & Finanças, pp. 88–103 (2015). doi:10.18405/RECFIN20150206

13. Mello, J.M., et al.: Análise do plano de desenvolvimento institucional de instituições de ensino superior participantes da associação de universidades grupo Montevideo – AUGM. GUAL, pp. 01–22 (2013). doi:10.5007/1983-4535.2013v6n4p1

14. Mizael, G.A., Boas, A.A.V., Pereira, J.R., Santos, T.S.: Análise do Plano de Desenvolvimento Institucional das universidades federais do Consórcio Sul-Sudeste de Minas Gerais. Revista de Administração Pública, pp. 1145–1164 (2013). doi:10.5007/1983-4535. 2012v5n4p21

15. Newman, J., Clarke, J.: Gerencialismo. Educação e Realidade (2012)

16. Oliveira, V.C.S.: Modelos de administração pública. In: Sanabio, M.T., Santos, G. J., David, M.V. (Org.) Administração pública contemporânea: política, democracia e gestão, Juiz de Fora (2013)

17. Paula, A.P.P.: Administração pública brasileira entre o gerencialismo e a gestão social. Revista de Administração de Empresas, pp. 36–49 (2005)

18. Picawy, M.M.: PDI-Plano de desenvolvimento institucional, PPI-projeto pedagógico institucional e PPC-projeto pedagógico de curso, entre o dito e o feito, uma análise da implementação em três IES/RS/Brasil. Programa de Pós-Graduação em Educação, Porto Alegre (2008). http://hdl.handle.net/10923/2743

19. Picchiai, D.: O plano de desenvolvimento institucional e o projeto pedagógico institucional de universidades públicas: limites organizacionais. GUAL, pp. 23–45 (2012). doi:10.5007/ 1983-4535.2012v5n3p23

20. Rieg, D.L., Araújo Filho, T.: O uso das metodologias "Planejamento Estratégico Situacional" e "Mapeamento Cognitivo" em uma situação concreta: o caso da pró-reitoria de extensão da UFSCar. Gestão & Produção, São Carlos, pp. 163–179 (2002)

21. Silva, C.R.O.: Metodologia do trabalho científico. Centro Federal de Educação Tecnológica do Ceará, Fortaleza (2004)

22. Sorensen, L., Vidal, R.V.V., Engstrom, E.: Using soft or in a small company: the case of Kirby. Eur. J. Oper. Res. 555–570 (2004). doi:10.1016/S0377-2217(03)00057-2

23. Souza, J.C.V.: Gestão universitária em instituições particulares: os documentos institucionais como indicadores do modelo de gestão. Pontifícia, São Paulo (2007). https://tede2.pucsp.br/ handle/handle/10015

24. Teixeira, S.M.C.B.: O Planejamento e a gestão para resultados na administração pública: o caso da SGA Acre. VI Congresso de Gestão Pública, Brasília (2013). http://banco.consad. org.br/handle/123456789/963

Author Index

Printed in the United States
By Bookmasters